CADOGAN

Dana Facaros & Michael Pauls

Venice Padua Verona

S0-AAD-430

Introduction	vii
Travel	1
Practical A–Z	17
History	37
Art and Architecture	53
Topics	65
Venice	79
Padua	149
Verona	189
Artistic, Architectural and Historic Terms	211
Language	213
Further Reading	223
Index	225

Cadogan Guides
West End House, 11 Hills Place, London W1R 1AG
becky.kendall@morrispub.co.uk

The Globe Pequot Press
246 Goose Lane, PO Box 480, Guilford
Connecticut 06437–0480

Copyright © Dana Facaros and Michael Pauls 2000
Illustrations © Horatio Monteverde 1996

Book and cover design by Animage

Cover photographs © front: CORBIS/Paul Almasy
                      back: Ellen Rooney
                      inside back: John Sims

Maps © Cadogan Guides, drawn by Map Creation Ltd

Editorial Director: Vicki Ingle
Series Editor: Linda McQueen

Editor: Kate Paice
Indexing: Isobel McLean
Production: Book Production Services

A catalogue record for this book is available from the British Library
ISBN 1-86011-965-4

The author and publishers have made every effort to ensure the accuracy of the information in this book at the time of going to press. However they cannot accept any responsibility for any loss, injury or inconvenience resulting from the use of information contained in this guide.

Printed and bound in Great Britain by the Cromwell Press Ltd.

About the Authors

Dana Facaros and Michael Pauls have now written over 30 Cadogan Guides. For three years they and their two children Jackson and Lily lived in a tiny Umbrian hilltop village, then an equally remote French village in the Lot. They now live in Ireland.

Acknowledgements

Thanks to Linda and Nico and Tania, who took care of Lily, and to Lily for being good and leaving some ice-cream at Krioneri for the other campers. Also thanks to Claudia for her Venetian updating, and to all the tourist offices who took the time to answer questions, even the stupid ones. And a big thank you to Linda and Kate at Cadogan.

Villa plans are from Andrea Palladio, *The Four Books of Architecture* (Dover Publications Inc., 31 East 2nd Street, Mineola N.Y. 11501).

Please help us to keep this guide up to date

We have done our best to ensure that the information in this guide is correct at the time of going to press. But places and facilities are constantly changing, and standards and prices in hotels and restaurants fluctuate. We would be delighted to receive any comments concerning existing entries or omissions, as well as suggestions for new features. Authors of the most helpful letters may be offered a copy of the Cadogan Guide of their choice.

Contents

Introduction   vii

Travel   1–16

Getting There	2	Getting Around	10
By Air	2	By Air	10
By Rail	5	By Rail	11
By Road	6	By Coach and Bus	13
Entry Formalities	7	By Car	13
Tour Operators and		Hitchhiking	15
Special Interest Holidays	8	By Motorcycle or Bicycle	15

Practical A–Z   17–36

Climate and When to Go	18	Packing	28
Crime	18	Photography	29
Disabled Travellers	19	Post Offices	29
Embassies and Consulates	19	Shopping	30
Festivals	20	Sports and Activities	30
Food and Drink	22	Telephones	31
Health and Emergencies	26	Time	32
Maps and Publications	26	Toilets	32
Money	27	Tourist Offices	32
National Holidays	27	Where to Stay	33
Opening Hours and Museums	28		

History   37–52

Prehistory, and the Rather		Italy in Chains,	
Mysterious Paleoveneti	38	but Venice Recovers	46
The Romans, Rise and Fall	39	The Age of Baroque	47
The Dark Ages	41	Napoleon and the Austrians	47
The Rise of the *Comuni*	43	The Risorgimento and	
Guelphs and Ghibellines	43	United Italy	48
Renaissance Italy	45	War, Fascism and War	49
The Wars of Italy	46	1945–the Present	51

Art and Architecture 53–64

Paleoveneti	54	The Venetian High Renaissance	
Roman Art	54	and Mannerism	57
Dark and Early Middle Ages	54	Baroque and Rococo	57
Veneto-Byzantine		Neoclassicism, Romanticism	
and Romanesque	55	and Other -Isms	58
Gothic and Early Renaissance	55	Artists' Directory	59
The Renaissance of the			
Quattrocento	56		

Tales of Tyranny and Harmony 65–78

The Son of Satan	66	The Gentle Art of Building Villas:	
Still the Best: Giovanni Bellini	68	Palladio and his Heirs	71
The Council of Trent	69	A Most Serene Civilisation	75

Venice 79–148

History	83	Cannaregio	118
Getting There	88	San Giorgio Maggiore	
Getting Around	90	and the Giudecca	120
The Grand Canal	95	Shopping	120
Piazza San Marco	98	Where to Stay	123
San Marco to Rialto	108	Eating Out	127
San Marco to the Accademia	109	Entertainment and Nightlife	130
Dorsoduro	111	The Lagoon and its Islands	133
San Polo and Santa Croce	112	Venice to Padua:	
San Marco to Castello	114	The Brenta Canal	143
San Marco			
to Santi Giovanni e Paolo	116		

Padua 149–88

History	150	Eating Out	164
The Cappella degli Scrovegni		Day Trips North of Padua	165
and the Museo Civico	152	Day Trips South of Padua	171
Caffè Pedrocchi		Vicenza	175
and the University	157	Monte Bérico, Villa Valmarana	
The Medieval Civic Centre	158	and La Rotonda	184
Where to Stay	163		

Verona 189–210

History	190	West of Piazza delle Erbe	198
Getting Around	191	East of Verona	201
Tourist Information	191	Where to Stay	201
Porta Nuova to the Arena	194	Eating Out	202
Around Piazza delle Erbe	194	Day Trips North of Verona	205
North of the Adige: Veronetta	197	Day Trips South of Verona	208

Artistic, Architectural and Historic Terms 211–12

Language 213–22

Further Reading 223–4

Index 225–31

Maps and Plans

The Veneto	*inside front cover*	Scuola di San Rocco	113
Venice	80–81	The Venetian Lagoon	134
Venice Transport	92–3	Padua	151
The Grand Canal	96–7	Cappelli degli Scrovegni	153
Piazza San Marco	99	Vicenza	176–7
St Mark's Basilica	100	Verona	192–3

The Italians are second to none in creating beautiful stages to act out their lives, although perhaps a better analogy would be to look at their cities as gardens, seeded in Etruscan, Greek or Roman times, tended, pruned, grafted and loved over generations with intense loyalty. City-state rivalry, in fact, made Italy's cities early bloomers in the Middle Ages, in spite of the storms of civic turmoil and war. When they weren't fighting their neighbours by fair means or foul, they were doing all they could to outdazzle them in art and architecture.

The three cities of this book are among the most stunning products of centuries of Italian city-cultivating, adorned with all the hothouse refinements of the Veneto's unique history. Padua and Verona were important Roman cities, a fact still reflected in their street plans; Venice

Introduction

was founded by these same Romans taking refuge from Attila the Hun. Out in its inviolable lagoon, it took root in the fertile peat of the Dark Ages, becoming a Most Serene Republic of merchants trading with the east, before pulling off the most profitable heist of all time by conquering and pilfering Constantinople in 1204. The other cities of the Veneto took the more traditional Italian route, bashing it out in the Guelph and Ghibelline imbroglios of the *terra firma*, ruled by powerful *signori*. All have extraordinary, precocious ornaments: the exotic orchid of St Mark's in Venice, the magnificent Romanesque Basilica of San Zeno in Verona, and Giotto's revolutionary Scrovegni Chapel in Padua.

By 1404, the Serenissima had annexed the Veneto— Padua came in screaming and kicking, but Verona (and Vicenza) asked to join the republic. United, they became the envy of Italy, peaceful and prosperous; as the century progressed the Venetian school of art came into its own. A jealous Pope and emperor tried to tear them asunder in 1508, but failed, and when Italy itself descended into the long twilight years under the thumb of Spain, the Veneto remained independent. Ever more elegant *palazzi* were planted along the streets, especially after Sansovino, Palladio and Scamozzi perfected their classical dream-visions; these were the brilliant late Renaissance humanist cities chosen by Shakespeare as settings for so many plays.

After a last hectic bloom in the 18th century, the cities lost their freedom; with their destinies in other hands, they grew a few weeds and suffered their share of pests and disasters, including the devastations of the Second World War. Afterwards, everything possible was rebuilt *dov'é era, comé era* ('where it was, as it was'), fitting the pieces back together, obsessively, but with the perfect understanding of what belonged where.

Today Venice, Padua and Verona are in better shape than they have been in centuries. The Veneto economy is one of the great success stories of post-war Italy, leading predictably to some rather severe overgrowth outside the garden walls, but to a more perfect tending of what lies inside them. Cars, the worst pests, have been zapped from their historic centres and they are delightful to wander in once again—Venice as colourful and shimmering on the lagoon as Monet's water lilies; Verona as red, elegant and precious as the rose bower in the medieval *Roman de la Rose*; and Padua, the intellectual, as bright and precise as the lily of her Saint Anthony.

Getting There	2
By Air	2
By Rail	5
By Road	6
Entry Formalities	7
Tour Operators and	
Special Interest Holidays	8
Getting Around	10
By Air	10
By Rail	11
By Coach and Bus	13

Travel

By Car	13
Hitchhiking	15
By Motorcycle or Bicycle	15

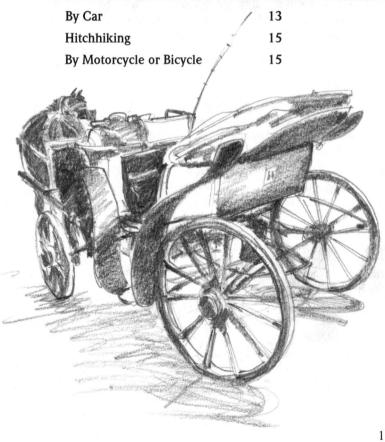

By Air

From the UK and Ireland

There are direct flights to Venice and Verona from several British airports, with good year-round services especially to Venice. Most scheduled flights are operated either by the Italian state airline **Alitalia**, ✆ (020) 7602 7111, or **British Airways**, ✆ (0345) 222 111. The best-value deals are usually **Apex** or **SuperApex** fares, which you must book seven days ahead, and which involve staying in Italy for a Saturday night—no alterations or refunds are possible without high penalties. Return scheduled fares range typically from around £149 off-season; midsummer fares will probably be well over £249. **Sabena**, ✆ (020) 8780 1444, to Venice only, and **Lufthansa**, ✆ (0345) 737 747, to Venice and Verona, can offer cheaper fares (around £180 return, sometimes less depending on time of travel), but these flights often have quite rigid restrictions and can involve flying via another European destination such as Brussels.

Two companies currently offer extremely cheap scheduled flights: **Go** airlines, ✆ (0845) 605 4321, a branch of British Airways, operates flights between London Stansted and Venice (seven times a week), which, if booked in advance, can cost as little as £80 return, although on a heavily booked flight this can rise to around £300. The starting prices for **Ryanair**, flights from Stansted to Venice Treviso, ✆ (0541) 569 569, are around £59 and most prices are below £215; catch them when they have special offers, and a return flight can cost as little as £50.

Early birds get the best seats in the airline business, so think well ahead when booking. If you're prepared to be flexible (and philosophical), last-minute stand-bys can be a snip. A certain number of cheap seats are allotted for young people or bona fide students, and senior citizens, but once they're gone, that's it.

From Ireland, **Alitalia,** ✆ (00353 1) 844 6035, and **Aer Lingus**, Dublin ✆ (00 353 1) 705 3333, or Belfast, ✆ (0645) 737 747, operate direct flights to Rome and Milan only. The frequency depends on the time of year; you may well save money by flying to London and picking up a Go or Ryanair flight from there.

charter flights

Many inexpensive charter flights are available to Venice and Verona in summer, though you are unlikely to find rock-bottom bargains. One of the biggest UK operators is **Italy Sky Shuttle**, which uses a variety of carriers. You may find cheaper fares by combing the small ads in the travel pages, or from a specialist agent. Use a reputable ABTA-registered one, such as **Trailfinders** or **Campus Travel** (*see* next page for addresses). All these companies offer particularly good student and youth rates too. The main problems with cheaper flights tend to be inconvenient or unreliable flight schedules, and booking restrictions, so that you may have to make reservations far ahead, accept given dates and, if you miss your flight, there's no redress. Taking out good travel insurance, however cheap your ticket, is your only precaution.

Italy Sky Shuttle, 227 Shepherd's Bush Road, London W6 7AS, ✆ (020) 8748 1333.

Italflights, 125 High Holborn, London WC1V 6QA, ✆ (020) 7405 6771.

Italia Nel Mondo, 6 Palace Street, London SW1E 5HY, ✆ (020) 7828 9171.

Budget Travel, 134 Lower Baggot Street, Dublin 2, ✆ (00353 1) 661 1866.

Trailfinders, 194 Kensington High Street, London, W8, ✆ (020) 7937 5400.

United Travel, Stillorgan Bowl, Stillorgan, Co. Dublin, ✆ (00353 1) 288 4346/7.

The Internet can be a very good source of cheap flights. Try *www.dhf.co.uk* (a useful site with lots of links) or *www.travelocity.co.uk*, or *www.discountairtravel.co.uk.*

students and youth travel

Besides saving 25 per cent on regular flights, young people under 26 have the choice of flying on special discount charters.

Campus Travel, 52 Grosvenor Gardens, London SW1W 0AG, or 174 Kensington High Street, London W8 7RG, ✆ (020) 7730 3402, with branches at most UK universities, including Bristol, ✆ (0117) 929 2494; Manchester, ✆ (0161) 833 2046; Edinburgh, ✆ (0131) 668 3303; Birmingham, ✆ (0121) 414 1848; Oxford, ✆ (01865) 242 067; Cambridge, ✆ (01223) 324 283, or find their website at *www.usitcampus.com.*

STA, 74 and 86 Old Brompton Road, London SW7 3LQ, or 117 Euston Road, London NW1 2SX, ✆ (020) 7361 6161; Bristol, ✆ (0117) 929 4399; Leeds, ✆ (0113) 244 9212; Manchester, ✆ (0161) 834 0668; Oxford, ✆ (01865) 792800; Cambridge, ✆ (01223) 366 966 and many other branches in the UK.

USIT, 19–21 Aston Quay, Dublin 2, ✆ (00353 1) 679 8833; Cork, ✆ (021) 270 900; Belfast, ✆ (01232) 324 073; Galway, ✆ (091) 565 177; Limerick ✆ (061) 415 064; Waterford, ✆ (051) 872 601. **Ireland**'s largest student travel agents.

From Mainland Europe

Air travel between Italy and other parts of Europe can be relatively expensive, especially for short hops, so check overland options unless you're in a great hurry. You may need to shop around a little for the best deals. Some airlines (**Alitalia, Qantas, Air France**, etc.) offer excellent rates on the European stages of intercontinental flights, and Italy is an important touchdown for many long-haul services to the Middle or Far East. Many of these may have inconvenient departure times and booking restrictions. Amsterdam, Paris and Athens are among the best centres for finding cheap flights.

From the USA and Canada

The main Italian air gateways for direct flights from North America are Rome and Milan, though, if you're doing a grand tour, check fares to other European destinations (Paris or Amsterdam, for example) which may well be cheaper. **Alitalia,** ✆ (800) 223 5730, Canada ✆ (800) 563 5954, the major carrier, may offer you a special deal if you're flying on to Verona or Venice. **TWA,** ℭ (800) 892 4141, **British Airways,** ℭ (800) 247 9297 and **Delta,** ℭ (800) 221 1212, also fly from a number of US cities to Italy. From Canada, **Air Canada,** ℭ (800) 776 3000, and **KLM** ℭ (800) 361 5330, operate from Toronto and Montreal. Summer round-trip fares from New York cost around US$1,000–1,300.

British Airways sometimes run World Offers when prices may well drop under the $1,000 mark. Otherwise, it may well be worth your while catching a cheap flight to London (New York–London fares are always very competitive) and then flying on from there. Prices are rather more from Canada, so you may prefer to fly from the States. As elsewhere, fares are very seasonal and much cheaper in winter, especially mid-week.

charters, discounts and special deals

From North America, standard scheduled flights on well-known airlines are expensive, but reassuringly reliable and convenient. Resilient, flexible and/or youthful travellers may be willing to shop around for budget deals on consolidated charters, stand-bys or perhaps even courier flights (remember you can usually only take hand luggage with you on the last). In the USA, **Airhitch,** ℭ (212) 864 2000, and **Council Charter,** ℭ (212) 822 2800, are leading reputable cheap-flight specialists. Check the *Yellow Pages* for listings of courier companies: **Now Voyager** is one of the largest USA ones, ℭ (212) 431 1616; or try *www.aircourier.org.*

For discounted flights, try the small ads in any of the newspaper travel pages (e.g. *New York Times, Chicago Tribune, Toronto Globe & Mail*). Firms like **STA** or Canada-based **Travel CUTS** are worth contacting for student fares. Numerous travel clubs and agencies also specialize in discount fares, but may require an annual membership fee; for the complete dope, pick up a copy of Michael McColl's *Worldwide Guide to Cheap Airfares*, published by Insider Publications.

Airhitch, 2641 Broadway, 3rd Floor, New York, NY 10025, ℭ (212) 864 2000.

Last Minute Travel Club, 100 Sylvan Road, Suite 600, Woburn, MA 01801, ℭ (800) 527 8646.

Now Voyager, 74 Varick Street, Suite 307, New York, NY 10013, ℭ (212) 431 1616.

STA, 48 East 11th Street, New York, NY 10003, ℭ (800) 777 0112.

Travel CUTS, 187 College Street, Toronto, Ontario M5T 1P7, ℭ (416) 979 2406.

Also, try the Internet for cheap flights. There are a lot of websites that can help: shop around. You could try the following: *www.travelshoppe.com, www.travelocity.com, www.cheaptickets.com.*

student and youth travel

STA Travel, 48 East 11th Street, New York City, ℭ (212) 627 3111, or toll-free, ℭ (800) 777 0112.

Travel CUTS, 187 College Street, Toronto, Ontario M5T 1P7, ℭ (416) 979 2406. Canada's largest student travel specialists; branches in most provinces.

From the UK and Europe

A train journey from London to Rome used to be something of a nightmare involving ferries and station changes and taking the best part of 24 hours. This experience can still be repeated, should you so desire it, and will cost you around £160 second class return plus an extra £14 for a couchette. There are, however, following the opening of the Channel Tunnel and the construction of new fast rail networks throughout Europe, alternatives. Take a Eurostar to France and a high-speed Eurocity train to Italy and your journey could be reduced by as much as 7 hours. London–Venice involves two changes of train, takes around 17 hours and costs about £160 return; London–Verona goes via Munich in about 19 hours and costs about the same. Train travel, at whatever speed, has its benefits—the opportunity to watch the changing scenery, to acclimatise, and relax—but in an age of low-cost airlines, it is not much of an economy. For more information, contact either **Rail Europe Travel Centre**, 179 Piccadilly W1V 0BA, ✆ (0990) 848 848, or **Eurostar**, EPS House, Waterloo Station, London SE1 8SE, ✆ (0990) 186 186, or, as a last resort, visit the **International Rail Centre** at Victoria Station, adjacent to Platform 2, ✆ (0990) 848 848—you can call this number but be warned, the operators cannot give out any information regarding prices, times, availability or anything vaguely useful.

One supremely luxurious way of reaching Italy by rail deserves a special mention: the **Orient Express** whirls you from London through Paris, Zurich, Innsbruck and Verona to Venice in a cocoon of traditional '20s–'30s glamour, with beautifully restored Pullman *wagon-lits*. It's fiendishly expensive—and quite unforgettable for a once-in-a-lifetime treat. Current prices are about £1,130/$1,900 per person (London–Venice one-way); prices include all meals. Several operators offer packages including smart Venice hotel accommodation and return flights home. Call Venice Simplon-Orient Express, Sea Containers House, 20 Upper Ground, London SE1 9PF, ✆ (020) 7928 6000 for more information.

Interail (UK) or **Eurail** passes (USA/Canada) give unlimited travel for under-26s throughout Europe for one or two months. Various other cheap youth fares (BIJ tickets, etc.) are also available; organize these before you leave home. Useful addresses for rail travel include **Eurotrain**, 52 Grosvenor Gardens, London SW1W 0AG, ✆ (020) 7730 8518; **Wasteels Travel**, adjacent Platform 2, Victoria Station, London SW1V 1JT, ✆ (020) 7834 7066; any branch of **Thomas Cook**, or **CIT** (*see* addresses below).

If you are just planning to see Italy, inclusive rail passes may not be worthwhile. Fares on FS (*Ferrovie dello Stato*), the Italian State Railway, are among the lowest (kilometre for kilometre) in Europe. A month's under-26 full Interail pass costs £259 (£349 for those over 26), though you can now buy cheaper zonal passes covering three or four countries only. If you intend travelling extensively by train, one of the special Italian tourist passes may be a better bet (*see* below, p.12).

A convenient pocket-sized **timetable** detailing all the main and secondary Italian railway lines is now available in the UK, costing £9 (plus 90p postage). Contact **Italwings**, Travel & Accommodation, 87 Brewer Street, London W1R 5TB, ✆ (020) 7287 2117. If you wait until you arrive in Italy, however, you can pick up the Italian timetable (in two volumes) at any station for about L4,500 each.

From the USA and Canada, contact **Rail Europe**, central office at 226–230 Westchester Ave, White Plains, NY 10604, ✆ (914) 682 2999 or ✆ (800) 438 7245. **Wasteels** also have a USA office at 5728 Major Boulevard, Suite 308, Orlando, 32819 Florida.

CIT Offices outside Italy

UK	Marco Polo House, 3–5 Lansdowne Road, Croydon, Surrey CR9 1LL, ✆ (0891) 715 151 (50p a minute), ✉ (020) 8681 1712.
USA	15 West 44th Street, 10th Floor, New York, NY 10036, ✆ (800) 248 7245, ✉ (888) FAX CIT.
Canada	1450 City Councillors Street, Suite 750, Montreal H3A 2E6, ✆ (514) 845 4310.

By Road
by bus and coach

Eurolines is the main international bus operator in Europe, with representatives in Italy and many other countries. In the UK, they can be found at Victoria Coach Station, London SW1W 0AG, ✆ (0990) 80 80 80, and are booked through National Express. Regular services run to many northern Italian cities, from where you can get other coaches. Needless to say, the journey is long (30 hours to Venice, including a change in Milan) and the relatively small savings on price (a return ticket from London to Venice costs £135; £122 for under-26s) make it a masochistic choice in comparison with a discounted air fare, or even rail travel. Within Italy, you can obtain more information on long-distance bus services from any CIT office.

by car

Driving to Venetia from the UK is a lengthy and expensive proposition. If you're only staying for a short period, check costs against airline fly-drive schemes. Plan for the best part of 30 hours' driving time, even if you stick to fast toll roads. The most scenic and hassle-free route is via the Alps, avoiding crowded Riviera roads in summer, but if you take a route through Switzerland, expect to pay for the privilege (around £14 or SF30 for motorway use). In winter the passes may be closed and you will have to stick to those expensive tunnels (one-way tolls range from about L22,000 for a small car). You can avoid some of the driving by putting your car on the train, though this is scarcely a cheap option. **Express Sleeper Cars** run to Milan from Paris or Boulogne (infrequently in winter). Foreign-plated cars are no longer entitled to free breakdown assistance from the **Italian Auto Club** (ACI), but their prices are fair. Phone ACI on ✆ (0039) 06 49 981 to find out the current rates.

To bring a GB-registered car into Italy, you need a **vehicle registration document, full driving licence** (and international driving permit if you have one of the old-fashioned licences) and **insurance papers**—these must be carried at all times when driving. Non-EU citizens should preferably have an **international driving licence** which has an Italian translation incorporated. Your vehicle should display a nationality plate indicating its country of registration. Before travelling, check everything is in perfect order. Minor infringements like worn tyres or burnt-out sidelights can cost you dear in any country. A **red triangular hazard sign** is obligatory; also recommended are a spare set of bulbs, a first-aid kit and a fire extinguisher. Spare parts for non-Italian cars can be difficult to find, especially Japanese models. Before crossing the Italian border, remember to fill up with petrol; *benzina* is still very expensive in Italy.

For more information on driving in Italy, *see* 'Getting Around By Car', pp.13–15, or contact the motoring organisations **AA**, ✆ (0990) 500 600, or **RAC**, ✆ (0800) 550 550 in the UK, and **AAA**, ✆ (407) 444 7000 in the USA and (416) 221 4300 in Canada.

Entry Formalities

Passports and Visas

EU nationals with a valid passport can enter and stay in Italy as long as they like. Citizens of the USA, Canada, Australia and New Zealand need only a valid passport to stay up to three months in Italy, unless they get a visa in advance from an Italian embassy or consulate.

UK	38 Eaton Place, London SW1X, ✆ (020) 7235 9371.
	32 Melville Street, Edinburgh EH3 7HA, ✆ (0131) 226 3631.
	111 Piccadilly, Manchester M1 2HY, ✆ (0161) 236 9024.
Ireland	63–65 Northumberland Road, Dublin, ✆ (00353 1) 660 1744.
USA	690 Park Avenue, New York, NY 10021, ✆ (212) 737 9100.
	12400 Wilshire Boulevard, Suite 300, Los Angeles CA, ✆ (323) 820 0622.
Canada	136 Beverley Street, Toronto, ✆ (416) 977 1566.
Australia	Level 45, The Gateway Building, Macquarie Place, Circular Quay, Sydney 2000, NSW, ✆ (2) 627 33 333.
New Zealand	34 Grant Road, Thorndon, Wellington, ✆ (4) 473 4339.
France	47 Rue de Varennes, 73343 Paris, ✆ (1) 49 54 03 00.
Germany	Karl Finkelnburgstrasse 49–51, 5300 Bonn 2, ✆ (228) 82 20.
Netherlands	Herengracht 609, 1017 CE Amsterdam, ✆ (3120) 624 0043.

By law you should register with the police within eight days of your arrival in Italy. In practice this is done automatically for most visitors when they check in at their first hotel. Don't be alarmed if the owner of your self-catering property proposes to 'denounce' you to the police when you arrive—it's just a formality.

Customs

EU nationals over the age of 17 can now import a limitless amount of goods for personal use. Non-EU nationals have to pass through the Italian customs. How the frontier police manage to recruit such ugly, mean-looking characters to hold the submachine guns and dogs from such a good-looking population is a mystery, but they'll let you be if you don't look suspicious and haven't brought along more than 200 cigarettes or 100 cigars, or not more than a litre of hard drink or three bottles of wine, a couple of cameras, a movie camera, 10 rolls of film for each, a tape-recorder, radio, record-player, one canoe less than 5.5m, sports equipment for personal use, and one TV (though you'll have to pay for a licence for it at Customs). Pets must be accompanied by a bilingual Certificate of Health from your local Veterinary Inspector. You can take the same items listed above home with you without hassle—except of course your British pet. US citizens may return with $400 worth of merchandise: keep your receipts.

Currency

There are no limits to the amount of money you may bring into Italy: legally you may not export more than L20,000 000 in Italian banknotes, a sum unlikely to trouble many of us, though officials rarely check.

Tour Operators and Special Interest Holidays

Dozens of general and specialist companies offer holidays in Italy. Some of the major ones are listed below. Not all of them are necessarily ABTA-bonded; we recommend you check before booking.

UK general

Cosmos, Dale House, Tiviot Dale, Stockport, Cheshire, SK1 1TB, ✆ (0161) 476 4768.

Cresta Italy, Tabley Court, Victoria Street, Altringham, Cheshire WA14 1EZ, ✆ (0161) 927 7000.

Crystal Premier, Crystal House, The Courtyard, Arlington Road, Surbiton, Surrey KT6 6BW, ✆ (020) 8390 5554.

Inghams Travel, 10–18 Putney Hill, London, SW15 6AX, ✆ (020) 8780 4411.

Italian Escapades, 227 Shepherds Bush Road, London W6 7AS, ✆ (020) 8748 2661.

Italiatour, 9 Whyteleafe Business Village, Whyteleafe Hill, Whyteleafe, Surrey CR3 0AT, ✆ (01883) 623 363.

In Ireland: 4–5 Dawson Street, Dublin 2, (01) 671 7821.

Magic of Italy, 227 Shepherds Bush Road, London W6 7AS, ✆ (020) 8748 7575.

Page & Moy, 136–140 London Road, Leicester LE2 1EN, ✆ (0116) 250 7979.

Sunvil, Sunvil House, 7–8 Upper Square, Old Isleworth, Middlesex TW7 7BJ, ✆ (020) 8568 4499.

Thomson, Albert House, Tindal Bridge, Edward Street, Birmingham B1 2RA, ✆ (0990) 502 555.

UK special interest

Abercrombie & Kent (city breaks), Sloane Square House, Holbein Place, London SW1W 8NS, ✆ (020) 7559 8686.

Alternative Travel (walking and cycling tours), 69–71 Banbury Road, Oxford OX2 6PE, ✆ (01865) 310 399.

Arblaster & Clarke (wine tours linked with opera), Clarke House, Farnham Road, West Liss, Hampshire, GU33 6JQ, ✆ (01730) 893 344.

Blair Travel for the Arts (opera), 117 Regent's Park Road, London NW1 8UR, ✆ (020) 7483 4466.

British Museum Tours (guest lecturers, art and architecture), 46 Bloomsbury Street, London WC1B 3QQ, ✆ (020) 7323 8895.

Brompton Travel (tailor-made and opera), Brompton House, 64 Richmond Road, Kingston-upon-Thames, Surrey KT2 5EH, ✆ (020) 8549 3334.

Citalia (opera), Marco Polo House, 3–5 Lansdowne Road, Croydon CR9 1LL, ✆ (020) 8686 5533.

Italia 2000 (golf and sport), 8 Timperley Way, Up Hatherley, Cheltenham, Gloucestershire, GL51 5RH, ✆ (01242) 234 215.

JMB (opera), Rushwick, Worcester WR2 5SN, ✆ (01905) 425 628.

Kirker (city breaks, tailor-made tours and trips to the Verona Opera), 3 New Concordia Wharf, Mill Street, London SE1 2BB, ✆ (020) 7231 3333.

Martin Randall Travel (cultural tours with expert guides: art and architecture, wines, gardens), 10 Barley Mow Passage, Chiswick, London W4 4PH, ✆ (020) 8742 3355.

Prospect Music and Art (Verona opera), 36 Manchester Street, London, W1M 5PE, ✆ (020) 8995 2151.

Ramblers (walking tours), Box 43, Welwyn Garden City, Hertfordshire AL8 6PQ, ✆ (01707) 331 133.

Saga (art and architecture—senior citizens), Enbrook Park, Sandgate high Street, Sandgate, Kent, CT20 3SE, ✆ (01303) 711 111.

Solo's (singles holidays), 54–8 High Street. Edgware, Middlesex HA8 7EJ, ✆ (020) 8951 2800.

Special Tours (escorted cultural tours: art, architecture, gardens), 81a Elizabeth Street, London SW1W 9PG, ✆ (020) 7730 2297.

Tasting Places (cookery courses near Verona), 40 Buspace Studios, Conlan Street, London W10 5AP, ✆ (020) 7460 0077.

Travelsphere (coach tours), Compass House, Rockingham Road, Market Harborough, Leicestershire LE16 7QD, ✆ (01858) 464 818.

Venice-Simplon Orient Express (luxury rail tours), Sea Containers House, 20 Upper Ground, London SE1 9PF, ✆ (020) 7928 6000.

Wallace Arnold (coach tours), Lowfield Road, off Gelderd Road, Leeds, LS12 6JN, ✆ (01132) 310 739.

American Express Vacations (prepacked or tailor-made tours), 300 Pinnacle Way, Norcross, GA 30093, ✆ (800) 241 1700.

CIT Tours, 342 Madison Avenue, Suite 3207, New York, NY 10173, ✆ (212) 697 2100.

Connaissance et Cie (wine tours), 790 Madison Avenue, New York, NY 10021, ✆ (212) 472 5772.

Dailey-Thorp Travel (music and opera), 330 West 58th Street, New York, NY 10019, ✆ (212) 307 1555.

Esplanade Tours (art and architecture tours), 581 Boyston Street, Boston, MA 02116, ✆ (617) 266 7465.

Italiatour (fly-drive in conjunction with Alitalia), 666 5th Avenue, New York, NY 10103, ✆ (212) 765 2183.

Maupintour, 1515 St Andrew's Drive, Lawrence, Kansas 66047, ✆ (913) 843 1211.

Olson Travelworld, 970 West 190th Street, Suite 425, Torrance, California, CA 90502, ✆ (310) 354 2600.

Stay and Visit Italy, 5506 Connecticut Avenue NW, Suite 28, Washington, DC 20015, ✆ (202) 237 5220, ✆ (800) 411 3728, 🖷 (202) 966 6972.

Travel Concepts (wine/food), 62 Commonwealth Avenue, Suite 3, Boston, MA 02116, ✆ (617) 266 8450.

For self-catering and camping specialists *see* **Practical A–Z**, 'Where to Stay', pp.35–6.

Getting Around

Strikes

Italy has an excellent network of airports, railways, highways and byways and you'll find getting around fairly easy—until one union or another takes it into its head to go on strike (to be fair, they rarely do it during the high holiday season). There's plenty of talk about passing a law to regulate strikes, but it won't happen soon if ever. Instead, learn to recognize the word in Italian: *sciopero* (SHO-per-o), and do as the Romans do—quiver with resignation. There's always a day or two's notice, and strikes usually last only a day, just long enough to throw a spanner in the works if you have to catch a plane. Keep your ears open and watch for notices posted in the stations.

By Air

Air traffic within Italy is intense, with up to ten flights a day on popular routes. Domestic flights are handled by **Alitalia** ✆ (020) 7602 7111, **ATI** (its internal arm) or **Avianova**. Air travel makes most sense when hopping between north and south. Shorter journeys are often just as quick (and much less expensive) by train or even bus if you take check-in and airport travelling times into account. Venice and Verona have direct flights to and from Rome and Milan.

Domestic flight **costs** are comparable to those in other European countries: a full-price return fare from Rome to Venice costs about £158 (one-way tickets are half-price). A complex system of discounts is available (some only at certain times of year) for night flights, weekend travel, senior (60 plus) and youth fares (12–26-year-olds; half-price or less for younger children). Family reductions are also available (up to 50%). Each airport has a bus terminal in the city; ask about schedules as you purchase your ticket to avoid hefty taxi fares. Baggage allowances vary between airlines. Tickets can be bought at CIT offices and other large travel agencies.

By Rail

FS information from anywhere in Italy, © 1478 88088, open 7am–9pm, www.fs-on-line.com.

Italy's national railway, the **FS** (*Ferrovie dello Stato*) is well run, inexpensive (despite recent price rises) and often a pleasure to ride. On the FS, some of the trains are sleek and high-tech, but much of the rolling stock hasn't been changed for fifty years. Possible FS unpleasantnesses you may encounter, besides a strike, are delays, crowding (especially at weekends and in the summer), and crime on overnight trains, where someone rifles your bags while you sleep. The crowding, at least, can become much less of a problem. Reserve a seat in advance (*fare una prenotazione*): the fee is small and can save you hours standing in some train corridor. On the more expensive trains, **reservations** are mandatory. Do check when you purchase your ticket in advance that the date is correct; tickets are only valid the day they're purchased unless you specify otherwise. A number on your reservation slip will indicate in which car your seat is—find it before you board rather than after. The same goes for sleepers and couchettes on overnight trains, which must also be reserved in advance. At sleepy rural train stations without information boards, the imminent arrival of a train is signalled by a platform bell.

Tickets may be purchased not only in the stations, but at many travel agents in the city centres. Fares are strictly determined by the kilometres travelled. The system is computerized and runs smoothly, at least until you try to get a reimbursement for an unused ticket (usually not worth the trouble). Be sure you ask which platform (*binario*) your train arrives at; the big permanent boards in the stations are not always correct. Always remember to stamp your ticket (*convalidare*) in the not very obvious yellow machines at the head of the platform before boarding the train, or else you may have to pay a fine. If you get on a train without a ticket you can buy one from the conductor, although you will have to pay an added 20% penalty. You can also pay a conductor to move up to first class or get a couchette, if there are places available.

There is a fairly straightforward **hierarchy of trains**. At the bottom of the pyramid is the humble *Locale* (also euphemistically known as an *Accelerato*) which often stops even where there's no station in sight; it can be excruciatingly slow. When you're checking the schedules, beware of what may look like the first train to your destination—if it's a *Locale*, it will be the last to arrive. A *Diretto* stops far less, an *Expresso* just at the main towns.

Intercity trains whoosh between the big cities. *Eurocity* trains link Italian cities with major European centres. Both of these services require a supplement—some 30% more than a regular fare. Lording it above these are the *ETR 500 pendolino* trains, similar to the French TGV service, which can travel at up to 186mph. Reservations are free, but must be made at least five hours before the trip, and on some trains there are only first-class coaches. Sitting on the pinnacle are the true Kings of the Rails, the super-swish and super-fast *Eurostars*. These make very few stops, have both first and second class carriages, and require you to pay a supplement which includes an obligatory seat reservation. So, the faster the train, the more you pay.

The FS offers several **passes**. A flexible option (naturally) is the 'Flexi Card' (marketed as a 'Freedom Pass' in the UK) which allows unlimited travel for either four days within a month (L206,000), eight days within a month (L287,000), 12 days within a month (L368,000) plus seat reservations and supplements on Eurostars. Another ticket, the *Kilometrico*, gives you 3,000 kilometres of travel, made on a maximum of 20 journeys and is valid for two months (second class L206,000, first class L338,000); one advantage is that it can be used by up to five people at the same time. However, supplements are payable on *Intercity* trains. Other discounts, available only once you're in Italy, are 15 per cent on same-day return tickets and three-day returns (depending on the distance involved), and discounts for families of at least four travelling together. Senior citizens (men 65 and over, women 60) can also get a *Carta d'Argento* ('silver card') for L44,000 entitling them to a 20 per cent reduction in fares. A *Carta Verde* bestows a 20% discount on people under 26 and also costs L44,000.

Refreshments on routes of any great distance are provided by bar cars or trolleys; you can usually get sandwiches and coffee from vendors along the tracks at intermediary stops. Station bars often have a good variety of takeaway travellers' fare; but you should consider at least investing in a plastic bottle of mineral water, since there's no drinking water on the trains and the journeys can become hot and stuffy.

Besides trains and bars, Italy's stations offer other **facilities**. Most have a *Deposito*, where you can leave your bags for hours or days for a small fee. The larger ones have porters (who charge L1,000–L1,500 per piece) and some even have luggage trolleys; major stations may well have an *Albergo Diurno* ('Day Hotel', where you can shower, shave and have a haircut, etc.), information offices, currency exchanges open at weekends (not at the most advantageous rates, however), hotel-finding and reservation services, kiosks with foreign papers, restaurants and so on. You can also arrange to have a **rental car** awaiting you at your destination—Avis, Hertz, Aurotrans and Maggiore are the firms most widespread in Italy, *see* p.15.

Beyond that, some words need to be said about riding the rails on the most serendipitous national line in Europe. The FS may have its strikes and delays, its petty crime and bureau-cratic inconveniences, but when you catch it on its better side it will treat you to a dose of the real Italy before you even reach your destination. If there's a choice, try for one of the older cars, depressingly grey outside but fitted with comfortably upholstered seats, Art Deco lamps and old pictures of the towns and villages of the country. Best of all, the FS is relatively reliable, and even if there has been some delay you'll have an amenable station full of clocks to wait in; some of the station bars have astonishingly good food (some do not), but at any of them you may accept a well-brewed cappuccino and look blasé until the train comes in. Try to avoid travel on Friday evenings, when the major lines out of the big cities are packed.

The FS is a lottery; you may find a train uncomfortably full of Italians (in which case stand by the doors, or impose on the salesmen in first class, where the conductor will be happy to change your ticket). Now and then, you may just have a beautiful 1920s compartment all to yourself for the night—even better if you're travelling with your beloved—and be serenaded on the platform.

By Coach and Bus

Inter-city coach travel is sometimes quicker than train travel, but also a bit more expensive. Coaches almost always depart from the vicinity of the train station, and tickets usually need to be purchased before you get on. In many regions they are the only means of public transport and well used, with frequent schedules. If you can't get a ticket before the coach leaves, get on anyway and pretend you can't speak a word of Italian; the worst that can happen is that someone will make you pay for a ticket. The base for all **country bus** lines will be the provincial capital.

City buses are the traveller's friend. Most cities (at least in the north) label routes well; all charge flat fees for rides within the city limits and immediate suburbs, at the time of writing around L1,500. Bus tickets must always be purchased before you get on, either at a tobacconist's, a newspaper kiosk, in bars, or from ticket machines near the main stops. Once you get on, you must 'obliterate' your ticket in the machines in the front or back of the bus; controllers stage random checks to make sure you've punched your ticket. Fines for cheaters are about L50,000, and the odds are about 12 to 1 against a check, so many passengers take a chance. If you're good-hearted, you'll buy a ticket and help some overburdened municipal transit line meet its annual deficit.

By Car

The advantages of driving in Italy generally outweigh the disadvantages, but, before you bring your own car or hire one, consider the kind of holiday you're planning. For a tour of art cities or a few days lounging on the beach, you'd be better off not driving at all: parking isimpossible, traffic impossible, deciphering one-way streets, signals and signs impossible. But for touring the countryside a car gives immea-surable freedom.

Third-party **insurance** is a minimum requirement in Italy (and you should be a lot more than minimally insured, as many of the locals have none whatever!). Obtain a Green Card from your insurer, which gives automatic proof that you are fully covered. Also get hold of a **European Accident Statement** form, which may simplify things if you are unlucky enough to have an accident. Always insist on a full translation of any statement you are asked to sign. Breakdown assistance insurance is obviously a sensible investment (e.g. AA's Five Star or RAC's Eurocover Motoring Assistance).

Petrol (*benzina*, unleaded is *benzina senza piombo*, and diesel *gasolio*) is still very expensive in Italy (around L1,800 per litre; fill up before you cross the border). Many petrol stations close for lunch in the afternoon, and few stay open late at night, though you may find a 'self-service' where you feed a machine nice smooth L10,000 notes. Motorway (*autostrada*) tolls are quite high. Rest stops and petrol stations along the motorways stay open 24 hours. Other roads—*superstrade* on down through the Italian grading system—are free of charge.

Italians are famously anarchic behind a wheel. The only way to beat the locals is to join them by adopting an assertive and constantly alert driving style. Bear in mind that whoever hesitates is lost (especially at traffic lights, where the danger is less great of crashing into someone at the front than being rammed from behind). All drivers from boy racers to elderly nuns tempt providence by overtaking at the most dangerous bend, and no matter how fast you are hammering along the *autostrada*, plenty of others will whizz past at apparently supersonic rates. North Americans used to leisurely speed limits and gentler road manners may find the Italian interpretation of the highway code somewhat stressful. Speed limits (generally ignored) are 130kph on motorways (110kph for cars under 1,100cc or motorcycles), 110kph on main highways, 90kph on secondary roads, and 50kph in built-up areas. Speeding fines may be as much as L500,000, or L100,000 for jumping a red light (a popular Italian sport).

If you are undeterred by these caveats, you may actually enjoy driving in Italy, at least away from the congested tourist centres. Signposting is generally good, and roads are usually excellently maintained. Some of the roads are feats of engineering that the Romans themselves would have admired—bravura projects suspended on cliffs, crossing valleys on vast stilts and winding up hairpins.

Buy a good road map (the Italian Touring Club series is excellent). The **Automobile Club of Italy** (ACI) is a good friend to the foreign motorist. Besides having bushels of useful information and tips, they can be reached from anywhere by dialling ℂ **116**—also use this number if you have to find the nearest service station. If you need major repairs, the ACI can make sure the prices charged are according to their guidelines.

Hiring a Car

Hiring a car, *autonoleggio*, is simple but not particularly cheap—Italy has some of the highest rates in Europe. A small car (Fiat Punto or similar) with unlimited mileage and collision damage waiver, including tax, will set you back around L70,000–90,000 per day although if you hire for the car for over three days, this will decrease slightly pro rata. The minimum age limit is usually 25 (sometimes 23) and the driver must have held their licence for over a year—this will have to be produced, along with the driver's passport, when hiring the car. Major rental companies have offices in airports or main stations, though it may be worthwhile checking prices of local firms. If you need a car for longer than three weeks, leasing may be a more economic alternative. The National Tourist Office has a list of firms that hire caravans (trailers) or camper vans. Non-residents are not allowed to buy cars in Italy.

Taking all things into account, it may make sense to arrange your car hire before leaving home and, in particular, to check-out fly-drive discounts. Notwithstanding the convenience of picking up the car when you arrive, it often works out cheaper. Prices tend towards the L70,000 per day mark, often with large discounts for a second week of hire.

Car Rental Agencies

UK and Ireland

Avis, ✆ 0990 900 500

Hertz, ✆ 0990 996 699

National Car Rental, ✆ 0990 365 365

Car Rental Direct, ✆ 020 7604 4688

Hertz, Dublin, ✆ (00353 1) 660 2255

USA and Canada

Avis, ✆ (800) 331 1084

Hertz, ✆ (800) 654 3131

Hertz, Canada (800) 263 0600

Hitchhiking

It is illegal to hitch on the *autostrade*, though you may pick up a lift near one of the toll booths. Don't hitch from the city centres; head for suburban exit routes. For the best chances of getting a lift, travel light, look respectable and take off your sunglasses. Hold a sign indicating your destination if you can. Never hitch at points which may cause an accident or obstruction; Italian traffic is bad enough already!

Risks for women are lower in northern Italy than in the more macho south, but it is not advisable to hitch alone. Two or more men may encounter some reluctance.

By Motorcycle or Bicycle

Mopeds, Vespas and scooters are the vehicles of choice for a great many Italians. You will see them everywhere. In the traffic-congested towns this is a ubiquity born of necessity; when driving space is limited, two wheels are always better than four. However, in Italy, riding a two-wheeler often seems to be as much a form of cultural and social expression as it does a means of getting from A to B. Italian youths tend to prefer chic Italian lines, Vespas, Lambrettas and the like, which they parade self-consciously through the town's main drags. Older members of society, in the main, tend to plump for mopeds, the type you can actually pedal should you feel so inclined.

Choosing your machine, however, is only the first stage of this cultural process; it then becomes necessary to master the Italian way of riding. This means dispensing with a crash helmet, despite the fact that they are compulsory, in order to look as stylishly laid-back as possible while still achieving an alarming rate of speed: riding sidesaddle, or whilst on the phone, or smoking, or holding a dog or child under one arm; all of these methods have their determined and expert adherents.

Despite the obvious dangers of this means of transport (especially if you choose to do it Italian-style), there are clear benefits to moped-riding in Italy. For one thing it is cheaper than car hire—costs for a *motorino* range from about L30,000 per day, scooters somewhat more (up to L50,000)—and can prove an excellent way of covering a town's sights in a limited space of time. Furthermore, because Italy is such a scooter-friendly place, car drivers are more conditioned to their presence and so are less likely to hurtle into them when taking corners. Nonetheless, you should only consider hiring a moped if you have ridden one before (Italy's alarming traffic is no place to learn) and, despite local examples, you should always wear a helmet. Also, be warned, some travel insurance policies exclude claims resulting from scooter or motorbike accidents—make sure you check. You must be at least 14 to hire a moped.

Italians are keen cyclists, racing drivers straight up the Dolomites, but if you're not training for the Tour de France consider the topography well before planning a bicycling tour. Much of the Veneto is fairly flat and prime cycling territory, but it can be sweltering in the summer. Prices begin at about L20,000 per day, which may make buying one interesting (L190,000–L300,000) if you plan to spend much time in the saddle, either in a bike shop or through the classified ad papers put out in nearly every city and region. If you bring your own bike, do check the airlines to see what their policies are on transporting them. Bikes can be transported by train in Italy, either with you or within a couple of days—apply at the baggage office (*ufficio bagagli*). Many towns in Venetia hire out bikes by the hour or day; ask at the tourist offices.

Climate and When to Go   18

Crime   18

Disabled Travellers   19

Embassies and Consulates   19

Practical A–Z

Festivals   20

Food and Drink   22

Health and Emergencies   26

Maps and Publications   26

Money   27

National Holidays   27

Opening Hours and Museums   28

Packing   28

Photography   29

Post Offices   29

Shopping   30

Sports and Activities   30

Telephones   31

Time   32

Toilets   32

Tourist Offices   32

Where to Stay   33

average temperatures in °C (°F)

January	April	July	October
3.8 (39)	12.6 (54)	23.6 (74)	15.1 (59)

average monthly rainfall in millimetres (inches)

January	April	July	October
58 (2)	77 (4)	37 (1)	66 (3)

O Sole Mio notwithstanding, Italy isn't always sunny; it rains just as much in Rome every year as in London. Summer comes on humid and hot in Venetia, especially along the Po; the Dolomites stay fairly cool, but the valleys just below can be little ovens, and, while the coasts are often refreshed by breezes, Venice in its lagoon tends to swelter. You can get by without an umbrella, but take a light jacket for cool evenings. For average touring, August is probably the worst month. Transport facilities are jammed to capacity, prices are at their highest, and the large cities are abandoned to hordes of tourists while the locals take to the beach. As compensation, summer is prime festival time (*see* below).

Spring and autumn are the loveliest times to go. In spring the blossoming apple and cherry orchards rival the wild flowers of Italy's countryside and mountains; by May and June the gardens are at their peak. But in many ways the best and certainly the most soulful season of Venetia is autumn, when the landscapes match the colours of Venetian art; the Po Delta and lagoon are at their most haunting and the vineyards are heavy with grapes. The weather is mild, places aren't crowded, and you won't need your umbrella too much, at least until November. During the winter the happiest visitors are either on skis, in the opera house, or at the table eating wild mushrooms and radicchio. It's the best time to go if you want the churches and museums to yourself, or want to meet Italians. Beware, though, that it can rain and rain, and mountain valleys can lie for days under banks of fog and mist.

Crime

Police or medical emergency number ✆ 113

There is a fair amount of petty crime in Italy, although relatively little in Venetia—purse-snatchings, pickpocketing, minor thievery of the white-collar kind (always check your change) and car break-ins and theft—but violent crime is rare. Nearly all mishaps can be avoided with adequate precautions. Scooter-borne purse-snatchers can be foiled if you stay on the inside of the pavement and keep a firm hold on your property (sling your bag-strap across your body, not dangling from one shoulder); pickpockets strike in crowded buses or trams and gatherings: don't carry too much cash, and split it so you won't lose the lot at once. In cities and popular tourist sites, beware groups of scruffy-looking women or children with placards, apparently begging for money. They use distraction techniques to perfection. The smallest and most innocent-looking child is generally the most skilful pickpocket. If you are targeted, the best technique is to grab sharply hold of any vulnerable possessions or pockets and shout furiously. Be extra careful in train stations, don't leave valuables in hotel rooms, and always park your car in garages, guarded lots or on well-lit streets, with portable temptations out of sight. Purchasing small quantities of soft drugs for personal consumption is technically legal in Italy, though what constitutes a small quantity is unspecified, and if the police don't like you to begin with, it will probably be enough to get you into big trouble.

Political terrorism, once the scourge of Italy, has declined greatly in recent years, mainly thanks to special quasi-military squads of black-uniformed national police, the *Carabinieri*. Local matters are usually in the hands of the *Polizia Urbana*; the nattily dressed *Vigili Urbani* concern themselves with directing traffic, and handing out parking fines. If you need to summon any of them, dial ✆ 113.

Disabled Travellers

Italy has been relatively slow off the mark in its provision for disabled visitors. Cobblestones, uneven or non-existent pavements, appalling traffic conditions, crowded transport and endless flights of steps in many public places are all disincentives. Progress is gradually being made, however. Venice has added ramps to many bridges; the tourist office's 'Venice's Lido' map no.1 indicates the parts of the city accessible by wheelchair. A national support organization in your own country may have specific information on facilities in Venetia, and the Italian tourist office or CIT (travel agency) can also advise on hotels, museums with ramps and so on. If you book rail travel through CIT, you can request assistance. In Italy, a cooperative of disabled organizations, ✆ 167 179 179, dispenses advice on accommodation and travel.

In the UK, contact the **Royal Association for Disability & Rehabilitation** (RADAR), and ask for their guide *Getting There* (£5 inc p&p). They are based at 12 City Forum, 250 City Road, London EC1V 8AF, ✆ (020) 7250 3222. Americans should contact SATH (**Society for the Advancement of Travel for the Handicapped**), 347 Fifth Avenue, Suite 610, New York 10016, ✆ (212) 447 7284, ✉ 725 8253. Another useful organisation providing help on both sides of the Atlantic is **Mobility International**, at 45 Broadway West, Eugene, Oregon 97403, USA, ✆ (541) 343 1284. Australians could try **Australian Council for the Rehabilitation of the Disabled** (ACROD), 24 Cabarita Road, Ryde, New South Wales, ✆ (61) 297 432 699. If you need help while you are in Italy, contact the local tourist offices.

Embassies and Consulates

UK	Milan: Via San Paulo 7, ✆ 02 723 001.
	Rome: Via XX Settembre 80/a, ✆ 06 482 5441.
Ireland	Rome: Largo Nazareno 3, ✆ 06 678 2541.
USA	Milan: Largo Donegani 1, ✆ 02 2900 1841.
	Rome: Via V. Veneto 119/a, ✆ 06 46741.

Canada	Milan: Via Vittorio Pisani 19, ✆ 02 669 7451.
	Rome: Via Zara 30, ✆ 06 440 3028.
Australia	Milan: Via Borgagna 2, ✆ 02 7601 1330.
	Rome: Via Alessandria 215, ✆ 06 852 721.
New Zealand	Rome: Via Zara 28, ✆ 06 440 2928.

Festivals

There are literally thousands of festivals answering to every description in Venetia. Every *comune* has at least one or two, celebrating a patron saint; others are sponsored by the political parties (especially the Communists and Socialists), where everyone goes to meet their friends and enjoy the masses of cheap food. No matter where you are, look at the posters; Italy is swamped with culture, and best of all, remains refreshingly unsnobbish or élitist about it all. On the other hand, don't expect anything approaching uninhibited gaiety. Italy is a rather staid place these days, and festivals are largely occasions to dress up, hear some music, re-enact a historic event or have a pleasant outdoor supper. If, at a festival, you happen to notice Italians laughing too loudly, drinking too much, or singing extemporaneously, drop us a line; we would love to see it.

Below is a calendar of the most popular annual events in Venetia. Always check at the tourist offices for precise dates, which tend to change from year to year.

January
Mid-month	Gold and silver fair, **Vicenza**.

February
1st week	*Padovantiquaria*, week-long antiques fair, **Padua**.
2nd week	Big agricultural fair, **Verona**.
Carnival	**Venice** is the place to see the most beautiful masks and costumes, and to attend big-name events as the Lagoon city strives to recreate the old magic. On Carnival Friday, **Verona** celebrates the *Bacanal del gnocco*, a parade with the king of gnocchi and a feast, all in 15th-century dress.
25	*Festa della Renga*, feasting on local specialities, Concordia Sagittaria (**Venice**).

March
25	Traditional horse fair, Lonigo (**Vicenza**).

April
Mid-month	Sagra del Gnocco, eating and dancing, in Teolo (**Padua**).
3rd week	Vinitaly, wine, spirits and olive oil fair, **Verona**; asparagus festival, San Michele al Tagliamento-Bibione (**Venice**); kite-flying festival, Badia Polesine (**Padua**).
End month	Giant antiques fair, and Città di Padova Rugby Tournament, both in **Padua**.

May

1st week	Sagra di Sansonessa, country fair of food, games, and dancing, Caorle (**Venice**).
Ascension	La Sensa, or re-enactment of the Doge's Wedding of the Sea, **Venice**.
End month	Cherry festival, Maróstica (**Vicenza**).

June

12–13	Sant'Antonio, **Padua**: historic re-enactment of the transition of saint's relics from Arcella, and torchlight procession along the Bacchiglione.
Mid-month	Gold, silver, jewellery and watch fair, **Vicenza**.
19–21	Palio di Noale (**Venice**), with 14th-century costumes, market, games.

July

July–Aug	Opera at the Arena, and Shakespeare in the Roman theatre, **Verona**; Festival delle Ville, theatre and other events in the villas along the Brenta Canal, Mira (**Venice**).
All month	International wood sculpture competition, Recoaro Terme (**Vicenza**).
3rd Sun	Feast of the Redentore, **Venice**, celebrating the end of the 1576 plague, with a tremendous fireworks show followed by a procession over a bridge of boats on the Giudecca Canal.

August

1st week	Pavana d'Estate, festival of popular and ethnic music, Teolo (**Padua**).
Mid-Aug–Sept	Musical festival, Portogruaro (**Venice**).
End Aug –early Sept	International Film Festival, **Venice**; Sagra di Santa Colomba, Piazzola sul Brenta (**Padua**), folk festival, with donkey palio, dances, food, etc.

September

1st Sun	Historical regatta in costume and gondola races in **Venice**; *Gioco dell'Oca in Piazza*, playing of the medieval Goose Game, in costume, Portogruaro (**Venice**).
2nd week	Human chess game at Maróstica (**Vicenza**), even-numbered years.
20	Re-enactment of 10th-century nabbing of the 12 Venetian brides by pirates on their wedding night, Caorle (**Venice**).
3rd Sun	*Festa Regionale dell'Uva*, Vò (**Padua**), festival of grapes from around Italy, with a parade and plenty of wine; wine festival, Gambellara (**Vicenza**).

October

1st week	*Salone dell'Antiquariato*, antiques and old books, **Vicenza**.
1st Sun	Feast of the Rosary, Galzignano Terme (**Padua**), procession in historical costume recalling the Battle of Lepanto, and a donkey race.
3rd Sun	Pumpkin festival, Salzano (**Venice**).

November

Mid-month	*Fieracavalli*, major horse fair in **Verona** (since 1908); DOC wine and food fair, **Vicenza**.
21	Feast of the Madonna della Salute, **Venice**, pilgrimage on bridge of boats over the Grand Canal, in thanksgiving for deliverance from the 1630 plague.

December

Throughout	Exhibition of *presepi* (Christmas cribs) in **Verona**.

Food and Drink

There are those who eat to live and those who live to eat, and then there are the Italians, for whom food has an almost religious significance, unfathomably linked with love, La Mamma and tradition. In this singular country, where millions of otherwise sane people spend much of their waking hours worrying about their digestion, standards both at home and in the restaurants are understandably high. Few Italians are gluttons, but all are experts on what is what in the kitchen; to serve a meal that is not properly prepared and more than a little complex is tantamount to an insult. For the visitor this national culinary obsession comes as an extra bonus to the senses—along with Italy's remarkable sights, music and the warm sun on your back, you can enjoy some of the best tastes and smells the world can offer, prepared daily in Italy's kitchens and fermented in its countless wine cellars. Eating *all'Italiana* is not only delicious and wholesome, but now undeniably trendy. Foreigners flock here to learn the secrets of Italian cuisine and the even more elusive secret of how the Italians can live surrounded by such delights and still fit into their sleek Armani trousers.

Breakfast (*colazione*) in Italy is no lingering affair, but an early morning sugar and caffeine wake-up shot to the brain: a *cappuccino* (espresso with hot foamy milk, often sprinkled with chocolate—incidentally, first thing in the morning is the only time of day any self-respecting Italian will touch the stuff), a *caffè latte* (white coffee) or a *caffè lungo* (a generous portion of espresso), accompanied by a croissant-type roll, called a *cornetto* or *briosce*, or a fancy pastry. This repast can be consumed in any bar and repeated during the morning as often as necessary. Breakfast in Italian hotels is seldom worth the price.

Lunch (*pranzo*), generally served around 1pm, is traditionally the most important meal of the day, with a minimum of a first course (*primo piatto*—any kind of pasta dish, broth or soup, or rice dish or pizza), a second course (*secondo*—a meat dish, accompanied by a *contorno* or side dish—a vegetable, salad, or potatoes usually), followed by fruit or dessert and coffee. You can, however, begin with a platter of *antipasti*—the appetizers Italians do so brilliantly, ranging from warm seafood delicacies to raw ham (*prosciutto crudo*), salami in a hundred varieties, lovely vegetables, savoury toasts, olives, pâté and many more. There are restaurants that specialize in *antipasti*, and they usually don't take it amiss if you decide to forget the pasta and meat and just nibble on these scrumptious hors-d'œuvres (though in the end it will probably cost more than a full meal). Most Italians accompany their meal with wine and mineral water—*acqua minerale*, with or without bubbles (*con* or *senza gas*), which supposedly aids digestion—concluding their meals with a *digestivo* liqueur.

Cena, the **evening meal**, is usually eaten around 8pm. This is much the same as *pranzo* although lighter, without the pasta; a pizza and beer, eggs or a fish dish. In restaurants, however, they offer all the courses.

In Italy the various terms for types of **restaurants**—*ristorante*, *trattoria*, or *osteria*—have been confused. A *trattoria* or *osteria* can be just as elaborate as a restaurant, though rarely is a *ristorante* as informal as a traditional *trattoria*. Unfortunately the old habit of posting menus and prices in the windows has fallen from fashion, so it's often difficult to judge variety or prices. In general, the fancier the fittings, the fancier the **bill**, though neither of these points has anything at all to do with the quality of the food. If you're uncertain, do as you would at home—look for lots of locals. When you eat out, mentally add to the bill (*conto*) the bread and cover charge (*pane e coperto*, between L2,000 and L4,000), and a 15% service charge. This is often included in the bill (*servizio compreso*); if not, it will say *servizio non compreso*, and you'll have to do your own arithmetic. Additional tipping is at your own discretion, but not expected in family-owned and -run places.

People who haven't visited Italy for years and have fond memories of eating full meals for under a pound will be amazed at how much **prices** have risen; though in some respects eating out in Italy is still a bargain, especially when you figure out how much all that wine would have cost you at home. In many places you'll often find restaurants offering a *menu turistico*—full, set meals of usually meagre inspiration for L20,000–30,000. More imaginative chefs often offer a *menu degustazione*—a set-price gourmet meal that allows you to taste their daily specialities and seasonal dishes. Both of these are cheaper than if you had ordered the same food à la carte.

Restaurant price categories

very expensive	over L80,000
expensive	L50,000–80,000
moderate	L30,000–50,000
inexpensive	below L30,000

When you leave a restaurant you will be given a receipt (*scontrino* or *ricevuto fiscale*) which according to Italian law you must take with you out of the door and carry for at least 60 metres. If you aren't given one, it means the restaurant is probably fudging on its taxes and thus offering you lower prices. There is a slim chance the tax police (*Guardia di Fianza*) may have their eye on you and the restaurant, and if you don't have a receipt they could slap you with a heavy fine.

As the pace of modern urban life militates against traditional lengthy home-cooked repasts with the family, followed by a siesta, alternatives to sit-down meals have mushroomed. Many office workers now behave much as their counterparts elsewhere in Europe and consume a rapid snack at lunchtime, returning home after a busy day to throw together some pasta and salad in the evenings. The original Italian fast food alternative, a buffet known as the 'hot table' (*tavola calda*) is becoming harder and harder to find among the international and made in Italy fast food franchises of various descriptions; bars often double as *panicotecas* (which make hot or cold sandwiches to order, or serve *tramezzini*, little sandwiches on plain, square white bread that are always much better than they look);

outlets selling pizza by the slice (*al taglio*) are common in city centres. At any grocer's (*alimentari*) or market (*mercato*) you can buy the materials for countryside or hotel-room picnics; some will make sandwiches for you.

What comes as a suprise to many visitors is the tremendous regional diversity at the table; often next to nothing on the menu looks familiar, or is disguised by a local or dialect name. Expect further mystification, as many Italian chefs have wholeheartedly embraced the concept of *nouvelle cuisine*, or rather *nuova cucina*, and are constantly inventing dishes with even more names. If your waiter's English fails to elucidate, the menu decoder at the back of this book may help.

Regional Specialities

Forget the Italian stereotypes; olives don't grow in Venetia (except around Lake Garda) so many dishes are prepared with butter. Tomatoes and oregano are used more sparingly here than in the south, and many dishes, for better or worse, are served with *polenta* (a pudding or cake of yellow maize flour), a brick-heavy substance to be approached with caution.

Venice

Venetian cuisine is delicious, although in Venice proper you'll have to pay way over the odds to have it done properly; you'll do much better, in quality and price, on the *terra firma*. In seaside or lagoonside restaurants, a typical meal might include oysters from Chioggia or *sarde in saor* (marinated sardines) for *antipasti*, followed by the classic *risi e bisi* (rice and peas, cooked with Parma ham and Parmesan) or the Veneto's favourite pasta, *bigoli in salsa* (thick spaghetti, served with a piquant onion, butter and anchovy sauce). Another favourite choice for primo are various types of *risotto*: *di mare*, with seafood, *in nero*, with cuttlefish cooked in its own ink, or *alla sbirraglia*, with vegetables, chicken and ham. For *secondo*, liver and onions (*fegato alla veneziana*) with polenta shares top billing with seafood dishes like scampi, cuttlefish in its own ink (*seppie alla veneziana*), *fritto* (Adriatic mixed fry) and lobster (*aragosta*), or the equally pricey large Venetian crab, the delicate *granceola*. Top it all off with a *tiramisù*, the traditional Veneto mascarpone, coffee and chocolate dessert.

Candied fruit has an important role in the sweet category, recalling Venice's long rule over the island that gave us both the name and Europe's first sugar cane—Candia (Crete). An enduring taste for sultanas and pine nuts was acquired from the Byzantines and Turks, studding not only pastries but dishes such as *stoccafisso* (salt cod) and fish prepared *in carpione* (fried or grilled, then marinated with vinegar, wine and fried onions—a favourite of Venetian sailors, as it lasted a long time at sea and helped to prevent scurvy).

The Veneto

Elsewhere along coastal areas look for fish soup, *brodetto di pesce*, often served with polenta. Catfish and other freshwater creatures are the speciality from Rovigo, served fried or in ragouts. Treviso's little river Sile yields the star ingredient of *anguilla* (or *bisato*) *in umido* (eel stew) while the province is renowned for its *radicchio*, red chicory, a favourite in winter salads. Since Roman times the Trevigiano was famous for its *soppressa* (salted meats) and spicy *divina lucanica tarvisiana*, a sausage better known these days as *luganeghe*. A traditional first course, *sopa coada*, is a rich chicken broth with pieces of meat and bread.

In springtime gastronomes flock to feast on white asparagus from Bassano del Grappa and the deep red cherries of Maróstica, while in the autumn wild mushrooms, especially from the hills of Montello, hold pride of place, along with game dishes served with *peverada* (a traditional sauce made of giblets, anchovies and lemons). Padua is the land of pumpkin dishes and poultry 'of the courtyard'—chicken and geese mainly, usually served roasted; if it's cooked *alla Padovana* it will be spit roast and very spicy. Vicenza is famous for its dried cod, *bacalà*, and tops its *bigoli* with duck sauce. Montagnana produces sweet hams, Verona is synonymous with gnocchi, tall golden Pandoro cakes, all kinds of fruit and peaches served in red wine; it also produces more cabbage than anywhere else in Italy. The latter features in the classic Veronese dish, *patissada de cavolo con gnocchi*. The Veneto's best known cheese is strong-flavoured Asiago, from the eponymous mountain plateau; another, Formaggio Monte Veronese DOC, is made at the Lessinia, above Verona, and hard to find outside the region.

Regional Wines

If Italy has an infinite variety of regional dishes, there is an equally bewildering array of **regional wines,** many of which are rarely exported because they are best drunk young. Unless you're dining at a restaurant with an exceptional cellar, do as the Italians do and order a carafe of the local wine (*vino locale* or *vino della casa*). You won't often be wrong. Most Italian wines are named after the grape and the district they come from. If the label says DOC (*Denominazione di Origine Controllata*) it means that the wine comes from a specially defined area and was produced according to a certain traditional method. DOCG (*Denominazione d'Origine Controllata e Garantia*) is allegedly a more rigorous classification, indicating that the wines not only conform to DOC standards, but are tested by government-appointed inspectors (who are now more in evidence since a hideous methanol scandal claimed 20 lives in 1986). *Classico* means that a wine comes from the oldest part of the zone of production, though is not necessarily better than a non-*Classico*. *Riserva, superiore* or *speciale* denotes a wine that has been aged longer and is more alcoholic; *Recioto*, a favourite in the Veneto, is a wine made from the outer clusters of grapes ('the ears') with a higher sugar (and therefore alcohol) content. Other Italian wine words are *spumante* (sparkling); *frizzante* (pétillant), *amabile* (semi-sweet), *abbocato* (medium dry) and *passito* (strong sweet wine made from raisins). *Rosso* is red, *bianco* white; between the two extremes lie *rubiato* (ruby), *rosato, chiaretto* or *cerasuolo* (rose). *Secco* is dry, *dolce* sweet, *liquoroso* fortified and sweet. *Vendemmia* means vintage, a *cantina* is a cellar, and an *enoteca* is a wine-shop where you can taste and buy wines.

The Veneto, one of Italy's top three wine regions (along with Tuscany and Piedmont) has made massive strides in improving quality since the war. Verona's Valpolicella is now one of Italy's most prestigious red wines, followed in fame by its lesser cousin Bardolino, from the shores of Lake Garda. Other lesser known reds worth seeking out in the region include Pramaggiore Cabernet and Merlot, Venegazzu della Casa and Piave Raboso. Of the whites, Soave is the best known and most abundant, if not the most reputable, although small Soave estates have been producing wines of quality; dry white Bianco di Custoza is a more flavoursome bet with its mix of Tocai, while Tocai di Lison from the border of Friuli has an excellent reputation. Most of the house wine in Venice is Piave, and the favourite aperitif throughout the region is Prosecco, that charming sparkler from Conegliano. Then there's that famous wine by-product, *grappa*, a mighty, Schnapps-like aquavit drunk in black coffee after a meal (a *caffè corretto*) or for breakfast if it's chilly; Bassano del Grappa has Italy's oldest distillery.

Health and Emergencies

You can insure yourself against almost any possible mishap—cancelled flights, stolen or lost baggage and illness. Check any policies you hold to see if they cover you while abroad, and under what circumstances, and judge whether you need a special **traveller's insurance** policy for the journey. Travel agencies sell them, as well as insurance companies.

Citizens of EU countries are entitled to **reciprocal health care** in Italy's National Health Service and a 90% discount on prescriptions (bring **Form E111** with you). The E111 does not cover all medical expenses (no repatriation costs, for example, and no private treatment), and it is advisable to take out separate travel insurance for full cover. Citizens of non-EU countries should check carefully that they have adequate insurance for any medical expenses, and the cost of returning home. Australia has a reciprocal health care scheme with Italy, but New Zealand, Canada and the USA do not. If you already have health insurance, a student card, or a credit card, you may be entitled to some medical cover abroad.

In an **emergency**, dial *©* **115** for fire (*incendio*) and *©* **113** for an ambulance in Italy (*ambulanza*) or to find the nearest hospital (*ospedale*). Less serious problems can be treated at a *Pronto Soccorso* (casualty/first aid department) at any hospital clinic (*ambulatorio*) or at a local health unit (*Unita Sanitaria Locale*—USL). Airports and main railway stations also have **first-aid posts**. If you have to pay for any health treatment, make sure you get a receipt, so that you can make any claims for reimbursement later.

Dispensing **chemists** (*farmacia*) are generally open from 8.30am to 1pm and from 4 to 8pm. Pharmacists are trained to give advice for minor ills. Any large town will have a *farmacia* that stays open 24 hours; others take turns to stay open (the address rota is posted in the window).

No specific **vaccinations** are required or advised for citizens of most countries before visiting Italy; the main health risks are the usual travellers' woes of upset stomachs or the effects of too much sun. Take a supply of **medicaments** with you (insect repellent, anti-diarrhoeal medicine, sun lotion and antiseptic cream), and any drugs you need regularly.

Most Italian doctors speak at least rudimentary English, but if you can't find one, contact your embassy or consulate for a list of English-speaking doctors.

Maps and Publications

The maps in this guide are for orientation only and, to explore in any detail, invest in a good, up-to-date regional map, produced by the **Touring Club Italiano**, and **Istituto Geografico de Agostini**. Get them in the UK at **Stanford's**, 12–14 Long Acre, London WC2 9LP, *©* (020) 7836 1321, or **The Travel Bookshop**, 13 Blenheim Crescent, London W11 2EE, *©* (020) 7229 5260. In the USA, try **The Complete Traveler**, 199 Madison Ave, New York, NY 10016, *©* (212) 685 9007. They are available at all major bookshops in Italy (e.g. Feltrinelli) or sometimes on news stands. Italian tourist offices are helpful and can often supply good area maps and town plans.

Money

It's a good idea to order a wad of lire from your home bank to have on hand when you arrive in the land of strikes, unforeseen delays and quirky banking hours (*see* below). Take great care how you carry it, however (don't keep it all in one place). Obtaining money is often a frustrating business involving much queueing and form-filling. The major banks and exchange bureaux licensed by the Bank of Italy give the best exchange rates for currency or traveller's cheques. Hotels, private exchanges in resorts and FS-run exchanges at railway stations usually have less advantageous rates, but are open outside normal banking hours. Weekend exchange offices can be found in most large cities, e.g. **Venice**: American Express, S. Moise 1471; CIT Piazza S. Marco. In addition there are exchange offices at most airports. Remember that Italians indicate decimals with commas and thousands with full points.

You can (for a significant commission) use your major credit card, Eurocheque card or British bank card (but check at your bank first) to take money out of Italian automatic tellers (*Bancomat*). You need a four-digit PIN number to use these. Make sure you read the instructions carefully, or your card may be retained by the machine. Besides traveller's cheques, most banks will give also you cash on a recognized credit card or Eurocheque with a Eurocheque card. Large hotels, resort area restaurants, most petrol stations, shops and car hire firms will accept plastic as well; many smaller places will not.

You can have money transferred to you through an Italian bank but this process may take over a week, even if it's sent urgent, *espressissimo*. You will need your passport as identification when you collect it.

National Holidays

Most museums, as well as banks and shops, are closed on the following national holidays.

1 January (New Year's Day)

6 January (Epiphany)

Easter Monday

25 April (Liberation Day)

1 May (Labour Day)

15 August (Assumption, also known as *Ferragosto*, the official start of the Italian holiday season)

1 November (All Saints' Day)

8 December (Immaculate Conception)

25 December (Christmas Day)

26 December (*Santo Stefano*, St Stephen's Day)

In addition to these general holidays, many towns also take their patron saint's day off.

Opening Hours and Museums

Although it varies from town to town, most of Venetia closes down at 1pm until 3 or 4pm to eat and properly digest the main meal of the day. Afternoon hours are from 4 to 7, often from 5 to 8 in the hot summer months. Bars are often the only places open during the early afternoon. Some cities close down completely during August when locals flee from the polluted frying pan to the hills, lakes or coast. In any case, don't be surprised if you find anywhere in Italy unexpectedly closed (or, indeed, open), whatever its official stated hours.

Banks: Banking hours vary, but core times in large towns are usually Monday to Friday 8.30am to 1pm and 3 to 4pm, closed weekends and on local and national holidays (*see* below). Outside normal hours, you will usually be able to find somewhere to change money (at disadvantageous rates).

Shops usually open Monday to Saturday from 8am to 1pm and 3.30pm to 7.30pm, though hours vary according to season and are shorter in smaller centres. In some large cities hours are longer. Some supermarkets and department stores stay open throughout the day.

Offices: Government-run dispensers of red tape (e.g. visa departments) often stay open for quite limited periods, usually during the mornings, Monday to Friday. It pays to get there as soon as they open (or before) to spare your nerves in an interminable queue. Anyway, take something to read, or write your memoirs.

Museums and galleries: Many of Italy's museums are magnificent, many are run with shameful neglect, and many have been closed for years for 'restoration' with slim prospects of reopening in the foreseeable future. With two works of art per inhabitant, Italy has a hard time financing the preservation of its heritage; ring the local tourist office to find out what is open and what is 'temporarily' closed before setting off on a wild-goose chase.

Churches: Italy's churches have always been a prime target for art thieves and as a consequence are usually locked when there isn't a sacristan or caretaker to keep an eye on things. All churches, except for the really important cathedrals and basilicas, close in the afternoon at the same hours as the shops, and the little ones tend to stay closed. Always have a pocketful of coins for the light machines in churches, or whatever work of art you came to inspect will remain clouded in ecclesiastical gloom. Don't do your visiting during services, and don't come to see paintings and statutes in churches the week preceding Easter—you will probably find them covered with mourning shrouds.

In general, Sunday afternoons and Mondays are dead periods for the sightseer—you may want to make them your travelling days. Places without specified opening hours can usually be visited on request, but it is best to go before 1pm. Entrance charges vary widely; major sights are fairly steep (L10,000 plus), but others may be completely free. EU citizens under 18 and over 65 get free admission to state museums, at least in theory.

Packing

You simply cannot overdress in Italy; whatever grand strides Italian designers have made on the international fashion merry-go-round, most of their clothes are purchased domestically, prices be damned. Whether or not you want to try to keep up with the natives is your own affair and your own heavy suitcase—you may do well to compromise and just bring a couple of smart outfits for big nights out. It's not that the Italians are very formal; they simply like to dress up with a gorgeousness that adorns their cities just as much as those old Renaissance churches and palaces. The few places with dress codes are the major churches and basilicas (no shorts, sleeveless shirts or strappy sundresses—women should tuck a light silk scarf in a bag to throw over the shoulders), casinos, and a few posh restaurants.

After agonizing over fashion, remember to pack small and light: trans-Atlantic airlines limit baggage by size (two pieces are free up to 1.5m in height and width; in second-class you're allowed one of 1.5m and another up to 110cm). Within Europe limits are by weight; 20kg (44lbs) in second-class, 30kg (66lbs) in first. You may well be penalized for anything larger. If you're travelling mainly by train, you'll want to keep bags to a minimum: jamming big cases in overhead racks in a crowded compartment isn't much fun for anyone. Never take more than you can carry; but do bring the following: any prescription medicine you need, an extra pair of glasses or contact lenses if you wear them; a pocket knife and corkscrew (for picnics), a flashlight (for dark frescoed churches, caves and crypts), a travel alarm (for those early trains) and a pocket Italian-English dictionary (for flirting and other emergencies; outside the main tourist centres you may well have trouble finding someone who speaks English). If you're a light sleeper, you may want to invest in ear-plugs. Your electric appliances will work in Italy if you adapt and convert them to run on 220 AC with two round prongs on the plug.

Photography

Film and developing are much more expensive than they are in either the UK or the USA, though there are plenty of outlets where you can obtain them. Note that you are not allowed to take pictures in most museums and in some churches. Most cities now offer one-hour processing if you need your pics in a hurry.

Post Offices

Dealing with *la posta italiana*, the most expensive and slowest postal service in Europe, has always been a risky, frustrating, time-consuming affair. Even buying the right stamps requires dedicated research and saintly patience. One of the scandals that mesmerized Italy in recent years involved the minister of the post office, who disposed of literally tons of backlog mail by tossing it in the Tiber. When the news broke, he was replaced—the new minister, having learned his lesson, burned all the mail the post office was incapable of delivering. Not surprisingly, fed-up Italians view the invention of the fax machine as a gift from the Madonna.

Post offices in Italy are usually open from 8am until 1pm (Monday to Saturday), or until 6 or 7pm in a large city. To have your mail sent poste restante (general delivery), have it addressed to the central post office (*Fermo Posta*) and expect three to four weeks for it to arrive. Make sure your surname is very clearly written in block capitals. To pick up your mail you must present your passport and pay a nominal charge. Stamps (*francobolli*) may be purchased in post offices or at tobacconists (*tabacchi,* identified by their blue signs with a white T). Prices fluctuate. The rates for letters and postcards (depending how many words you write!) vary according to the whim of the tobacconist or postal clerk.

You can also have money telegraphed to you through the post office; if all goes well, this can happen in a mere three days, but expect a fair proportion of it to go into commission.

Shopping

'Made in Italy' has become a byword for style and quality, especially in fashion and leather, but also in home design, ceramics, kitchenware, jewellery, lace and linens, glassware and crystal, chocolates, bells, Christmas decorations, hats, straw work, art books, engravings, handmade stationery, gold and silverware, bicycles, sports cars, woodworking, a hundred kinds of liqueurs, aperitifs, coffee machines, gastronomic specialities, and antiques (both reproductions and the real thing). You'll find the best variety of goods in Verona and Venice—in other words, where the money is. Be sure to save receipts for Customs (or tax rebates, if you're not an EU resident) on the way home.

If you are looking for antiques, be sure to demand a certificate of authenticity—Venetia is Italy's top manufacturer of reproductions, and they can be very, very good. Monthly weekend antique markets are a thriving business, run on the following calendar:

1st Sunday: Battaglia Terme.

2nd Saturday: Àsolo.

2nd Sunday: Noale.

3rd Saturday and Sunday: Montagnana.

3rd Sunday: Padua and Este.

4th Saturday: Monsélice.

4th Sunday: Dolo.

To get your antique or modern art purchases home, you will have to apply to the Export Department of the Italian Ministry of Education—a possible hassle. You will have to pay an export tax as well; your seller should know the details.

Sports and Activities

Football: Soccer (*il calcio*) is a national obsession. For many Italians its importance far outweighs tedious issues like the state of the nation, the government of the day, or any momentous international event—not least because of the weekly chance (slim but real) of becoming an instant lira billionaire in the Lotteria Sportiva. All major cities, and most minor ones, have at least one team of some sort. The sport was actually introduced by the English, but a Renaissance game, something like a cross between football and rugby, has existed in Italy for centuries. Modern Italian teams are known for their grace, precision, and coordination; rivalries are intense, scandals, especially involving bribery and cheating, are rife. The tempting rewards offered by such big-time entertainment attract all manner of corrupt practices, yet crowd violence is minimal compared with the havoc wreaked by Britain's lamentable fans. Big-league matches are played on Sunday afternoons from September to May. For information, contact the Federazione Italiana Giuoco Calcio, Via G Allegri 14, 00198 Rome, ✆ 06 84911. Rugby and baseball are also played in most cities; even American football and basketball have their devotees.

Rowing and canoeing: The annual regatta between the four ancient maritime republics of Venice, Amalfi, Genoa and Pisa (held in turn at each city) is a splendidly colourful event. The fast rivers of the mountain areas provide exciting white-water sport. For information contact Federazione Italiana Canoa e Kayak, Viale Tiziano 70, 00196 Rome, ℗ 06 368 58215.

Tennis: If soccer is Italy's most popular spectator sport, tennis is probably the game most people play. Every *comune* has public courts for hourly hire, especially resorts. Private clubs may offer temporary membership to passing visitors, and hotel courts can often be used by non-residents for a reasonable fee. Contact local tourist offices for information.

Watersports: Despite Italy's notorious coastal pollution, watersports are immensely popular, especially sailing and windsurfing. Waterskiing is possible on all the major lakes, as well as at many coastal resorts. Boat and equipment hire tends to be quite expensive.

Venetia is not remarkable for its **beaches** and, although you'll find plenty of sand at major resorts such as Venice's Lido, much of the coast is disappointingly flat and dull and many seaside resorts are plagued by that peculiarly Italian phenomenon, the concessionaire, who parks ugly lines of sunbeds and brollies all the way along the best stretches of beach, and charges all comers handsomely for the privilege. During the winter you can see what happens when the beaches miss out on their manicures; many get depressingly rubbish-strewn. No one bats an eye at topless bathing, though nudism requires more discretion. For further information, write to the following organizations:

> **Federazione Italiana Vela** (Italian Sailing Federation), Via Brigata Bisagno 2/17, Genoa, ℗ 010 56 57 23.

> **Federazione Italiana Motonautica** (Italian Motorboat Federation), and **Federazione Italiana Sci Nautico** can both be found at Via Piranesi 44b, Milan, ℗ 02 76 10 50.

Telephones

Public telephones for international calls may be found in the offices of **Telecom Italia**, Italy's telephone company. They are the only places where you can make reverse-charge calls (*a erre*, collect calls) but be prepared for a wait, as all these calls go through the operator in Rome. Long-distance rates are among the highest in Europe. Calls within Italy are cheapest after 10pm; international calls after 11pm. Most phone booths now take either coins (L100, 200, 500 or 1,000) or phone cards (*schede, telefoniche*) available in L5,000, L10,000 and sometimes L15,000 amounts at tobacconists and news-stands—you will have to snap off the small perforated corner in order to use them. In smaller villages, you can usually find *telefoni a scatti*, with a meter on it, in at least one bar (a small commission is generally charged).

Direct calls may be made by dialling the international prefix (for the UK ℗ 0044, Ireland ℗ 00353, USA and Canada ℗ 001, Australia ℗ 0061, New Zealand ℗ 0064). If you're calling Italy from abroad, dial the country code, ℗ 0039, and then the whole number, including the first zero.

Time

Italy is on Central European Time, one hour ahead of Greenwich Mean Time and six hours ahead of Eastern Standard Time. From the last weekend of March to the end of September, Italian Summer Time (daylight saving time) is in effect.

Toilets

They 'let down their breeches wherever and before whomsoever they please; according all St Mark's Place, and many parts of the sumptuous building, the Doge's Palace, are dedicated to Cloacina, and you may see Votaries at their devotions every hour of the day.' Thus Samuel Sharp in the 18th century. It's not so bad now, although don't expect Italy to makes its conveniences very convenient even in city centres—look for them in places like train and bus stations and bars. Ask for the *bagno*, *toilette*, or *gabinetto*; in stations and the smarter bars and cafes, there are washroom attendants who expect a few hundred lire for keeping the place decent. Don't confuse the Italian plurals; *signori* (gents), *signore* (ladies).

Tourist Offices

Known under various initials as EPT, APT or AAST, Italian tourist offices usually stay open from 8am to 12.30 or 1pm, and from 3 to 7pm, possibly longer in summer. Few open on Saturday afternoons or Sundays. Information booths can also be found at major railway stations and can provide hotel lists, town plans and terse information on local sights and transport. Queues can be maddeningly long. English is spoken in the main centres. If you're stuck, you may get more sense out of a friendly travel agency than an official tourist office. The Veneto regional government has a free phone tourist information number you can use while in Italy ✆ 167 853 040. Or contact your Italian State Tourist Office:

UK	1 Princes Street, London W1R 8AY, ✆ (020) 7408 1254, ✉ (020) 7493 6695.
USA	630 Fifth Avenue, Suite 1565, New York NY 10111, ✆ (212) 245 4822, ✉ (212) 586 9249.
	12400 Wilshire Boulevard, Suite 550, Los Angeles, CA 90025, ✆ (310) 820 0098, ✉ (310) 820 6357.
	500 North Michigan Avenue, Suite 1046, Chicago IL 60611, ✆ (312) 644 0990/6, ✉ 644 3019.
Australia	c/o Italian Embassy, 61–69 Macquerie Street, Sydney 2000, NSW, ✆ (02) 9247 8442.
Canada	1 Place Ville Marie, Suite 1914, Montréal, Quebec H3B 3M9, ✆ (514) 866 7667.
Japan	2–7–14 Minimi, Aoyama, Minato-Ku, Tokyo 107, ✆ (813) 347 82 051.
France	23 Rue de la Paix, 75002 Paris, ✆ 01 42 66 66 68.
	14 Avenue de Verdun, 06048 Nice, ✆ 04 93 87 75 81.

Germany	Berliner Allee 26, 4 Düsseldorf, ✆ (211) 13 22 32.
	Kaiserstrasse 65, 6000 Frankfurt/Main 1, ✆ (069) 2374.
	Goethestrasse 20, 80336 München, ✆ (089) 53 03 69.
Netherlands	Stadhouderskade 6, 1054 ES Amsterdam, ✆ (020) 616 8244.
New Zealand	c/o Italian Embassy, 36 Grant Road, Thomdon, Wellington, ✆ (04) 736 065.

Tourist and travel information may also be available from **Alitalia** (Italy's national airline) or **CIT** (Italy's state-run travel agency) offices in some countries. In the UK, contact the **Italian Travel Centre**, 30 St James's Street, London SW1A 1HB, ✆ (020) 7853 6464.

Where to Stay

All accommodation in Italy is classified by the Provincial Tourist Boards. Price control, however, has been deregulated since 1992. Hotels set their own tariffs from then on, which means that prices rocketed. After a period of rapid and erratic price fluctuation, tariffs are at last settling down again to more predictable levels under the influence of market forces. Good-value, interesting accommodation in cities can be very difficult to find.

The quality of furnishings and facilities has generally improved in all categories in recent years. Many hotels have installed smart bathrooms and electronic gadgetry. At the top end of the market, Italy has a number of exceptionally sybaritic hotels, furnished and decorated with real panache. But you can still find plenty of older-style hotels and *pensioni*, whose eccentricities of character and architecture (in some cases undeniably charming) may frequently be at odds with modern standards of comfort or even safety.

Accommodation prices

Category	Double with bath
luxury (*****)	L450–800,000
very expensive (****)	L300–450,000
expensive (***)	L200–300,000
moderate (**)	L120–200,000
cheap (*)	up to L120,000

Hotels and Guesthouses

Italian *alberghi* come in all shapes and sizes. They are rated from one to five stars, depending what facilities they offer (not their character, style or charm). The star ratings are some indication of price levels, but for tax reasons not all hotels choose to advertise themselves at the rating to which they are entitled, so you may find a modestly rated hotel just as comfortable (or more so) than a higher rated one. Conversely, you may find a hotel offers few stars in hopes of attracting budget-conscious travellers, but charges just as much as a higher-rated neighbour. *Pensioni* are generally more modest establishments, though nowadays the distinction between these and ordinary hotels is becoming blurred. *Locande* are traditionally an even more basic form of hostelry, but these days the term may denote somewhere fairly chic. Other inexpensive accommodation is sometimes known as *alloggi* or *affittacamere*. There are usually plenty of cheap dives around railway stations; for somewhere more salubrious, head for the historic quarters. Whatever the shortcomings of the décor, furnishings and fittings, you can usually rely at least on having clean sheets.

Price lists, by law, must be posted on the door of every room, along with meal prices and any extra charges (such as air-conditioning, or even a shower in cheap places). Many hotels display two or three different rates, depending on the season. Low-season rates may be about a third lower than peak-season tariffs. Some resort hotels close down altogether for several months a year. During high season you should always book ahead to be sure of a room (a fax reservation may be less frustrating to organize than one by post). If you have paid a deposit, your booking is valid under Italian law, but don't expect it to be refunded if you have to cancel. Tourist offices publish annual regional lists of hotels and pensions with current rates, but do not generally make reservations for visitors. Major city business hotels may offer significant discounts at weekends.

Main railway stations generally have accommodation booking desks; inevitably, a fee is charged. Chain hotels or motels are generally the easiest hotels to book, though not always the most interesting to stay in. Top of the list is CIGA (*Compagnia Grandi Alberghi*) with some of the most luxurious establishments in Italy, many of them grand, turn-of-the-century places that have been exquisitely restored. Venice's legendary Cipriani is one of its flagships. The French consortium *Relais et Châteaux* specializes in tastefully indulgent accommodation, often in historic buildings. At a more affordable level, one of the biggest chains in Italy is *Jolly Hotels*, always reliable if not all up to the same standard; these can generally be found near the centres of larger towns. Many motels are operated by the ACI (Italian Automobile Club) or by AGIP (the oil company) and usually located along major exit routes.

If you arrive without a reservation, begin looking or phoning round for accommodation early in the day. If possible, inspect the room (and bathroom facilities) before you book, and check the tariff carefully. Italian hoteliers may legally alter their rates twice during the year, so printed tariffs or tourist board lists (and prices quoted in this book!) may be out of date. Hoteliers who wilfully overcharge should be reported to the local tourist office. You will be asked for your passport for registration purposes.

Prices listed in this guide are for double rooms; you can expect to pay about two-thirds the rate for single occupancy, though in high season you may be charged the full double rate in a popular beach resort. Extra beds are usually charged at about a third more of the room rate. Rooms without private bathrooms generally charge 20–30% less, and most offer discounts for children sharing parents' rooms, or children's meals. A *camera singola* (single room) may cost anything from about L25,000 upwards. Double rooms (*camera doppia*) go from about L60,000 to L250,000 or more. If you want a double bed, specify a *camera matrimoniale*.

Breakfast is usually optional in hotels, though obligatory in *pensioni*. You can usually get better value by eating breakfast in a bar or café if you have any choice. In high season you may be expected to take half-board in resorts if the hotel has a restaurant, and one-night stays may be refused.

There aren't many youth hostels in Italy (where they are known as *alberghi* or *ostelli per la gioventù*), but they are generally pleasant and sometimes located in historic buildings. The **Associazione Italiana Alberghi per la Gioventù** (Italian Youth Hostel Association, or AIG) is affiliated to the International Youth Hostel Federation. For a full list of hostels, contact AIG at Via Cavour 44, 00184 Roma (✆ 06 487 1152; ✆ 06488 0492). An international membership card will enable you to stay in any of them. You can obtain these in advance from the following organizations.

UK　　Youth Hostels Association of England and Wales, 14 Southampton Street, London, WC2, ✆ (020) 7836 1036.

USA　　American Youth Hostels Inc., Box 37613, Washington DC 20013-7613, ✆ (202) 783 6161.

Australia　Australian Youth Hostel Association, 60 Mary Street, Surry Hills, Sydney, NSW 2010, ✆ (02) 9621 1111.

Canada　Canadian Hostelling Association, 1600 James Naismith Drive, Suite 608, Gloucester, Ontario K1B 5N4, ✆ (613) 237 7884.

(Cards can usually be purchased on the spot in many hostels if you don't already have one.)

Religious institutions also run hostels; some are single sex, some will accept Catholics only. Rates are usually somewhere between L15,000 and L20,000, including breakfast. Discounts are available for senior citizens, and some family rooms are available. You generally have to check in after 5pm, and pay for your room before 9am. Hostels usually close for most of the daytime, and many operate a curfew. During the spring, noisy school parties cram hostels for field trips. In the summer, it's advisable to book ahead. You should contact the hostels directly.

Villas, Flats and Chalets

If you're travelling in a group or with a family, self-catering can be the ideal way to experience Italy. The National Tourist Office has lists of agencies in the UK and USA which rent places on a weekly or fortnightly basis. CIT offices also rent flats and villas. If you have set your heart on a particular region, write ahead to its tourist office for a list of local agencies and owners, who will send brochures or particulars of their accommodation. Maid service is included in the more glamorous villas; ask whether bed linen and towels are provided. A few of the larger operators are listed below.

in the UK

Eurovillas, 36 East Street, Coggeshall, Essex CO6 1SH, ✆ (01376) 561 156.

Inghams, 10–18 Putney Hill, London SW15 6AX, ✆ (020) 8780 4411.

Interhome, 383 Richmond Road, Twickenham, Middlesex, TW1 2EF, ✆ (020) 8891 1294, website *www.interhome.co.uk*, e-mail *interhome.uk@ibm.net*.

International Chapters, 47–51 St John's Wood High Street, London NW8 7NJ, ✆ (020) 7722 9560.

Magic of Italy, 227 Shepherds Bush Road, London W6 7AS, ✆ (020) 8748 7575.

Vacanze in Italia, Manor Courtyard, Bignor, Pulborough, West Sussex RH20 1QD, ✆ (01798) 869 461.

in the USA

At Home Abroad, 405 East 56th Street 6-H, New York, NY 10022-2466, ✆ (212) 421 9165, ✉ 752 1591, *athomabrod@aol.com*

Rentals for Italy (and Elsewhere!), Suzanne T. Pidduck, 1742 Calle Corva, Camarillo, CA 93010, ✆ (800) 726 6702/(805) 987 5278, ✉ (805) 482 7976, *mail@ rentvillas. com*; they also offer car rentals schemes.

Hideaways International, 767 Islington Street, Portsmouth NH 03801, ✆ (617) 486 8955.

Hometours International, PO Box 11503, Knoxville, TN 37938, ✆ (423) 690 8484/(800) 367 4668.

RAVE, (Rent-a-Vacation Everywhere), 135 Meigs Street, Rochester, New York, NY 14607, ✆ (716) 256 0760.

Camping

Life under canvas is not the fanatical craze it is in France, nor necessarily any great bargain, but there are over 2,000 sites in Italy, particularly popular with holidaymaking families in August, when you can expect to find many sites at bursting point. Unofficial camping is generally frowned on and may attract a stern rebuke from the local police. Camper vans (and facilities for them) are increasingly popular. You can obtain a list of local sites from any regional tourist office. Campsite charges generally range from about L6–8,000 per adult; tents and vehicles additionally cost about L7,000 each. Small extra charges may also be levied for hot showers and electricity. A car-borne couple could therefore spend practically as much for a night at a well equipped campsite as in a cheap hotel. To obtain a camping carnet and to book ahead, write to the **Centro Internazionale Prenotazioni Campeggio**, Casella Postale 23, 50041, Calenzano, Firenze, ✆ 055 882 381; ✉ 055 882 3918 (ask for their list of campsites as well as the booking form). The **Touring Club Italiano** (TCI) publishes a comprehensive annual guide to campsites and tourist villages throughout Italy which is available in bookshops for L29,5000. Write to TCI, Corso Italia 10, Milan, ✆ 02 85261/852 6245.

History

1100–3rd century BC: Prehistory, and the
Rather Mysterious Paleoveneti   38

283 BC–AD 475: The Romans, Rise and Fall   39

476–1000: The Dark Ages   41

1000–1154: The Rise of the *Comuni*   43

1154–1300: Guelphs and Ghibellines   43

1300–1550: Renaissance Italy   45

1494–1529: The Wars of Italy   46

1529–1600: Italy in Chains, but Venice Recovers   46

1600–1796: The Age of Baroque   47

1796–1830: Napoleon and the Austrians   47

1848–1915: The Risorgimento and United Italy   48

1915–1945: War, Fascism and War   49

1945–the Present   51

1100–3rd century BC: Prehistory, and the Rather Mysterious Paleoveneti

Some of the most creative cultures grow up from some of the messiest historical composts. The Mediterranean is a case in point, and Italy an extreme case, and its northeast corner as historically messy and creative as any place on this planet. Venetia's earliest inhabitants (5th–4th millennium BC) were peaceful shepherds, but little else was known about them until 1991 and the sensational discovery of the '**Ice Man**' who perished in an alpine storm 5,300 years ago; his frozen, miraculously intact mummy is now on display in Bolzano, complete with all his gear and the stone statue steles carved by his Neolithic/early Copper Age contemporaries. Many of those contemporaries were lake-dwellers, who built their houses on piles in the water—an art their descendants would one day perfect when they turned the mud flats in a lagoon into Venice.

The Ice Man's world was invaded in the Bronze Age (2nd millennium BC) by proto-Celtic tribes from the Caucasus, some of whom settled on the Black Sea in Paphlagonia (now part of Turkey) and others in northeast Italy, making their home in the fertile lands between the Alps and the Adriatic. These invaders seem to have been the first of the **Paleoveneti** (a.k.a. the ancient Veneti or even Heneti in some accounts). They maintained contact with their Veneti kinfolk back in Paphlagonia, and the Mycenaean Greeks traded with them and others along the Po near Adria.

Catastrophic floods, war, and migrations in the 12th–9th centuries, symptomatic of the great upheavals plaguing the entire Mediterranean at this time, brought the onset of the Western World's first Dark Age. According to Titus Livy, the great Roman historian from Padua, the Veneti living in Paphlagonia had fought as allies of the Trojans under their leader **Antenor**, and in the turmoil after the fall of Troy (c. 1180 BC) Antenor brought his tribes to the promised lands of their cousins, and founded Padua in the same way that Aeneas founded Rome. Livy, of course, wanted to give his folk a pedigree as good as the Romans, and whether or not Antenor and company ever fought at Troy, it is true the Veneti were long considered a race apart, of 'Illyrian' origin, different from the other Italic tribes; in their own myths they were raisers of horses from a place called 'Tessalia'. They were certainly more advanced than Venetia's natives, at least in an equine way: they had light, fast chariots, and knew how to ride.

By the 9th century BC, the Veneti of the coastal areas began to trade again with their old acquaintances across the Adriatic and Black Sea, most notably acting as agents between the Greek world and the wealthy Etruscans of Felsina (Bologna). The inland Veneti became known for their vineyards, cloth and bronze working. The intricate working and detail of their artefacts places them firmly in the Celtic tradition, evidence of Polybius' description, that 'the Veneti differed only slightly from the Gauls in their customs and dress, but had a different language.'

This different language, the Indo-European-based **Venet** or **Venetic**, has been the subject of much debate. Once widespread in Venetia and eastern Lombardy, from Bergamo as far east as Istria and into the Dolomites, it was first written in the Etruscan alphabet in the 6th century BC. According to some linguists, its closest cousin is Latin prior to its infiltration by Etruscan. Pliny the Elder confirms a bond between the two, and cites the link between people of the Veneti and the ancient (pre-Rome) Latin league of Alba Longa. It makes sense, if Livy and Virgil are to believed and the Veneti and Latins both washed ashore in Italy from the east, if not all as glorious descendants of Trojan warriors.

The original Veneti capital was **Ateste** (Este); by the time of their first contact with Rome in the 5th century BC, the Veneti had at least fifty towns, a population reckoned at a million and a half, and a new capital at Padua. This was their golden age, enjoyed even as trouble appeared in this same century, in the shape of **Gauls** who came from over the Alps in wave after wave—and stayed, infiltrating south of Venetia into Etruscan lands north of the Apennines. Extremely talented in art and metalworking, they present the singular paradox of a nomadic people, caring little for the comforts of home and everything for their freedom, yet culturally and technologically up to date.

The Gauls invented one significant though overlooked military advance—horseshoes—and carried better swords than most of their foes. The native Veneti allied themselves with Rome against them, but got little thanks for it; on the Roman map, everything north of the Rubicon was lumped together as **Cisalpine Gaul**.

283 BC–AD 475: The Romans, Rise and Fall

More rumblings came, this time from the south as **Rome** gradually subjugated the Etruscans, Latins, and neighbouring tribes. The little republic with the military camp ethic was successful on all fronts, and a sack by marauding Gauls in 390 BC proved only a brief interruption in Rome's march to conquest. Their arch-enemies, the Samnites, formed an alliance with the Northern Etruscans and Celts, leading to a general Italian commotion in which the Romans beat everybody, annexing almost all of Italy by 283 BC.

All the while, the Romans had been diabolically clever in managing their new demesne, maintaining most of the tribes and cities as nominally independent states (among them Verona, Trieste, Oderzo, Este, Adria, Treviso, Vicenza, Feltre, Belluno and Padua) while planting Latin colonies at important transport nodes (Aquileia, Chioggia, Concordia, Cividale del Friuli, Trento, and Altinum, which became the region's biggest port and something of a Roman holiday resort). A major Roman contribution was the great network of roads, beginning with the Via Postumia (148 BC) from Genoa to Verona and Aquileia, and the Via Popilia, linking the Adriatic coast as far south as Rimini, all of which made a truly united Italy seem close to reality.

The northeast, the Roman Tenth Augustine Region of **Venetia et Histria**, 'the flower of Italy, that ornament of the people of Rome,' as Cicero once flattered it, actually turned out to be one of the sleepier corners. The famous men it contributed (the poet Catullus, architect-author Vitruvius, the historian Livy) and the events it saw, such as the meeting of Augustus and Herod the Great in Aquileia, made their mark elsewhere. What the Romans loved best about Venetia was its lagoons, a major source of salt (an imperial monopoly). The Veneti preserved fish in salt to create those favourite Roman condiments, garum and allec, which must have tasted something like Vietnamese fish sauce; they produced it all along the coast from the Po to the River Timavo on an ancient industrial scale, and imported it all over the empire.

The sparsely populated northern section of what is now Alto Adige was conquered in 15 AD by Augustus' stepson Nero Drusus as a buffer between Italy and the hostile Germanic tribes. These mountains were divided into the Imperial provinces of **Raetia** (along with Switzerland) and **Norico** (along with Austria), which were even sleepier than Venetia et Histria. The Romans did however busy themselves with more roadworks in the Dolomites, laying out the originals of the modern *autostrade* that link Italy with the great alpine passes.

The 2nd century AD saw the emergence of the well-known north-south economic divide in Italy. The south—the former lands of Magna Graecia—ruined by Hannibal, impoverished by the Roman Republic, now sank deeper into decline, wrecked by foreign competition. In the north, a sounder economy led to the growth of new centres; in Venetia Padua, Verona and Aquileia were among the most prominent. On balance, though, both politically and economically Italy was becoming an increasingly less significant part of the empire. Of the 2nd-century emperors, fewer came from Italy than from Spain, Illyria or Africa.

By the 3rd century, the legions were no longer the formidable military machine of Augustus' day. In 256 the **Franks** and **Alemanni** invaded Gaul descending as far as the Adige, and in 268 much of the east detached itself from the empire under the leadership of Odenathus of Palmyra. Somehow Rome recovered and prevailed, under four soldier-emperors led by **Diocletian**, who completely revamped the structure of the state and economy, replacing it with a gigantic bureaucracy. Taxes reached new heights as people's ability to pay them declined, and society became increasingly militarized. The biggest change was the division of the empire into halves, each ruled by a co-emperor called 'Augustus'; the western emperors after Diocletian usually kept their court at army head-quarters in Milan, and Rome itself became a marble-veneered backwater.

The confused politics of the 4th century are dominated by **Constantine** (306–337), who ruled both halves of the empire, and favoured Christianity, by now the majority religion in the East but largely identified with the ruling classes and urban populations in Italy and the West. But even the new faith wasn't able to stay the disasters that began in 406. Visigoths, Franks, Vandals, Alans and Suevi overran Gaul and Spain. Italy's turn came in 408, when Western Emperor **Honorius**, ruling from the empire's new capital of Ravenna, had his brilliant general Stilicho (who himself happened to be a Vandal) murdered. A Visigothic invasion followed, including Alaric's sack of Rome in 410. St Augustine, probably echoing the thoughts of most Romans, wrote that the end of the world must be near. Rome should have been so lucky; judgement was postponed long enough for **Attila the Hun** to pass through Italy in 451, decimating Venetia, uprooting its vineyards and burning Padua and Altinum to the ground.

So completely had things changed, it was scarcely possible to tell the Romans from the barbarians. By the 470s, the real ruler in Italy was a Goth general named **Odoacer**, who led a half-Romanized Germanic army and thought of himself as the genuine heir of the Caesars. In 476, he decided to dispense with the lingering charade of the Western Empire, and had himself crowned King of Italy at Pavia. In the confusion, Venetia was left as a province of the Eastern Empire, but a faraway, and fairly autonomous one. The fall of Rome was to prove its big chance; Attila in his rampage had indirectly founded a new city of refugees called **Venice**.

476–1000: The Dark Ages

In Italy, the Dark Ages were never as dark as common belief would have it. One key to understanding the period is that the Roman cities never entirely disappeared. A few expired totally, like Altinum, but most of the rest shrank to provincial market centres, their theatres, arenas and aqueducts abandoned. Amidst the confusion of Rome's fall, popes and monks and battling barons, Goths, Greeks and Lombards were weaving a strange cocoon for Roman Italy. From its silence, centuries later, would be born a new Italian people, suddenly bursting with talent and energy.

Odoacer's government was a peaceful parenthesis for Italy until Byzantine Emperor Zeno in 488 commissioned young King **Theodoric of the Ostrogoths** to invade, a ploy meant to take Ostrogoth pressure off Constantinople. Odoacer's army was waiting, but the Goths defeated them decisively near Verona. Most of the peninsula was speedily occupied, though Odoacer held out in impregnable Ravenna for another three years. At last Theodoric tricked him out with a promise to share Italy with him, then performed the traditional murder at what was supposed to be a reconciliation banquet.

Despite that black mark, Theodoric—a strapping fellow with long Asterix moustaches, typical of the half-cultured, half-barbaric protagonists of the Roman twilight—reorganized his new dominions with remarkable sophistication. Inheriting a civil service that had come down from Odoacer, and before him the Empire, Theodoric used it well to stabilize his realm. The Church was a harder nut to crack. In the disorders of the first barbarian invasions, the Roman pope and scores of local bishops had achieved a great degree of temporal power, filling the vacuum left by the collapse of the Roman system. This temporal power gave the Church a diabolical incentive to oppose any strong government in Italy—especially one of heretical Arian Christians. Theodoric himself had no use for theological disputes, but his policy of religious tolerance proved as intolerable to the Church as his Arianism. Most of his subjects, at least, were thankful for it.

The old guard Romans and Veneti, however, continued to regard the Goths as usurpers; religious bigotry grew, and many looked towards Constantinople in hopes of a restoration of legitimate government. Embittered and increasingly paranoid, Theodoric died in 526, leaving as heir a young grandson named Athalaric, who, with his good Gothic warrior's upbringing, drank himself to death. His mother Amalasuntha was then forced to marry her cousin Theodehad, who had her murdered. With no strong hand in control, the kingdom was ripe for mischief. There was no doubt in anyone's mind that the next move would come from Constantinople.

The Eastern Empire had just the right sort of emperor to take up the challenge: the great **Justinian**. Amalasuntha's murder in 536 gave him his excuse to invade Italy, in the person of his young and brilliant general **Belisarius**. The historical irony was profound; in the ancient homeland of the Roman Empire, Roman troops now came not as liberators, but as foreign, largely Greek-speaking conquerors. Belisarius, and his successor, the eunuch Narses, ultimately prevailed over the Goths in a series of terrible wars that lasted until 563, but the damage to an already stricken society and economy was incalculable.

Italy's total exhaustion was exposed a mere five years later, when the **Lombards**, a Germanic tribe who drank out of their enemies' skulls and otherwise worked hard to earn the title of barbarians, overran the north, setting up their capital at Cividale del Friuli. Although first sharing Italy with semi-independent Byzantine dukes, the Exarchs (Byzantine Viceroys) of Ravenna, and the remarkable new trading city of Venice, the Lombards, under the ruthless and crafty **King Aistulf**, saw their chance to go for the whole boot. Aistulf conquered almost all of the Byzantine Exarchate; in 753, even the old Imperial capital of Ravenna fell into his hands. If the Lombards' final solution were to be averted, the popes would need help from outside. The logical people to ask were the Franks.

At the time, the popes had something to offer in return. For years, the Mayors of the Palace had wanted to supplant the Merovingian dynasty, but lacked the appearance of legitimacy that only the mystic pageantry of the papacy could provide. At the beginning of Aistulf's campaigns, Pope Zacharias quickly gave his blessing to the change of dynasties, and **Pepin**, the new king of the Franks, sent his army over the Alps, in 753 and 756, to foil Aistulf's designs. His unsuccessful attempt to tame Venice, which refused to take sides, helped set that city on its idiosyncratic track.

By 773 the conflict remained the same, though with a different cast of characters. The new Lombard king was Desiderius, the Frankish king was his cordially hostile son-in-law **Charlemagne**, who also invaded Italy twice, in 775 and 776, deposed his father-in-law and took the Iron Crown of Italy for himself. In 799, Pope Leo III set an imperial crown on his head, resuscitating not only the idea of empire, but of an empire that belonged to the successors of St Peter to dispose of as they wished. It changed the political face of Italy for ever, beginning the contorted *pas de deux* of pope and emperor that was to be the mainspring of Italian history throughout the Middle Ages.

With the disintegration of Charlemagne's empire, Italy reverted to a finely balanced anarchy. In Venetia, forests and marshes replaced the ravaged and abandoned farmland, creating a physical as well as a psychological barrier between the precocious maritime city of Venice and the people who remained on the mainland. For the latter, the 9th and early 10th centuries were a bad time of endless wars of petty nobles and battling bishops, forcing many cities to look to their own resources, defending their interests against the Church and nobles alike. An invasion by the Magyars from Hungary in the early 10th century forced the cities to build their first walls and the rural nobles their first castles, which became a source of control over the populations who sought their shelter—hence the origins of the fabulous Este family, and the demonic Ezzelini.

A big break for the cities came in 961, with the invasion of the German **Otto the Great**, the conqueror of the Hungarians, at the request of the powerful Count of Tuscany at Canossa. Otto deposed the last feeble King of Italy, Berengar II, married his widow and was crowned Holy Roman Emperor in Rome the following year. Not that any of the Italians were happy to see him, but the strong government of Otto and his successors beat down the great nobles, gave more power to the bishops, and allowed the growing cities to expand their power and influence. A new pattern was established; the Germanic emperors would be meddling in Italian affairs for centuries, not powerful enough to establish total control, but at least usually able to keep out important rivals.

1000–1154: The Rise of the *Comuni*

Like the rest of Christendom, Italy looked ahead to the year 1000 fearing nothing but the worst—the old legends prophesied that this nice round number would bring with it the end of the world. Perhaps only historical hindsight could see the sprouts of new life and growth that were appearing everywhere on Italian soil at this time, perhaps most remarkably symbolized by the building of St Mark's in Venice. In the towns, business was very good, and the political prospects even brighter. The first mention of a truly independent *comune* (a term used throughout this book, meaning a free city state; the best translation might be 'commonwealth') was in Milan, in 1024; before long, similar *comuni* appeared in Verona, Padua, Vicenza and Treviso.

Throughout this period the papacy had declined greatly in power. In the 1050s, a remarkable monk named Hildebrand controlled papal policy, working behind the scenes to reassert the influence of the Church. When he became pope himself in 1073, **Gregory VII** immediately set himself in conflict with the emperors over the issue of investiture—whether the church or secular powers would appoint church officials. Fifty years of intermittent war followed, including the famous penance in the snow of **Emperor Henry IV** at Canossa (1077) and his donation, that same year, of the lands of Friuli, from the Cadore to Slovenia and Istria, to the **Patriarchate of Aquileia**. Elsewhere, the cities of the north used the long struggle between pope and emperor as an opportunity to increase their influence, and in some cases achieve outright independence.

A different fate was in store for the Dolomites. Keen to keep the road to Rome open and well-disposed for their all-important papal coronations, the German emperors in the 1020s made powerful feudal princes of the bishops at the important crossroads towns of Trento and Bressanone. As time went on, the vassals of the prince-bishops were equally keen to escape their clutches, and littered the mountains with castles to defend their relatively autonomous fiefs.

1154–1300: Guelphs and Ghibellines

While all this was happening, of course, the **First Crusade** (1097–1130) occupied the headlines, partially a result of the new militancy of the papacy begin by Gregory VII. For Italy, and especially for Pisa and Genoa, with plenty of boats to help ship Crusaders, the affair meant nothing but pure profit. Venice sat this Crusade out, not wanting to disrupt its own trade in the East, but it quickly moved to get in on the new action. It also financed the continued independence of the *comuni*, with a big enough surplus for building projects like the Verona's San Zeno and Padua's Palazzo della Ragione. After a thousand years, Venetia and the other cities of the north were as prosperous as they had been in Roman times. Nor had those good old days ever been forgotten. Free *comuni* in the north called their elected leaders 'consuls' or 'senators', and artists and architects turned ancient Roman styles into the Romanesque.

Emperors and popes were still embroiled in the north. **Frederick I Barbarossa** of the Hohenstaufen or Swabian dynasty was strong enough back home in Germany, and he made it the cornerstone of his policy to reassert imperial power in Italy. Beginning in 1154, he crossed the Alps five times, molesting free cities that asked nothing more than the right to fight one another continually. After he brutally sacked and pillaged Lodi and Milan, the cities forgot their differences, formed a united front called the **Lombard League**, and joined up with **Pope Alexander III** (whom Frederick had exiled from Rome in favour of his antipope) to defeat him in 1176. Frederick was forced to recognize Italian freedoms, and equally galling, he was forced to kiss Alexander's foot in Venice. For all that, Frederick triumphed south of the Alps by arranging a marriage that left his grandson **Frederick II** not only emperor but King of Sicily, thus giving him a strong power base in Italy itself.

The second Frederick's career dominated Italian politics for thirty years (1220–50). With his brilliant court, in which Italian was used for the first time (alongside Arabic and Latin), his half-Muslim army, his processions of dancing girls, eunuchs and elephants, he provided Europe with a spectacle the like of which it had never seen. The popes excommunicated him at least twice, while all Italy divided into factions: the **Guelphs**, under the leadership of the popes, supported religious orthodoxy, the liberty of the *comuni* and the interests of their emerging merchant class. The **Ghibellines** stood for the emperor, state economic control, the interests of the rural nobles and religious and intellectual tolerance.

When fierce family feuds tore Verona apart (the germ of the Romeo and Juliet story), Frederick appointed his lieutenant in the region, **Ezzelino III da Romano**, as *podestà* to restore order. As he dragged the rebellious Guelph *comuni* of Padua, Vicenza and Treviso back into the imperial fold, Ezzelino, the first of the Italian self-made despots, or signori, was so wickedly effective that he earned the nickname 'the son of Satan' (*see* pp.66–7). Frederick's other campaigns and diplomacy in the north met with very limited success; nothing he gained was secure, revolts were frequent, and the Bolognese defeated and captured his son Enzo in 1249; Frederick died the next year.

To fight Frederick's other son, Manfred, Pope Urban IV set an ultimately disastrous precedent by inviting in foreign assistance, in the person of **Charles of Anjou**, brother of the King of France. As protector of the Guelphs, Charles defeated Manfred (1266) and murdered the last of the Hohenstaufens, Conradin (1268). He held unchallenged sway over Italy until 1282, creating the perfect conditions to produce a whole new crop of Ezzelino wannabes in every town, until the revolt of the **Sicilian Vespers** started the wars up again. By now, however, the terms Guelph and Ghibelline had ceased to have much meaning; men and cities changed sides as they found expedient, and the old parties began to seem like the black and white squares on a chessboard. If your neighbour and enemy were Guelph, you became for the moment Ghibelline, and if he changed so would you.

Some real changes did come out of all this sound and fury. In 1208 Venice hit its all-time biggest jackpot when it diverted the **Fourth Crusade** to the sack of Constantinople, winning itself a small empire of islands in the Adriatic and Levant. Other cities fell under the rule of military despots, the signori, whose descendants would style themselves counts and dukes: the da Carrara of Padua, the della Scala of Verona. Everywhere the freedom of the *comuni* was in jeopardy; after so much useless strife the temptation to submit to a strong leader often proved overwhelming. Still, trade and money flowed as never before; cities built new cathedrals and incredible skyscraper skylines, with the tall tower-fortresses of the now urbanized nobles. Above all, it was a great age of culture. The time of Guelphs and Ghibellines was also the time of Dante (b. 1265) and Giotto (b. 1266).

1300–1550: Renaissance Italy

This paradoxical Italy continued into the 14th century, with a golden age of culture and an opulent economy alongside continuous war and turmoil. With no serious threats from any other foreign power, the myriad Italian states were able to menace each other joyfully without interference. By now most wars had become a sort of game, conducted on behalf of cities by bands of paid mercenaries, led by hired captains called *condottieri*, who were never allowed to enter the cities themselves. The arrangement suited everyone well. The soldiers had lovely horses and armour, and no real desire to do each other serious harm. The cities were usually free from grand ambitions; everyone was making too much money to want to wreck the system. Best of all, the worst schemers and troublemakers on the Italian stage were fortuitously removed from the scene. With the election of the French Pope **Clement V** in 1303, the papacy moved to Avignon, a puppet of the French king and temporarily without influence in Italian affairs.

By far the biggest event of the 14th century was the **Black Death** of 1347–48, in which it is estimated that Italy lost one-third of its population. The shock brought a rude halt to what had been four hundred years of almost continuous growth, though its effects did not prove a permanent setback for the economy. In fact, the plague's grim joke was that it actually made life better for most who survived; working people in the cities, no longer overcrowded, found their rents lower and their labour worth more, while in the country farmers were able to increase their profits by tilling only the best land.

By now the peninsula was split up by long-established, cohesive states pursing different ends and often warring against each other. Italian statesmen well understood the idea of a balance of power long before political theorists invented the term, and most of them probably believed Italy was enjoying the best of all possible worlds. Foremost among the major states was Venice, the oldest and most glorious, with its oligarchic but singularly effective constitution, and its exotic career of trade and contacts with the East (*see* **Venice**, 'History' pp.83–6). The Venetians waged a series of wars against arch-rival Genoa, finally exhausting her after the **War of Chioggia** in 1379. Once serenely aloof from Italian politics, Venice then added to her sea realms a small land empire, including by 1428 Ùdine, Treviso, Verona, Padua, Vicenza, Belluno, Brescia and Bergamo. One city she subdued but never captured was her Adriatic rival Trieste, which in 1382 had come under the protection of the Austrian emperors. In the north the independent prince-bishops of Trento served to create a kind of demilitarized zone between Venice and their vassals who had managed to achieve real independence, the Counts of Tyrol, and their 14th-century successors, the up and coming **Habsburg** dynasty.

Meanwhile, the Renaissance—the new art and scholarship that began in Florence in the 1400s from a solid foundation of medieval accomplishment—found a happy home in northeast Italy. Masters like Giotto (back in 1309), Donatello and Antonello da Messina spent time in the region, leaving seeds of the imagination for Venetia's artists. Àsolo, under the exiled Queen of Cyprus, became a courtly ideal of Renaissance art and literature and the University of Padua led Europe in the study of medicine.

1494–1529: The Wars of Italy

The Italians brought the trouble down on themselves, when Duke Lodovico of Milan invited the French King **Charles VIII** to cross the Alps and assert his claim to the throne of Milan's enemy, Naples. Charles did just that, and the failure of the combined Italian states to stop him (at the inconclusive Battle of Fornovo, 1485) showed just how helpless Italy was at the hands of emerging new nation-states like France or Spain. When the Spaniards saw how easy it was, they, too, marched in, and before long the German emperor and even the Swiss entered this new market for Italian real estate. The popes did as much as anyone to keep the pot boiling. Alexander VI and his son Cesare Borgia carried the war across central Italy in an attempt to found a new state for the Borgia family, and Julius II's madcap policy saw him unite the emperor and the Italian states in the **League of Cambrai**, which soundly defeated Venice in 1508, sapping her strength just when it was most needed to fight the Turks. Julius egged on the Swiss, French and Spaniards in turn, before finally crying 'Out with the barbarians!' when it was already too late.

By 1516, with the French ruling Milan and the Spanish in control of the south, it seemed as if a settlement would be possible. The worst possible luck for Italy, however, came with the accession in Spain of the insatiable Habsburg megalomaniac **Charles V** who got enough loans from the Fugger banks to buy himself the crown of the Holy Roman Empire in 1519, making him the most powerful ruler in Europe since Charlemagne. As soon as he had emptied Spain's treasury, driven her to revolt and plunged Germany into civil war, he turned his tender attentions to Italy. The wars began anew, bloodier than anything Italy had seen for centuries.

1529–1600: Italy in Chains, but Venice Recovers

Two years after the dramatic 1527 **Sack of Rome** by Imperial troops and German mercenaries, Charles V met Pope Clement VII in Bologna for his fateful coronation as Holy Roman Emperor (he was to be the last ever crowned by a pope) and to draw the map of Italy, which, save only the Republic of Venice, was at the mercy of the Spaniards.

It also marked the beginning of the bitter struggles of the **Counter-Reformation**. In Italy, the Spaniards found a perfect ally in the papacy. One had the difficult job of breaking the spirit of a nation that, though conquered, was still wealthy, culturally sophisticated and ready to resist; the other saw an opportunity to recapture by force the hearts and minds it had lost long before. The job of re-educating Italy was put in the hands of the new Jesuit order; their schools and propaganda machine bored the pope's message deeply into the Italian mind. The Church's **Council of Trent** (1545–63, *see* pp.69–71) provided long-needed reforms, and although it was too little too late to bring the Protestants back to the fold, it initiated the creation of sumptuous new churches, spectacles and dramatic sermons that helped redefine Catholicism. Protected by its lagoon, and clever enough to avoid the Spaniards and most of the Jesuits, Venice quickly recovered its conquered territories of the Veneto lost in the War of Cambrai and went about perfecting a way of life that came to be the envy of Italy (*see* pp.75–8). Venetian artists attained a brilliance and virtuosity never seen before, just in time to embellish the scores of new churches, palaces, and villas of the mid-16th-century building boom. In one issue, however, Venice combined with Spain: in turning back the Ottoman threat at the **Battle of Lepanto** (1571), a victory that provided a tremendous boost to morale throughout Christendom.

1600–1796: The Age of Baroque

Palladio's country villas for the magnates of the Veneto are landmarks in architecture but were also an early symptom of decay. The old mercantile economy was failing, and the wealthy began to invest their money less productively in land instead of risking it in business. Despite Lepanto, Venice's position in the east continued to be eroded, damaged by the Portuguese discovery of the spice route to the Indies, by endless warfare with the Ottomans and the Austrian-backed pirates, the Uskoks, in the north Adriatic. Yet when the chips were down, Venice had the spirit to stand up to Pope Paul V and his Spanish allies during the **Great Interdict** (1606), striking an irreversible blow to papal temporal authority while all Europe watched. It was her last starring role in European affairs, but the Venetians kept their head and made their decline remarkably serene and a great deal of fun.

Decline was not limited to Venice. After 1600 nearly everything started to go wrong for Italy across the board. The textiles and banking of the north, long the engines of the economy, both withered in the face of foreign competition; the popes soaked whoever they could for money to redecorate Rome. Bullied, humiliated and impoverished, 17th-century Italy tried hard to keep up its prominence in the arts and sciences. Galileo looked through telescopes and taught at Padua, Monteverdi wrote the first operas, and hundreds of talented though uninspired artists cranked out pretty pictures to meet the continuing high demand. Baroque art—the florid, expensive coloratura style that serves as a perfect symbol for the age itself—impressed everyone with the majesty of Church and State. Baroque impresarios managed the wonderful pageantry of Church holidays, state occasions and carnivals that kept the crowds amused; manners and clothing were decorously berserk.

By the 18th century, there were very few painters or scholars or scientists. There were no more heroic revolts either. Italy in this period hardly has any history at all; with Spain's increasing decadence, the great powers decided the futures of Italy's major states, and used the minor ones as a kind of overflow tank to hold surplus princes. Gambling revenues became one of the main props of the Venetian state. There, carnival was exended to six months in order to bring in decadent aristocrats from around Europe; this was the age of blundering spies and scamps like Casanova, of the glittering brilliance of Vivaldi, of Grand Tourists, opera at La Fenice, and Canaletto.

1796–1830: Napoleon and the Austrians

Napoleon (that greatest of Italian generals) arrived in 1796 on behalf of the French Revolutionary Directorate, winning at Rivoli north of Verona and sweeping away Austrians, Spaniards, the Pope, the prince-bishops of the Dolomites and the Doge, replacing them with the '**Cisalpine Republic**' and '**Kingdom of Illyria**' in the east. Italy woke up with a start from its baroque slumbers, and local nobles gaily joined the French cause. In 1799, however, while Napoleon was off in Egypt, the advance through Italy by an Austro-Russian army, aided by Nelson's fleet, restored the status quo.

In 1800 Napoleon returned in a campaign that saw the great victory at Marengo, which gave him the opportunity once more to reorganize Italian affairs as the nation's self-crowned king. Napoleonic rule lasted only until 1814, but in that time important public works were begun and laws, education and everything else reformed after the French model; immense Church properties were expropriated, and medieval relics everywhere put to rest—including the Venetian Republic, which Napoleon for some reason took a special delight in liquidating. The French, however, soon outstayed their welcome. Besides hauling much of Italy's artistic heritage off to the Louvre, implementing high war taxes and conscription (some 25,000 Italians died on the Russian front), and brutally repressing a number of local revolts, they systematically exploited Italy for the benefit of the Napoleonic élite and the crowds of speculators who came flocking over the Alps. When the Austrians and English came to chase all the little Napoleons out, no one was sad to see them go.

But the experience had given Italians a taste of the opportunities offered by the modern world, as well as a sense of national feeling that had been suppressed for centuries. The 1815 **Congress of Vienna** put the clock back to 1796; indeed the Habsburgs and Bourbons thought they could pretend the Napoleonic upheavals had never happened, and the political reaction in the territories was fierce. The only major change from the *ancien régime* was that all of Venetia now unwillingly (except for the South Tyrol) belonged to Austria.

1848–1915: The Risorgimento and United Italy

Simmering discontent kindled into action across Italy in the revolutionary year of 1848. On 22 March, the fire spread to Venice. The Austrian authorities simply fled, and the Venetian Republic was back in business. Within a few days, a democratic assembly was elected; leadership passed to **Daniele Manin**, a lawyer who had distinguished himself in liberal struggles in Venice for a decade. A day after the events in Venice, **King Carlo Alberto** of Piedmont-Savoy declared war on Austria.

At first, the odds seemed to favour Piedmont, the strongest state and leading force in Italian unification. Austria's army was disorganized and outnumbered, and for the time being it could expect little help from Vienna. The Piedmontese won early victories, but under the timid leadership of the King they failed to follow them up. The Austrians fell back to the base of their defences in Italy, the circuit of fortresses called the Quadrilateral (Peschiera, Verona, Mantua and Legnano, in the western Veneto). Here they won a resounding victory, at Custozza, on 25 July, that knocked Piedmont ingloriously out of the war.

Shutting out the disappointments of 1848, Venice put up a brave and determined resistance. Though blockaded by the Austrian fleet, the Venetians nevertheless had a large quantity of arms and men to complement the natural protection of their lagoon in withstanding a siege. The Austrians bombarded the city continuously from May of 1849. An outbreak of cholera, as much as a total absence of outside support, decided the issue. The city surrendered on 22 August.

Despite failure on a grand scale, at least the Italians knew they would get another chance. Unification was inevitable, but there were two irreconcilable contenders for the honour of accomplishing it. On one side, the democrats and radicals dreamed of a truly reborn, revolutionary Italy, and looked to the popular hero **Garibaldi** to deliver it; on the other, moderates wanted the Piedmontese to do the job, ensuring a stable future by making **Vittorio Emanuele II** King of Italy. Vittorio Emanuele's minister, the polished, clever Count Camillo Cavour, spent the 1850s getting Piedmont into shape for the struggle, building its economy and army, participating in the Crimean War to earn diplomatic support, and plotting with the French for an alliance against Austria.

War came in 1859, just as a rebellion chased the pope's troops out of Bologna. The French and Piedmontese defeated Austria in two inconclusive, extremely bloody battles, at Magenta and Solferino. Piedmont annexed Lombardy and the Marches, and the armistice of 1850 was arranged so that France picked up Nice and Savoy, while Tuscany, Emilia-Romagna and the duchies of Parma and Modena went to Piedmont. These gains were increased in the next two years, when Garibaldi and his Thousand picked up Sicily and the south.

With Austria still in control of Venetia, most Italians felt that the first duty of the nation was to complete the work of unification. The logical place to look for an ally against Austria was with Bismarck and **Prussia**, then preparing for the climax of their own nation's struggle for unification. In April 1866, Italy and Prussia signed a treaty, proposing the Veneto as reward for Italian aid in the coming war with Austria. That war was not long in coming. Hostilities began in June, and before the year was out the Italians had been decisively defeated on land, at Custozza (again), and on sea, at Lissa. Fortunately for them, von Moltke's Prussian army was causing even greater embarrassments to the Austrians up north. The Veneto and western Friuli joined Italy—a gift from Prussia.

Despite popular feeling, and its conquest by Garibaldi, Trentino remained a part of Austria, as did eastern Venezia Giulia. In these regions secret revolutionary committees for unity with Italy soon gave politics a new word: **irredentism**, from *irredenta* or 'unredeemed'. Unfortunately the price of their 'redemption' as part of Italy was to cost the country dear—its entrance into the First World War.

After 1900, with the rise of a strong socialist movement, strikes, riots and police repression often occupied centre stage in Italian politics. But at the same time new industries, at least in the north, made the country a fully integral part of the European economy. The fifteen years before the war, prosperous and contented ones for many, came to be known by the slightly derogatory term *Italietta*, the 'little Italy' of modest bourgeois happiness, an age of sweet Puccini operas, the first motorcars, blooming 'Liberty'-style architecture, and Sunday afternoons on the beach.

1915–1945: War, Fascism and War

Besides the hope of gaining Trentino, Trieste and Istria, Italy's entrance into the **First World War** was influenced by a certain segment of the intelligentsia who found Italietta boring and disgraceful: followers of the artistic Futurists and the perverse, idolized poet **Gabriele D'Annunzio**. These helped Italy leap blindly into the war in 1915. Venetia saw the bulk of the fighting—especially along the Piave and Isonzo rivers, at Asiago and at Monte Grappa. Italian armies fought with their accustomed flair, masterminding an utter catastrophe at Caporetto (October 1917) that any other nation but Austria would have parlayed into a total victory. No thanks to their incompetent generals, the poorly armed and equipped Italians somehow held firm for another year, until Austria's total exhaustion let them prevail at **Vittorio Veneto**, capturing some 600,000 prisoners in November 1918.

In return for 650,000 dead, a million casualties, severe privation on the home front and a war debt higher than anyone could count, Italy received Trieste, Gorizia, Trentino and the South Tyrol up to the natural frontier of the Brenner Pass, where many German-speakers who suddenly found themselves Italian began in turn a new Irredentist movement, yearning to be reunited with Austria.

Led somehow to expect much more, Italians felt they had been cheated, and nationalist sentiment increased, especially when D'Annunzio led a band of freebooters to seize the half-Italian city of Fiume in September 1919, after the peace conferences had promised it to Yugoslavia. The Italian economy was a shambles, and, at least in the north, revolution was in the air. The trouble had encouraged extremists of both right and left, and many Italians became convinced that the liberal state was finished.

Enter **Benito Mussolini**, a professional intriguer with bad manners and no fixed principles. Before the War he had found his real talent as editor of the Socialist Party paper *Avanti!*—the best it ever had, tripling the circulation in a year. When he decided that what Italy really needed was war, he left to found a new paper, and contributed mightily to the jingoist agitation of 1915. In the post-War confusion, he found his opportunity. A little bit at a time, he developed the idea of Fascism, at first less a philosophy than an astute use of mass propaganda and a sense of design. With a little discreet money supplied by frightened industrialists, Mussolini had no trouble finding recruits for his black-shirted gangs, who had their first successes bashing Slavs in the city of Trieste.

The basic principle, combing left- and right-wing extremism into something the ruling classes could live with, proved attractive to many Italians, and a series of weak governments chose to stand by while the fascist *squadre* (organised thugs) cast their shadow over more and more of Italy. Mussolini's accession to power was the result of an improbable gamble. In the particularly anarchic month of October 1922, he announced that his followers would march on Rome. **King Vittorio Emanuele III** refused to sign a decree of martial law to disperse them, and there was nothing to do but offer Mussolini the post of prime minister. At first, he governed Italy with undeniable competence. Order was restored, and the economy and foreign policy handled intelligently by non-fascist professionals. Mussolini increased his popularity by singling out especially obnoxious unions and corrupt leftist local governments for punishment. In the 1924 elections, despite the flagrant rigging and intimidation, the Fascists won only a slight majority.

Mussolini evolved a new economic philosophy, the 'corporate state', where labour and capital were supposed to live in harmony under a syndicalist government control. But the longer Fascism lasted, the more unreal it seemed, a patchwork government of Mussolini and his ageing cronies, magnified and rendered heroic by cinematic technique—stirring rhetoric before oceanic crowds, colourful pageantry, magnificent, larger-than-life post offices and railway stations built of travertine and marble, dashing aviators and winsome gymnasts from the Fascist youth groups on parade. In a way it was the baroque all over again, and Italians tried not to think about the consequences. In the words of one of Mussolini's favourite slogans, painted on walls all over Italy, 'Whoever stops is lost.'

Mussolini couldn't stop, and the only possibility for new diversions lay with the chance of conquest and empire. His invasion of Ethiopia and his meddling in the Spanish Civil War, both in 1936, compromised Italy into a close alliance with Nazi Germany. Under Hitler's prodding, Mussolini invited all the unhappy German speakers in the Alto-Adige to leave, which they immediately did, in droves. Nevertheless, Mussolini's confidence and rhetoric never faltered as he led an entirely unprepared nation into the biggest war ever. The Allies invaded; the Germans poured in divisions to defend the peninsula. In 1943 they set Mussolini up in a puppet state called the Italian Social Republic at **Saló** on Lake Garda. In September, the Badoglio government finally signed an armistice with the Allies, too late to keep the War from dragging on another year and a half, as the Germans made good use of Italy's difficult terrain to slow the Allied advance. Meanwhile Italy finally gave itself something to be proud of, a determined, resourceful Resistance that established free zones in many areas, and harassed the Germans with sabotage and strikes. The *partigiani* caught Mussolini in April 1945, while he was trying to escape to Switzerland; after shooting him and his mistress, they hung him by the toes from the roof of a petrol station in Milan.

1945–the Present

Post-War Italian *cinema-verità*—Rossellini's *Rome, Open City* or de Sica's *Bicycle Thieves*—captures the atmosphere better than words ever could. In a period of serious hardships that older Italians still remember, the nation slowly picked itself up and returned things to normal. The eastern border with Yugoslavia was the most lingering problem in the north—**Trieste**, as the major bone of contention, was made a neutral zone from 1947 to 1954, when it was finally given to Italy in exchange for what bits of Istria it still controlled.

A referendum in June 1946 made Italy a republic, but only by a narrow margin. The first governments fell to the new **Christian Democrats** under Alcide di Gasperi, the party that would run the show for decades in coalitions with a preposterous band of smaller parties. The main opposition was provided by the Communists, surely one of the most remarkable parties of modern European history. With the heritage of the only important socialist philosopher since Marx, Antonio Gramsci, and the democratic and broadminded leaders Palmiere Togliatti and Enrico Berlinguer, Italian communism took the moral high ground and stayed there.

The economic miracle that began in the 1950s continues today, propelling the Italians into sixth place among the world's national economies. 'God made the world and Italy made everything in it,' was the slogan of the '60s. The rotten Christian Democratic corruption behind the glittering mask was revealed in the early 1990s, when a small group of judges and prosecutors in Milan took a minor political kickback scandal and from it unravelled the golden string that held together the whole tangle of Italian political depravity—what the Italians call the ***tangentopoli***, or 'bribe city'. The Christian Democrats and the Socialists, the two leading parties, collapsed like a house of cards, leaving a vacuum filled by a jostling array of new parties and personalities, none of whom so far has been able to put the brakes on the merry-go-round of Italian politics: noisiest of all was media tycoon **Silvio Berlusconi**'s rightist *Forza Italia*, which won Mr Television a brief tenure as prime minister in 1994. Plagued by allegations of scandals and bribery, Berlusconi was soon forced out by the more enduring, middle-of-the-road Olive party of **Romano Prodi**, with the support of the former Communists. Prodi's stringent economic measures allowed Italy to squeak into Euroland in January 1999, but led to the Communists' withdrawing their support of his government in late 1998, and giving it to current prime minister **Massimo d'Alema**'s DS (*Democrazia di Sinistra*) party, Italy's 60th government since the Second World War.

One of the jokers in the Italian deck is the neo-fascist MSI party of Alberto Fini, and another is Milanese lawyer **Umberto Bossi**, the only Italian political figure to dress badly since the time of King Aistulf. Bossi's new Lombard League, or **Lega Lombarda**, was around even before *tangentopoli*, breaking though in the 1990 elections in Lombardy; by 1994 he had united with similar northern leagues to form the Lega Nord. Although many of the Lega's positions change by the hour, its basic tenet of federalism, to cut out the voracious politicians and bureaucrats of Rome and allow the wealthy north of Italy to keep more of its profits for itself, has understandably struck a deep chord in Venetia. In September 1996, Bossi attracted a lot of attention by declaring the north (as far south as Umbria and the Marches) as the independent Republic of Padania, and made a three-day march down the Po to Venice. Unlike Mussolini's march on Rome, the whole affair turned out to be a badly staged comedy, although it did put federalism, perhaps on the Spanish model, a little higher up on the politicians' agenda.

In Venetia, with its history of separateness from the rest of Italy, there is a growing interest in reviving the glories of the Serenissima. New groups such as the Società Filologica Veneta have sprouted up, with the goal of defending the Veneto language and culture, and there's a Liga Veneta for greater regional autonomy and greater recognition for the German speakers in the Sud Tirol. As of 1998, you can take classes in Venetic, and listen to long-winded arguments about how the Paleoveneti were Celts (one of Bossi's favourite topics), in the hopes of showing that they aren't like the rest of the Italians and should go their separate ways.

But, truer to the spirit of the once great cosmopolitan Republic of Venice, the natives seem rather more impressed with their economy. The Veneto has become a vast metropolis of four and a half million people, connected by the A4 highway. Its economy, with a gross domestic product of over $95 billion, is larger than that of Israel and Greece; its exports are worth more than those of Portugal and Argentina. People talk of the 'Veneto model' that has evolved since the war, creating a climate that encourages small, mainly family-run businesses (some 65 per cent are of recent origin) aimed towards the export market, employing a devoted workforce making something that is unique or at least better than foreign competition: Benetton is a case in point. Luxury goods (fashion, jewellery, housewares and everything else related to the cleverly promoted mystique of Italian design) are a mainstay, just as they were during the Renaissance and Middle Ages. Before the war, 60% of the work was in agriculture; today only 6% of the population are farmers, while the unemployment rate, at a measly 5%—microscopic in European terms—has brought emigrants from around the world in search of a job, restoring some of Venetia's old international feel, more noticable the further east you go; if old Venice is cosmopolitan because of international tourism, Trieste is so because of its newfound status as Mitteleurope on the Med.

Paleoveneti (8th–2nd centuries BC)   54

Roman Art (3rd century BC–5th century AD)   54

Dark and Early Middle Ages (5th–10th centuries)   54

Veneto-Byzantine and Romanesque
  (11th–12th centuries)   55

Gothic and Early Renaissance
  (13th–14th centuries)   55

The Renaissance of the Quattrocento   56

Art and Architecture

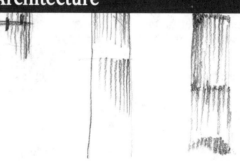

The Venetian High Renaissance and Mannerism
  (16th century)   57

Baroque and Rococo (17th and 18th centuries)   57

Neoclassicism, Romanticism and Other -Isms
  (19th and 20th centuries)   58

Artists' Directory   59

Venetia produced one of the three great schools of Italian art—not a spiritual or intellectual school like the Tuscan, or anything half as imposing or classical as the Roman, but an art of visual delight and sensuality. A love of decoration, of gold and glitter and gorgeous colours, is the thread that links the glimmering richness of the 11th-century Byzantine style mosaics of St Mark with the effervescent sparkle of Tiepolo in the 18th century. Architecture, too, was showy—you'll find little of that sombre, rusticated stone monumentality that characterizes Tuscany or Rome, but instead palaces meant to dazzle, and villas set like gems in the landscape.

Paleoveneti (8th–2nd centuries BC)

The mysterious Paleoveneti excelled in metal work, and many of their artefacts are indistinguishable from Celtic. The museums in Este and Adria have the most extensive collections of Paleoveneti and other pre-Roman artefacts, but all the archaeology museums in Venetia have evocative bits and bobs. Among their most striking works are the little metal plaques, or *laminette*, from the 5th century BC, engraved with warriors and women, in the Santa Corona museum in Vicenza.

Roman Art (3rd century BC–5th century AD)

Roman art may have been derivative of Etruscan and Greek models, but it showed a special talent for mosaics, portraiture, wall paintings and glasswork; architecturally, the Romans were brilliant engineers, grand exponents of the arch and inventors of concrete. Verona is one of the best places in Italy to admire their ability to build large and well, in its Ponte della Pietra, the ancient theatre, Porta dei Borsari, and especially the Arena, a pink marble oval that rivals the Colosseum in size and grandeur. The city was the birthplace of Vitruvius, the only classical writer on architecture whose works have come down to us.

Other Roman odds and ends remain in the museums of Padua and Venice. The latter has a fair share of Greek originals as well, donated by collectors, although none that can match Venice's finest Greek work—the four horses of St Mark, the only surviving bronze *quadriga* from antiquity.

Dark and Early Middle Ages (5th–10th centuries)

Artistically, at least, the decline of Rome was a bonus for Venetia, especially when Emperor Honorius transferred the capital of the Western Empire to nearby Ravenna. Although Roman sculpture and painting were degraded, mosaics thrived, a decorative art patronized by the rich. It was a strange time; a 5th-century chronicle declares: 'Those who are alive perish from thirst, while corpses float in the water…priests practise usury and Syrians sing psalms…eunuchs learn the art of war and barbarian mercenaries study literature.'

The Greek artists working in Ravenna drifted into Venetia—the 7th-century frescoes in the cathedral crypt in Adria are a rare record of their migration. Their still, 'hieratic' art, really an inheritance from decadent Rome, was to remain prominent until the 13th century, and found its greatest expression in mosaics, where highly stylized, spiritual beings live in a gold-ground paradise, with no need of shadows or perspective or other such worldly tricks. Beautiful examples remain, such as that at **Torcello** in Venice, where the style lingered long enough to adorn St Mark's. In architecture, forms that originated in the time of Constantine prevailed—basilican churches, derived directly from Roman law courts and octagonal baptistries.

In the 7th–10th centuries, while Byzantine artists painted and created mosaics of their ethereal almond-eyed creatures, the native population under the Lombards produced works in a vigorous style that had little use for Roman or Byzantine models. Instead of mosaics, the Lombards' talent lay in architecture, sculpture and metalwork; there is art from the period in the Castelvecchio museum in Verona.

Veneto-Byzantine and Romanesque (11th–12th centuries)

By the 11th century, Venice had taken over the artistic crown in northeast Italy from Ravenna, in a typically lavish if rather conservative way: the Veneto-Byzantine style of the magnificent mosaics and Pala d'Oro in St Mark's basilica is still 90% Byzantine. But influences from other parts of Italy were seeping into the heart of the lagoon: the vigorous reliefs of the Labours of the Months on St Mark's central portal and St Mark's Campanile are in the new Romanesque style from Lombardy.

Lombard Romanesque churches are characterized by broad, triangular façades, blind arcading, gabled porches, rib vaulting, and presbyteries raised above the nave and crypt. The best examples are in Verona, near the Lombard frontier (the Palazzo della Ragione, S. Fermo, S. Lorenzo, the Duomo and, most magnificently, San Zeno, with its superb Romanesque decoration and unique bronze doors, a 'poor man's Bible' that predates the church by a century). Other architects in the 12th century opted for a Veneto-Byzantine and Romanesque compromise, as in Santa Sofia in Padua. In the next century Padua would witness the most amazing Veneto-Byzantine-Romanesque wedding of all, in the fabulous multi-domed Basilica of St Anthony.

The 11th and 12th centuries also saw the erection of urban skyscrapers by the nobility, family fortresses and towers built when the *comuni* forced the barons to move into the towns. Larger cities once had hundreds of them, although municipal authorities gradually succeeded in having most of them demolished. This same period is marked by an epidemic of castle building, especially in the Dolomites.

Gothic and Early Renaissance (13th–14th centuries)

The Italians never really appreciated Gothic; trapped in their Roman sensibilities and snobbishness, they looked on the soaring flying-buttressed cathedrals from the Ile-de-France as barbaric. Still, they weren't entirely immune to its charms. Bonino's ornately chivalric Scaliger tombs in Verona are a prime example of what they could do when they bothered. Most Italian Gothic, however, is austere, coinciding with back-to-basics Franciscan and Dominican religious revivals of the 13th century, resulting in piously plain Gothic-barn churches that loom over city rooftops like beached whales, among them Santa Corona in Vicenza, the Frari and SS. Giovanni e Paolo in Venice, and the most beautiful, the Dominican Santa Anastasia in Verona.

At the same time the Venetians were rolling in swag from the Fourth Crusade (1204) and for their secular buildings they took Gothic and twisted it merrily around to suit their flamboyant, cosmopolitan tastes. Gothic arches took on Byzantine and Islamic designs, and plain walls were enlivened with coloured marbles in different shapes and patterns, reliefs, round paterae of semi-precious stones, and even gold. The resulting hybrid, Venetian Gothic, became the city's own distinct style, seen in scores of magnificent palaces from the Fondaco dei Turchi to the Ca' d'Oro, culminating in the Palazzo Ducale. Venetian Gothic became so closely identified with Venice that the style took on a second life in the 16th century, in public buildings designed to mark the Republic's presence on the *terra firma* (Ùdine's Piazza della Libertà and Belluno's Palazzo dei Rettori).

In painting, the colourful, decorative fairytale style called International Gothic also lingered longer in Venetia than elsewhere in Italy. The great Pisanello of Pisa and Stefano da Verona were its major exponents in Verona; in Venice painters like Paolo Veneziano, Jacobello del Fiore and Michele Giambono and the Vivarini family remained popular into the 15th century. The Gothic spirit endured for centuries in the Dolomites, especially in polychrome sculpture and ornate altarpieces that often combine a powerful expressiveness with a love of rich decoration.

In Tuscany, the 14th century was one of the most exciting and vigorous phases in Italian art, when great imaginative leaps occurred in architecture, painting, and sculpture. In 1308, the most influential of all early Tuscans, Giotto, left the Veneto the seeds of the future in the Cappella degli Scrovegni or Arena Chapel in Padua, teaching local artists about forms in space, composition, and a new, more natural way to paint figures. His chief followers of the Paduan school, Altichiero and Menabuoi, frescoed Padua's Baptistry, Oratory of San Giorgio and the Ermitani church; another, Tommaso da Modena, left beautiful works in Treviso and almost nowhere else.

The Renaissance of the Quattrocento

The visit to Padua by Giotto was followed up in the next century by a prolonged stay by another Tuscan genius, Donatello; the perfect harmony and classical calm of his great equestrian statue of Gattamelata (now in Verona, *see* p.199) and his complex reliefs in the Basilica of Sant'Antonio were formative influence on Venice's Lombardo and Bon families, as well as on Antonio Rizzo of Verona. The Lombardi and Bons went on to create an overwhelming share of Venice's best Renaissance churches, palaces, sculptures, and tombs along with Mauro Codussi, who instilled a certain amount of Tuscan order and classicism into the Venetian imagination.

The great revolution in Venetian painting began in the mid-15th century, and owes much to the brothers-in-law Andrea Mantegna and Giovanni Bellini. Mantegna influenced generations of artists and sculptors with his strong interest in antiquity, his scientific perspective, and his powerfully sculpted figures, while Giovanni Bellini (*see* pp.68–9) perfected a luminous oil painting technique to express natural light and rich, autumnal colours. Other major figures of the quattrocento include narrative masters Gentile Bellini and Vittore Carpaccio, the more rustic Cima da Conegliano and the more elegant Carlo Crivelli.

The Venetian High Renaissance and Mannerism (16th Century)

While the rest of Italy, increasingly oppressed by reaction and war, followed the artists of Rome in learning drawing and anatomy, the Venetians followed Giovanni Bellini and his obsession with the expressive qualities of atmosphere and colour. The shooting star among his many pupils was Giorgione of Castelfranco, a major if tragically short-lived figure in the new manner; his *Tempest* in the Accademia is a remarkable study in brooding tension. Giorgione is credited with inventing 'easel painting'—art that served neither Church nor State nor the vanity of a patron, but stood on its own for the pleasure of the viewer.

Another Bellini alumnus, Titian, the High Renaissance master of the Venetian school, was a revolutionary in his own right, one of the first painters to put the 'art' into art, in his dramatic compositions and striking tonal effects produced by large brushstrokes, or even finger-painting. His contemporary, Tintoretto, took these Mannerist tendencies to extremes, while Paolo Veronese painted lavish canvases that are the culmination of all that Venice had to teach in decoration and magnificence. Veronese's followers, Zelotti, Battista Franco and others, laboured beaverishly across the Veneto, filling patrician villas with allegories, mythologies and virtues.

One of the greatest sculptors in cinquecento Venice was Jacopo Sansovino, who adapted his training in Tuscany and Rome to create a distinctive Venetian architectural style, richly decorated with sculpture and classical motifs. He was greatly admired by Andrea Palladio, whose creamy white temple-fronted villas, which are as characteristic of the rural Veneto as Venetian Gothic is of Venice, would inspire architects as far away as England and colonial America (*see* pp.71–5). Palladio's colleague and artistic heir, Vincenzo Scamozzi, added a Mannerist touch that became the rage for the next century in the Veneto, even when the more populist baroque style squashed Mannerism and its intellectual fancies elsewhere in Italy.

Baroque and Rococo (17th and 18th centuries)

Art shall move to devotion the heart of the beholder.

The Council of Trent

As an art designed to induce temporal obedience and psychological oblivion, baroque's effects are difficult to describe. On the whole, however, history saw that little of its most excessive moods (much in evidence in Rome and Naples) touched Venetia; the Venetians kicked the Jesuits out, and the Spaniards had little influence in the Republic. In short, the 17th century saw more of the same: Palladian villas, Venetian palaces, atmospheric painting and decorated churches, but squared into baroque. The age does provide some exceptions to the rule that in art, less is more: the church of La Salute in Venice, or the uncanny paintings of Francesco Maffei of Vicenza, or the furniture of Andrea Brustalon (Ca' Rezzonico, in Venice).

In the 18th century Venice bloomed like Camille on her death bed, when its charming, elegant school of painting was in demand across Europe, thanks almost entirely to one great figure: Giambattista Tiepolo. Tiepolo's buoyant ceiling art and narrative frescoes, shimmering with light, added a fresh, scintillating rococo fizz to Veronese's grandeur. If Giotto's Cappella degli Scrovegni is the majestic overture in the art of Italian fresco, Tiepolo's Villa Valmara in Vicenza and the Palazzo Labia in Venice are the grand finale.

Less majestic but extremely popular 18th-century figures include Antonio Canaletto, who produced countless views of Venice snapped up by English and French travellers on the Grand Tour; another now famous painter of views, proto-Impressionist Francesco Guardi, had to wait until the 19th century to gain recognition. Pietro Longhi, their contemporary, devoted himself to little genre scenes that offer an insight into the Venice of 200 years ago; Rosalba Carriera's pastel portraits were the rage of Europe's nobility. Meanwhile, Venetian architect Giorgio Massari translated their rococo sensibility into stone, specializing in churches that doubled as concert halls, while in the countryside neo-Palladian villas grew bigger and bigger in Venice's hectic *Götterdämmerung*: Villa Pisani on the Brenta Canal is a monster of the genre.

Neoclassicism, Romanticism and Other -Isms (19th and 20th centuries)

Whatever artistic spirit remained at the end of the 18th century evaporated with Napoleon and remained evaporated for a long time. Although Europe's greatest neoclassical sculptor, Antonio Canova, hailed from Possagno in the northern Veneto, he left very few of his pseudo-Greeks and Romans in the region. Giuseppe Jappelli left his famous coffeehouse in Padua and designed romantic gardens for villas. A good collection of 19th-century art can be seen in Palazzo Pésaro (Venice).

Italians began to regain some of their artistic panache in the 20th century. The first years saw new grand hotels built on Venice's Lido, many with a delightful Liberty-style (Italian Art Nouveau) touch. Other artistic trends also came from elsewhere. There was Futurism, an artistic movement that made dynamism, velocity and modernity its creed and, at the same time, the so-called Metaphysical school led by Giorgio De Chirico and Carlo Carra, filled with a hallucinatory nostalgia and stillness; the Peggy Guggenheim museum in Venice has a good representative collection.

The Fascist style (Art Deco at the service of Mussolini's illusions of grandeur) often makes us smile, but as the only Italian school in the last two hundred years to achieve a consistent sense of design it presents a challenge to all modern Italian architects—one they have so far been unable to meet. Venetia has only a few examples, such as the Palazzo del Cinema on the Lido in Venice.

In 1946, Renato Guttuso and Emile Vedova founded an avant-garde group in Venice, the Fronte Nuova, but without very noticeable improvement in the local art scene, then or now. Misplaced atavism prevented the construction of Frank Lloyd Wright's palace on the Grand Canal (although, when the same authorities vetoed a hospital designed by Le Corbusier, even Corby agreed they were right). But Venice does get its share of contemporary art, in special exhibitions and at the Biennale, although at times the latter has all the panache of a Eurovision art contest. Besides the Peggy Guggenheim, you'll find collections of modern and contemporary art—notably in Verona.

This short list of the principal architects, painters and sculptors of Venetia is bound to exasperate partisans of some artists and do scant justice to the rest, but we've tried to include the most representative works you'll find in the region.

Alticheiro (da Zevio, 1320–95): top Veronese painter of his day, and a talented follower of Giotto (S. Anastasia, S. Stefano, Verona; Oratorio de S. Giorgio, Padua).

Antonello da Messina (*c.* 1430–79): a Sicilian painter who visited Venice. Antonello became one of the first Italians to perfect the Van Eyckian oil painting techniques of Flanders; his compelling mastery of light, shadows, and the simplification of forms was a major influence on Giovanni Bellini (see the great but damaged *Pietà* in the Museo Correr, Venice).

Basaiti, Marco (1470–*c.* 1530): student and collaborator of Alvise Vivarini (Accademia, Venice).

Bassano, Jacopo (da Ponte; 1510–92): son of village painter Francesco senior and head of a clan of artists working mainly from Bassano del Grappa, from whom they took their name. Jacopo began by painting in the monumental style of Parmigianino, but is better known for cranking out a succession of religious night scenes in rustic barnyards that became increasingly dramatic à la Tintoretto. Of his four painter sons, Francesco the Younger (1549–92) was his most skilled assistant and follower, until he jumped out of a window; the more prolific Leandro was less talented (Palazzo Ducale, Venice; also the museum in Vicenza).

Bastiani, Lazzaro (*c.* 1420–1512): probably Carpaccio's master, and the painter responsible for the charming 'Baby Carpaccios' in Venice's S. Alvise.

Bella, Gabriel (1730–99): painter of city scenes, a valuable source of information about 18th-century Venice despite their sublime ineptitude (Palazzo Querini-Stampalia).

Bellini, Gentile (1429–1507): elder son of Jacopo, famous for his meticulous depictions of Venetian ceremonies and narrative histories (*Miracles of the True Cross*, Accademia, Venice). Unfortunately, his histories painted for the Doge's Palace were lost in the fire.

Bellini, Giovanni (1435–1516): the greatest early Renaissance painter of Northern Italy. No artists before him painted with such sensitivity to light, atmosphere, colour, and nature; none since have approached the almost magical tenderness and empathy he conveyed in his Madonnas and other religious works (Accademia, San Zaccaria, and the Frari in Venice; S. Corona, Vicenza).

Bellini, Jacopo (1400–70): pupil of Gentile da Fabriano, father of Giovanni and Gentile, father-in-law of Mantegna, all of whom were influenced by Jacopo's beautiful drawings from nature (in the Louvre and British Museum); in Venetia his best works are his Madonnas, more natural and lifelike than others of his generation (Accademia, Venice; Castelvecchio, Verona).

Bon, Bartolomeo (d. 1464): prolific Venetian sculptor and architect, who worked with his brother Giovanni to produce some of Venice's most lavishly decorative work (Porta della Carta and statues of the Ducal Palace, Ca' d'Oro).

Bonifazio Veronese (Bonifazio de' Pitati; 1487–1553): native of Verona who moved to Venice and fell under the spell of Titian and company; as he rarely signed anything, secondary paintings in their style have been so often attributed to him that he has become posthumously one of the most prolific painters of his generation.

Bonino (*c.* 1335–75): flamboyant Gothic sculptor from Campione (Lake Lugano), the cradle of northern builders and sculptors; in Verona he carved most of the Scaliger tombs.

Bordone, Paris (1500–71): a pupil of Titian and follower of Giorgione, whose pastoral landscapes were a seminal influence on his work and earned him commissions from across Europe (*The Presentation of the Ring of St Mark to the Doge*, Accademia, Venice, is his masterpiece; also Scuola del Carmine, Padua).

Brustalon, Andrea (1662–1732) of Belluno: rococo sculptor and furniture maker of imagination and whimsy (Ca' Rezzonico, Venice).

Campagnola, Domenico (1500–1550s): adopted son and pupil of the great Paduan engraver Giulio Campagnola, a student of Mantegna; like Giulio he made bucolic landscapes a speciality (Scuola di S. Rocco and Scuola del Carmine, Padua).

Canaletto, Antonio (Giovanni Antonio Canal, 1697–1768): master of meticulous, colourful, and postcard-accurate Venetian *vedute*, or views, but go to England to see them—there is but one in the Accademia, and two in the Ca' Rezzonico (Venice).

Canova, Antonio (1757–1821): born near Àsolo, a neoclassical celebrity sculptor—the favourite of Napoleon and Benjamin Franklin and everyone in between, including the popes, one of whom made him Marchese d'Ischia. The Museo Correr in Venice has a naturalistic early work, *Daedalus and Icarus*, but most of his sculptures went elsewhere; his studio in Possagno is now a museum of casts, while the village is crowned with a huge temple he built to hold his ashes.

Caroto, Giovanni (1480–1555): not the greatest Veronese artist, but an endearing one; the Big Carrot is best known for his portrait of a child in the Castelvecchio; also works in S. Fermo, both in Verona.

Carpaccio, Vittore (c. 1465–1525): a probable student of Gentile Bellini and the most charming of Venetian artists, with fairytale paintings full of documentary details from his life and times. The distinctive red tones he loved gave his name to paper-thin slices of raw beef fillet. His major cycles can be found at Scuola di S. Giorgio Schiavone and the Accademia; also the *Two Courtesans*, in the Museo Correr, all in Venice.

Carriera, Rosalba (1675–1757): a Venetian portraitist and miniaturist, and the first woman to make a good living as an artist; her soft, pastel portraits were the rage of the powdered wig set not only in Venice, but in Paris and Vienna, until she lost her eyesight in 1749 (Venice, Accademia and Ca' Rezzonico).

Castagno, Andrea del (1423–57): a Tuscan master of striking form and composition, who visited Venice in 1445 and left the city some Renaissance food for thought in St Mark's and S. Zaccaria.

Catena, Vincenzo (1480–1531): a well-born Venetian merchant, humanist and friend of Giorgione who painted as a hobby, increasingly well as time went on (*Judith*, in the Palazzo Querini-Stampalia in Venice, is his masterpiece).

de Chirico, Giorgio (1888–1978): a Greek-Italian and a founding father of the Metaphysical School (1916–18); best known for his enigmatic, often uncanny empty urban landscapes dotted with classical odds and ends and dressmakers' mannequins (Peggy Guggenheim, Venice).

Cima da Conegliano, Giovanni Battista (1459–1518): his luminous autumnal colours and landscapes were inspired by Bellini—as Bellini was inspired by several of his compositions (Madonna del Orto and Accademia in Venice).

Codussi, Mauro (c. 1420–1504): architect from Bergamo, who worked mainly in Venice; a genius at synthesizing traditional Venetian styles with the classical forms of the Renaissance (S. Michele in Isola, Venice's first Renaissance church; also S. Zaccaria, staircase at the Scuola di S. Giovanni Evangelista, Palazzo Vendramin-Calergi).

Crivelli, Carlo (c. 1435–95): meticulous Venetian enamoured of luminous perspective, crystalline forms, garlands and cucumbers in his exclusively religious work; he spent most of his time in the Marches (Accademia, Venice; Castelvecchio, Verona).

De Pisis, Filippo (1896–1956): a neo-Impressionist from Ferrara who spent a long period in Venice (Peggy Guggenheim, Venice).

Donatello (1386–1466), of Florence: the greatest European sculptor of the quattrocento, never equalled in technique, expressiveness or imaginative content. He spent 1443–50 in Padua, casting his Gattamelata statue and sculptures and reliefs for the high altar for the Basilica di S. Antonio, a major inspiration to young Andrea Mantegna; also a statue in the Frari, Venice.

Falconetto, Giovanni Maria (1468–1534): Veronese architect who built in a charming anti-quarian style that inspired Palladio, leading the way in the transformation of Gothic Padua (especially the Loggia della Gran Guardia and Loggia Cornaro) into a Renaissance city; he also designed the villa at Luvigliano in the Euganean Hills.

Fogolino, Marcello (1480–1550): a fine painter from Vicenza, who became court artist to Prince-Bishop Bernardo Cles, introducing the Renaissance to Trento (works in Santa Corona, Vicenza).

Giambono, Michele (c. 1420–62): one of the princes of Venetian retro; while everyone else moved on to the Renaissance, Giambono was still cranking out rich paintings in International Gothic (Accademia, altarpieces in St Mark's, Venice).

Giorgione (Giorgio da Castelfranco, c. 1478–1510): got his nickname 'Big George' not only for his height, but for the huge influence he had on Venetian painting. Although he barely lived past thirty and only several paintings are undisputedly by his hand, his poetic evocation of atmosphere and haunting, psychological ambiguity was echoed not only by Titian and Sebastiano del Piombo, his followers, but by his master Giovanni Bellini (paintings in the Accademia in Venice and Castelfranco).

Giotto di Bondone (c. 1267–1337): a Florentine, one of the most influential painters in history, the first Italian to break away from stylized Byzantine forms in favour of a more 'natural' and narrative style. Although associated with Florence and Assisi, he painted his masterpiece in Padua: the Cappella degli Scrovegni.

Giovanni da Verona (1457–1525): a Dominican friar and greatest marquetry artist of the century (S. Maria in Organo, Verona).

Guardi, Francesco (1712–93): brother-in-law of Giambattista Tiepolo and younger brother of Gianantonio (1699–1760) with whom he worked, making early attributions difficult. Guardi's favourite subject was Venice, but his views, unlike those of Canaletto, are suffused with light and atmosphere; many of his canvases approach Impressionism in their handling—hence his revival in the 19th century, after a life of obscurity and poverty (Ca' d'Oro, Accademia, Angelo Raffaele, all in Venice).

Guariento (14th century): a follower of Giotto and founder of the Paduan school. His master-piece, a massive fresco of *Paradise* in Venice's Ducal Palace, burned in a fire, though fragments hint at what was lost. His work has much of the same humane quality as Giotto (Ermitiani, Padua).

Jacobello del Fiore (c. 1370–1439): Venetian master of International Gothic, fond of raised gold embossing (Accademia, Venice).

Jappelli, Giuseppe (1783–1852): stylish Paduan neoclassical/eclectic architect and romantic landscape gardener; designed the Caffè Pedrocchi and several other buildings around Padua as well as the Grand Hotel Orologio in Àbano Terme.

Liberale da Verona (c. 1445–1529): genteel painter of frescoes (Duomo, Castelvecchio, S. Fermo).

Lombardo, Pietro (c. 1455–1516): native of Lombardy and founder of Venice's greatest family of sculptors and architects, strongly influenced by the Tuscan Renaissance and antique models (SS. Giovanni e Paolo, S. Giobbe, S. Francesco della Vigna, and his masterpiece, S. Maria dei Miracoli, all in Venice).

Lombardo, Tullio (c. 1455–1532): son of Pietro, with whom he often worked. Tullio was an exquisite marble-sculptor, best known for his tombs, especially the Vendramin tomb in Venice's SS. Giovanni e Paolo. His brother Antonio (c. 1458–1516) assisted him in the classical reliefs in the Basilica of S. Antonio, Padua.

Longhena, Baldassare (1598–1682): Venetian architect, a student of Scamozzi, whose best work was one of his first commissions: the church of the Salute (also Ca' Pesaro, both in Venice).

Longhi, Pietro (1702–85): there weren't photographers in 18th-century Venice, but there was Pietro Longhi, dutifully portraying society's foibles (Ca' Rezzonico, Accademia, Querini-Stampalia, all in Venice; also Palazzo Leoni Montanari, Vicenza). His son Alessandro (1733–1813) was official portrait painter of the Accademia, and in 1762 he published a biography of Venetian painters, with portraits of each.

Lorenzo Veneziano (active 1356–79): disciple of Paolo Veneziano (no relation) and painter in a luxuriant, golden International Gothic style (Duomo, Vicenza; Accademia, Venice).

Lotto, Lorenzo (c. 1480–1556): a neurotic Venetian trained under Giovanni Bellini, best known for religious paintings—some great, some uninspired—and portraits that seem to catch their sitters off guard, capturing his own restless energy on canvas. Lotto was run out of Venice by Titian and Aretino and spent much his life in the Marches (Accademia, Venice).

Maffei, Francesco (*c.* 1600–60) of Vicenza: dissonant and unorthodox baroque painter, whose nervous brush often brings out the dark side of the age of curlicues (Museo Civico and Oratorio di S. Nicola, Vicenza; Castelvecchio, Verona).

Mansueti, Giovanni (*c.* 1465–1527): under-rated student of Giovanni Bellini and a talented painter of narrative histories (Accademia, Venice; Museo Civico, Vicenza).

Mantegna, Andrea (*c.* 1420–1506): remark-able painter born near Padua, whose use of antiquity, sculptural forms as hard as coral and unusual perspectives dominated art in the Veneto until the rise of his brother-in-law Giambellini (Eremitani, Padua; S. Zeno and Castelvecchio, Verona; Accademia, Venice).

dalle Masegne, Jacobello and Pier Paolo: 14th-century Venetian architects and sculptors, influenced by the works of Tuscan Nicolò Pisano, creator of a new, realistic, classically inspired style (S. Marco, Venice).

Massari, Giorgio (1687–1766): Venetian archi-tect who collaborated with G.B. Tiepolo and Vivaldi to create some of the most delightful baroque churches in Venice (La Pietà and Gesuati).

Mazzoni, Sebastiano (1611–78): irrepressible Florentine baroque master who loved to go over the top (Museo Civico, Padua).

Menabuoi, Giusto de' (d. 1397): Florentine painter who followed Giotto to Padua, where his masterpiece is the Baptistry (also frescoes in the Palazzo della Ragione).

Montagna, Bartolomeo (1450–1523): a painter of heavy dignity inspired by Antonello da Messina, founder of the Vicentine school (Monte Bérico, Museo Civico, Vicenza).

Muttoni, Francesco (1668–1747): architect from Como and one of the most talented propo-nents of the Palladian revival in the Veneto (Palazzo Valmarano-Trento, Vicenza).

Palladio (Andrea di Pietro della Gondola, 1508–80): the Veneto's most influential architect, not only for his buildings, but for his books and drawings that imaginatively reinterpreted the clas-sics to fit the needs of the day (major buildings in Vicenza, Venice, Masèr, and on the Brenta Canal).

Palma Giovane (Jacopo Palma, 1544–1628): the most prolific painter of his day, the great-nephew of Palma Vecchio and a pupil of Titian, who specialized in large but usually vapid narra-tive paintings (every church in Venice seems to have at least one).

Palma Vecchio (Jacopo Negretti, *c.* 1480–1528): a student of Giovanni Bellini who success-fully adopted the new sensuous style of Giorgione and young Titian, and is best known for his volup-tuous Venetian blondes, often disguised as saints (S. Maria Formosa, Venice; S. Stefano, Vicenza).

Paolo Veneziano (*c.* 1290–1360): the leading painter of his day, a powerful Byzantine influence in Venetian art that would linger longer in the lagoon than elsewhere (Venice, Accademia; Padua, Museo Civico).

Piazzetta, Giambattista (1683–1754): Venetian baroque painter extraordinaire, who went to extremes in his use of light and dark, favouring the latter. An early influence on Giambattista Tiepolo, he became the first director of the Accademia (Accademia, SS. Giovanni e Paolo, and other churches, Venice).

Pisanello, Antonio (*c.* 1395–*c.* 1455): origi-nator of the Renaissance medal and one of the leading and most graceful painters of the Gothic International school; he collaborated with Gentile da Fabriano on the lamented lost frescoes in the Doges' Palace (Castelvecchio, S. Fermo and S. Anastasia, Verona; medals in Ca' d'Oro, Venice).

Pittoni, Giovanni Battista (1687–1767): one of the most popular painters of his day in Venice, who went from dark baroque to a lighter rococo under Tiepolo's influence (S. Corona, Vicenza).

Pordenone (Giovanni de' Sacchis, 1484–1539): Titian's main rival, with a more monumental, Roman style inspired by Michelangelo, combined with quick brushstrokes and often bizarre iconog-raphy and expressions; Vasari claims that he was self-taught (S. Giovanni Elemosinario, Venice).

Ricci, Sebastiano (1659–1734): decorative painter from Belluno inspired by the scenographic monumentality of Roman baroque; his work at its best is fresh and colourful, while other times it shows slapdash haste—Ricci was a terrible womanizer and often had to flee jealous husbands (S. Giustina, Padua; Museo Civico, Vicenza). He often worked with his nephew Marco Ricci (1670–1730; landscapes in the Accademia, Venice).

Il Riccio (Andrea Briosco, c. 1470–1532): High Renaissance sculptor and architect and great friend of humanist scholars, famous for his intricate bronze work and statuettes (Padua, Museo Civico, S. Antonio, where the Pascal candelabrum is his masterpiece; also S. Giustina).

Rizzo, Antonio (c. 1445–98): pure Renaissance sculptor and architect from Verona, who worked mostly in Venice (Tron monument, Frari; courtyard of the Palazzo Ducale).

Sammicheli, Michele (1484–1559): born in Verona, Sammicheli was a sometimes heavy-handed Renaissance architect and sculptor, as well as the Serenissima's master builder of walls and fortifications (walls, Padua; also walls, S. Bernardino and Palazzo Bevilacqua, Verona; Palazzo Grimani, Venice).

Sansovino, Jacopo (Jacopo Tatti, 1486–1570): sculptor and architect from Florence who took his name from his master Andrea Sansovino. Jacopo fled the Sack of Rome in 1527 and came to Venice, where he became chief architect to the Procurators of St Mark's and a good buddy of Titian and poison pen master Aretino. Sansovino created a new Venetian High Renaissance style— the rhythmic use of columns, arches, loggias and reliefs, with sculpture playing an integral role (Venice, where he rebuilt St Mark's Square and designed the famous Library; sculptures in the Ducal Palace).

Scamozzi, Vincenzo (1552–1616): from Vicenza, Palladio's closest collaborator who completed many of his projects according to his own imagination; and a brilliant Mannerist architect in his own right (villas, palaces and Teatro Olimpico, Vicenza; Procuratie Nuove, Venice; Via Sacra, Monsélice).

Sebastiano del Piombo (Sebastiano Luciani, 1485–1547): pupil of Giorgione, and a rich autumnal colourist. Sebastiano became the chief notary of the Vatican (hence his nickname, for the lead seals that still haunt the Posta Italiana); most works are in Rome, but *see* S. Giovanni Crisostomo, Venice.

Squarcione, Francesco (c. 1394–1474): a Paduan tailor and self-taught painter, one of the first antique dealers, and teacher of Mantegna; not much of his documented work survives beyond a polyptych in the Museo Civico, Padua.

Stefano da Verona (or da Zevio, c. 1375–1450): delightful International Gothic master, lead painter in Verona in the generation after Turone (S. Fermo Maggiore, Castelvecchio, both Verona).

Tiepolo, Giambattista (1691–1770): Venice's rococo wizard, generally considered the greatest European painter of the 18th century. He initially worked in the style of Piazzetta, but soon left all that gloomy chiaroscuro behind for one of the most colourful palettes in art; Tiepolo's subjects, many mythological, live in the delightful warm afterglow of Venice's decline (Palazzo Labia, Scuola dei Carmini, and Gesuati, Venice; Villa Valmarana, Vicenza).

Tiepolo, Giandomenico (1727–1804): son of Giambattista, with whom he frescoed Villa Valmarana. While he could imitate his father's grand heroic manner to the point that attribution of some frescoes could go either way, Giandomenico's work tends to be more introspective and often wistful, especially his masquerades (Ca' Rezzonico, S. Polo, Venice).

Tintoretto (Jacopo Robusti, 1518–94): he was given his name, 'little dyer', because of his father's profession. A proud, ill-tempered workaholic, his ideal was to combine Michelangelo's drawing with the colouring of Titian, but his most amazing talent was in his visionary, unrestrained and original composition, often delighting in startling sleight-of-hand foreshortening. His most talented follower was a Greek who ended up in Spain—El Greco (Scuola di S. Rocco series; the world's largest painting, in the Palazzo Ducale; Accademia and S. Giorgio Maggiore, all in Venice; also Museo Civico, Vicenza).

Titian (Tiziano Vecellio, *c.* 1480s–1576): from Pieve di Cadore in the Dolomites; he became, with the death of Giovanni Bellini, official painter to the Venetian Republic. Generally regarded as the greatest painter of the Venetian school, Titian was a pupil of Giovanni Bellini at the same time as Giorgione, and followed the latter so closely that many of his early works have often been attributed to his colleague. Titian made his reputation with the monumental altarpiece of the *Assumption* in Venice's Frari, a bold handling of form and colour that cast a spell on Tintoretto, Veronese and countless others. In his long career, his work evolved through several phases, influenced by Mannerism in the 1540s after a trip to Rome, and then in his last years, taking his revolutionary free brushwork to an extreme, most violently in his last unfinished work, the *Pietà* in the Accademia. Although Titian spent most of his life in Venice, his international reputation saw most of his canvases scattered across Europe: Emperor Charles V was such an admirer that he made Titian a Count Palatine, an extraordinary honour for a painter. Besides the Frari altarpieces, Venice keeps a few of his works in S. Salvatore, the Accademia, the Salute; also the cathedral of Verona.

Tommaso da Modena (*c.* 1325–76): delightful, humane 14th-century painter, a follower of Giotto who worked for a long period in Treviso; also in Castelvecchio, Verona.

Tura, Cosmè (*c.* 1430–90): of the Ferrara school, whose singularly intense, craggy and weirdly tortured style is immediately recognizable and, for many, an acquired taste (Museo Correr, Venice).

Turone (active in the 1360s): Veronese master influenced by German miniaturists, teacher of Altichiero (Castelvecchio, S. Anastasia, Verona).

Veronese (Paulo Caliari, 1528–88): the most sumptuous and ravishingly decorative painter of the High Renaissance, fond of striking illusionism, shimmering colours, and curious perspectives set in Palladian architectural fancies (Villa Bàrbaro at Masèr; Accademia, Ducal Palace, and S. Sebastiano, Venice; S. Corona, Vicenza).

Verrocchio, Andrea del (Andrea di Cioni, 1435–88): painter, sculptor, and alchemist nicknamed 'true eye', Verrocchio was a follower of Donatello and teacher of Leonardo da Vinci. The greatest bronze sculptor of the day, he was hired by Venice to create the dynamic equestrian statue of Colleoni.

Vittoria, Alessandro (1525–1608): Venetian sculptor, a student of Sansovino famous for his elegant bronze statuettes and portrait busts (S. Francesco della Vigna, Frari, Ca' d'Oro, Venice).

Vivarini: 15th-century clan of painters from Murano, the chief rivals of the Bellini dynasty in Venice, noted for their rich, decorative and retro style. Antonio (*c.* 1415–76/84) collaborated with Giovanni d'Alemagna to paint altarpieces (S. Giobbe, Venice); brother Bartolomeo (1432–99) was more imaginative in his use of colour and rhythm (S. Maria Formosa, Frari, Venice); Alvise (1446–1503), son of Antonio, was influenced by Antonello da Messina (Frari, S. Giovanni in Brágora, Venice).

Zelotti, Giambattista (1526–78) of Verona: a collaborator of Veronese who became one of Palladio's chief and most interesting interior decorators (La Malcontenta, on the Brenta Canal).

Tales of Tyranny and Harmony

The Son of Satan   66

Still the Best: Giovanni Bellini   68

The Council of Trent   69

The Gentle Art of Building Villas:
 Palladio and his Heirs   71

A Most Serene Civilisation   75

In stark contrast to the benign flock of winged lions left behind by Venice, in Venetia you'll find older, darker relics—walls, castles, towers, prisons and torture chambers—recalling one of the meanest hombres who ever lived. The very name Ezzelino still evokes a shiver in this part of the world, even though he's been frying in hell for over 700 years. Medieval Italy was precocious in so many ways, in banking, in trade, in art, in architecture, in literature—the list goes on and on. Ezzelino III da Romano was another first: Europe's first self-made tyrant.

He lived in interesting times. Two generations previously, in 1176, the Lombard League, including Verona, Vicenza, Padua, Belluno and Treviso, had battled to win the guarantee of their civic freedoms from the German Holy Roman Emperor, Frederick I Barbarossa. This came as a blow to the Ezzelini, the feudal lordlings of what is now northern Vicenza province, and staunch members of the Emperor's Ghibelline party. Now the pro-papal Guelph *comuni* were open rivals, especially Vicenza, which had taken advantage of its new freedoms to snatch a chunk of Ezzelino turf.

Ezzelino hopes rose again with the advent of Barbarossa's grandson, Emperor Frederick II, Stupor Mundi, 'the Wonder of the World'. A man with a brilliant mind, a poet fluent in six languages, Frederick was the first 'Italian' emperor, having grown up in cosmopolitan Arab-Greek-Norman Sicily. This also made him singularly open-minded and tolerant. But these were the tub-thumping days of the Crusades, and the popes hated him from the start; when he regained Jerusalem by treaty in 1229, rather than by massacring the infidels, the popes excommunicated him.

Frederick hated the popes right back. They presented the biggest obstacle to his plans for a modern centralized empire, and it came as a major blow in 1230 when the *comuni* of northern Italy re-formed the Lombard League, declaring themselves the allies of Pope Gregory IX. It was an act that many *comuni* soon regretted, as Gregory made them prove their allegiance by accepting the Church's new weapon, the Inquisition, to roust out the Paterini and Cathar heretics they had hitherto tolerated. Many of these heretics belonged to the nobility, including Ezzelino II da Romano. Gregory demanded that his son, Ezzelino III, then serving as *podestà* (feudal mayor or imperial representative) of Verona, turn his father over for burning. The younger Ezzelino refused; it was the only good deed of his life.

Ezzelino III was born 1194, the same year as Frederick. He was the most skilled military commander of his day, ruthless and ambitious, a bachelor who despised luxury and women. He was also completely devoted to the emperor. In 1234, when Frederick amassed a Saracen army from Sicily (immune from papal bans and excommunications) to attack the *comuni* of the Lombard League, he naturally chose Ezzelino as his lieutenant in Venetia, and, in Verona in 1236, put 3,000 German cavalry and his Saracens under his command.

Ezzalino, advised by his astrologers, at once pounced on Vicenza and Padua, then the most powerful city on the *terra firma*. He did this with a brutality shocking even by the standards of the day, torturing his victims to death to extract names of other potential enemies, flinging others in dungeons to starve to death, then killing all their relatives. Stories of his cruelty dominate the literature of the 13th century and feature prominently in the *Cento Novelle Antiche*, gathered together in 1525. His subjects called him the 'Son of Satan'.

Although Frederick regained much of northern Italy, it was at the price of taking the blame for Ezzelino's atrocities and another excommunication. The emperor's colleagues, fearful for their own souls, began to abandon and betray him, and Frederick grew increasingly bitter. If he was alarmed by the monster he had created in the Veneto, he could at least trust him. In 1250, Stupor Mundi died of dysentery while preparing to crusade with St Louis in the hope of returning to the pope's good graces.

Ezzelino, for his part, was never bothered by remorse. In Padua alone he kept eight overflowing prisons 'notwithstanding the incessant toil of the executioner to empty them'. In 1256 Pope Alexander IV preached an anti-Ezzelino Crusade, offering all who fought him the same indulgences offered to Crusaders in the Holy Land. The offer attracted all the riffraff in Italy, who took Padua by sheer numbers; the gates were opened to welcome the 'liberators' who then raped and pillaged the city for a week. In revenge for that open gate, Ezzelino tortured and killed all but 200 of the 11,000 Paduans in his army.

The Pope's Crusaders were so incompetent that Ezzelino actually grew stronger, and gained Brescia when the Ghibellines there delivered their *comune* to him, free of charge. This gave Ezzelino a bad case of hubris, and in 1259, aged 65, he decided to take all of Lombardy and Milan itself, believing the nobles there, as in Brescia, would hand their city to him. Off he marched with the most splendid army of his career, but the Brescians, by now disgusted by his cruelty, had secretly dealt with the Guelphs of Milan, Cremona, Ferrara and Mantua; when Ezzelino was well into Lombardy, at Cassiano on the Adda, the Brescians abandoned him and his enemies closed in. Ezzelino fought until he was severely wounded in the foot. The Guelphs chained him up in the castle at Soncino, where he refused to speak or accept any aid, but furiously tore his bandages off with his teeth and died eleven days later.

His brother, the *podestà* of Treviso, and all his family were slain to make sure the family never plagued Venetia again. But in reality Ezzelino had more than his share of heirs: the mafia-like signori, the Carrara of Padua, the Scaligers of Verona, the Visconti of Milan, the Medici of Florence who would dominate Italian politics for centuries. In *The Civilization of the Renaissance in Italy* (1867) Jacob Burckhardt wrote Ezzelino's chilling epitaph:

> *The conquests and usurpations which had hitherto taken place in the Middle Ages rested on real or pretended inheritance and other such claims... Here for the first time the attempt was openly made to found a throne by wholesale murder and endless barbarities, by the adoption, in short, of any means with a view to nothing but the end pursued. None of his successors, not even Cesare Borgia, rivalled the colossal guilt of Ezzelino; but the example once set was not forgotten, and his fall led to no return of justice among nations, and served as no warning to future transgressors.*

Renaissance artists tended to be pernickity, proud individualists, not averse to pulling a pistol on one another, and their lives often make for colourful reading. One great exception to the rule was Giovanni Bellini, who apparently never quarrelled, married, travelled, designed buildings, wrote letters or poetry, hobnobbed with princes, or in brief did anything at all except paint during a career that lasted for 65 years. In most art histories he gets a nod as the father of the Venetian school and master of Giorgione and Titian, but many visitors to the Veneto overlook him, bedazzled by the greater fireworks of the Three Ts (Titian, Tintoretto and Tiepolo). Next to theirs, Bellini's work is very still, but like many quiet voices he often has more to say at the end of the day.

Giambellini, as our ancestors liked to call him, was born in Venice around 1430, with a paintbrush in his baby fist. His father Jacopo, a student of the great International Gothic master Gentile da Fabriano, was an innovator in his own way; one of the first artists to draw from nature, he also did a number of perspectivist studies in his notebooks. Giovanni and his older brother Gentile learned their craft at their father's knee, but early on they went separate ways: Gentile inherited Jacopo's workshop and style, while Giovanni inherited his love of the natural world. His heaven was on earth, in the Veneto; his saints were human, and his faith, while pure, was above all humane, and expressed itself not through halos and gold paint, but through a warm and sensuous empathy. Only Raphael, that other great painter of madonnas, had a similar gift. But while Raphael's are beautiful, tender loving mammas bursting with charm, Bellini's have the balance and measure of the quattrocento. They are women doing their bit in the divine scheme, brave yet wistful, perhaps knowing what's in store for their *bambino*. They never emote, or appeal for the viewer's sympathy, which makes them all the more poignant.

In 1453 family played another formative role in Bellini's development, when his older sister married Andrea Mantegna. Mantegna, already the top master of perspective in Italy, showed Giovanni how to place solid figures in three-dimensional settings, lessons revealed in a number of works now in Venice's Museo Correr: *Transfiguration*, the *Frizzoni Madonna*, *Crucifixion* and the *Dead Christ Supported by Two Angels*. Some time around 1460, Andrea and Giovanni both produced paintings from a drawing of the *Agony in the Garden* in old Jacopo's notebooks. Both are in London's National Gallery: Mantegna's landscape is as precise as his figures, while Bellini has a more lyrical bent in his use of colour and light. His most important work of the period, the *Polyptych of S. Vincenzo Ferreri* in Venice's SS. Giovanni e Paolo (1464–8), shows his rapid progress—the pediment, which he painted first, is awkward, but the last figure he added, the Angel Gabriel, is exquisite.

The last key ingredient for Bellini came to Venice with Antonello da Messina in 1475. Antonello had just learned the art of oil painting from Jan Van Eyck, and among the Italians Bellini led the way in adopting the new medium, then mastering it to a degree that few painters since have ever equalled, painstakingly building up colour and depth in transparent glazes, enabling him to achieve a remarkable richness of tone and luminosity.

Critics call Bellini's mature style 'tonalism', for its emphasis on light and colour and atmosphere at the expense of design and line. In his experiments, the borders between solids and space begin to dissolve, replaced by melting transitions of light and shadow. Backgrounds and landscapes play a larger role in the composition than they ever had before, until they become as integral to the meaning as the central figures. An early example is the *Saint Francis* (1480, Frick Collection, New York City), while the *Pala Barbarigo* (1484, San Pietro Martire, Murano), the *Pala di San Giobbe* and *Madonna of the Little Trees* (1487, both in the Accademia) represent the culmination.

Bellini's splendid late style dates from around 1500, when he was seventy and could count nearly every young Venetian painter of distinction as a pupil. He was the Official Painter of Venice and had singlehandedly brought his home town into the first ranks of the Renaissance, alongside Florence and Rome. But he never stopped learning or innovating. His *Portrait of Doge Leonardo Loredan* (National Gallery, London; 1501) shows the first use of *impasto* (the building up of paint to produce texture)—this was the first individualist use of a brushstroke and the first step in the great revolution in western art that would separate art from the object represented. Other beautiful examples of Bellini's late style are the *Baptism of Christ* (Santa Corona, Vicenza) and the sublime *Sacra Conversazione* (San Zaccaria, Venice), where the complex shadings of colour and glazings are sheer wizardry— Leonardo da Vinci's famous *sfumato* technique but in colour, all merging to create a perfect lyrical unity.

And he still had time for young artists. Albrecht Dürer wrote home from Venice in 1507, 'Giambellino praised me in front of many gentlemen. He wanted something done by me, and he came in person to ask me, telling me he would pay me well. And everyone said that it really was very gracious of him to have favoured me in this way. He is very old, but he's still the best in painting.'

And he still had nine good years in him. He greatly admired the work of his pupil Giorgione, who had taken his tonalism a step further by emphasizing mood over matter, and painted for the delight of private patrons. Giambellini, after 60 years of painting for Church and State, was ready for a change. Five of his small mythological paintings remain in Venice's Accademia, while the others are abroad, including the *Feast of the Gods* (1514) in the National Gallery, Washington D.C. Perhaps most remarkable of all is his *Lady with a Mirror* (1515) in Vienna's Kunsthistorisches Museum—perhaps the most touchingly optimistic and dreamily sensuous work ever painted by an artist in his late 80s, in Bellini's case a year before his death.

The Council of Trent

In the 1520s Emperor Charles V, haughty ruler of much of Europe and the Americas, found his Germanic possessions in the throes of the Reformation, and his Catholic domains bracing themselves for a hysterical reaction. A staunch Catholic himself, Charles sought to heal the rift by asking the Pope to call a council—an idea first suggested by Luther himself—to look into some urgently needed reforms in the Church. Pope Clement VII refused point blank (the last thing any pope wanted was a revival of Conciliarism, with the threat that papal authority could be overruled in a general council), but after Charles V taught him a lesson by sacking Rome in 1527, Clement agreed that perhaps a council wasn't such a bad idea after all.

His successor, Paul III, let the uncongenial idea slide until 1538, when the Germans threatened to call a national council of their own, minus the Pope. But where to convoke it? Charles insisted that it take place on Imperial turf, while the Pope wanted an Italian city where he could influence the outcome. Eventually, Trento, an Italian city ruled by a prince-bishop under the Holy Roman Empire, proved to be the perfect compromise. After more delays, the Council finally convened in Trento on December 1545 to study the three goals Paul III had placed before it: to reunite Christendom, reform the Church's administration and procedures, and form a league of Christian princes against the Ottomans.

The council had hardly began when a typhus epidemic sent the prelates scurrying off to Bologna for safety, and it was another six years before a new pope, Julius III, ordered them back to Trent. Other events in Germany, such as the military advance of the Protestant princes, soon caused a new break-up. The last session of the Council, under Pius IV, met for two years, from January 1562 to December 1563, when a long list of decrees were promulgated and approved by the pope.

If the Council of Trent had signally failed to unite the Christians (after all the dithering, it was far too late for compromise) or unite their princes against the Turk, it did result in a new unified, clear-cut doctrine to confront the Protestant threat. This provided for vast improvements in pastoral care and the education of priests, and an end of clerical concubinage; there was to be a new edition of the Bible and a new catechism. In the face of Protestant doubt, the rites of the Seven Sacraments in themselves were confirmed as signs of grace (the spiritual state of the minister or recipient being incidental), and the Office of Propaganda was created to convert Protestant (and other) unbelievers.

The Council's last salvos, decided at the last minute during the last session, were aimed straight at the Protestants, confirming the existence of Purgatory, the veneration of saints, images and relics, and the value of indulgences. The Counter-Reformation had blasted off, and the 'Jesuit style', precursor of the baroque, incorporating all the richness, pomp and sensuality that the Protestants hated, inspired a wave of church-building to provide a visual symbol for the new Catholicism. It was a hothouse orchid that blossomed on a scorched and increasingly fearful Christendom.

In his famous *History of the Council of Trent* (first published in 1619, in London), Paolo Sarpi, the great Venetian monk and historian, called the controversies in Trent 'the *Iliad* of our age' and believed that the resulting Council's doctrines were an unmitigated disaster. According to Sarpi, the original goal of its well-meaning leaders—the restoration of the primitive Church, poor and democratic, to coax back the Protestants—had been distorted by the political intrigues of the Roman Curia, Jesuits and Spaniards.

> *This Council, which pious men desired and procured to reunite the Church (which was beginning to split apart), has, on the contrary, made the split a permanent one and the parties to it irreconcilable. It was planned by the princes to reform the Church; but it has brought about the greatest corruption of the Church since the name of 'Christian' was first heard.*
>
> Paolo Sarpi, *History of the Council of Trent*

Sarpi's *Iliad* analogy was certainly right in one respect. Instead of making peace, the Council of Trent turned out to be a Trojan horse for an ever grander, ever more militant Church, re-armed with its most fearful weapon, the Inquisition (reinstated by Paul III), an excess soon followed by the Wars of Religion and the even more horrific Thirty Years War—the worst Europe would see until the 20th century.

The Gentle Art of Building Villas: Palladio and his Heirs

The man who would change the face of Western architecture could not have had a more unlikely background. Andrea di Pietro della Gondola was born in 1508 into a poor family in Padua, who apprenticed him to a stonecutter at age 13. Treated harshly, he ran away 18 months later, taking refuge in Vicenza, where he found a job as an assistant with a kinder family of stonecutters. And so he would have remained, chiselling away, had not Dame Fortune smiled on him in 1537 and sent him to the humanist scholar Giangiorgio Trissino, to work on the villa he was redesigning at Crioli, just outside Vicenza.

Able to see a spark in Andrea that no one else had bothered to notice, Trissino became his fairy godfather, teaching him the essentials of a Renaissance education and the principles of classical architecture, especially *De Architectura* of Vitruvius, a treatise that had been redis-covered in the 1400s. The 30-year-old stonecutter blossomed. Trissino proudly introduced him to his humanist cronies in Vicenza, Padua, and Venice. He got him his first commission as an architect, designing the Villa Godi at Lonedo di Lugo (1538). At the same time Trissino was working on an epic poem, *L'Italia liberata dai Goti* (Italy freed from the Goths), with Justinian's General Belisarius and his guardian angel Palladio (from Pallas Athena, the goddess of wisdom) as the heroes. Trissino was so pleased with both the name he invented and his protégé that he united the two forever in 1540.

To complete Palladio's education, Trissino took him on a two-year study tour of Rome (1540–1), giving him first-hand knowledge not only of the ancients, but of the pioneer architects of his day—Michele Sammicheli, Giulio Romano, Giovanni Maria Falconetto, and Sebastiano Serlio. Palladio would return to Rome four times, measuring and analyzing; he even wrote a best-selling guidebook to the ruins. Yet rather than direct inspiration, ancient Rome and Vitruvius would act primarily as emotional reference in all his work, as he created idylls that reflected an antiquity that was partly real (notably in Italy, where Roman ruins were everywhere), and partly the dream antiquity that infused the Renaissance. Palladio liked to flatter his villa clients by comparing them to Pliny and Seneca, philosophising in their country retreats.

But there was far more to Palladio than Roman play-acting; more than any other architect of that talented age, he was able to invent a style that was at once imposing yet sensuous, perfect for his time and place. Venetia's patrician élite, increasingly unable to risk their fortunes in new trade ventures or Middle Eastern derring-do, now sought to escape city business in the summer, seeking a life of balance and harmony in the country, enjoying the beauties of nature while supervising their new-found interests in agriculture. While they required the structures necessary for a working farm (*barchesse*), defence was no longer a consideration, even in the open country; by the time Palladio came on the scene, Venetia had recovered from the War of the Cambrai and was at peace. He led the way in abandoning the old fortified country residence in favour of light and comfort. His famous temple-fronts and airy double loggias, derived from his mistaken notions of Roman domestic architecture, were revolutionary in the 16th century and lend the villas an openness and serenity that feel at home in the surrounding countryside.

There are over three thousand of these villas in the Veneto alone. But why are Palladio's eighteen surviving houses the most satisfying? One lesson from Vitruvius that Palladio engraved on his heart was the ideal of harmony and proportion. According to his own writings, the elements of a building must correspond to the whole and to each other, the careful consonance of parts and dimensions that was the original meaning of the word symmetry. Within those restrictions, what he called 'the certain truth of mathematics which is final and unchangeable', he managed a subtle variation of size and shape according to each commission, although always with the idea that no matter where one stood inside a villa, the whole would be immediately comprehensible. Rudolph Wittkower, in his *Architectural Principles in the Age of Humanism* (1949) noted that Palladio's dimensions are based on the harmonic proportions of music, as in Pythagoras' musical scale. This was no accident—in the 16th century, music and architecture were praised as the most artificial of arts, based on science alone, and free from attempts to imitate or better nature.

> *...in all works it is requisite that their parts should correspond together, and have such proportions, that there may be none whereby the whole cannot be measured, and likewise all the other parts.*
>
> *I Quattro Libri dell'Archittura*
> *Book IV, chapter 5,*

Based on Pythagoras' musical scale, and the Renaissance concept that architecture can mirror music to reveal the universal harmonic ratios inherent in nature, Palladio proposes seven sets of beautiful and harmonious proportions for rooms:

1. Circular
2. Square (1:1)
3. The diagonal of the square for the room length (1:√2)
4. A square plus a third (3:4)
5. A square plus a half (2:3)
6. A square plus two-thirds (3:5)
7. Double square (1:2)

The double square is the *diapason*, or octave, as a lyre string of a given length will produce a note one octave above the note of a string half its size. Two strings of lengths in the ratio of 2 to 3 will produce harmony, a *diapente* or musical fifth. If the ratio is 3:4, you get a different harmony, a *diatesseron*, or fourth.

The ratio of 3:5 isn't musical, but it is extremely close to the famous proportion called the Golden Section, found throughout nature and in much ancient and medieval architecture. All of these relationships are commensurable—expressible in whole numbers, and easy for an architect to work with. The non-musical, incommensurable exception, the diagonal of a square, or √2, comes straight out of Vitruvius, and is believed to hark straight back to ancient Greek theories of proportions. The Romans never used it in building, and to tell the truth Palladio didn't either.

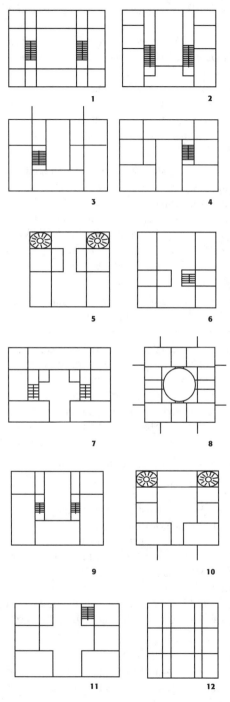

1 Villa Thiene
2 Villa Sarego
3 Villa Badoera
4 Villa Zeno
5 Villa Pisani, Montagnana
6 Villa Emo, p.167
7 Villa Pisani, Bagnolo
8 La Rotonda, p.185
9 Villa Pojana
10 Villa Cornaro, p.166
11 La Malcontenta, p.143
12 general pattern of villas

The country villa, more than any other building, was an isolated ideal that united the artificial and natural in perfect harmony (*see* grey box, p.72).

Because of the innate classical grandeur of his designs, Palladio didn't need to rely as much as past architects on expensive stone, marbles, reliefs, exterior frescoes and gilding for effect; his finest villas are endowed with a serene clarity and geometric simplicity, all white surfaces and columns, set against lush green lawns and gardens. And as buildings go they were bargains; what looks like stone is cheap brick coated with a sheen of stucco-like material called *intonaco* (one imagines Palladio had seen enough stone for a lifetime in his former career). Most of the capitals crowning the brick columns are made of terracotta, while other features that look like marble are nearly always wood, coated with straw and stucco. Because the villas were only for the summer, there was no need to worry about heating them and no need for expensive tapestries to insulate the walls; frescoes were the answer, a nice family allegory perhaps, or mythological allusions to suit the owner's private fancy.

Unlike Alberti, Michelangelo, Raphael, Sansovino, Giulio Romano and the other great architects of the Renaissance,

Palladio was the first who did nothing but build. He was the first professional architect. But he also found the time to pass his knowledge on. Besides his very popular guide to Rome, he illustrated Daniele Barbaro's annotated edition of Vitruvius' *De Architectura*, and then, in 1570, published his own monumental *I Quattro Libri dell' Architettura*, offering practical advice for builders, illustrated with fine woodcuts of his own buildings. *I Quattro Libri* has never gone out of print, with good (and perhaps not so good) reason: 'With the touch of pedantry that suited the times and invested his writings with a fallacious air of scholarship, he was the very man to summarize and classify, and to save future generations of architects the labour of thinking for themselves,' as Sir Reginald Blomfield wrote in his *Studies in Architecture*.

These future generations would give Palladio a curious afterlife. The first foreign president of his fan club was Inigo Jones, who came to the Veneto in 1613, toured the villas and met Palladio's collaborator, Vincenzo Scamozzi. Smitten, Jones returned to England and designed stage sets in the Italian manner, collaborating on elaborate masques with Ben Jonson. By 1615, he had worked his way up to the post of Surveyor of the King's Works, in effect the court architect. Even after that, he still had time for theatrical work. The very first masque he staged after gaining his royal post was called *The Golden Age Restored*, and this proved a fitting motto for what was to follow.

Jones may have brought the Renaissance in building to Britain, but he was hardly a slavish follower. His Banqueting House at Whitehall, the Queen's House at Greenwich and Covent Garden were highly original interpretations of the Palladian style. They induced a revolution in British tastes; Jones even had the effrontery to tack a Palladian façade on the old Gothic St Paul's in London, which so embarrassed the old cathedral that it burned up along with the rest of London in 1666. After the fire, Jones's precocious Vitruvian visions were bumped aside for Christopher Wren's more genial mix of Renaissance and Continental baroque. For a whole century, British fashion would ignore Inigo Jones; even in the Veneto, Palladio's reputation took a nosedive in the 1600s, his fame entirely eclipsed by that of Scamozzi.

But in the early 18th century change was again in the air, and as John Charlton put it 'a new architectural religion was born, with Palladio as Mahomet, his *Four Books of Architecture* as the sacred text, and Inigo Jones as a major prophet. Of the new cult Lord Burlington was to be high priest and Chiswick House the temple.' After reading *Vitruvius Britannicus* by Colen Campbell (1715) and Venetian Giacomo Leoni's 'translation' of Palladio's *Four Books of Architecture* (1715), the young aristocrat-architect Burlington went to Vicenza in 1719 to study the master's works in person and to purchase every drawing by Palladio he could lay his hands on. The fresh interest by foreigners inspired a Palladian revival in Venetia itself, just when the booming economy ignited a veritable villa building spree. But while the architects of the settecento packed their houses with Palladian decorative elements and references, few even tried to follow the old master's recipes for harmonic proportions.

Neither did any of his foreign followers. Burlington, who loved Palladio for his re-interpretation of the ancients, was dogmatically more Palladian than Palladio (forgetting that Palladio himself often broke his own rules), and his greatest work, Chiswick House, seems cold compared to its model, La Rotonda. Burlington's strict interpretations influenced 18th-century domestic architecture in England more than Palladio himself, both through his own designs and the books he financed, especially *The Designs of Inigo Jones* by William Kent (1727).

Other influential works that followed, *Palladio Londinensis: Of the London Art of Building* by William Salmon (1738) and *The City and Country Builders and Workman's Treasury of Designs* by Batty Langley (1740), were sent to colonial America as pattern books, illustrated with Anglo-Palladian designs. There, in the more congenial climate and landscapes of Virginia and the Carolinas, Palladian architecture was to find its true home. The planters' houses and public buildings of the Old South in the 18th century are still revered as some of America's finest buildings, and Palladio's stamp is on most of them.

The northern colonies' first accomplished architect, Peter Harrison, carried the fashion up to Newport, Rhode Island, but the crowning achievement of Palladian architecture in America was to come courtesy of the copy of the *Quattro Libri* in the library of Thomas Jefferson. Jefferson once wrote to an architect friend, 'Palladio is the Bible. You should get it and stick close to it.' His three great works, the State Capitol at Richmond, his home at Monticello and the august rotunda of the University of Virginia, stand as reminders that, in architecture, America's first national style was a gift from Venice.

A Most Serene Civilization

Esto perpetua (May it last forever).

Paolo Sarpi's last words

There was nothing quite like the Serenissima, and there never will be again. The eight centuries in which the lagoon city kept her own counsel, plus the three and a half centuries when her government embraced the *terra firma* of Venetia, are marked by a way of life so distinct and original as to be a civilization apart. It wasn't perfect, but the last two hundred years of Italian history would have been far different, and probably far happier, had Venice rather than Rome had been put in charge of the show. Of course the Italians themselves never considered any such thing; even today, in their national family, Venice is the quirky cousin born on the wrong side of the blanket who spent most of her life in exotic lands. She stands apart, proud and diffident and perhaps a little misunderstood. Modern Italians tend to find Rome far more beautiful.

Although Venetia was fragmented after the fall of Rome, and separated throughout the Middle Ages into two distinct camps, the precocious seagoing Republic and the more traditional states of the terra firma, there was always a close relationship between the sea Venetians and the land Venetians. They shared a common ancient history and language— Venet, the official language of the Serenissima until the Austrian occupation. And even though Venice remained aloof from mainland politics for centuries, avoiding the Ghibelline-Guelph gang rumbles that troubled the rest of the peninsula, her famous network of spies kept a close eye on potentially troublesome tyrants like Ezzelino da Romano and the Carrara of Padua. Protected by her impenetrable lagoon, Venice intervened only when it suited her interest or pleasure.

It was not exactly an attitude that won her many friends in Italy, but there wasn't much anyone could do about it, either—until the pincer-like siege by Genoa and its ally Padua cut off Venice's food supplies in the Battle of Chioggia (1379). This scared the pants off Venice, and changed her mind; holding her nose, she plunged into the murk of mainland affairs. By 1454 she had conquered (mostly by diplomacy) all of the present Veneto, Friuli, the Dolomites as far as Belluno, as well as Bergamo, Brescia and Istria. It proved to be an act of some prescience: as Venice's sway grew on the mainland, her traditional livelihood, trade in the East, was being drained away by Ottoman conquests, the opening of new markets in the Americas and, after Vasco da Gama, the opening up of alternative trade routes around the horn of Africa.

Unlike most empires, the *terra firma* cities were given the choice of whether or not they wanted to stay in or get out. Pope Julius II, who had the artistic foresight to muscle Michelangelo into painting the Sistine Chapel ceiling, was an imbecile at statecraft. Rather than support Venice as Europe's main bulwark against the Turks, he grew jealous and raised the international League of the Cambrai against her in 1509. In face of the massive invasion, Venice released the *terra firma* from its oaths of allegiance. And as soon as the coast was clear, every last *comune* returned to St Mark's.

This hate and envy by outsiders gave the people of Venetia a strong sense of solidarity with one another—a bond strengthened by the law that compelled the mainlanders and over-seas colonists to buy and sell with Venice alone. That this monopoly actually ran smoothly is testimony to the spirit of internal harmony in the Republic; outside conspirators and insti-gators notoriously found it hard to latch on to a discontented citizen to work their schemes. People were happy and proud to be part of the Most Serene Republic. You can see it in the lions of St Mark that remain in place on gates and portals, columns and towers from Asiago to Ùdine. No two lions are alike; the symbol was never standardized, true to the Republic's unity in plurality. Veronese's banquet scenes are prototypes of UN cocktail parties. Even women, notoriously absent from Venetian life in the Middle Ages, increasingly distin-guished themselves: Cassandra Fedele was one of Italy's first female poets, followed by Gaspara Stampa and Veronica Franco, while Elena Lucrezia Corner Piscopia became the first woman in Europe to earn a degree (a doctorate in philosophy, from Padua, in 1678).

Tales of Tyranny and Harmony

Another source of solidarity arose from the sincere if quaint Venetian conviction that their destiny was mystical and divine. Like the Blues Brothers, they were on a mission from God. They had in Mark (never mind that they shanghaied him from Alexandria) a saint as good as Peter, not to mention all the other holy relics they swiped from Constantinople and elsewhere, in which they placed the most naïve and credulous belief. Other Italians commented in astonishment on the masses the Venetians held before going into battle; the Doge was not only a secular ruler but high priest, the Vicar of the Republic. The Venetians credited all their victories to heaven and all their defeats to the bungling of their leaders, whom more often than not they tossed in the clink. Failure was against the law.

Yet at the same time, religious fanaticism was as alien to their pragmatic nature as nationalism; throughout their history the Venetians would be condemned for doing business with Muslims. They bear the shame for having invented the Ghetto, yet Venetia was considered Europe's safest refuge for Jews. Under their spiritual leader Fra Paolo Sarpi, the Venetians hemmed and hawed over the Reformation, until many Protestants thought they would join them. The Jesuits were banned outright or strictly controlled. At the Council of Trent, it was Venetia's special ambassador who defended the rights of the Orthodox Christians in the west. Papal interference in the Republic was kept to a minimum, and the Venetians defied the Pope to keep it that way, even when he laid an Interdict on the whole Republic that lasted nearly two years (1606–07).

For all their superstition, the Venetians didn't entirely rely on the bones of St Rocco to keep away the plague and epidemics (and they had perhaps more than their share, with 70 major outbreaks in 700 years). The Republic was famous for its hospitals—the University at Padua was the chief medical school of the Renaissance—and in times of war the Venetians astonished the world by caring not only for their own wounded, but the enemy's. In the 18th century, Venice was the first state in Europe to abolish torture.

The Venetians accumulated power and wealth with the aim of enjoying life, spending what they made on luxuries and spices and courtesans; they were besotted by music (a well-sung aria was about the only thing that could shut them up), and little bothered by intellectual debates, philosophical speculations or literature. They may have been proud that Petrarch, a Tuscan, had chosen to retire in the Euganean Hills south of Padua, but they absent-mindedly misplaced the great library he left them; they were far more interested in imitating his pioneering country villa lifestyle than reading any of his books.

But the Venetians also planned ahead for future generations in ways that shame modern democracies. Programmes such as diverting the River Brenta into canals to prevent the silting up of the lagoon took centuries to complete; special forests such as Cansiglio, deemed essential to future shipbuilding, were protected to the extent that it was death to chop down a tree. The Venetians put their considerable energy into land reclamation schemes and the draining of pestilent marshes; even in their decadent 18th century, when the State derived much of its income from gambling, they managed to find the money to build the wide quay of the Riva degli Schiavoni and the Murazzi, the great sea walls that shielded the lagoon from catastrophic floods, at least until 1966. Their villas were not just the pleasure domes most of them have become, but were working agricultural estates that fed the growing population of the cities. Although Columbus is a villain in Venetian eyes, they could thank him for a new crop—maize from the New World; Villa Emo, near Castelfranco, was one of the first places in Europe to sow it. Smart investments in silk and wool paid off with an economic boom in the late 17th and 18th century. Even in 1790, when the rest of the world looked at Venice as a non-stop party, it had the guts to teach the Barbary pirates a lesson, when even the English were paying them tribute.

All of this happened of course without the people having the slightest voice in politics. Yet they enjoyed more social justice than any one else in Italy, if not Europe. The mercantile oligarchy understood that the best way to maintain their exclusive grip on power and privilege was to keep the people happy and secure, and to that end, they, by their own strict laws, devoted themselves to the public good, paying heavy taxes and serving at the state's beck and call from age sixteen until the grave. Other aristocrats in Europe thought they were nuts. The Republic's biggest social problem was what to do with all the bankrupt noblemen.

As for the people, by contemporary standards they had it made. The government encouraged co-operative, independent guilds and confraternities (*scuole*): at the fall of the Republic, there were over 300 of these—either large religious charitable confraternities (the *scuole* connected to the churches), or guilds, from the arsenal workers on down to the greengrocers. These *scuole* were the backbone of society; each had its own constitution, senate and 'doge'; they regulated pay, set standards of craftsmanship, settled disputes and selected apprentices. Members paid dues to their *scuola* according to their earnings, and in return had access to the guild hospital and school, old age pensions, and the knowledge that the *scuola* would support their widows and orphans. Napoleon, busily melting the priceless treasure of St Mark's to pay his troops and stripping the Veneto of its art to beautify Paris, thought the whole system was a load of anachronistic rubbish, and he destroyed it along with everything else.

History 83

Getting There and Around 88

The Grand Canal 95

Piazza San Marco 98

San Marco to Rialto 108

San Marco to the Accademia 109

Dorsoduro 111

San Polo and Santa Croce 112

San Marco to Castello 114

San Marco to Santi Giovanni e Paolo 116

Cannaregio 118

San Giorgio Maggiore and the Giudecca 120

Where to Stay 123

Eating Out 127

Entertainment
and Nightlife 130

The Lagoon and its Islands 133

Venice to Padua:
The Brenta Canal 143

Venice

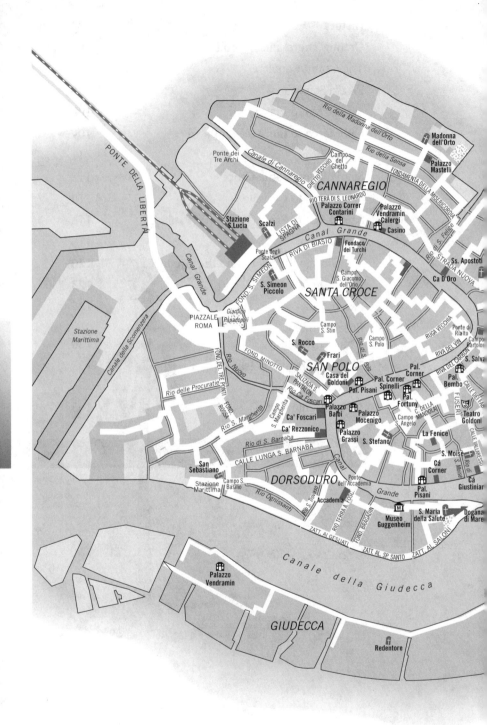

S. Michele

N

Venice

500 metres
500 yards

Gesuiti

FONDAMENTA NUOVE

Rio dei SS. Apostoli

S. Giovanni Crisostomo

SS. Giovanni
e Paolo

ndaco dei
edeschi

S. Lio

Campo S.
Maria Formosa

SALIZZADA
DI S. LIO

S. Maria Formosa

S. Zulian

Rio di S. Francesco

Pal. Querini
Stampalia

RUGA GIUFFA

Campo SS.
Filippo e
Giacomo

S.
Zaccaria

S. Giorgio
dei Greci

Rio di S. Lorenzo

Scuola di
S. Giorgio
degli Schiavoni

Rio del Vin

Canale delle Galeazze

Arsenale

MERCERIE

Basilica

Piazza S.
Marco

Museo
Correr

Pal.
Ducale

Giardini
Reali

RIVA DEGLI SCHIAVONI

Pal. Dandolo
Gritti

CASTELLO

S. Pietro

VIA GARIBALDI

S. Giorgio
Maggiore

S. Giorgio
Maggiore

Canale di San Marco

Giardini
della Biennale

S. Elena

S. Elena

Venice seduces, Venice irritates, but Venice rarely disappoints. She is a golden fairy-tale city floating on the sea, a lovely mermaid with agate eyes and the gift of eternal youth. On the surface she is little changed from the days when Goethe called her the 'market-place of the Morning and the Evening lands', when her amphibious citizens dazzled the world with their wealth and pageantry, their magnificent fleet, their half-Oriental doges, their crafty merchant princes, their splendidly luminous art, their silken debauchery and their decline and fall into a seemingly endless carnival. One can easily imagine Julius Caesar bewildered by today's Rome, or Romeo and Juliet missing their rendezvous in the traffic of modern Verona, but Marco Polo, were he to return from Cathay today, could take a familiar gondola up the familiar Grand Canal to his house in the Rialto, astonished more by the motor-boats than anything else. Credit for this unique preservation goes to the Lagoon, the amniotic fluid of Venice's birth, her impenetrable 'walls' and the formaldehyde that has pickled her more thoroughly than many far more venerable cities on the mainland.

For a thousand years Venice called herself the Most Serene Republic (*la Serenissima*), and at one point she ruled 'a quarter and a half' of the Roman Empire. The descent to an Italian provincial capital was steep and bittersweet; and sensitive souls find gallons of melancholy, or, like Thomas Mann, even death, brewed into the city's canals that have nothing to do with the more flagrant microbes. In the winter, when the streets are silent, Venice can be so evocative that you have to kick the ghosts out of the way to pass down the narrower alleys. But most people (some million or so a year) show up in the summer and, like their ancestors, have a jolly good time.

For Venice is a most experienced old siren in her boudoir of watery mirrors. International organizations pump in the funds to keep her petticoats out of the water and smooth her wrinkles. Notices posted throughout the city acknowledge that she 'belongs to everybody', while with a wink she slides a knowing hand deep into your pocket. Venice has always lived for gold, and you can bet she wants yours—and you might just as well give it to her, in return for the most enchanting, dream-like favours any city can grant.

When to Go

Venice (Venezia) is as much a character as a setting, and the same may be said of its weather. In no other city will you be so aware of the light; on a clear, fine day no place could be more limpid and clear, no water as crystal bright as the Lagoon. The rosy dawn igniting the domes of St Mark's, the splash of an oar fading in the cool mist of a canal, the pearly twilit union of water and sky are among the city's oldest clichés.

If you seek solitude and romance with a capital R, go in **January**. Pack a warm coat, water-resistant shoes and an umbrella, and expect frequent fogs and mists. It may even snow—in 1987 you could actually ski jump down the Rialto bridge. But there are also plenty of radiant diamond days, brilliant, sunny and chill; any time after October you take your chances.

As **spring** approaches there is Carnival, a game and beautiful but rather bland attempt to revive a piece of old Venice; Lent is fairly quiet, though in the undercurrent the Venetians are building up for their first major invasion of sightseers at Easter. By **April** the tourism industry is cranked up to full operational capacity; the gondolas are un-mothballed, the café tables have blossomed in the Piazza, the Casino has re-located to the Lido. In **June** even the Italians are considering a trip to the beach.

In **July** and **August** elbow-room is at a premium. Peripheral camping grounds are packed, queues at the tourist office's room-finding service stretch longer and longer, and the police are kept busy reminding the hordes that there's no picnicking in St Mark's Square. The heat can be sweltering, the ancient city gasping under a flood of cameras, shorts, sunglasses and rucksacks. Scores head off to the Lido for relief; a sudden thunderstorm over the Lagoon livens things up, as do the many festivals, especially the Redentore and its fireworks in July. In the **autumn** the city and the Venetians begin to unwind, the rains begin to fall, and you can watch them pack up the parasols and *cabanas* on the Lido with a wistful sigh.

History

Venice has always been so different, so improbable, that one can easily believe the legend that the original inhabitants sprang up from the dew and mists on the mud banks of the Lagoon. Historians who don't believe in fairies say that Venice was born of adversity: the islands and treacherous shallows of the Lagoon provided the citizens of the Veneto with a refuge from Attila the Hun and the Arian heresies sweeping the mainland. According to the Venetians' own legends, the city was founded at exactly noon on 25 March AD 413, when the refugees laid the first stone on the Rialto. Twelve Lagoon townships grew up between modern Chioggia and Grado; when Theodoric the Great's secretary Cassiodorus visited them in 523 he wrote that they were 'scattered like sea-birds' nests over the face of the waters'.

In 697 the 12 townships united to elect their first duke, or Doge. Fishing, trading—in slaves, among other things—and their unique knowledge of the Lagoon brought the Venetians their first prosperity, but their key position in between the Byzantine empire and the 'barbarian' kings on the mainland also made them a bone of contention. In 810, the Franks, who had defeated the Lombards in the name of the Pope and claimed dominion over the whole of northern Italy, turned their attention to the last hold-out, Venice: Doge Obelario de'Antenori, engaged in a bitter internal feud with other Venetian factions, even invited Charlemagne's son Pepin to send his army into the city.

The quarrelling Venetians, until then undecided whether to support Rome or Constantinople, united at the approach of Pepin's fleet, deposed the Doge, declared for Byzantium, and entrenched themselves on the Rialto. The shallows and queer humours of the Lagoon confounded Pepin, and after a gruelling six-month siege he threw in the towel.

A subsequent treaty between the Franks and the Eastern Emperor Nicephorus (814) recognized Venice as a subject of Byzantium, with important trading concessions. As Byzantine authority over the city was never more than words, it in effect marked the birth of an independent republic.

The Venetians lacked only a dynamic spiritual protector; their frumpy St Theodore with his crocodile was simply too low in the celestial hierarchy to fulfil the destiny they had in mind. In 829 Venetian merchants, supposedly on secret orders from the Doge, carried off one of the Republic's greatest coups when they purloined the body of St Mark from Alexandria, smuggling him past Egyptian customs by claiming that the saint was pickled pork. To acquire an Evangelist for themselves was, in itself, a demonstration of the Venetians' new ambition.

Marriage to the Sea

As the East–West trade expanded, the Venetians designed their domestic and external policies to accommodate it. At home they required peace and stability, and by the beginning of the 11th century had squelched all notions of an hereditary dogeship by exiling the most hyper-active families; Venice would never have the despotic *signori* who plagued the rest of Italy.

Raids by Dalmatian pirates spurred the Venetians to fight and win their first major war in 997, under Doge Pietro Orseolo, who captured the pirates' coastal strongholds. The Venetians were so pleased with themselves that they celebrated the event with a splendidly arrogant ritual every Ascension Day, the *Sensa* or 'Marriage of the Sea', in which the Doge would sail out to the Lido in his sumptuous barge, the *Bucintoro*, and cast a diamond ring into the sea, proclaiming 'We wed thee, O sea, in sign of our true and perpetual dominion'.

Venice, because of her location and fleet, supplied a great deal of the transport for the first three Crusades, and in return received her first important trading concessions in the Middle East. Her arch-rival Genoa became increasingly envious, and in 1171 convinced the Byzantine Emperor to all but wipe out the Venetian merchants in Constantinople. Rashly, the Doge Vitale Michiel II set off in person to launch a revenge attack upon the Empire, and failed utterly, and on his return he was killed by an angry mob. The Venetians were always sore losers, but they learned from their mistakes: the Great Council, the *Maggior Consiglio*, was brought into being to check the power of the Doge and avert future calamities.

Vengeance stayed on the back-burner until the next Doge, the spry and crafty Enrico Dandolo, was contracted to provide transport for the Fourth Crusade. When the Crusaders turned up without their fare, Dandolo offered to forgo it in return for certain services: first, to reduce Venice's rebellious satellites in Dalmatia, and then, in 1204, to sail to Constantinople instead of Egypt. Aged 90 and almost blind, Dandolo personally led the attack; Christendom was scandalized, but Venice had gained, not only a glittering hoard of loot, but three-eighths of Constantinople and 'a quarter and a half' of the Roman Empire— enough islands and ports to control the trade routes in the Adriatic, Aegean, Asia Minor and the Black Sea.

To ensure their dominance at home, in 1297 the merchant élite limited membership in the *Maggior Consiglio* to themselves and their heirs (an event known in Venetian history as the *Serrata*, or Lock-out), their names inscribed in the famous *Golden Book*. The Doges were slowly reduced to honorary chairmen of the board, bound up by an increasingly complex web of laws and customs to curb any possible ambitions; for the patricians, fear of revolution from above was as powerful as fear of revolt from below.

A Rocky 14th Century

First the people (1300) and then the snubbed patricians (the 1310 Tiepolo Conspiracy) rose up against their disenfranchisement under the *Serrata*. Both were unsuccessful, but the latter threat was serious enough that a committee of public safety was formed to hunt down the conspirators, and in 1335 this committee became a permanent institution, the infamous Council of Ten. Because of its secrecy and speedy decisions, the Council of Ten (in later years it was streamlined into a Council of Three) was more truly executive than the figurehead Doge: it guarded Venice's internal security, looked after foreign policy and, with its sumptuary laws, kept tabs on the Venetians' moral conduct as well.

Away from home the 14th century was marked by a fight to the death with Genoa over eastern trade routes. Each republic annihilated the other's fleet on more than one occasion before things came to a head in 1379, when the Genoese, fresh from a victory over the Venetian commander Vittor Pisani, captured Chioggia and waited for Venice to starve, boasting that they had come to 'bridle the horses of St Mark'. As was their custom, the Council of Ten had imprisoned Pisani for his defeat, but Venice was now in such a jam, with half of its fleet far away, that the people demanded his release to lead what remained of their navy. A brilliant commander, Pisani exploited his familiarity with the Lagoon and blockaded the Genoese in Chioggia. When the other half of Venice's fleet came dramatically racing home, the Genoese surrendered (June 1380) and never recovered in the East.

Fresh Prey on the Mainland

Venice was determined never to feel hungry again, and set her sights on the mainland—not only for the sake of farmland, but to control her trade routes into the west that were being increasingly harried and taxed by the signori of the Veneto. Treviso came first, then opportunity knocked in 1402 with the sudden death of the Milanese duke Gian Galeazzo Visconti, whose conquests became the subject of a great land grab. Venice picked up Padua, Bassano, Verona and Belluno, and in 1454 added Ravenna, southern Trentino, Friuli, Crema and Bergamo. In 1489 the republic's overseas empire reached its greatest extent when it was presented with Cyprus, a somewhat reluctant 'gift' from the king's widow, a Venetian noblewoman named Caterina Cornaro, who received the hilltown of Àsolo as compensation.

But just as Venice expanded, Fortune's wheel gave a creak and conspired to squeeze her back into her Lagoon. The Ottoman Turks captured Constantinople in 1453, and although the Venetians tried to negotiate trading terms with the sultans (as they had previously done with the infidel Saracens, to the opprobrium of the West), they would be spending the next three centuries fighting a losing battle for their eastern territories. The discovery of the New World was another blow, but gravest to the merchants of Venice was Vasco da Gama's voyage around the Cape of Good Hope to India in 1497, blazing a cheaper and easier route to Venice's prime markets that broke her monopoly of oriental luxuries; Western European merchants no longer had to pay Venice for safe passage to the East. In just 44 years nearly everything that Venice had worked for over 500 years was undermined.

On the mainland, Venice's rapid expansion had excited the fear and envy of Pope Julius, who rallied Italy's potentates and their foreign allies to form the League of Cambrai to humble the proud republic. They snatched her *terra firma* possessions after her defeat at Agnadello in 1509, but quarrelled amongst themselves, and before long all the territories they conquered voluntarily returned to Venice. Venice, however, never really recovered from this wound inflicted by the very people who should have rallied to her defence, and although her Arsenal produced a warship a day, and her captains helped to win a glorious victory over the Ottomans at Lepanto (1571), she was increasingly forced to retreat.

A Most Leisurely Collapse

The odds were stacked against her, but in her heyday Venice had accumulated enough wealth and verve to cushion her fall. Her noble families consoled themselves in the classical calm of Palladio's villas, while the city found solace in masterpieces of Venice's golden age of art. Carnival, ever longer, ever more licentious, was sanctioned by the state to bring in moneyed visitors, like Lord Byron, who dubbed it 'the revel of the earth, the masque of Italy'. In the 1600s the city had 20,000 courtesans, many of them dressed as men to whet the Venetians' passion. It didn't suit everyone: 'Venice is a stink pot, charged with every virus of hell,' fumed one Dr Warner, in the 18th century.

In 1797, Napoleon, declaring he would be 'an Attila for the Venetian state', took it with scarcely a whimper, ending the story of the world's longest-enduring republic, in the reign of its 120th doge. Napoleon took the horses of St Mark to Paris as his trophy, and replaced the old *Pax tibi, Marce, Evangelista Meus* inscribed in the book the lion holds up on Venice's coat of arms with 'The Rights of Men and Citizens'. Reading it, a gondolier made the famous remark, 'At last he's turned the page'. Yet while many patricians danced merrily around his Liberty trees, freed at last from responsiblity, the people wept.

Napoleon gave Venice to Austria, whose rule was confirmed by the Congress of Vienna after the Emperor's defeat in 1815. The Austrians' main contribution was the railway causeway linking Venice irrevocably to the mainland (1846). Two years later, Venice gave its last gasp of independence, when a patriotic revolt led by Daniele Manin seized the city and re-established the republic, only to fall to the Austrian army once again after a heroic one-year siege.

Modern Venice

The former republic did, however, finally join the new kingdom of Italy in 1866, after Prussia had conveniently defeated the Austrians. Already better known as a magnet to visitors than for any activity of its own, Venice played a quiet role in the new state. Things changed under Mussolini: the industrial zones of Mestre and Marghera were begun on the mainland, and a road was added to the railway causeway. The city escaped damage in the two World Wars, despite heavy fighting in the environs; according to legend, when the Allies finally occupied Venice in 1945 they arrived in a fleet of gondolas.

But Venice was soon to engage in its own private battle with the sea. From the beginning the city had manipulated nature's waterways for her own survival, diverting a major outlet of the Po, the Brenta, the Piave, the Adige and the Sile rivers to keep her Lagoon from silting up. In 1782, Venice completed the famous *murazzi*, the 4km-long, 20ft-high sea walls to protect the Lagoon. But on 4 November 1966 a deadly combination of wind, torrential storms, high tides and giant waves breached the *murazzi*, wrecked the Lido and left Venice under record *acque alte* (high waters) for 20 hours, with disastrous results to the city's architecture and art. The catastrophe galvanized the international community's efforts to save Venice. Even the Italian state, notorious for its indifference to Venice (historical grudges die slowly in Italy) passed a law in 1973 to preserve the city, and contributed to the construction of a new flood barricade similar to the one on the Thames.

This giant sea gate, known as 'Moses', has now been completed, but arguments continue over whether it will ever be effective if needed, and what its ecological consequences might be. Venice today is perennially in crisis, permanently under restoration, and seemingly threatened by a myriad potential disasters—the growth of algae in the Lagoon, the effects of the outpourings of Mestre on its foundations, the ageing of its native population, or perhaps most of all the sheer number of its tourists. Fears of an environmental catastrophe have, though, receded of late; somehow, the city contrives to survive, as unique as ever, and recent proposals to give it more of a function in the modern world, as, for example, a base for international organizations, may serve to give it new life as well.

The Face of Venice

Venice stands on 117 islets, divided by over 100 canals that are spanned by some 400 bridges. The longest bridges are the 4.2km rail and road causeways that link Venice to the mainland. The open sea is half that distance across the Lagoon, beyond the protective reefs or *lidi* formed by centuries of river silt and the Adriatic current. The Grand Canal, Venice's incomparable main street, was originally the bed of a river that fed the Lagoon; the other canals, its tributaries (called *rio*, singular, or *rii*, plural), were shallow channels meandering through the mud banks, and are nowhere as grand—some are merely glorified sewers.

A warren of 2,300 alleys, or *calli*, handle Venice's pedestrian-only traffic, and they come with a colourful bouquet of names—a *rio terrà* is a filled-in canal; a *piscina* a filled-in pool; a *fondamenta* or *riva* a quay; a *salizzada* is a street that was paved in the 17th century; a *ruga* is one lined with shops; a *sottoportico* passes under a building. A Venetian square is a *campo*, recalling the days when they were open fields; the only square dignified with the title of 'piazza' is that of St Mark, though the two smaller squares flanking the basilica are called *piazzette*, and there's one fume-filled *piazzale*, the dead end for buses and cars.

All the *rii* and *calli* have been divided into six neighbourhoods, or *sestieri*, since Venice's earliest days: **San Marco** (by the piazza), **Castello** (by the Arsenal) and **Cannaregio** (by the Ghetto), all on the northeast bank of the Grand Canal; and **San Polo** (by the church), **Santa Croce** (near the Piazzale Roma), and **Dorsoduro**, the 'hard-back' by the Accademia, all on the southwest bank. Besides these, the modern *comune* of Venice includes the towns on the Lagoon islands, the Lido, and the mainland *comuni* of Mestre and Marghera, Italy's version of the New Jersey Flats, where most Venetians live today. There is some concern that historic Venice (population around 79,000, down from 200,000 in its heyday) may soon become a city of second homes belonging to wealthy northern Italians and foreigners.

Signs, Directions, Piles and Hair

The Venetian language, Venetic or Venet, is still commonly heard—to the uninitiated it sounds like an Italian trying to speak Spanish with a numb mouth—and it turns up on the city's street signs. Your map may read 'San Giovanni e Paolo' but you should inquire for 'San Zanipolo'; 'San Giovanni Decollato' (decapitated John) is better known as 'San Zan Degola'. Still, despite the impossibility of giving comprehensible directions through the tangle of alleys (Venetians will invariably point you in the right direction, however, with a blithe *'sempre diritto!'*— 'straight ahead!'), it's hard to get hopelessly lost in Venice. It only measures about 1.5 by 3 kilometres, and there are helpful yellow signs at major crossings, pointing the way to San Marco, Rialto and the Accademia, or the Piazzale Roma and the Ferrovia if you despair and want to go home. When hunting for an address in Venice, make sure you're in the correct *sestiere*, as quite a few *calli* share names. Also, beware that houses in each *sestiere* are numbered consecutively in a system logical only to a postman from Mars; numbers up to 5,000 are not unusual.

To support their houses on the soft mud banks, the Venetians drove piles of Istrian pine 18ft into the solid clay—over a million posts hold up the church of Santa Maria della Salute alone. If Venice tends to lean and sink, it's due to erosion of these piles by the salty Adriatic, pollution, and the currents and wash caused by the deep channels dredged into the Lagoon for the large tankers sailing to Marghera. Or, as the Venetians explain, the city is a giant sponge.

Most Venetian houses are between four and six storeys high; some of the grander palazzi have gondola garages below. Others have wooden rooftop loggias, or *altane*, where the Renaissance ladies of Venice were wont to idle, bleaching their hair in the sun; they wore broad-brimmed hats to protect their complexions, and spread their tresses through a hole cut in the crown.

Getting There

by air

Venice's **Marco Polo Airport** is 13km north of the city near the Lagoon, and has regularly scheduled connections from London, New York (via Milan), Paris, Vienna, Nice, Zürich, Frankfurt, Düsseldorf, Rome, Milan, Palermo and Naples. For flight information in Venice, ✆ 041 260 9260.

The airport is linked with Venice by water-taxi (© 041 966 870 or © 041 523 5775), the most expensive option (L140,000); or by *motoscafi* to San Marco (Zecca) roughly every hour (L17,000 per person), connecting with most flights from March to October, and if you're catching an early flight, you can reserve a departure (© 041 541 5058). There is also an ATVO bus to the Piazzale Roma (L7,000) or, cheapest of all, the ACTV city bus no.5 (L1,500), which passes by twice an hour.

Some **charter flights** arrive at Treviso, 30km to the north. If a transfer is not included with your ticket, catch bus no.6 into Treviso, from where there are frequent trains and buses to Venice.

by sea

Adriatica lines (Zattere 1412, © 041 520 4322 or © 041 522 8018), has connections every 10 days June–Sept with Split (15 hours) and Dubrovnik (24 hours). There are also daily car-ferries between Venice, Corfu and Patras, Greece (2 days), and Alexandria (3½ days). An easier way to approach Venice on water is by taking the *Burchiello* from Padua along the Brenta Canal (*see* p.143).

by train

Venice's **Stazione Santa Lucia** (the **Ferrovia**) is the terminus of the *Venice Simplon-Orient Express* and less glamorous trains from the rest of Europe and Italy. All trains from Santa Lucia stop in Mestre, where you may have to change for some destinations. For rail information, © 1478 88088.

Water-taxis, *vaporetti* and gondolas (*see* below) wait in front of the station to sweep you off into the city. If you've brought more luggage than you can carry, one of Venice's infamous porters (distinguished by their badges) will lug it to your choice of transport and, if you pay his fare on the water-taxi, will take it and you to your hotel (official price for one or two pieces of luggage is L30,000 between any two points in the historic centre, extra bags are L10,000). Sometimes you can track down a porter once you disembark at one of the main landings or the Lido. Since rates for baggage-handling are unregulated everywhere other than at the station, be sure to negotiate a price in advance.

by car

All roads to Venice end at the monstrous municipal parking towers in **Piazzale Roma** or its cheaper annexe, **Tronchetto**, © 041 520 7555, nothing less than the largest car park in Europe. You can leave your car there for L25,000 a day, or less for longer stays. In the summer, at Easter and Carnival, when the causeway turns into a solid conga-line of cars waiting to park, consider the Italian Auto Club's three alternative car parks (open to non-members): **Fusina**, © 041 547 0055, with a shady, year-round campsite, located at the mouth of the Brenta Canal south of Marghera (car park open summer only; *vaporetto* no.16 to Venice); **S. Giuliano**, in Mestre near the causeway (bus service to Venice), and **Punta Sabbioni**, © 041 530 0455, in between the Lido and Jesolo (ferry no.17 from Tronchetto).

vaporetti and motoscafi

Public transport in Venice means by water, by the grunting, canal-cutting **vaporetti** (the all-purpose water-buses), or the sleeker, faster **motoscafi**, run by the ACTV (✆ 041 528 7886). Note that the only canals served by public transport are the Grand Canal, the Rio Nuovo, the Canale di Cannaregio and the Rio dell'Arsenale; between them, you'll have to rely on your feet, which is not as gruelling as it sounds, as Venice is so small you can walk across it in an hour.

Single **tickets** (a flat rate of L6,000) should be purchased and validated in the machines at the landing-stages (random inspections aren't very frequent, but if you get caught without a validated ticket you'll have to pay a L30,000 fine on the spot). As some landing stages don't sell tickets, it's best to stock up (most *tabacchi* sell them in blocks of ten). Or, if you intend being on a boat at least three times in a given day, purchase a **24-hour tourist pass**, for L18,000, valid for unlimited travel on all lines, or the **3-day pass**, for L35,000. If you plan to spend more than a few days in Venice, the cheapest option is to buy a *tesserino di abbonamento* from the ACTV office at Piazzale Roma (L10,000) and a passport photo—there's a machine

Line 1	(*accelerato*, the Italian euphemism for slow-coach): runs in an hour from Piazzale Roma and the Ferrovia down the Grand Canal to San Marco and the Lido, and vice versa, stopping everywhere; every 10mins (every 20mins after 9pm).
Line 82	(orange) (*diretto*): does a speedier circular tour from S. Zaccaria (S. Marco), including the extension to the Lido, the Giudecca and S. Giorgio Maggiore. Every 10mins during the day, approximately once an hour at night.
Line 82	(green) (*diretto*): has a smaller itinerary, beginning and ending at S. Zaccaria with stops at S. Giorgio Maggiore, all along the Giudecca, Zattere and S. Marta. Every 10mins.
Line 52	(red 'barred'): a *motoscafo* linking various major landmarks (Piazzale Roma, Giudecca, S. Zaccaria, Campo della Tana and Fondamente Nuove) with the islands of Murano (all six stops) and S. Michele. Every 20mins.
Line 52	(green): a *motoscafo* between the Lido and all stops to S. Zaccaria, Zattere, Piazzale Roma, Ferrovia, Fondamente Nuove and Murano. Every 20mins.
Line 6	(*diretto motonave*): the large steamer from S. Zaccaria to the Lido (every 20mins).
Line 11	(the 'mixed' line): begins at the Lido on a bus to Alberoni, from where you catch a boat for Pellestrina, then one for Chioggia, or vice versa (about once an hour, sometimes more often).
Line 12	Fondamente Nuove to Murano, Burano, Torcello and Treporti (about once an hour).
Line 13	Fondamente Nuove to Murano, Vignole and S. Erasmo (about once an hour).
Line 14	S. Zaccaria to the Lido and Punta Sabbioni (every half hour).
Line 16	(L8,000) a private service, Zattere to the Fusina car park (summer only, every 50mins).
Line 17	car ferry from Tronchetto (Piazzale Roma) throught the Giudecca to the Lido and Punto Sabbione (every 50mins).
Line N	(*servizio notturno*) runs all night (every 20mins from about 11pm) doing a sweep which includes the Lido, S. Zaccaria, Accademia, S. Toma, Rialto, Piazzale Roma, Zattere, Zitelle and S. Giorgio Maggiore.

at the Ferrovia) which is valid for three years and entitles you to buy monthly season tickets (L45,000) or single tickets at greatly reduced rates.

Lines of most interest to visitors are listed on p.90; most run until midnight. Precise schedules are listed in the tourist office's free monthly guide, *Un Ospite di Venezia*.

At San Marco you can also find a number of **excursion boats** to various points in the Lagoon; they are more expensive than public transport, but may be useful if you're pressed for time.

water-taxis

These are really more tourist excursion boats—they work like taxis, but their fares are de luxe. Stands are at the station, Piazzale Roma, Rialto, San Marco, Lido and the airport. These jaunty motor boats can hold up to 15 passengers, and fares are set for destinations beyond the historic centre, or you can pay L150,000 per hour. Within the centre the minimum fare for up to four people is L50,000; additional passengers are up to L10,000 each, and there are surcharges for baggage, holiday or nocturnal service (after 10pm), and for using a radio taxi (✆ 041 522 2303 or ✆ 041 240 6711).

gondolas

Gondolas, first mentioned in the city's annals in 1094, have a stately mystique that commands all other boats to give way. Shelley and many others have compared them to a funeral barque or the soul ferry to Hades, and not a few gondoliers share the infernal Charon's expectation of a solid gold tip for their services. Like Ford Model Ts, gondolas come in any colour as long as it's black, still obeying the Sumptuary Law of 1562, though nowadays hardly any gondolas have cabins for clandestine trysts.

Once used by all and sundry, gondolas now operate frankly for tourists (and weddings). Official prices are L120,000 for a 50-minute ride (L150,000 after 8pm). Before setting out, agree with the gondolier on where you want to go and how long you expect it to take to avoid any unpleasantness later on.

In addition, gondolas retired from the tourist trade are used for **gondola traghetti** services across the Grand Canal at various points between its three bridges—your only chance to enjoy an economical, if brief, gondola ride for L700. *Traghetto* crossings are signposted in the streets nearby. For appearance's sake you'll have to stand up: only sissies ever sit down on *traghetti*.

hiring a boat

Perhaps the best way to spend a day in Venice is by bringing or hiring your own boat—a small motor boat or a rowing boat—though beware of the Venetian type of oar, which requires practice to use. It can be difficult to find a boat for hire, but ask in the Piazza San Marco tourist office for suggestions. *Motoscafi* for hire are easier to find, especially with chauffeurs: try Cooperativa San Marco, S. Marco 4267, ✆ 041 523 5775; Narduzzi & Solemar, S. Marco 2828, ✆ 041 716 000; or Serenissima Motoscafi, Castello 4545, ✆ 041 522 4281.

Venice Transport

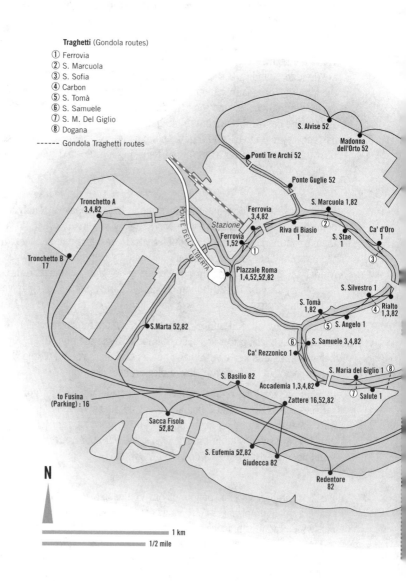

Traghetti (Gondola routes)

① Ferrovia
② S. Marcuola
③ S. Sofia
④ Carbon
⑤ S. Tomà
⑥ S. Samuele
⑦ S. M. Del Giglio
⑧ Dogana

------ Gondola Traghetti routes

S. Alvise 52

Madonna dell'Orto 52

Ponti Tre Archi 52

Ponte Guglie 52

Tronchetto A 3,4,82

S. Marcuola 1,82

Ferrovia 3,4,82

Stazione

Ferrovia 3,4,82

Riva di Biasio 1

S. Stae 1

Ca' d'Oro 1

Ferrovia 1,52

Tronchetto B 17

PONTE DELLA LIBERTA

Plazzale Roma 1,4,52,52,82

S. Silvestro 1

S. Tomà 1,82

Rialto 1,3,82

S.Marta 52,82

S. Angelo 1

S. Samuele 3,4,82

Ca' Rezzonico 1

S. Maria del Giglio 1 ⑧

S. Basilio 82

Accademia 1,3,4,82

Salute 1

to Fusina (Parking) : 16

Zattere 16,52,82

Sacca Fisola 52,82

S. Eufemia 52,82

Giudecca 82

Redentore 82

N

1 km

1/2 mile

Regular Lines

1: *(accelerato)* Piazzale Roma–Ferrovia–Grand Canal–San Marco–Lido: stops every where; around the clock, every 10min (20mins after 9pm). The entire one-way journey takes an hour.

6: *(diretto motonave)* S. Zaccaria–Lido; every 20mins.

11: (the 'mixed' line) Lido–Alberoni (by bus)–Pellestrina (by boat)–Chioggia (by boat); about once an hour. (Not shown.)

12: Fondamente Nuove–Murano–Torcello–Burano–Treporti; about once an hour.

13: Fondamente Nuove–Murano–Vignole–S. Erasmo; about once an hour.

14: S. Zaccaria–Lido–Punta Sabbioni–Treporti–Burano–Torcello (every half-hour).

17: (car ferry) Tronchetto (Piazzale Roma)–Giudecca–Lido–Punta Sabbione; every 50mins.

52: (red 'barred') *(motoscafo)* Piazzale Roma–Giudecca–S. Zaccaria–Campo della Tana (the Arsenale)–Fondamente Nuove–Murano (all six stops)–S. Michele; every 20mins.

52: (green) *(motoscafo)* Lido–S. Zaccaria–Zattere–Piazzale Roma–Ferrovia–Fondamente Nuove–Murano; every 20mins.

82: (orange) *(diretto)* S. Zaccaria (S. Marco)–Lido–Giudecca–S. Giorgio Maggiore; a speedy circular tour; every 10min during the day, approx. once an hour at night.

82: (green) *(diretto)* S. Zaccaria–S. Giorgio Maggiore–Giudecca–Zattere–S. Marta; every 10mins.

N: *(servizio notturno)* Lido–S. Zaccaria–Accademia–S. Toma–Rialto–Piazzale Roma–Zattere–Zitelle–S. Giorgio Maggiore; every 20mins from about 11pm all night.

Summer only

3: Tronchetto–Grand Canal–S. Zaccaria–Tronchetto

4: S. Zaccaria–Grand Canal–Tronchetto–S. Zaccaria

16: (private service *L8000*) Zattere–Fusina car park; every 50mins.

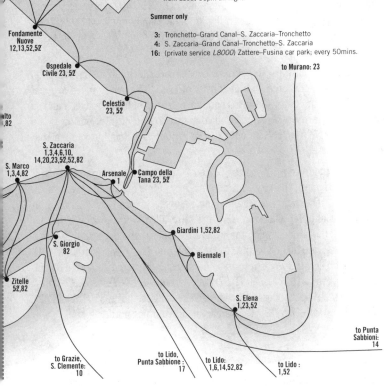

93

Piazzale Roma is Venice's bus terminus; there are frequent city buses from here to Mestre, Chioggia, Marghera and Malcontenta; and regional buses every half hour to Padua, and less frequently to other Veneto cities and Trieste. It has its own helpful tourist information office, ✆ 041 528 7886.

car hire

If you want to explore the mainland by car, several hire firms have offices at Piazzale Roma, the airports, or Mestre station: **Avis** (Marco Polo Airport) ✆ 041 541 5030; **Europcar** (Piazzale Roma) ✆ 041 523 8616, (Treviso Airport) ✆ 0422 23396; **Maggiore** (Marco Polo) ✆ 041 541 5040, (Mestre) ✆ 041 935 300.

Tourist Information

The main information office is in one corner of Piazza San Marco, to the far left as you face the square from the basilica (Ascensione 71/c, ✆ 041 522 6356). Branch offices at Palazzetto Selva, right by the S. Marco *vaporetto* stop (✆ 041 529 8730), the railway station (✆ 041 529 8727) and the bus station in Piazzale Roma (✆ 041 522 7402) offer accommodation services. There are also offices on the Rotonda Marghera (✆ 041 937 764), Marco Polo Airport (✆ 041 541 5887) and on the Lido at Gran Viale 6 (✆ 041 526 5721).

The main source in English on any current events is the fortnightly magazine *Un Ospite di Venezia*, distributed free at tourist offices. Otherwise, the two local papers *Il Gazzettino* and *Nuova Venezia* both have listings of films, concerts and so on in Venice and the *terra firma*. Another detailed source of information is the monthly city magazine *Marco Polo*, with articles written in Italian but summarized in English.

For L5,000, people between the ages of 14 and 29 can buy a *Rolling Venice* card, which gives discounts on the city's attractions, from films at the Film Festival to museums, hostels, shops and restaurants (and access to the university canteen in Palazzo Badoer, Calle del Magazen 2840). It also allows you to buy a special reduced-price ticket for travelling on the *vaporetti*. Apply at one of these three associations: the Assessorato alla Gioventù, Corte Contarina 1529, San Marco, ✆ 041 274 7650/1 (*Mon–Fri 9.30–1, Tues and Thurs also 3–5*); Agenzia Arte e Storia, Corte Canal 659, Santa Croce, ✆ 041 524 0232 (*Mon–Fri 9–1 and 3.30–7*); or Associazone Italiana Alberghi per la Gioventu, Calle del Castelforte 3101, San Polo, ✆ 041 520 4414 (*Mon–Sat 8–2*). Take a photo and your passport.

Practical A–Z

If you lose something in the city, try the Municipio, ✆ 041 274 8111; or if you lost it on a train, ✆ 041 785 238; or on a *vaporetto*, ✆ 041 780 310.

Ambulance, ✆ 041 523 000.

If you have an accident or become seriously ill, go to the *Pronto Soccorso* department of the **city hospital** in Campo Santi Giovanni e Paolo, Castello, or the **Ospedale del Mare**, 1 Lungomare d'Annunzio, Lido (© 041 529 4111); if you need a doctor at night or on holidays ring the *Guardia Medica*, © 041 529 4060.

Several *farmacie* are open all night on a rotating basis: the addresses are in the window of each, or you can ring © 041 523 0573 for a list.

Places that exchange money outside normal banking hours include:

American Express: S. Moisè 1471, © 041 520 0844, *open April–Oct Mon–Sat 8–8*; **CIT**: Piazza S. Marco 4850, © 041 528 5480, *open Mon–Sat 8–6*; **INTRAS**: Piazza S. Marco, at the corner of the Procuratie Nuove and clock tower, *open Mon–Sat 8.30–6*; **World Vision**: (Thomas Cook), Calle delle Ostreghe 2457, S. Marco.

The **main post office** is in the Fóndaco dei Tedeschi, near the Ponte Rialto (*open Mon–Sat 8.15–7.25*). There are also smaller offices at the foot of Piazza San Marco (Calle dell'Ascensione) and at the western end of the Zattere, although you can buy stamps at any tobacco shop.

The Grand Canal

A ride down Venice's bustling and splendid main artery is most visitors' introduction to the city, and there's no finer one. The Grand Canal has always been Venice's highest-status address, and along its looping banks the patricians of the Golden Book, or *Nobili Homini*, as they liked to call themselves, built a hundred marble palaces, each with its front door giving on to the water, framed by the peppermint-stick posts where the nobles moored their watery carriages.

The highlights, from Piazzale Roma to Piazza San Marco, include the 12th-century **Fóndaco dei Turchi** (with rounded arches, on the right after the Station Bridge), which was the Ottoman merchants' headquarters until 1838, and is now the Natural History Museum. Nearly opposite, Mauro Codussi's Renaissance **Palazzo Vendramin-Calergi**, where Richard Wagner died in 1883, is now the winter home of the casino. Back on the right bank, just after the San Stae landing, the baroque **Palazzo Pésaro** is adorned with masks by Longhena. And then comes the loveliest palace of all, the **Ca' d'Oro**, with a florid Venetian Gothic facade, formerly etched in gold, now housing the Galleria Franchetti (*see* pp.117–8).

After the Ca' d'Oro Europe's most famous bridge, the **Ponte di Rialto**, swings into view. 'Rialto' recalls the days when the canal was the Rio Alto; originally it was spanned here by a bridge of boats, then by a 13th-century wooden bridge. When that was on the verge of collapse, the republic held a competition for the design of a new stone structure. The winner, Antonio da Ponte, was the most audacious, proposing a single arch spanning 157ft; built in 1592, it has defied all the dire predictions of the day and still stands, even taking the additional weight of two rows of shops. The reliefs over the arch are of St Mark and St Theodore.

The Grand Canal

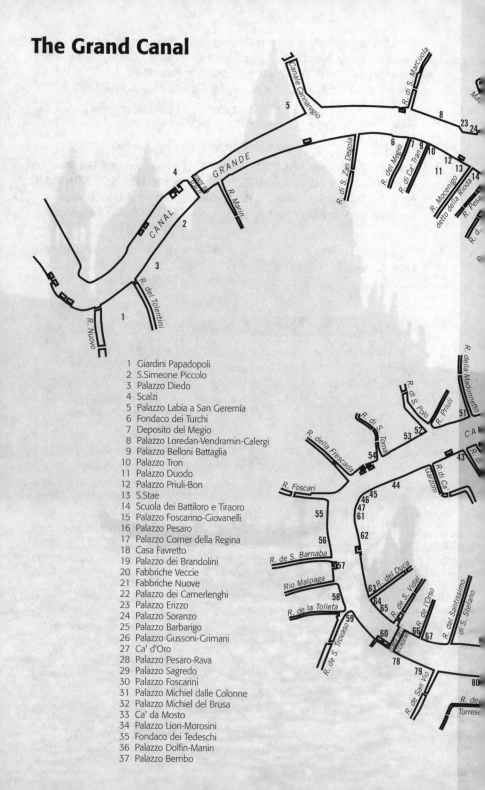

1 Giardini Papadopoli
2 S.Simeone Piccolo
3 Palazzo Diedo
4 Scalzi
5 Palazzo Labia a San Geremía
6 Fondaco dei Turchi
7 Deposito del Megio
8 Palazzo Loredan-Vendramin-Calergi
9 Palazzo Belloni Battaglia
10 Palazzo Tron
11 Palazzo Duodo
12 Palazzo Priuli-Bon
13 S.Stae
14 Scuola dei Battiloro e Tiraoro
15 Palazzo Foscarino-Giovanelli
16 Palazzo Pesaro
17 Palazzo Corner della Regina
18 Casa Favretto
19 Palazzo dei Brandolini
20 Fabbriche Veccie
21 Fabbriche Nuove
22 Palazzo dei Camerlenghi
23 Palazzo Erizzo
24 Palazzo Soranzo
25 Palazzo Barbarigo
26 Palazzo Gussoni-Grimani
27 Ca' d'Oro
28 Palazzo Pesaro-Rava
29 Palazzo Sagredo
30 Palazzo Foscarini
31 Palazzo Michiel dalle Colonne
32 Palazzo Michiel del Brusa
33 Ca' da Mosto
34 Palazzo Lion-Morosini
35 Fondaco dei Tedeschi
36 Palazzo Dolfin-Manin
37 Palazzo Bembo

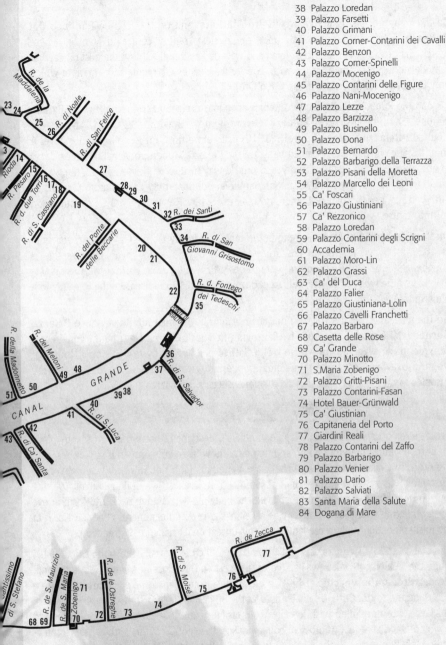

38 Palazzo Loredan
39 Palazzo Farsetti
40 Palazzo Grimani
41 Palazzo Corner-Contarini dei Cavalli
42 Palazzo Benzon
43 Palazzo Corner-Spinelli
44 Palazzo Mocenigo
45 Palazzo Contarini delle Figure
46 Palazzo Nani-Mocenigo
47 Palazzo Lezze
48 Palazzo Barzizza
49 Palazzo Businello
50 Palazzo Dona
51 Palazzo Bernardo
52 Palazzo Barbarigo della Terrazza
53 Palazzo Pisani della Moretta
54 Palazzo Marcello dei Leoni
55 Ca' Foscari
56 Palazzo Giustiniani
57 Ca' Rezzonico
58 Palazzo Loredan
59 Palazzo Contarini degli Scrigni
60 Accademia
61 Palazzo Moro-Lin
62 Palazzo Grassi
63 Ca' del Duca
64 Palazzo Falier
65 Palazzo Giustiniana-Lolin
66 Palazzo Cavelli Franchetti
67 Palazzo Barbaro
68 Casetta delle Rose
69 Ca' Grande
70 Palazzo Minotto
71 S.Maria Zobenigo
72 Palazzo Gritti-Pisani
73 Palazzo Contarini-Fasan
74 Hotel Bauer-Grünwald
75 Ca' Giustinian
76 Capitaneria del Porto
77 Giardini Reali
78 Palazzo Contarini del Zaffo
79 Palazzo Barbarigo
80 Palazzo Venier
81 Palazzo Dario
82 Palazzo Salviati
83 Santa Maria della Salute
84 Dogana di Mare

To the right stretch the extensive **Rialto Markets**, and on the left the **Fóndaco dei Tedeschi** (German Warehouse), once the busiest trading centre in Venice, where merchants from all over the north lived and traded. The building (now the post office) was remodelled in 1505 and adorned with exterior frescoes by Giorgione and Titian, of which only fragments survive (now in the Ca' d'Oro).

Beyond the Ponte di Rialto are two Renaissance masterpieces: across from the S. Silvestro landing, Sanmicheli's 1556 **Palazzo Grimani**, now the Appeals Court, and Mauro Codussi's **Palazzo Corner-Spinelli** (1510) just before the Sant'Angelo landing stage. A short distance further along the left bank are the **Palazzi Mocenigo**, actually three palaces in one, where Byron lived for two years. A little way further on the same side, the wall of buildings gives way for the Campo San Samuele, dominated by the **Palazzo Grassi**, an 18th-century neoclassical residence, now renovated by Fiat as a modern exhibition and cultural centre.

On the right bank, just after the bend in the canal, the lovely Gothic **Ca' Foscari** was built in 1437 for Doge Francesco Foscari: two doors down, by its own landing-stage, is Longhena's 1667 **Ca' Rezzonico**, where Robert Browning died. Further on, the canal is spanned by the wooden **Ponte dell'Accademia**, built in 1932 to replace the ungainly iron 'English bridge'.

On the left bank, before S. Maria del Giglio landing, the majestic Renaissance **Palazzo Corner** (Ca' Grande) was built by Sansovino in 1550. On the right bank, Longhena's baroque masterpiece **Santa Maria della Salute** is followed by the Customs House, or **Dogana di Mare**, crowned by a golden globe and weathervane of Fortune, guard the entrance to the Grand Canal. The next landing-stage is San Marco.

Piazza San Marco

Venice's self-proclaimed Attila, Napoleon himself, described this asymmetrical showpiece as 'Europe's finest drawing-room', and no matter how often you've seen it in pictures or in the flesh, its charm never fades. There are Venetians (and not all of them purveyors of souvenirs) who prefer it in the height of summer at its liveliest, when Babylonians from the four corners of the earth outnumber even the pigeons, who swoop back and forth at eye level, while the rival café bands provide a Fellini-esque accompaniment. Others prefer it in the misty moonlight, when the familiar seems unreal under hazy, rosy streetlamps.

The piazza and its two flanking *piazzette* have looked essentially the same since 1810, when the 'Ala Napoleonica' was added to the west end, to close in Mauro Codussi's long, arcaded **Procuratie Vecchie** (1499) on the north side and Sansovino's **Procuratie Nuove** (1540) on the south. Both, originally used as the offices of the 'procurators' or caretakers of St Mark's, are now filled with jewellery, embroidery and lace shops. Two centuries ago they contained an equal number of coffee-houses, the centres of the 18th-century promenade. Only two survive—the **Caffè Quadri** in the Procuratie Vecchie, the old favourite of the Austrians, and **Florian's**, in the Procuratie Nuove, its hand-painted décor unchanged since it opened its doors in 1720, although with espressos at L7,000 a head the proprietors could easily afford to remodel it in solid gold.

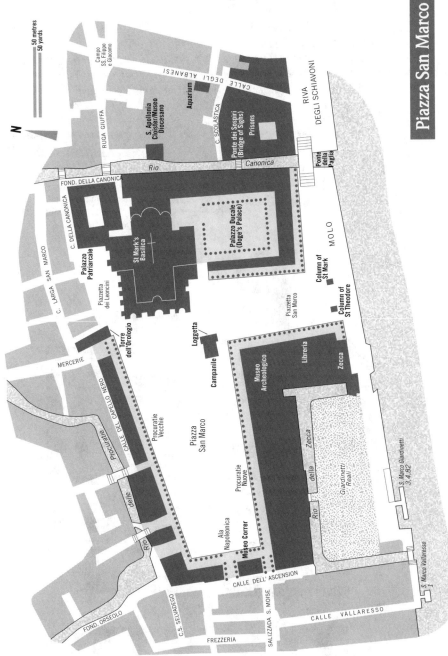

Piazza San Marco

N

50 metres
50 yards

Campo
SS. Filippo
e Giacomo

CALLE DEGLI ALBANESI

RUGA GIUFFA

S. Apollonia
Cloister/Museo
Diocesano

Aquarium

C. SOLASTICA

Ponte dei Sospiri
(Bridge of Sighs)

Prisons

RIVA
DEGLI SCHIAVONI

FOND. DELLA CANONICA

Rio   Canonica

Ponte
della
Paglia

C. DELLA CANONICA

Palazzo
Patriarcale

St Mark's
Basilica

Palazzo Ducale
(Doge's Palace)

MOLO

C. LARGA SAN MARCO

Piazzetta
dei Leoncini

Column of
St Mark

Column of
St Theodore

Torre
dell'Orologio

MERCERIE

Loggetta

Campanile

Piazzetta
San Marco

Procuratie
Vecchie

Museo
Archeologico

Libreria

Zecca

CALLE DEL CAPELLO NERO

Piazza
San Marco

Rio   della   Zecca

Procuratie

Procuratie
Nuove

Giardinetti
Reali

delle

Ala
Napoleonica

Museo Correr

S. Marco Giardinetti
3.4.82

Rio

CALLE DELL'ASCENSION

S. Marco Vallaresso
1

C.S. SELVADEGO

SALIZZADA S. MOISE

CALLE   VALLARESSO

FOND. ORSEOLO

FREZZERIA

St Mark's Basilica

Open to visitors Mon–Sat 10–4.30, Sun and hols 2–5. No shorts, and women must have their shoulders covered and a minimum of décolletage, or risk being peremptorily dismissed from the head of the queue, which can be diabolically long in season. There are separate admission charges for many of the smaller chapels and individual attractions; different sections are frequently closed for restoration. Disabled ramp access from Piazzetta dei Leoncini.

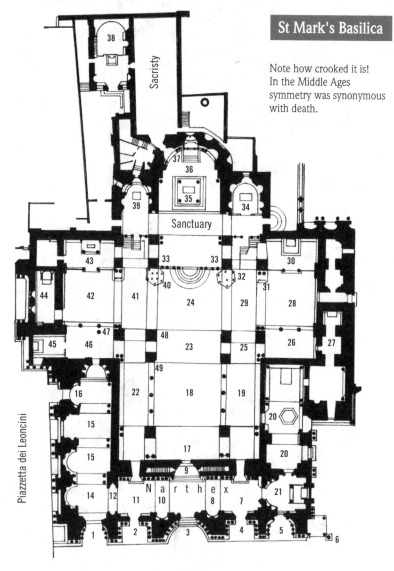

St Mark's Basilica

Note how crooked it is! In the Middle Ages symmetry was synonymous with death.

Sacristy

Sanctuary

Piazzetta dei Leoncini

N a r t h e x

Piazza San Marco

Names in *italics* refer to mosaics.

1 *Translation of the Body of St Mark* (1270)

2 *Venice Venerating the Relics of St Mark* (1718)

3 Central door, with magnificent 13th-century carvings in arches

4 *Venice Welcoming the Relics of St Mark* (1700s)

5 *Removal of St Mark's Relics from Alexandria* (1700s)

6 Pietra del Bando, stone from which the Signoria's decrees were read

7 *Scenes from the Book of Genesis* (1200) and 6th-century Byzantine door of S. Clemente

8 *Noah and the Flood* (1200s), tomb of Doge Vitale Falier (d. 1096)

9 *Madonna and Saints* (1060s); red marble slab where Emperor Barbarossa submitted to Pope Alexander III (1177); stair up to the Loggia and Museo Marciano

10 *Death of Noah* and the *Tower of Babel* (1200s)

11 *Story of Abraham* (1230s)

12 *Story of SS. Alipius and Simon*, and *Justice* (1200s)

14 Tomb of Doge Bartolomeo Gradenigo (d. 1342)

15 *Story of Joseph*, remade in 19th century

16 Porta dei Fiori (1200s); Manzù's bust of Pope John XXIII

17 *Christ with the Virgin and St Mark* (13th century, over the door)

18 Pentecost Dome (the earliest, 12th century)

19 On the wall: *Agony in the Garden* and *Madonna and Prophets* (13th century)

20 Baptistry, *Life of St John the Baptist* (14th century) and tomb of Doge Andrea Dandolo

21 Cappella Zen, by Tullio and Antonio Lombardo (1504–22)

22 On the wall: *Christ and Prophets* (13th century)

23 In arch: *Scenes of the Passion* (12th century)

24 Central Dome, the *Ascension* (12th century)

25 Tabernacle of the Madonna of the Kiss (12th century)

26 On wall: *Rediscovery of the Body of St Mark* (13th century)

27 Treasury

28 Dome of S. Leonardo; Gothic rose window (15th century)

29 In arch, *Scenes from the Life of Christ* (12th century)

30 Altar of the Sacrament; pilaster where St Mark's body was rediscovered, marked by marbles

31 Altar of St James (1462)

32 Pulpit where newly elected doge was shown to the people; entrance to the sanctuary

33 Rood screen (1394) by Jacopo di Marco Benato and Jacobello and Pier Paolo Dalle Masegne

34 Singing Gallery and Cappella di S. Lorenzo, sculptures by the Dalle Masegnes (14th century)

35 Dome, *Prophets Foretell the Religion of Christ* (12th century); Baldacchino, with Eastern alabaster columns (6th century?)

36 Pala d'Oro (10th–14th century)

37 Sacristy door, with reliefs by Sansovino (16th century)

38 Sacristy, with mosaics by Titian and Padovanino (16th century) and Church of St Theodore (15th century), once seat of the Inquisition, and now part of the sacristy: both are rarely open

39 Singing Gallery and Cappella di S. Pietro (14th century): note the Byzantine capitals

40 Two medieval pulpits stacked together

41 *Miracles of Christ* (16th century)

42 Dome, with *Life of St John the Evangelist* (12th century)

43 Cappella della Madonna di Nicopeia (miraculous 12th-century icon)

44 Cappella di S. Isidoro (14th-century mosaics and tomb of the Saint)

45 Cappella della Madonna dei Máscoli: *Life of the Virgin* by Andrea del Castagno, Michele Giambono, Jacopo Bellini

46 On wall: *Life of the Virgin* (13th century)

47 Finely carved Greek marble stoup (12th century)

48 *Virgin of the Gun* (13th century—rifle *ex voto* from 1850s)

49 Il Capitello, altar topped with rare marble ciborium, with miraculous Byzantine Crucifixion panel

This is nothing less than the holy shrine of the Venetian state. An ancient law decreed that all merchants trading in the East had to bring back from each voyage a new embellishment for St Mark's. The result is a glittering robbers' den, the only church in Christendom that would not look out of place in Xanadu. Yet it was dismissed out of hand for centuries. 'Low, impenetrable to the light, in wretched taste both within and without,' wrote the Président de Brosses in the 18th century.

Until 1807, when it became Venice's cathedral, the basilica was the private chapel of the doge, built to house the relics of St Mark after their 'pious theft' in 828, a deed sanctioned by a tidy piece of apocrypha that had the good Evangelist mooring his ship on the Rialto on the way from Aquileia to Rome, when an angel hailed him with the famous '*Pax tibi...*' or 'Peace to you, Mark, my Evangelist. Here your body shall lie.'

The present structure, consecrated in 1094, was begun after a fire destroyed the original St Mark's in 976. Modelled after Constantinople's former Church of the Apostles, five rounded doorways, five upper arches and five round Byzantine domes are the essentials of the exterior, all frosted with a sheen of coloured marbles, ancient columns and sculpture ('As if in ecstasy,' wrote Ruskin, 'the crests of the arches break into marbly foam...'). The spandrils of the arches glitter with gaudy, Technicolor mosaics—the High Renaissance, dissatisfied with the 13th-century originals, saw fit to commission new painterly scenes, leaving intact only the *Translation of the Body of St Mark* on the extreme left, which includes the first historical depiction of the basilica itself. The three bands of 13th-century **reliefs** around the central portal, among Italy's finest Romanesque carvings, show Venetian trades, the Labours of the Months, and Chaos in the inner band.

Front and centre, seemingly ready to prance off the façade, the controversial 1979 copies of the bronze **horses of St Mark** masquerade well enough—from a distance. The ancient originals (cast some time between the 3rd century BC and 2nd century AD, and now inside the basilica's Museo Marciano) were one of the most powerful symbols of the Venetian Republic. Originally a 'triumphal *quadriga*' taken by Constantine the Great from Chios to grace the Hippodrome of his new city, it was carried off in turn by the artful Doge Dandolo in the 1204 Sack of Constantinople. The four porphyry 'Moors' huddled in the corner of the south façade near the Doge's Palace are also prizes from Byzantium; according to legend, they were changed into stone for daring to break into St Mark's treasury, though scholars prefer to believe that they are four chummy 3rd-century Roman Emperors known as the Tetrarchs.

The Interior

The best mosaics, most of them from the 13th century, cover the six domes of the **atrium**, or narthex, their old gold glimmering in the permanent twilight. The oldest mosaic in St Mark's is that of the *Madonna and Saints* above the central door, a survivor of the original 11th-century decoration of the basilica. A slab of red marble in the pavement marks the spot where the Emperor Barbarossa knelt and apologized to 'St Peter and his pope'—Alexander III, in 1177. This, a favourite subject of Venetian state art, is one of the few gold stars the republic ever earned with the papacy; an atmosphere of mistrust and acrimony was far more common.

The interior, in the form of a Greek cross, dazzles the eye with the intricate splendour of a thousand details. The domes and upper vaults are adorned with golden mosaics on New Testament subjects, the oldest dating back to the 1090s, though there have been several restorations since. Ancient columns of rare marbles, alabaster, porphyry and verdantique, sawn into slices of rich colour, line the lower walls; while the 12th-century pavement is a magnificent geometric mosaic of marble, glass, and porphyry. Like a mosque, the nave is covered with carpets.

The first door on the right leads to the 14th-century **baptistry**, much beloved by John Ruskin and famous for its mosaics on the life of John the Baptist, featuring a lovely Salome in red who could probably have had just as many heads as she pleased (*with luck this may have reopened by the time you visit*). Attached to the baptistry is the **Cappella Zen**, which was designed by Tullio Lombardo in 1504 to house the tomb of one Cardinal Zen, who had left a fortune to the Republic on the condition that he should be buried in St Mark's.

Further along the right transept you can visit the **treasury** (*open 9.45–5; adm*), containing the loot from Constantinople that Napoleon overlooked—golden bowls and crystal goblets studded with huge coloured gems, straight from the cavern of Ali Baba. Near the Altar of the Sacrament, at the end of the right transept, a lamp burns 'eternally' next to one pillar: after the 976 fire, the body of St Mark was lost, but in 1094 (after Bari had beaten Venice to the relics of St Nicolaus) the good Evangelist staged a miraculous reappearance, popping his hand out of the pillar during Mass. St Mark is now safely in place in a crypt under the high altar, in the **sanctuary** (*open 9.45–5; adm*). You can't visit his relics, but you can see the altar's retablo, the fabulous, glowing **Pala d'Oro**, a masterpiece of medieval gold and jewel work. The upper section may originally have been in the Church of the Pantocrator in Constantinople, and the lower section was commissioned in that same city by Doge Pietro Orseolo I in 976. Over the years the Venetians added their own scenes, and the Pala took its present form in 1345.

In the left transept, the **Chapel of the Madonna of Nicopeia** shelters a much-venerated 10th-century icon hijacked from Constantinople, the *Protectress of Venice*, which was formerly carried into battle by the Byzantine Emperors. More fine mosaics are further to the left in the Chapel of St Isidore (the Venetian bodysnatchers kidnapped his relics from Chios—and in the mosaic he seems happy to go, grinning like a chimp). In the **Chapel of the Madonna dei Máscoli**, the mosaics on the *Life of the Virgin* by Tuscan Andrea Castagno and Michele Giambono (1453) were among the first harbingers of the Renaissance in Venice.

Before leaving, climb the steep stone stair near the west door of the narthex, to the **Museo Marciano, Galleria and Loggia dei Cavalli** (*open 9.45–5; adm*), for a closer look at the dome mosaics from the women's gallery and a visit to the loggia, where you can inspect the replica horses and compare them with the excellently restored, gilded, almost alive originals in the museum.

The Campanile

Open summer 9–7.30; winter 9.30–3.30; other months in between; adm.

St Mark's bell tower, to those uninitiated in the cult of Venice, seems like an alien presence, a Presbyterian brick sentinel in the otherwise delicately wrought piazza. But it has always been there, at least since 912; it was last altered in 1515, and when it gently collapsed into a pile of rubble on 14 July 1902 (the only casualty a cat) the Venetians felt its lack so acutely that they began to construct an exact replica, only a few hundred tons lighter and stronger, completed in 1912. It is 332ft tall, and you can take the lift up for a bird's-eye vision of Venice and its Lagoon; from up here the city seems amazingly compact. Though you have to pay for the view, misbehaving priests had it for free; the Council of Ten would suspend them in cages from the windows. Under the campanile, Sansovino's elegant **loggetta** adds a graceful note to the brick belfry. Its marbles and sculptures glorifying Venice took it on the nose when the campanile fell on top of them, but they have been carefully restored.

The Correr Museum and Clock Tower

At the far end of the piazza, in the Procuratie Nuove, the **Museo Correr** (*open 9–7, last tickets at 6; adm exp, but includes entrance to Palazzo Ducale*) contains an interesting collection of Venetian memorabilia—the robes, ducal bonnets and old-maidish nightcaps of the doges, the 20-inch-heeled *zoccoli*, once the rage among Venetian noblewomen, and a copy of the statue of Marco Polo from the temple of 500 Genies in Canton. Upstairs, the fine collection of Venetian paintings, includes two great works by Carpaccio, *The Courtesans* (or Ladies—in Venice it was notoriously hard to tell) and the *Young Man in a Red Beret*, with his archetypal Venetian face; Antonello da Messina's damaged but luminous *Pietà*, and others by Cosme Turà and a young Giovanni Bellini; a lively early sculpture by Canova, *Daedalus and Icarus* (1779); and the Bosch-esque *Temptation of St Anthony* by Il Civetta (the 'little owl').

At the head of the Procuratie Vecchie, two bronze wild men, called the 'Moors', sound the hours atop the clock tower, the **Torre dell'Orologio** (*due to reopen for its 500th anniversary in 1999*), built to a design by Mauro Codussi in 1499 above the entrance to Venice's main shopping street, the Merceria. The old Italians were fond of elaborate astronomical clocks, but none is as beautiful as this, with its richly coloured enamel and gilt face, its Madonna and obligatory lion. The Council of Ten (which actually encouraged fearsome false rumours about itself, to make its job easier) supposedly blinded the builders to prevent them from creating such a marvel for any other city. Below, flanking the basilica's north façade, a fountain and two porphyry lions, just right for children to ride, stand in **Piazzetta Giovanni XXIII,** named after the beloved Venetian patriarch who became pope in 1959.

Piazzetta San Marco

To the south of the basilica, the Piazzetta San Marco was the republic's foyer, where ships would dock under the watchful eye of the doge. The view towards the Lagoon is framed by two tall Egyptian granite **columns**, trophies brought to Venice in the 1170s. The Venetians had a knack for converting their booty into self-serving symbols: atop one of the columns several Roman statues were pieced together to form their first patron saint, St Theodore with his crocodile (or dragon, or fish), while on the other stands an ancient Assyrian or Persian winged lion, under whose paw the Venetians slid a book, creating their symbol of St Mark.

Opposite the Doges' Palace stands the **Libreria**, built in 1536 by Sansovino and considered by Palladio to be the most beautiful building since antiquity, especially notable for the play of light and shadow in its sculpted arcades. Sansovino, trained as a sculptor, was notorious for paying scant attention to architectural details, and the library was scarcely completed when its ceiling collapsed. The goof-up cost him a trip to the Council of Ten's slammer, and he was only released on the pleading of Titian. Scholars who have obtained permission from the director can examine such treasures as the 1501 *Grimani breviary*, a masterwork of Flemish illuminators; Homeric *codices*; the 1459 world map of Fra Mauro; and Marco Polo's will. But not the famous library Petrarch willed to the Republic—the Venetians misplaced it.

Next to the library, at No.17, Venice's **Archaeology Museum** (*closed for restoration at the time of writing; due to reopen in 1999*) is one of the few museums in the city heated in the winter. It has an excellent collection of Greek sculpture, including a violent *Leda and the Swan* and ancient copies of the famous *Gallic Warriors of Pergamon*, all given to the city by collector Cardinal Grimani in 1523. On the other side of the Libreria, by the waterfront, is another fine building by Sansovino, the 1547 **Zecca**, or Old Mint, which once stamped out thousands of gold *zecchini* and gave English a new word: 'sequin'.

The Palace of the Doges (Palazzo Ducale)

> *Open 15 April–Oct 9–7; winter 8.30–1; other months somewhere in between; adm exp—includes entry to the Museo Corror. Ticket office through Porta della Carta and in the courtyard.*

What St Mark's is to sacred architecture, the **Doges' Palace** is to the secular—unique and audacious, dreamlike in a half-light, an illuminated storybook of Venetian history and legend. Like the basilica, it was founded shortly after the city's consolidation on the Rialto, though it didn't begin to take its present form until 1309—with its delicate lower colonnade, its loggia of lacy Gothic tracery, and the massive top-heavy upper floor, like a cake held up by its own frosting. Its weight is partly relieved by the diamond pattern of white Istrian stone and red Verona marble on the façade, which from a distance gives the palace its wholesome peaches-and-cream complexion. Less benign are the two reddish pillars in the loggia (on the Piazzetta façade), said to have been dyed by the blood of Venice's enemies, whose tortured corpses were strung out between them.

Some of Italy's finest medieval sculpture crowns the 36 columns of the lower colonnade, depicting a few sacred and many profane subjects—animals, guildsmen, Turks and Venetians. Beautiful sculptural groups adorn the corners, most notably the 13th-century *Judgement of Solomon*, near the palace's grand entrance, the 1443 **Porta della Carta** (Paper Door), a Gothic symphony in stone by Giovanni and Bartolomeo Bon.

Fires in 1574 and 1577 destroyed much of the palace, and at the time there were serious plans afoot to knock it down and let Palladio start again, *à la* Renaissance. Fortunately, however, you can't teach an old doge new tricks, and the palace was rebuilt as it used to be, with some Renaissance touches added in the interior. Just within the Porta della Carta, don't miss Antonio Rizzo's delightful arcaded courtyard and his finely sculpted grand stairway, the **Scala dei Giganti**, named for its two Gargantuan statues of *Neptune* and *Mars* by Sansovino.

Visitors enter the palace via another grand stairway, Sansovino's **Scala d'Oro**. The first floor, which once housed the private apartments of the doge, is now used for frequent special exhibitions (*separate adm*), while the golden stairway continues up to the *Secondo Piano Nobile*, from where the Venetian state was actually governed. After the fire that destroyed its great 15th-century frescoes, Veronese and Tintoretto were employed to paint the newly remodelled chambers with mythological themes and scores of allegories and apotheoses of Venice—a smug, fleshy blonde in the eyes of these two. These paintings are the palace's chief glory, and signboards in each room identify them.

Visiting ambassadors and other foreign official guests would be required to wait in the first room, the **Anticollegio**, so the frescoes (Tintoretto's *Bacchus and Ariadne* and Veronese's *Rape of Europa*) had to be especially impressive; in the next room, the **Sala del Collegio**, which has several masterpieces by both artists, they would be presented to the hierarchy of the Venetian state.

Tintoretto's brush dominates in the **Sala del Senato**—less lavish, since only Venetians were admitted here—while the main work in the **Sala del Consiglio dei Dieci** is Veronese's ceiling, *Old Man in Eastern Costume with a Young Woman*. Under this the Council of Ten deliberated and pored over the accusations deposited in the *Bocche dei Leoni*—the lions' mouths spread over the Republic. To be considered, an accusation had to be signed and supported by two witnesses, and anyone found making a false accusation would suffer the punishment that would have been meted out to the accused had it been true. Next to the Ten's chamber, the old **Armoury** (Sala d'Armi) houses a fine collection of medieval and Renaissance arms and armour.

From here the visit continues downstairs, to the vast and magnificent **Sala del Maggior Consiglio**, built in 1340 and capable of holding the 2,500 patricians of the Great Council. At the entrance hangs Tintoretto's crowded, and recently restored, *Paradiso*—the biggest oil painting in the world (23ft by 72ft), showing all the Blessed looking up at Veronese's magnificent *Apotheosis of Venice* on the ceiling. The frieze along the upper wall portrays the first 76 doges, except for the space that would have held the portrait of Marin Falier (1355), had he not led a conspiracy to take sole power; instead, a black veil bears a dry note that he was decapitated for treason. The portraits of the last 44 doges, each painted by a contemporary painter, continue around the **Sala dello Scrutinio**, where the votes for office were counted. Elections for doge were Byzantine and elaborate—and frequent; the Maggior Consiglio preferred to choose doges who were old, and wouldn't last long enough to gain a following.

A Doge's Life: Gormenghast with Canals

Senator in Senate, Citizen in City were his titles, as well as Prince of Clothes, with a wardrobe of gold and silver damask robes, and scarlet silks. Once the Doge was dressed, the rest of his procession would fall in line, including all the paraphernalia of Byzantine royalty: a naked sword, six silver trumpets, a damask parasol, a chair, cushion, candle and eight standards bearing the Lion of St Mark in four colours symbolizing peace, war, truth and loyalty. Yet for all the pomp this was the only man in Venice not permitted to send a private note to his wife, or receive one from her, or from anyone else; nor could he accept any gift beyond flowers or rose-water, or go to a café or theatre, or engage in any money-making activity, while nevertheless having to meet the expenses of his office out of his own pocket. Nor could he abdicate, unless requested to do so.

The office was respected, but often not the man. When a Doge died he was privately buried in his family tomb before the state funeral—which used a dummy corpse with a wax mask. First, an 'Inquisition of the Defunct Doge' was held over the dummy, to discover if the Doge had kept to his *Promissione* (his oath of coronation), if his family owed the state any money, and if it were necessary to amend the *Promissione* to limit the powers of his successor still further. Then the dead Doge's dummy was taken to St Mark's to be hoisted in the air nine times by sailors, to the cry of 'Misericordia!' (Mercy), and then given a funeral service at Santi Giovanni e Paolo.

At the end of the tour the **Bridge of Sighs** (*Ponte dei Sospiri*) takes you to the 17th-century **Palazzo delle Prigioni**, mostly used for petty offenders. Those to whom the Republic took real exception were dumped into uncomfortable *pozzi*, or 'wells' in the lower part of the Palazzo Ducale, while celebrities like Casanova got to stay up in the *piombi* or 'leads' just under the roof (*see* below).

The Secret Itinerary

In 1984 the section of the palace where the real nitty-gritty business of state took place, a maze of narrow corridors and tiny rooms, was restored and opened to the public. Because the rooms are so small the 1½-hour guided tour, the Itinerari Segreti ('Secret Itinerary') is limited to 20 people, and the reason why it's not better known is that it's only available in Italian (*mornings at 10 and 12; book at least a day in advance at the director's office on the first floor, or ring © 041 522 4951*).

The tour begins at the top of the Scala d'Oro, with the snug wood-panelled offices of the **Chancellery** and the 18th-century **Hall of the Chancellors**, lined with cupboards for holding treaties, each bearing the arms of a Chancellor. In the justice department is the **Torture Chamber**, where the three Signori della Notte dei Criminali (judges of the night criminals) would 'put to the question' anyone suspected of treason, hanging them by the wrists on a rope that is still in place. This ended in the early 1700s, when Venice, along with Tuscany, became one of the first states in Europe to abolish torture.

Next is the ornate **Sala dei Tre Capi**, the chamber of the three magistrates of the Council of Ten, who had to be present at all state meetings. As this chamber might be visited by foreign dignitaries, it was lavishly decorated with works by Veronese, Antonello da Messina and Hieronymus Bosch. From here it's up to the notorious **Piombi**, which despite their evil reputation appear downright cosy, as prisons go. Casanova's cell is pointed out, and there's an elaborate explanation of his famous escape through a hole in the roof.

Near the end of the tour comes one of Venice's marvels: the **attic of the Sala del Maggior Consiglio**, where you can see how the Arsenale's shipwrights made a vast ceiling float unsupported over the room below; built in 1577, it has yet to need any repairs.

San Marco to Rialto

The streets between the piazza and the market district of the Rialto are the busiest in Venice, especially the **Mercerie**, which begin under the clock tower and are lined with some of the city's smartest shops. It was down the Mercerie that Baiamonte Tiepolo, miffed at being excluded from the Golden Book, led his rebel aristocrats in 1310, when an old lady cried 'Death to tyrants!' from her window and hurled a brick at his standard-bearer, killing him on the spot, and causing such disarray that Tiepolo was forced to give up his attempted coup. It was a close call that the republic chose never to forget: the site, above the Sottoportego del Capello Nero, is marked by a stone relief of the heroine with her brick.

The Merceria continues to the church of **San Zulian**, redesigned in 1553 by Sansovino, with a façade most notable for Sansovino's statue of its pompous and scholarly benefactor, Tommaso Rangone. Sansovino also had a hand in **San Salvatore** in the next campo, adding the finishing touches to its noble Renaissance interior and designing the monument to Doge Francesco Venier. An 89-year-old Titian painted one of his more unusual works for this church, the *Annunciation*, which he signed with double emphasis *Titianus Fecit*— '*Fecit*' because his patrons refused to believe that he had painted it. In a chapel north of the altar is the *Supper at the House of Emmaus*, by the school of Giovanni Bellini.

Humming, bustling **Campo San Bartolomeo**, next on the Mercerie, has for centuries been one of the social hubs of Venice, and still gets packed with after-work crowds every evening. Its centre is graced by the **statue of Goldoni**, whose comedies in Venetian dialect still make the Venetians laugh; and by the look on his jolly face he still finds their antics amusing. Follow the crowds up to the **Ponte di Rialto** (*see* 'The Grand Canal', p.95), the geographical heart of Venice, and the principal node of its pedestrian and water traffic.

The city's central markets have been just across the bridge for a millennium, divided into sections for vegetables and for fish. Near the former you may pay your respects to Venice's oldest church, little **San Giacomo di Rialto**, founded perhaps as long ago as the 5th century and substantially reworked in 1071 and 1601. In the same campo stands a famous Venetian character, the 16th-century granite hunchback **Gobbo di Rialto**, who supports a little stairway and marble podium from which the decrees of the Republic were proclaimed.

San Marco to the Accademia

Following the yellow signs 'To the Accademia' from the Piazza San Marco (starting by the tourist office), the first campo belongs to baroque **San Moisè** (1668), Italy's most grotesque church, with a grimy opera-buffa façade, rockpile and altarpiece. For more opera and less buffa, take a detour up Calle Veste (the second right after Campo San Moisè) to monumental Campo San Fantin and **La Fenice** (1792), the Republic's last hurrah and one of Italy's most renowned opera houses, which saw the premieres of Verdi's *Rigoletto* and *La Traviata*. A fire set by a contractor during renovations ripped it apart in 1996, so expect to see only scaffolding for a long time to come. Venice has a venerable musical tradition, albeit one that had become more tradition than music by the time of the era of grand opera—although Mozart's great librettist, Lorenzo da Ponte, was a Venetian.

Back en route to the Accademia, in the next campo stands **Santa Maria Zobenigo** (or del Giglio), on which the Barbaro family stuck a fancy baroque façade in 1680, not for God but for the glory of the Barbari; the façade is famous for its total lack of religious significance. The signs lead next to the Campo Francesco Morosini, named after the doge who recaptured the Morea from the Turks, but who is remembered everywhere else as the man who blew the top off the Parthenon. Better known as **Campo Santo Stefano**, it's one of the most elegant squares in Venice, a pleasant place to sit outside at a café table—particularly at **Paolin**, Venice's best *gelateria*. At one end, built directly over a canal, the Gothic church of **Santo Stefano** has the most gravity-defying campanile of all the leaning towers in Venice (most alarmingly viewed from the adjacent Campo Sant'Angelo). The interior is worth a look for its striking wood ceiling, soaring like a ship's keel, as well as its wooden choir stalls (1488).

The Accademia

Open daily; hours vary slightly throughout the year; summer Tues–Sat 9am–10pm, Sun 9am–8pm, Mon 9–2; closed 1 May, 25 Dec and 1 Jan; adm exp, free for under-18s and over-60s if members of the EU. It's a good idea to get there early since a maximum of 300 visitors are allowed at a time.

Just over the bridge and Grand Canal from Campo Santo Stefano stands the Galleria dell'Accademia, the grand cathedral of Venetian art, ablaze with light and colour. The collection is arranged chronologically, beginning in the former refectory of the Scuola (**Room I**): among them are 14th-century altarpieces by Paolo and Lorenzo Veneziano, whose half-Byzantine Madonnas look like fashion models for Venetian silks. Later altarpieces fill **Room II**, most importantly Giovanni Bellini's *Pala di San Giobbe*, one of the key works of the quattrocento. The architecture of the piece repeats its original setting in the church of San Giobbe; on the left St Francis invites the viewer into a scene made timeless by the music of the angels at the Madonna's feet. There are other beautiful altarpieces in the room, by Carpaccio, Basaiti and Cima da Conegliano (the subtle *Madonna of the Orange Tree*).

The next rooms are small but, like gifts, contain the best things: Mantegna's confidently aloof *St George*, the little allegories and a trio of Madonnas by Giovanni Bellini (including the lovely, softly coloured *Madonna of the Little Trees*) and Piero della Francesca's *St Jerome and Devotee*, a youthful study in perspective. In **Room V** you will find Giorgione's *La Vecchia*, with the warning '*Col Tempo*' ('With Time') in her hand, and the mysterious *The Tempest*, two of the few very paintings scholars accept as being indisputably by Big George, but how strange they are! It is said Giorgione invented easel painting for the pleasure of bored, purposeless courtiers in Catherine Cornaro's Àsolo but the paintings seem to reflect rather than lighten their ennui and discontent.

Highlights of the next few rooms include Lorenzo Lotto's *Gentleman in his Study*, which catches its sitter off-guard before he could clear the nervously scattered scraps of paper from his table, and Paris Bordenone's masterpiece, *Fisherman Presenting St Mark's Ring to the Doge* (1554) celebrating a miracle of St Mark.

The climax of the Venetian High Renaissance comes in **Room X**, with Veronese's *Christ in the House of Levi* (1573), set in a Palladian loggia with a ghostly white imaginary background, in violent contrast to the rollicking feast of Turks, hounds, midgets, Germans and the artist himself (in the front, next to the pillar on the left). The painting was originally titled *The Last Supper*, and fell foul of the Inquisition, which took umbrage (especially at the Germans). Veronese was cross-examined, and ordered to make pious changes at his own expense; the artist, in true Venetian style, saved himself both the trouble and the money by simply giving it the title by which it has been known ever since.

Room X also contains Veronese's fine *Annunciation*, and some early masterworks by Tintoretto—*Translation of the Body of St Mark*, and *St Mark Freeing a Slave*, in which the Evangelist, in true Tintoretto-esque fashion, nosedives from the top of the canvas. The last great painting in the room was also the last ever by Titian, the sombre *La Pietà*, which he was working on when he died in 1576, aged about 90, from the plague; he intended it for his tomb, and smeared the paint on with his fingers.

Alongside several more Tintorettos, the following few rooms mainly contain work from the 17th and 18th centuries (Tiepolo, Sebastiano and Marco Ricci, Piazzetta, Longhi, Rosalba Carriera). Canaletto and Guardi, whose scenes of 18th-century Venice were the picture postcards of the British aristocracy on their Grand Tour, are represented in **Room XVII**.

The final rooms of the Accademia were formerly part of the elegantly Gothic church of Santa Maria della Carità, and house more luminous 15th-century painting by Alvise Vivarini, Giovanni and Gentile Bellini, Marco Basaiti and Crivelli. **Room XX** has a fascinating series depicting the *Miracles of the True Cross* with Venetian backgrounds, painted by Gentile Bellini, Carpaccio and others. **Room XXI** contains the dreamily compelling and utterly charming *Cycle of S. Ursula* by Carpaccio, from the former Scuola di Sant'Orsola. Finally, the last room, **Room XXIV**, the former *albergo* of the church, contains two fine paintings that were originally made for it: Titian's striking *Presentation of the Virgin* (1538) and a triptych by Antonio Vivarini and Giovanni d'Alemagna (1446).

Dorsoduro

The Accademia lies in the *sestiere* of Dorsoduro, which can also boast the second-most-visited art gallery in Venice, the **Peggy Guggenheim Collection** (*open Easter–Oct, Wed–Mon 11–6; closed Tues; adm exp*), just down the Grand Canal from the Accademia in her 18th-century Venetian palazzo. In her thirty years as a collector, until her death in 1979, Ms Guggenheim amassed an impressive quantity of brand-name 20th-century art—Bacon, Brancusi, Braque, Calder, Chagall, Dali, De Chirico, Duchamp, Dubuffet, Max Ernst (her second husband), Giacometti, Gris, Kandinsky, Klee, Magritte, Miró, Moore, Mondrian, Picasso, Pollock, Rothko and Smith. Administered by the Solomon R. Guggenheim Foundation in New York, the collection can come as a breath of fresh air after so much high Italian art, and also sponsors temporary exhibitions, even in winter; look out for posters.

From here it's a five-minute stroll down to the serene, octagonal basilica of **Santa Maria della Salute,** 'of Health' (1631–81, *open 9–12, 3–6*), on the tip of Dorsoduro. One of five votive churches built after the passing of one or another bout of the plague (Venice, a busy international port, was particularly susceptible), La Salute is the masterpiece of Baldassare Longhena, its snow-white dome and marble jelly rolls dramatically set at the entrance of the Grand Canal. The interior is a relatively restrained white and grey baroque, and the **sacristy** (*adm*) contains the *Marriage at Cana* by Tintoretto and several works by Titian, including his *St Mark Enthroned Between Saints*. Almost next to the basilica, on the point, stands the distinctive profile of the **Dogana di Mare**, the Customs House (*see* 'The Grand Canal', p.98).

The **Fondamenta delle Zattere**, facing away from the city towards the freighter-filled canal and the island of Giudecca, leads around to the **Gesuati**, the only church in Venice decorated by Umbrian artists. For a more elaborate feast, take the long stroll along the Fondamenta (or take *vaporetto* Line 5 to San Basegio) to Veronese's parish church of **San Sebastiano** on Rio di San Basilio. Veronese, it is said, murdered a man in Verona and took refuge in this neighbourhood, and over the next 10 years he and his brother Benedetto Caliari embellished San Sebastiano—beginning in 1555 with the ceiling frescoes of the sacristy and ending with the magnificent ceiling, *The Story of Esther*, and illusionistic paintings in the choir (*the custodian is usually there on weekday mornings or Sunday afternoons; tip him for turning on the lights*).

From San Sebastiano you can head back towards the Grand Canal (Calle Avogaria and Calle Lunga S. Barnaba); turn left up Calle Pazienza to visit the 14th-century church of the **Carmini** with a landmark red campanile and lovely altars by Cima da Conegliano and Lorenzo Lotto. The **Scuola Grande dei Carmini** (*open Mon–Sat 9–12 and 3–6; adm; sometimes open for concerts*), next door, was designed by Longhena in the 1660s, and contains one of G.B. Tiepolo's best and brightest ceilings, *The Virgin in Glory.*

The Carmini is on the corner of the delightful **Campo Santa Margherita**. Traditionally the main marketplace of Dorsoduro, it's also a good spot to find relatively inexpensive pizzerias, restaurants and cafés that are not aimed primarily at tourists. It is also close to **Ca' Rezzonico** (Rio Terrà Canal down to the Fondamenta Rezzonico), home to the **Museo del Settecento Veneziano** (*open Oct–April 10–4, May–Sept 10–5; closed Fri; adm exp; at the time of writing only the first floor is open*), Venice's attic of 18th-century art, with bittersweet paintings by Giandomenico Tiepolo, some wild rococo furniture by Andrea Brustolon, a pharmacy, genre scenes by Longhi (*The Lady and Hairdresser*), and a breathtaking view of the Grand Canal. The house was owned in the last century by Robert Browning's son Pen, and the poet died there in 1889. One of the palaces you see opposite belonged to Doge Cristoforo Moro, whom the Venetians claim Shakespeare used as his model for Othello, confusing the doge's name with his race.

San Polo and Santa Croce

From the Ponte di Rialto, follow the yellow signs to Piazzale Roma, passing the pretty **Campo** and church of **San Polo** (*open Mon–Sat 7.10–5.30, Sun 3–5.30; adm*), with Giandomenico Tiepolo's dramatic *Stations of the Cross* in the Oratory of the Crucifix. The signs next take you before a venerable Venetian institution: the huge brick Gothic church of the **Frari** (*open Mon–Sat 9–6, Sun and hols 3–6; adm*), one of the most severe medieval buildings in the city, built between 1330 and 1469. Monteverdi, one of the founding fathers of opera and choir director at St Mark's, is buried here, as is Titian, whose tomb follows the Italian rule—the greater the artist, the worse the tomb (for proof, see Michelangelo's in Florence).

The strange pyramid with a half-open door was intended by Antonio Canova to be Titian's tomb, but it eventually became the sculptor's own last resting place. The Frari is celebrated for its great art, and especially for the most overrated painting in Italy, Titian's *Assumption of the Virgin* (1516–18), in the centre of the Monk's Choir. Marvel at the art, at Titian's revolutionary Mannerist use of space and movement, but its big-eyed, heaven-gazing Virgin has as much artistic vision as a Sunday school holy card.

That, however, is not true of Giovanni Bellini's *Triptych of Madonna with Child and Saints* in the sacristy, or Donatello's rustic statue of *St John the Baptist* in the choir chapel. In the north aisle Titian's less theatrical *Madonna di Ca' Pésaro* was modelled on his wife Celia; the painting had a greater influence on Venetian composition than the *Assumption*. Also note the beautiful Renaissance **Tomb of Doge Nicolò Tron** in the sanctuary, from 1476 by Antonio Rizzo.

The Scuola di San Rocco

Next to the Frari, the **Scuola di San Rocco** (*open summer 9–5.30; winter mornings only; adm*) was one of Venice's most important *scuole* (*see* p.78). San Rocco, renowned for his juju against the Black Death, was so popular among the Venetians that they stole his body from Montpelier and canonized him before the pope did, and his confraternity was one of the city's wealthiest. The *scuola* has a beautiful, lively façade by Scarpagnino, and inside it contains one of the wonders of Venice—or rather, 54 wonders—all painted by Tintoretto, who worked on the project from 1562 to 1585 without any assistance.

Chapter House

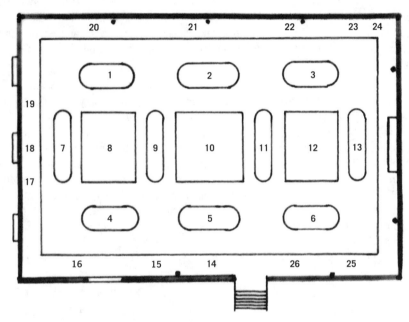

Tintoretto's Paintings

Ceiling:

1   God appearing to Moses
2   Vision of Ezekiel
3   Elisha Feeding the Multitude
4   Moses and the Pillar of Fire
5   Jacob's Ladder
6   Elisha Fed by an Angel in the Desert
7   Adam and Eve
8   Moses Bringing Forth Water from the Rock
9   Jonah Emerging from the Whale

10   The Miracle of the Brazen Serpent
11   The Sacrifice of Isaac
12   The Fall of Manna in the Desert
13   The Passover

Walls:

14   Ascension
15   Christ at Bethesda
16   The Temptation of Christ
17   San Rocco

18   Vision of San Rocco
19   San Sebastiano
20   Adoration of the Shepherds
21   Baptism of Christ
22   Resurrection
23   Christ in the Garden of Gethsemane
24   Last Supper
25   Miracle of the Loaves and Fishes
26   Resurrection of Lazarus

Tintoretto always managed to look at conventional subjects from a fresh point of view; while other artists of the High Renaissance composed their subjects with the epic vision of a Cecil B. de Mille, Tintoretto had the eye of a 16th-century Orson Welles, creating audacious, dynamic 'sets', often working out his compositions in his little box-stages, with wax figures and unusual lighting effects. In his work in the *scuola*, especially in the upper floor, he was at the peak of his career, and painted what is considered by some to be the finest painting cycle in existence, culminating in the *Crucifixion*, where the event is the central drama of a busy human world. Vertigo is not an uncommon response—for an antidote, look at the funny carvings along the walls by Francesco Pianta. In the same room there are also several paintings on easels by Titian, and a *Christ* that some attribute to Titian, some to Giorgione.

Just north, beyond Campo San Stin, the **Scuola Grande di San Giovanni Evangelista** (*open in theory if you ring the bell Mon–Fri 9.30–12.30, but it's best to call ahead, © 041 522 4134*) deserves a look for its beautiful Renaissance courtyard and double-ramp stairway (1498), Mauro Codussi's masterpiece, noted for the rhythms of its domes and barrel vaults.

From Campo San Stin, if you start along Calle Donà and keep as straight as possible, you should end up at **Ca' Pésaro** on the Grand Canal, a huge 17th-century pile by Longhena that is occupied by the **Galleria d'Arte Moderna** (*due to reopen in 1999; call © 041 721 127 to check*), with a collection principally made up of works exhibited in the Biennale exhibitions. Italian contemporary art, much of it unfamiliar to a foreign audience, is the mainstay, but some international figures are also represented, such as Gustav Klimt. Ca' Pésaro also houses a **Museum of Oriental Art** (*open 9–2, Sat and Sun 9–1; closed Mon; adm*), with a higgledy-piggledy collection of Asian artefacts collected in the last century. If you really want to escape the crowds, however, head further up the canal to the stuffed Lagoon fowl in the **Natural History Museum** (*closed for restoration at the time of writing; due to reopen in 2000; call © 041 524 0885 to check*) in the Venetian-Byzantine **Fóndaco dei Turchi**.

San Marco to Castello

From Piazzetta San Marco, the gracefully curving, ever-thronging **Riva degli Schiavoni** took its name from the Slavs of Dalmatia; in 1782, Venice was doing so much business here that the quay had to be widened. A few steps beyond the Palazzo Ducale, one of the city's finest Gothic palazzi was converted in 1822 to the famous **Hotel Danieli**, its name a corruption of the 'Dandolo' family who built it. The quay also has a robust **Memorial to Vittorio Emanuele II** (1887) where two of Venice's over 10,000 lions shelter—as often as not, with members of Venice's equally numerous if smaller feline population between their paws.

From Riva degli Schiavoni, the Sottoportico San Zaccaria leads back to the lovely Gothic-Renaissance **San Zaccaria** (*open 10–12 and 4–6*), begun by Antonio Gambello in 1444 and completed by Mauro Codussi in 1515. Inside, look for Bellini's extraordinary *Madonna and Saints* in the second chapel to the right, and the refined Florentine frescoes by Andrea del Castagno in the chapel of San Tarasio. Another church, back on the Riva itself, **La Pietà**, served the girls' orphanage which the red-headed priest Vivaldi made famous during his years as its concert master and composer (1704–38). The church was rebuilt shortly afterwards by Giorgio Massari with a remarkable oval interior, in luscious cream and gold with G.B. Tiepolo's extravagant *Triumph of Faith* on top. It has particularly fine acoustics—Vivaldi helped design it—and is still frequently used for concerts.

Due north of La Pietà stands the city's Greek Orthodox Church, the 16th-century **San Giorgio dei Greci**, with its tilting tower and *scuola*, now the **Museum of Byzantine Religious Painting** (*open Mon–Sat 9–1 and 2–5, Sun 9–1; adm*). Run by the Hellenic Centre for Byzantine Studies, many of its icons were painted in the 16th and 17th centuries by artists who fled the Turkish occupation. In Venice the Greeks came into contact with the Renaissance; the resulting Venetian-Cretan school nourished, most famously, El Greco.

Close by, another ethnic minority, the Dalmatians—present in Venice almost throughout the history of the Republic—began their tiny **Scuola di San Giorgio degli Schiavoni** in 1451 (*open 9.30–12.30 and 3.30–6.30; closed Mon; adm*). Its minute interior is decorated with the most beloved art in all Venice: Vittore Carpaccio's frescoes on the lives of the Dalmatia's patron saints—Augustine writing, watched by his patient little white dog; Jerome bringing his lion into the monastery, George charging a petticoat-munching dragon in a landscape strewn with maidenly leftovers from lunch, and more. Some of the greatest paintings by Carpaccio's more serious contemporaries, the Vivarini and Cima da Conegliano, hold pride of place in **San Giovanni in Brágora** (between San Giorgio degli Schiavoni and the Riva); the best work, Cima's *Baptism of Christ*, is in the sanctuary.

The Arsenale

From the Riva degli Schiavoni, the Fondamenta dell'Arsenale leads to the twin towers guarding the **Arsenale**. Founded in 1104, this, the first of all arsenals, derived its name from the Venetian pronunciation of the Arabic *darsina'a*, or workshop; and up until the 17th century these were the greatest dockyards in the world, the very foundation of the Republic's wealth and power. In its heyday the Arsenale had a payroll of 16,000, and produced a ship a day to fight the Ottomans. Dante visited this great industrial complex twice, and as Blake would later do with his Dark Satanic Mills, found its imagery perfect for the *Inferno*.

Today the Arsenale is occupied by the Italian military, but you can look at the **Great Gateway** next to the towers, built in 1460—almost entirely from marble trophies nicked from Greece. Among the chorus line of lions is an ancient beast that Doge Francesco Morosini found in Piraeus, with 11th-century runes carved in its back in the name of Harold Hardrada, the member of the Byzantine Emperor's Varangian Guard who was later crowned king of Norway. Other very innocent-looking lions, eroded into lambs, were taken from the island of Delos in 1718 when the Turks weren't looking. The only way to get a look at the inside of the Arsenale is by taking the Line 52 *vaporetto*, which goes through the middle of it.

Venice's glorious maritime history is the subject of the fascinating artefacts and models in the **Museo Storico Navale** (*open Mon, Tues, Wed, Sat 8.45–1.30, Thurs 2.30–5; closed Fri, Sun and hols; adm*)—the most dazzling exhibit of all is the model of the doge's barge, the *Bucintoro*. The museum is just past the gateway to the Arsenale, near the beginning of Via Garibaldi. In a neighbouring house lived two seafarers, originally from Genoa, who contributed more to the history of Britain than that of Venice, Giovanni and Sebastiano Caboto, also known as John Cabot, explorer of North America for Henry VII, and his son Sebastian, a navigator and cartographer of Brazil.

Via Garibaldi and Fondamenta S. Anna continue to the Isola di San Pietro, site of the unmemorable **San Pietro di Castello** (*open Mon–Sat 10–5.30, Sun 3–5.30; adm*), until 1807 Venice's cathedral, its lonely, distant site a comment on the Republic's attitude towards the papacy. The attractive, detached campanile is by Codussi, and, inside, there is a marble throne incorporating a Muslim tombstone with verses from the Koran, which for centuries was said to have been the Throne of St Peter in Antioch. To the south are the refreshing pines and planes of the **Public Gardens**, where the International Exhibition of Modern Art, on Biennale, takes place in even-numbered years in the artsy pavilions. Recently the Russians put on a display of photographs of Red Square taken by a chimpanzee. The Public Gardens and the **Parco delle Rimembranze** further on were a gift to this sometimes claustrophobic city of stone and water by Napoleon, who knocked down four extraneous churches to plant the trees. From here you can take Line 1 or 2 back to San Marco, or to the Lido.

San Marco to Santi Giovanni e Paolo

The *calli* that lead from the Piazzetta dei Leoncini around the back of San Marco and over the Rio di Palazzo will take you to the Romanesque cloister of Sant'Apollonia and one of Venice's newest museums, the **Museo Diocesano** (*open Mon–Sat 10.30–12.30*), containing an exceptional collection of trappings and art salvaged from the city's churches. Through a web of alleys to the north there's more art in the 16th-century Palazzo Querini-Stampalia, home of the **Fondazione Querini-Stampalia** (*open Tues, Wed, Thurs and Sun 10–1 and 3–6, Fri and Sat 10–1 and 3–10; closed Mon; adm exp*), which has an endearing assortment of genre paintings—scenes of 18th-century Venetian convents, dinner parties, music lessons, etc. by Pietro Longhi and Gabriel Bella, as well as works by Bellini, Palma il Vecchio, Vincenzo Catena (a 16th-century merchant and the first known amateur to dabble in painting) and G.B. Tiepolo—all in a suitably furnished 18th-century patrician's *palazzo*.

Santa Maria Formosa (*open Mon–Sat 10–5.30, Sun 3–5.30; adm*), in its charming campo just to the north, was rebuilt in 1492 by Codussi, who made creative use of its original Greek-cross plan. The head near the bottom of its campanile is notorious as being the most hideous thing in Venice, while, inside, Palma il Vecchio's *Santa Barbara* is famed as the loveliest of all Venetian blondes, modelled on the artist's own daughter. Another celebrated work, Bartolomeo Vivarini's *Madonna della Misericordia* (1473), is in the first chapel on the right; the parishioners shown under the protection of the Virgin's mantle earned their exalted position by paying for the painting.

The next campo to the north is dominated by **Santi Giovanni e Paolo** (or *San Zanipolo*), after St Mark's the most important church on the right bank (*open 7–12.30 and 3–7.15*). A vast Gothic brick barn begun by the Dominicans in 1246, then almost entirely rebuilt after 1333 and finally completed in 1430, no one could accuse it of being beautiful, despite its fine front doorway. San Zanipolo was the pantheon of the doges; all their funerals were held here after the 1300s, and some 25 of them went no further, but lie in splendid Gothic and Renaissance tombs. Scattered among them are monuments to other honoured servants of the Venetian state, such as the unfortunate Marcantonio Bragadin, the commander who was flayed alive by the Turks in 1571 after he had surrendered Famagusta, in Cyprus, after a long siege; his bust sits on an urn holding his neatly folded skin. The adjacent chapel contains Giovanni Bellini's polyptych of *St Vincent Ferrer*, a fire-eating subject portrayed by the gentlest of painters; nearby there's a buoyant baroque ceiling by Piazzetta in St Dominic's chapel, and a small shrine containing the foot of St Catherine of Siena. The right transept has paintings by Alvise Vivarini, Cima da Conegliano and Lorenzo Lotto; the finest tomb is in the chancel, that of Doge Andrea Vendramin, by Tullio and Antonio Lombardo (1478), while the **Chapel of the Rosary** in the north transept, which was severely damaged by fire in the last century, has a ceiling by Veronese from the church of the Umiltà, long demolished.

Adjacent to San Zanipolo, the **Scuola Grande di San Marco** has one of the loveliest Renaissance façades in Italy, the fascinating *trompe-l'œil* lower half by Pietro and Tullio Lombardo, the upper floor by Mauro Codussi, finished in 1495. The *scuola* is now used as Venice's municipal hospital, but it is possible to enter to see the lavish coffered ceiling in the library with the permission of the *Direttore di Sanità*.

Opposite stands the superbly dynamic **Equestrian Statue of Bartolomeo Colleoni**, the *condottiere* from Bergamo (1400–76) who had served the Republic so well on the mainland. In his lifetime proud of his emblem of *coglioni* (testicles—a play on his name), Colleoni envied Donatello's statue of his predecessor Gattamelata erected by the Venetians in Padua, and in his will he left the Republic 100,000 ducats if it would erect a similar statue of him in front of St Mark's. Greedy for the money but unable to countenance a monument to an individual in their sacred Piazza, the wily Venetians put the statue up before the *scuola* of St Mark. Verrocchio, the master of Leonardo and Botticelli, had only finished the plaster moulds when he died in 1488, leaving Alessandro Leopardi to do the casting. Verrocchio never saw a portrait of his subject, and all resemblences to Klaus Kinski are purely accidental.

Santa Maria dei Miracoli and the Ca' d'Oro

From Campo San Zanipolo, Largo G. Gallini leads to the perfect little Renaissance church of **Santa Maria dei Miracoli** (*open Mon–Sat 10–5.30, Sun and hols 3–5.30; adm*), built by Pietro Lombardo in the 1480s and often compared to an exquisite jewel box, elegant, graceful, and glowing with a soft marble sheen, inside and out. Just to the south are two enclosed courtyards, known as the **Corte Prima del Milion** and the **Corte Seconda del Milion**, where Marco Polo used to live. The latter in particular looks much as it did when the great traveller lived there; 'Million', his nickname in Venice, referred to the million 'tall' tales he brought back with him from China. Nearby, Codussi's **San Giovanni Crisostomo** (1504) was his last work, a seminal piece of Renaissance architecture that contains Giovanni Bellini's last altar painting (*SS. Jerome, Christopher, and Augustine*), as well as a beautiful high altarpiece by Sebastiano del Piombo.

Further towards the railway station up the Grand Canal, signposted off the Strada Nuova (Via 28 Aprile), stands the enchanting Gothic **Ca' d'Oro**, finished in 1440 and currently housing the **Galleria Franchetti** (*open daily 9–2; adm*). In its collection are Mantegna's stern *St Sebastian*, Guardi's series of Venetian views, an excellent collection of Renaissance bronzes and medallions by Pisanello and Il Riccio, Tullio Lombardo's charming *Double Portrait*, and now sadly faded fragments of the famous frescoes by Giorgione and Titian from the Fóndaco dei Tedeschi. Also present are minor works by Titian, including a voluptuous *Venus*. The building itself is famous for the intricate traceries of its façade, best appreciated from the Grand Canal, and the court-yard, with a beautifully carved well-head by Bartolomeo Bon.

Ca' d'Oro

Due north, near the Fondamente Nuove, stands the unloved, unrestored church of the **Gesuiti** (*open daily 10–12 and 5–7*), built by the Jesuits when the republic relaxed its restrictions against them, in 1714–29: a baroque extravaganza, full of *trompe-l'œil* of white and green-grey marble draperies that would make a fitting memorial for Liberace. A previous church on this same site was the parish church of Titian, to which he contributed the *Martyrdom of St Lawrence*—the saint on a grill revered by Titian's patron, Philip II of Spain.

Cannaregio

Crumbling, piquant Cannaregio is the least visited *sestiere* in Venice, and here, perhaps, more than anywhere else in the city, you can begin to feel what everyday life is like behind the tourist glitz—children playing tag on the bridges, old men in shorts messing around in unglamorous, unpainted boats on murky canals, neighbourhood greasy spoons and bars, banners of laundry waving gaily overhead.

Northern Cannaregio was Tintoretto's home base, and he is buried in the beautiful Venetian Gothic **Madonna dell'Orto** (*open Mon–Sat 10–5.30, Sun and hols 3–5.30; adm*). It also contains several of his jumbo masterpieces, such as the *Sacrifice of the Golden Calf*, in which Tintoretto painted himself bearing the idol—though he refrained from predicting his place in the *Last Judgement*, which hangs opposite it. He also painted the highly original *Presentation of the Virgin* in the south aisle, near one of Cima da Conegliano's greatest works, *St John the Baptist.* The first chapel by the door has a *Madonna* by Giovanni Bellini.

From the Campo Madonna dell'Orto, take a short walk down the Fondamenta Contarini, where, across the canal, in the wall of the eccentric **Palazzo Mastelli** you can see one of Venice's curiosities: an old, stone relief of a Moor confronting a camel. There are three more 'Moors' in the **Campo dei Mori**, just in front of the Madonna dell'Orto. The original identities of these mysterious figures has long been forgotten, although a fourth one, embedded in one corner of the square and with a metal nose like Tycho Brahe, is named Signor Antonio Rioba. He featured in many Venetian pranks of yore: anonymous satires or denunciations would be signed in his name, and new arrivals in the city would be sent off to meet him.

Also in the area is another church, **Sant'Alvise** (*currently under restoration*), which must be the loneliest church in Venice. Its main features are a forceful *Calvary* by Giambattista Tiepolo and a set of charming tempera paintings that Ruskin called the 'Baby Carpaccios', but are now attributed to Carpaccio's master, Lazzaro Bastiani, as Carpaccio himself would only have been about eight years old when they were painted.

Three *rii* to the south of Sant'Alvise is the **Ghetto**—*the* Ghetto, that is, for, like '*Arsenal*', the Venetians invented it: *ghetto* derives from the word '*getto*' meaning 'casting in metals', and there was an iron foundry here which preceded the establishment of a special quarter to which all Jews were ordered to move in 1516. The name is poignantly, coincidentally apt, for in Hebrew 'ghetto' comes from the root for 'cut off'. And cut off its residents were in Venice, for the Ghetto is an island, surrounded by a moat-like canal, and at night all Jews had to be within its windowless walls. Cramped for space, the houses are tall,with very low ceilings, which, as many people have noted, eerily presages ghetto tenements of centuries to come. But the Venetians did not invent the mentality behind the Ghetto; Spanish Jews in the Middle Ages were segregated, as were the Jews of ancient Rome. In fact, Venetian law specifically protected Jewish citizens and forbade preachers from inciting mobs against them—a common enough practice in the 16th century. Jewish refugees came to Venice from all over Europe; here they were relatively safe, even if they had to pay for it with high taxes and rents. When Napoleon threw open the gates of the Ghetto in 1797, it is said that the impoverished residents who remained were too weak to leave. The island of the **Ghetto Nuovo**, the oldest section, is a melancholy place, its small campo often empty and forlorn. The **Scuola Grande Tedesca** is the oldest of Venice's five synagogues, built by German Jews in 1528, and is in the same building as the small **Museo Comunità Israelitica/Ebraica** (*open 10.30–5; closed Sat and Jewish holidays; adm exp for the guided tour at 30mins past the hour*). The informative tours (in English) organized by the museum visit this synagogue and two others, the **Scuola Spagnola**—an opulent building by Longhena—and the **Scuola Levantina**.

Light years from the Ghetto in temperament, but only three minutes away on foot, the **Palazzo Labia** (next to the 1580 **Ponte delle Guglie**), has a ballroom with Giambattista Tiepolo's lavish, sensuous frescoes on the *Life of Cleopatra.* The palazzo is now owned by

RAI, the Italian state broadcaster, and the ballroom is open for concerts (*or call © 041 524 812 well in advance to arrange an appointment between 3 and 4pm*). Away from the palazzo towards the railway station runs the garish, lively **Lista di Spagna**, Venice's tourist highway, lined with restaurants, bars, hotels and souvenir stands that are not always as cheap as they should be.

San Giorgio Maggiore and the Giudecca

The little islet of San Giorgio Maggiore, crowned by Palladio's church of **San Giorgio Maggiore** (*open daily 10–12.30 and 2.30–6.30; adm, including the campanile*), dominates the view of the Lagoon from the Piazzetta San Marco (*vaporetto* Line 82). Built according to his theories on harmony, with a temple front, it seems to hang between the water and the sky, bathed by light with as many variations as Monet's series on the Cathedral of Rouen. The austere white interior is relieved by Tintoretto's *Fall of Manna* and his celebrated *Last Supper* on the main altar, which is also notable for the fine carving on the baroque choir stalls. A lift can whisk you to the top of the **Campanile** for a remarkable view over Venice and the Lagoon. The old monastery, partly designed by Palladio, is now the headquarters of the Giorgio Cini Foundation, dedicated to the arts and the sciences of the sea, and a venue for frequent exhibitions and conferences.

La Giudecca (Lines 32 and 82) actually consists of eight islands that curve gracefully like a Spanish *tilde* just south of Venice; prominent among its buildings are a string of empty mills and factories—the product of a brief 19th-century flirtation with industry—and for the most part the atmosphere is relatively quiet and homely. Like Cannaregio, it's seldom visited, though a few people wander over to see Palladio's best church, **Il Redentore** (*open Mon–Sat 10–5.30, Sun 3–5.30; adm*). In 1576, during a plague that killed 46,000 Venetians, the doge and the senate vowed that if the catastrophe ended they would build a church and visit it once a year until the end of time. Palladio completed the Redentore in 1592, and on the third Sunday of each July a bridge of boats was constructed to take the authorities across from the Zattere. This event, the *Festa del Redentore*, is still one of the most exciting events on the Venetian calendar. The Redentore itself provides a fitting backdrop; Palladio's temple front, with its interlocking pediments, matches it basilican interior, with curving transpects and dome. The shadowy semi-circle of columns behind the altar adds a striking, mystical effect, all that survives of Palladio's desire to built a circular church, which he deemed most perfect to worship the essence of God.

Shopping

Venice is a fertile field for shoppers, whether you're looking for tacky bric-a-brac to brighten up the mantelpiece (just walk down the Lista di Spagna) or the latest in hand-crafted Italian design—but be warned that bargains are hard to find. Everything from fresh fish to lovely inlaid wooden boxes and huge quantities of tourist junk can be found at the **Rialto markets**. You will also come across food stalls in any number of squares and on barges along the smaller canals, but there is another large food and produce market in Castello, on **Via Garibaldi**. The main public auction house is **Franco Semezato**, Palazzo Giovanelli, Cannaregio 2292.

antiques

A flea market appears periodically in Campo San Maurizio, near Campo Santo Stefano, which is also the area with the largest concentration of antique shops. **Antonietta Santomanco della Toffola**, Frezzeria 1504, S. Marco, has Russian and English silver, prints, and antique jewellery and glass, while the establishments of the print dealer **Pietro Scarpa** at Campo S. Moisè 1464 and Calle XXII Marzo 2089, S. Marco, are as much museums as shops. Away from the San Marco area, **Salizzada**, S. Lio 5672, in Castello, has old prints of Venice, clocks, and many other curious odds and ends, and **Xanthippe**, Dorsoduro 2773, near Ca' Rezzonico, is a highly eclectic shop specializing in the 19th century and Art Deco Venetian glass.

books

Venice has a good selection of bookshops. **Fantoni Libre Arte**, Salizzada di S. Luca 4121, S. Marco, has a monumental display of monumental art books, while **Sansovino**, Bacino Orseolo 84, S. Marco (just outside the Procuratie Vecchie), also has a large collection of art and coffee-table books combined with a huge stock of postcards. The best stock of books in Italian about every aspect of Venice, including some rare editions, is in **Filippi**, Calle del Paradiso 5763, Castello. If you're looking for books in English, try **Sangiorgio**, Calle Larga XXII Marzo 2087, S. Marco; **Alla Toletta**, Sacca della Toletta 1214, Dorsoduro, or **Serenissima**, Merceria dell'Orologio 739, San Marco.

fashion, fabrics and accessories

Most of Venice's high-fashion designer boutiques are located in the streets to the west of Piazza San Marco; fashion names like **Missoni**, with some of Italy's most beautiful knitwear, at Calle Vallaresso 1312, S. Marco, near Harry's Bar; **Krizia**, Mercerie del Capitello 4949, S. Marco, for more youth-oriented, colourful knits; **Laura Biagiotti**, Via XXII Marzo 2400/a, S. Marco; **Roberta di Camerino**, Lungomare Marconi 32, on the Lido, one of Venice's home-grown designers; and Giorgio Armani, at both **Giorgio Armani da Elysée**, Frezzeria 1693, S. Marco, and **Emporio Armani**, Calle dei Fabbri 989, S. Marco, with more accessible prices. For fashions by maverick Italian and French designers, try **La Coupole**, Via XXII Marzo or its sister shop, **La Fenice**, 1674, for more everyday-wear designers. Then there's **M. Antichità**, S. Marco 1691, offering velour dresses of Renaissance richness, and jewels to match.

Most Venetians, however, buy at least some of their clothes at the **COIN** department store, Salizzada San Giovanni Crisostomo, just north of Campo San Bartolomeo, part of a national chain, and a variety of cheap clothes stalls spread along Rio Terra San Leonardo, Cannaregio. Fashionable second-hand clothes are the mainstay at **Aldo Strausse**, Campo S. Giustina, in Castello, but **Emilio Ceccato**, Sottoportico di Rialto, S. Polo, is the place to find something very typically Venetian—gondoliers' shirts, jackets and tight trousers. Meanwhile, at the **Camiceria San Marco**, at Calle Vallaresso 1340, S. Marco, they will make up men's shirts and women's dresses to order for you within 24 hours.

For sensuous and expensive lingerie, visit **Jade Martine**, S. Marco 1645. The great place to find Venetian lace, whether for lingerie or tablecloths, is on Burano (*see* p.140), although be aware that the bargains you'll find there are neither handmade nor even Buranese. Back in Venice itself, **Jesurum**, Piazza S. Marco 60/61, has a vast quantity of Venetian lace and linen of all kinds on display in a 12th-century former church behind St Mark's Basilica, as well as a selection of swimwear and summer clothes.

Not just lace but also other high-quality fabrics have figured equally among Venice's traditional specialities, using skills that in many cases have been reinvigorated in recent years. **Trois**, Campo S. Maurizio, S. Marco 2666, is an institution selling colourful pleated Fortuny silks, invented in Venice and made to traditional specifications on the Giudecca. More modern designs in silks and fabrics can be found at **Valli**, Merceria S. Zulian 783, S. Marco.

For posh shoes, **La Fenice**, Via XXII Marzo 2255, S. Marco, has a good selection by French and Italian designers. The greatest name in Venetian leather is **Vogini**, Via XXII Marzo 1300, S. Marco, which has a comprehensive selection of bags and luggage, and a complete range by Venetian designer Roberta di Camerino.

Jewellery in Venice tends to be expensive and conservative—particularly in the many shops in and around San Marco—and so may be of more interest for looking than buying. **Codognato**, S. Marco 1295, is one of the oldest jewellers in Venice, with some rare Tiffany, Cartier and Art Deco items; at **Missiaglia**, Piazza S. Marco 125, you can see some of the most elegant pieces produced by Venetian gold- and silversmiths working today.

food and drink

As well as in the markets (*see* above), other good places to pick up local specialities include **Pastificio Artigiano**, Strada Nuova 4292, Cannaregio, where Paolo Pavon has for fifty years created Venice's tastiest and most exotic pastas, among them *pasta al cacao* (chocolate pasta) and lemon, beetroot and curry varieties. Similarly, **Il Pastaio**, Calle del Varoteri 219, in the Rialto market, offers pastas in over a score of different colours. **Colussi**, Rugheta S. Apollonia 4325, near Campo Santi Filippo e Giacomo, is a *pasticceria* with an enormous range of unusual pastries.

If you do want to picnic as you make your way round Venice then **Rizzo Pane**, Calle delle Botteghe, S. Marco, just off Campo F. Morosini, is an *alimentari* where you'll find everything you need. For wines and spirits, **Cantinone Già Schiavi**, Fondamenta S. Trovaso 992, Dorsoduro, has plenty to choose from.

gifts

Anyone seeking unusual gifts will find plenty to look at in Venice, though, again, prices sometimes need to be handled with care. At **La Scialuppa**, Calle Seconda dei Saoneri 2695, S. Polo, you can buy the wares of woodworker Gilberto Penzo, who makes beautiful *forcole* (gondola oar locks, made of walnut), replicas of Venetian guild signs and many other things. **Calle Lunga 2137**, in Dorsoduro, is a workshop specializing in decorative wrought-iron, and **Fondamenta Minotto 154**, S. Croce, near S. Nicolò Tolentino and the railway station, has all sorts of gold and brass items, such as Venetian doorknockers. For children, **Signor Blum**, Calle Lunga S. Barnaba 2864, Dorsoduro, has beautiful jigsaw puzzles and brightly painted wooden toys. For an overview, the **Consorzio Artigianato Artistico Veneziano**, Calle Larga S. Marco 412, S. Marco, has a fair selection of all kinds of handmade Venetian crafts.

The most renowned of Venice's ancient crafts are, of course, an obvious choice. As Burano is the centre for lace, so too Murano (*see* below) is still the place to go for glassware, but in the city one of the grand names in Venetian glass is **Pauly**, at the end of Calle Larga, near Ponte Consorzi, S. Marco, which has 30 rooms of both traditional and contemporary designs in glass housed in a former doge's palazzo. At a less exalted level, **Paolo Rossi**, Campo S. Zaccaria 4685, S. Marco, has attractive reproductions of ancient glassware at still-reasonable prices, and **Arte Veneto**, Campo S. Zanipolo 6335, Castello, offers glass and ceramic trinkets that escape looking tacky or ridiculous.

If you can contemplate carrying them home then mosaics, one of the oldest Venetian crafts, are also available, as individual *tessere* or larger items. Try **Arte del Mosaico**, Calle Erizzo 4002, Castello, or **Angelo Orsoni**, Campiello del Battello 1045, Cannaregio. For exquisite handmade paper, blank books and photo albums try **Paulo Olbi**, Calle della Mandorla 3653 (near Campo S. Angelo), and for paper designs, silk ties and masks made by Alberto Valese fusing Persian and Italian styles, visit **Alberto Valese-Ebrû**, Campo S. Stefano 3471, S. Marco (nearly opposite the church door).

Sports and Activities

Most of Venice's sporting facilities are found on the Lido or outer islands (*see* p.136).

Venice ✉ *30100*   **Where to Stay**

The rule of thumb in Venice is that whatever class of hotel you stay in, expect it to cost around a third more than it would on the mainland, even before the often outrageous charge for breakfast is added to the bill. Reservations are near-essential from about April to October and for Carnival; many hotels close in the winter, although many that do stay open offer substantial discounts at this time. Single rooms are always very hard to find. If you arrive at any time without reservations, tourist offices at the station and Piazzale Roma have a free room-finding service (a deposit is required, which is deducted from your hotel bill), though they get very busy in season. Also, the tourist office in Piazza San Marco has a list of agencies that rent self-catering flats.

***** **Cipriani**, Giudecca 10, ℂ 041 520 7744. Since 1963 this has been one of Italy's most luxurious hotels, a villa isolated in a lush garden at one end of the Giudecca that's so quiet and comfortable you could forget Venice exists, even though it's only a few minutes away by the hotel's 24-hour private launch service. An Olympic-size pool, sauna, jacuzzis in each room, tennis courts, and a superb restaurant are just some of its facilities, and no hotel anywhere could pamper you more.

***** **Danieli**, Riva degli Schiavoni 4196, ℂ 041 522 6480, 🖂 041 520 0208. The largest and most famous hotel in Venice, in what must be the most glorious location, overlooking the Lagoon and rubbing shoulders with the Palazzo Ducale. Formerly the Gothic palazzo of the Dandolo family, it has been a hotel since 1822; Dickens, Proust, George Sand and Wagner checked in here. Nearly every room has some story to tell, in a beautiful setting of silken walls, Gothic staircases, gilt mirrors and oriental rugs. The new wing, much vilified ever since it was built in the 1940s, is comfortable but lacks the charm and the stories.

***** **Gritti Palace**, S. Maria del Giglio 2467, S. Marco, ℂ 041 794 611. The 15th-century Grand Canal palace that once belonged to the dashing glutton and womanizer Doge Andrea Gritti has been preserved as a true Venetian fantasy and elegant retreat, now part of the CIGA chain. All the rooms are furnished with Venetian antiques, but for a real splurge do as Somerset Maugham did and stay in the Ducal Suite. Another of its delights is the restaurant, the **Club del Doge**, on a terrace overlooking the canal.

very expensive

**** **Concordia**, Calle Larga S. Marco 367, ℂ 041 520 6866, 🖂 041 520 6775. The only hotel overlooking Piazza S. Marco, the Concordia was swishly renovated in 1994 with a touch of Hollywood in some of its furnishings. Central air-conditioning is an added plus, as well as substanial off season discounts.

**** **Londra Palace**, Riva degli Schiavoni 4171, Castello, ℂ 041 520 0533, 🖂 041 522 5032. Tchaikovsky wrote his *Fourth Symphony* in room 108 of this hotel, and it was also a favourite of Stravinsky. The hotel was created by linking two palaces together, and it has an elegant interior, over half the rooms with a stunning canal view, one of the cosiest lobbies in Venice, and exceptionally good service. There is also an excellent restaurant, **Les Deux Lions**.

**** **Saturnia & International**, Via XXII Marzo 2398, S. Marco, ℂ 041 520 8377, 🖂 041 520 7131. A lovely hotel in a romantic quattrocento palazzo that has preserved centuries of accumulated decoration. Very near S. Marco, it has a garden court, faced by the nicest and quietest rooms. Off-season discounts.

expensive

*** **Accademia 'Villa Maravege'**, Fondamenta Bollani 1058, Dorsoduro, ℂ 041 521 0188, 🖂 041 523 9152. A hotel that offers a generous dollop of slightly faded charm in a 17th-century villa with a garden, just off the Grand Canal. Its 26 rooms are furnished with a menagerie of antiques, some of which look as if they were left behind by the villa's previous occupant—the Russian Embassy. The Accademia is a favourite of many, so book well in advance. Off-season discounts.

★★★ **La Fenice et Des Artistes**, Campiello de la Fenice 1936, S. Marco, ✆ 041 523 2333, 🖷 041 520 3721. A favourite of opera buffs in Venice (though that's not much use until La Fenice re-opens). Inside there are lots of mirrors, antiques and chandeliers to make artistes feel at home. Fully air-conditioned.

★★★ **Flora**, Calle Bergamaschi 2283/a, S. Marco, ✆ 041 520 5844. A small hotel on a little street that's remarkably quiet so near to the Piazza, with a charming garden and patio, spilling flowers. It's comfortably furnished, but ask for a large room. Air-conditioning and off-season discounts.

★★★ **Do Pozzi**, Corte do Pozzi 2373, S. Marco, ✆ 041 520 7855, 🖷 041 522 9413. With a bit of the look of an Italian country inn, this hotel has 29 quiet rooms on a charming little square, only a few minutes from Piazza San Marco. It's friendly and well run. Optional air-conditioning in all rooms.

★★★ **Malibran**, S. Giovanni Crisostomo 5864, Cannaregio, ✆ 041 522 8028. In the Corte del Milion, next to, or perhaps even incorporating, the house of Marco Polo.

★★★ **Sturion**, Calle del Sturion 679, San Polo, ✆ 041 523 6243, 🖷 041 522 8378. A popular choice, it's one of the least expensive hotels actually on the Grand Canal. It's advisable to book well ahead for one of its eight large, finely furnished rooms.

★★★ **Agli Alboretti**, Rio Terrà Foscarini 884, Dorsoduro, ✆ 041 523 0058, 🖷 041 520 4048 A charming little hotel, recently refurbished, on a rare tree-lined lane near the Accademia; 19 rooms.

★★★ **La Calcina**, Zattere ai Gesuati 780, Dorsoduro, ✆ 041 520 6466. Near the Gesuati church and overlooking the Giudecca canal, this was Ruskin's *pensione* in 1877. Totally refurbished in 1996 with all mod cons. Book well ahead.

moderate

★★ **Falier**, Salizzada S. Pantalon 130, S. Croce, ✆ 041 710 882, 🖷 041 520 6554. A small hotel near Campo San Rocco. Elegantly furnished, it has two flower-filled terraces for lounging around when your feet rebel; one room has its own terrace.

★★ **Messner**, Salute 216, Dorsoduro, ✆ 041 522 7443. A nicely modernized hotel only a hop from the Salute, and very suitable for families. Great showers, awful coffee.

★★ **Mignon**, SS. Apostoli 4535, Cannaregio, ✆ 041 523 7388, 🖷 041 520 8658. In a fairly quiet area, not far from the Ca' d'Oro, the Mignon boasts a little garden for leisurely breakfasts, though the rooms are rather plain. Has a loyal following.

★★ **La Residenza**, Campo Bandiera e Moro 3608, Castello, ✆ 041 528 5315, 🖷 041 588 5042. Located in a lovely 14th-century palace in a quiet square between San Marco and the Arsenale. The public rooms are flamboyantly decorated with 18th-century frescoes, paintings and antique furniture, though the bedrooms are simpler.

The largest concentration of cheaper hotels in Venice is around the Lista di Spagna, running eastwards into Cannaregio from the train station, though they can be pretty tacky and noisy. A more relaxed, pleasant and attractive area in which to find less expensive accommodation is in Dorsoduro, particularly around Campo S. Margherita.

* **Antico Capon**, Campo S. Margherita 3004/b, Dorsoduro, ✆ 041 528 5292. Being refurbished by new management at the time of writing, this hotel has seven simple rooms, and, thankfully, no breakfast. It owes most of its charm to its sociable *Campo*.

* **Casa Carettoni**, Lista di Spagna 130, Cannaregio, ✆ 041 716 231. The most pleasant and comfortable cheap hotel near the station; no breakfast is a plus, as you can do as Venetians do and take it in a nearby bar.

* **Casa Petrarca**, Calle delle Fuseri 4393, S. Marco, ✆ 041 520 0430. Petrarch didn't really sleep in one of these six friendly rooms near the Piazza, but who cares?

* **Casa Verardo**, Ruga Giuffa 4765, Castello, ✆ 041 528 6127, ✉ 041 523 2765. A classy, nine-room *locanda* with friendly owners.

* **Sant'Anna**, Corte Bianco 269, Castello, ✆ 041 528 6466. A fine little hotel popular with those who want to escape tourist Venice, located just north of the Giardini Pubblici. Only eight rooms, including some triples.

* **Silva**, Fondamenta Rimedio 4423, Castello, ✆ 041 522 7643. A bit hard to find— on one of the most photographed little canals in Venice, between the S. Zaccaria *vaporetto* stop and S. Maria Formosa. The rooms are fairly basic, but quiet, and the staff are friendly.

hostels and campsites

The tourist office has a list of all inexpensive hostel accommodation in Venice; as sleeping in the streets is now discouraged, schools are often pressed into use to take in the summer overflow, charging minimal rates to spread out a sleeping bag.

Camping is big business in the northeast corner of the Lagoon, around Cavallino, Jesolo and Punta Sabbioni, where there are any number of plushly appointed sites. The tourist office provides a complete list. Otherwise, the nearest campsite to Venice is **San Nicolò**, Riviera S. Nicolò 65, on the Lido, ✆ 041 526 7415 (International Camping Card required) (*closed at the time of writing; hoping to reopen in 1999*); another good site, open all year, is **Fusina**, Via Moranzani, Malcontenta, near Fusina, ✆ 041 547 0055, ✉ 041 547 0050. The *vaporetto* Line 16 from there to Venice runs every hour in summer, less frequently at other times.

Ostello Venezia, Fondamenta delle Zitelle 86, Giudecca, ✆ 041 523 8211. Venice's official youth hostel enjoys one of the most striking locations of any in Italy, with views across the Giudecca canal to San Marco. They don't take reservations over the phone, and to be assured of a place in July or August you have to write well in advance. At other times, you can chance it and book in person—the office opens as 6pm, but doors open at noon for waiting. IYHF cards required (but available at the hostel) and there's an 11.30pm curfew. Bed and breakfast L25,000; meals L14,000.

Foresteria Valdese, Calle della Madonnetta 5170, Castello, ✆ 041 528 6797. An old palazzo converted into a dormitory/*pensione* by the Waldensians. Check-in 9–1 and 6–8; beds in dorm L20,000, with breakfast; in rooms L24,000 per person.

Domus Cavanis, Rio Terrà Foscarini 912, Dorsoduro, ✆ 041 528 7374. A Catholic-run hostel open June–Sept only. Single (L45,000), double (L65,000) and triple (L90,000) rooms; students get about a 10% discount. There's an optional breakfast for L7,000.

Venice ✉ *30100*   **Eating Out**

The Venetians themselves are traditionally the worst cooks in Italy, and their beautiful city bears the ignominy of having a highest percentage of dud restaurants per capita. Not only is cooking in general well below the norm in Italy, but prices tend to be about 15% higher, and even the moderate ones can give you a nasty surprise at *conto* time with excessive service and cover charges. The cheap ones, serving up 500 tourist menus a day, are mere providers of calories to keep you on your feet; pizza is a good standby if you're on a budget. The restaurants listed here have a history of being decent or better, so chances are they still will be when you visit.

luxury

Antico Martini, Campo S. Fantin 1983, S. Marco, ✆ 041 522 4121. This is a Venetian classic, all romance and elegance. It started out as a Turkish coffee house in the early 18th century, but nowadays is better known for its seafood, a fantastic wine list and the best *pennette al pomodoro* in Venice. The intimate piano bar-restaurant stays open until 2am. Its romantic flavour is temporarily swallowed up by La Fenice's rebuilding operations directly outside. *Closed Tues, Wed midday, Dec and Feb.*

Danieli Terrace, in the Danieli Hotel, Riva degli Schiavoni 4196, Castello, ✆ 041 522 6480. The Danieli's rooftop restaurant is renowned for classic cuisine (try the *spaghetti alla Danieli*, prepared at your table) and perfect service in an incomparable setting overlooking Bacino San Marco.

very expensive

La Caravella, Calle Larga XXII Marzo 2397, S. Marco, ✆ 041 520 8901, in an annexe to the Saturnia Hotel (*see* above). For sheer variety of seasonal and local dishes, prepared by a master chef, few restaurants in Italy can top this merrily corny reproduction of a dining hall in a 16th-century Venetian galley. Try gilthead with thyme and fennel. Despite the décor, the atmosphere is fairly formal. *Open Oct–April, closed Wed.*

Do Forni, Calle dei Specchieri 468, S. Marco, ✆ 041 523 2148. For many Italians as well as foreigners, this is *the* place to eat in Venice. There are two dining rooms, one 'Orient Express'-style, the other rustic, and both always filled with diners partaking of its excellent seafood *antipasti*, polenta and seafood. *Closed Thurs in winter.*

Harry's Bar, Calle Vallaresso 1323, S. Marco, ✆ 041 523 6797. In a class by itself, a favourite of Hemingway and assorted other luminaries, this is as much a Venetian institution as the Doge's Palace, though food has become secondary to its celebrity atmosphere. Best to avoid the restaurant upstairs and just flit in for a quick hobnob while sampling a sandwich or the justly famous cocktails (a Bellini, Tiziano or Tiepolo—delectable fruit juices mixed with Prosecco) at a table downstairs near the bar. *Closed Mon.*

expensive

Dall'Amelia, Via Miranese 113, Mestre, ✆ 041 913 951. A restaurant that, despite its inconvenient mainland location, is absolutely necessary to include, as all Italian gourmets cross the big bridge to dine here at least once. The oysters are delicious and there's a divine *tortelli di bronzino* (sea bass), plus wine from one of Italy's most renowned cellars.

Antica Besseta, Salizada da Ca'Zusto (at the end of Calle Savio), S. Croce, ✆ 041 524 0428. A family-run citadel of Venetian homecooking, where you can experience an authentic *risi e bisi*, or *bigoli in salsa*, scampi, and the family's own wine. *Closed Tues, Wed lunch, and part of July and Aug.*

Corte Sconta, Calle del Pestrin 3886, Castello, ✆ 041 522 7024. It may be off the beaten track, but the reputation of this trattoria rests solidly on its exquisite molluscs and crustaceans, served in a setting that's a breath of fresh air after the exposed beams and copper pots that dominate the typical Venetian restaurant. The Venetians claim the Corte Sconta is even better in the off-season; be sure to order the house wine. *Closed Sun, Mon, and most of July and Aug.*

Hostaria da Franz, Fondamenta San Isepo (or Giuseppe) 754, Castello, facing the side of the church, ✆ 041 522 7505. A restaurant well out of the way just north of the Giardini Pubblici, but it's well worth the trouble of getting lost *en route*. This is one of Venice's best: great oysters, *gnocchi* and seafood cooked the way it should be if all Venetians tried harder. The house wine is lovely. *Closed Tues.*

Antica Locanda Montin, Fondamenta di Borgo or Eremite 1147 (near S. Trovaso), Dorsoduro, ✆ 041 522 7151. This has long been Venice's most celebrated artists' eaterie, with a vast garden, but the food can range erratically in quality from first to third division. *Closed Tues evening, Wed, and half of Aug.*

Trattoria Vini da Arturo, Calle degli Assassini 3656, S. Marco, ✆ 041 528 6974. In an infamous little street near La Fenice, this is a tiny trattoria that marches to a different drum from most Venetian restaurants, with not a speck of seafood on the menu. Instead, try the *papardelle al radicchio* or Venice's best steaks; its *tiramisù* is famous. *Closed Sun and half Aug.*

A La Vecia Cavana, Rio Terrà dei SS. Apostoli 4624, Cannaregio, ✆ 041 523 8644. Cannaregio's smartest restaurant; dine on Adriatic specialities. *Closed Tues.*

moderate

Altanella, Calle della Erbe 268, Giudecca, ✆ 041 522 7780. A delightful old seafood restaurant with an attractive setting on the Rio del Ponte Longo and a sideways glimpse of the Giudecca canal thrown in. Any of the grilled fish will be superb, and the *risotto di pesce* and *fritto* are worth the trip in themselves. *Closed Mon evening, Tues, and half of Aug. Reserve.*

Antica Mola, Fondamenta degli Ormesini 2800, Cannaregio (no telephone), near the Ghetto. All the old favourites—fish, risotto, *zuppa di pesce*—and tables by the canal. *Closed Wed.*

Antico Giardinetto da Erasmo, S. Croce 2315, ✆ 041 721 301, located behind the church of S. Cassiano. The star feature here is their delicious seafood cooked in a variety of styles. In good weather you can eat out in the little garden. *Closed Sat, Sun and Aug.*

Alla Madonna, Calle della Madonna 594, S. Polo (off Fond. del Vin, Rialto), ✆ 041 523 3824. A large, popular and very Venetian fish restaurant. *Closed Wed and Jan.*

Ai Promessi Sposi, Calle dell'Oca 4367, Cannaregio, near Campo SS. Apostoli (no tel). Cheerful bar/trattoria with good, basic, fairly traditional food and a garden at the back. *Closed Wed.*

Da Remigio, Salizzada dei Greci 3416, Castello, ✆ 041 523 0089. A neighbourhood favourite, with solid Venetian cooking. Very popular with the locals. *Closed Mon, and Tues eve.*

Tre Spiedi, Salizzada S. Canciano 5906, Cannaregio, ✆ 041 528 0035, near the Campiello F. Corner and the central post office. A cosy atmosphere to go with good local specialities like *spaghetti alla veneziana* and *braciola Bruno* (pork chops). *Closed Mon.*

cheap

Aciughetta, Campo SS. Filippo e Giacomo, Castello, ✆ 041 522 4292. One of the best cheap restaurants and bars near the Piazza San Marco, with good pizzas and atmosphere to boot. *Closed Tues.*

Pizzeria alle Oche, Calle del Tentor 1552, S. Croce, ✆ 041 524 1161, just before Ponte del Parucheta, south of S. Giacomo dell'Orio. Cheery, young atmosphere with 85 types of pizza, and take-away. *Closed Mon in winter.*

Rosticceria San Bartolomeo, Calle della Bissa 5424, San Marco, ✆ 041 522 3569. Honest cooking for honest prices, a no-frills trattoria with an cheaper snack bar downstairs.

San Tomà, Campo San Tomà 2864, San Polo, ✆ 041 523 8819. A good trattoria/pizzeria with convivial outdoor tables.

Da Crecola, S. Giacomo dell'Orio 1459, S. Croce, © 041 524 1496. Set in a quiet corner by a canal with outdoor tables. Good pasta dishes, like *tagliatelle alla gorgonzola*, and 50 different kinds of pizza, and a delightfully *pétillant* house wine.

Casa Mia, Calle dell'Oca 4430, Cannaregio, © 041 528 5590, near Campo SS. Apostoli. A lively pizzeria full of locals, and six courtyard tables. *Closed Tues.*

Vino Vino, Campo S. Fantin 1983, S. Marco, © 041 522 4121. A trendy offspring of the élite Antico Martini, where you can eat a well-cooked, filling dish (cooked by the same chefs!) with a glass of good wine at prices even students can afford. *Closed Tues, Wed midday, Dec and Feb.*

Entertainment and Nightlife

Sadly, in a city that's clearly made-to-order for pleasure, revelry and romance, life after dark is notoriously moribund. The locals take an evening stroll to their local *campo* for a chat with friends and an *aperitivo*, before heading home to dinner and the TV—the hotblooded may go on to bars and discos in Mestre, Marghera or the Lido. Visitors are left to become even poorer at the **Municipal Casino**, out on the Lido from April to October, and at other times in the Palazzo Vendramin on the Grand Canal (*hours are 3pm–2am, dress up and take your passport*). You might prefer to spend less more memorably on a moonlit gondola ride, or you can do as most people do—wander about. Venice is a different city at night, when the *bricole* lights in the Lagoon are a fitting backdrop for a mer-king's birthday pageant.

Even so, there are places to go among all this peace and quiet, and stacked against the absence of everyday nightlife there's Venice's packed calendar of special events. For an up-to-date calendar of current events, exhibitions, shows, films, and concerts in the city, consult *Un Ospite di Venezia*, free from tourist offices.

opera, classical music and theatre

Venice's music programme is heavily oriented to the classical. Opera (from December to May only), ballet, recitals and symphonic concerts, once at **La Fenice** are now performed in a temporary pavillion at Tronchetto; tickets available through the Cassa di Risparmio, Campo S. Luca, © 041 529 1111. At Venice's main theatre **Teatro Goldoni**, Calle Goldoni 4650/b, S. Marco, © 041 520 5422, the Goldoni repertory holds pride of place, but there are other plays, as well as concerts; in summer performances are often moved to Campo S. Polo.

Two other concert venues, worth visiting as much for the décor as the music, are the **Palazzo Labia**, Campo S. Geremia, Cannaregio (call ahead for tickets, © 041 524 2812), and Vivaldi's lovely rococo church of **La Pietà** (information and tickets, © 041 520 8711), where prices are high but the acoustics are well-nigh perfect.

cafés and bars

The classic cafés of Venice face each other across Piazza San Marco: **Florian's** and its great rival **Quadri**, both beautiful, and both correspondingly exorbitant. More fashionable with smart Venetians today, particularly on Sundays, is **Harry's Dolci**, Fondamenta S. Biagio 773 on the Giudecca, noted for its elegant teas, ice creams and cakes; also the Cipriani's **Cips**, which is now open for scrumptious sandwiches and cakes. **Caffè Costarica**, on Rio Terrà di S. Leonardo, Cannaregio, brews Venice's most powerful *espresso* and great iced coffee (*frappé*), and also sells ground coffees and beans over the counter.

Throughout the day Venetians frequently drop into bars and wine bars (*bacaro*) for a 'shadow' (an *ombra*, a tiny glass of wine generally downed in one go) and *cichetti*, the Venetian equivalent of tapas. For the greatest variety of wines, try Venice's oldest wine bar, **Al Volta**, Calle Cavalli di S. Marco 4081, S. Marco, with over 2,000 Italian and foreign labels to choose from and a sumptuous array of *cichetti*. *Open 9–2.30 and 5–9; closed Sun.* **Do Mori**, a resolutely traditional Rialto market bar, north of Ruga Vecchia San Giovanni, has delicious snacks (but no tables) to go with your *ombra*. *Open 8.30–9; closed Sun.*

Between 5pm and dinner is the time to indulge in a beer and *tramezzini*, finger sandwiches that come in a hundred varieties, and some of the best are to be found at eccentric **Bar alla Toletta**, Calle della Toletta 1191, Dorsoduro, run by a temperamental middle-aged couple with a voracious appetite for jazz.

The title of best *gelateria* in the city has by convention been accorded to **Paolin**, on the Campo Santo Stefano, S. Marco, above all for their divine pistachio. However, **Nico**, on the Zattere ai Gesuati, Dorsoduro, is also a must on anyone's ice cream tour, if the late night queues are anything to go by.

jazz, clubs and nightspots

Venice's few late-night bars and music venues can be fun, or just posy and dull, and what you find is pretty much a matter of pot luck. **Paradiso Perduto**, Fondamenta della Misericordia 2540, Cannaregio, ✆ 041 720 581, is the city's best-known and most popular late-night bar/restaurant with inexpensive though variable food, and a relaxed, bohemian atmosphere popular with a mix of locals and English visitors. Once known for live jazz, they now often have a bit of trouble with their late-night licence, so live events are rare. *Open 6pm–midnight, sometimes later; closed Wed.* A current favourite for young trendies is **Taverna l'Olandese Volante** (Flying Dutchman), Campo S. Lio 5658, Castello, ✆ 041 528 9349, Venice's answer to a pub, open late with snacks and simple food. The relaxed and informal wine bar **Osteria da Codroma**, Fondamenta Briati 2540, Dorsoduro, ✆ 041 520 4161, hosts a backgammon club, art shows and occasional live jazz. *Open 7pm–2am; closed Thurs.* Another restaurant/bar with music, dancing and sometimes live rock or jazz is **Ai Canottieri**, Ponte Tre Archi 690, Cannaregio, ✆ 041 715 408. *Open 7pm–2am; closed Sun.*

There are also quite a few fairly glitzy piano bars, such as **Linea d'Ombra**, Zattere ai Saloni, near the Salute, ✆ 041 528 5259. *Open 8pm–1am; closed Wed.* A favourite place for Venetians to make off to in Marghera is **Al Vapore**, Via Fratelli Bandiera 8, ✆ 041 930 796, which hosts live rock and jazz. In July and August there's a disco on the Lido: **Acropolis**, Lungomare Marconi 22, ✆ 041 526 0466. The Lido is also the place to hie for a late-night game of billiards, *chez* **Al Delfino**, an 'American Bar' with music and snacks at Lungomare Marconi 96, ✆ 041 526 8309. *Open until 2am.* Or **Villa Eva**, Gran Viale 49, ✆ 041 526 1884, with music and snacks from midnight until 4am. *Closed Thurs except in the summer.*

The main late-night drinking holes are **Harry's Bar** (*see* above, 'Eating Out'), especially if someone else is paying. **Osteria ai Assassini**, Calle degli Assassini, S. Marco, has wines, beers, and good *cichetti. Open till midnight; closed Sun.* For more filling victuals, try **Vino Vino** (*see* above, 'Eating Out'). *Open till 2am.* The **Creperia Poggi**, Cannaregio 2103, ✆ 041 715 971, has music and also stays open till 2am, flipping crêpes until midnight. *Closed Sun.* The last chance for an ice cream is at 3am at the Lido's **Gelateria Bar Maleti**, Gran Viale 47. *Closed Wed.*

exhibitions and art festivals

Venice is one of Europe's top cities for exhibitions: major international shows fill the **Palazzo Grassi**, Campo S. Samuele, S. Marco, which Fiat has transformed into a lavishly equipped exhibition and cultural centre. High calibre art and photographic exhibitions also appear frequently at the **Palazzo Querini-Stampalia**, the **Peggy Guggenheim Collection**, and **Ca' Pésaro**.

Then there's the **Biennale**, the most famous contemporary art show in the world, founded in 1895 and now held, in principle, in even-numbered years. The main exhibits of the forty or so countries officially represented are set up in the permanent pavilions in the Giardini Pubblici, but there is also an open section for younger and less-established artists, in venues across the city.

The city's other great cultural junket is the **Venice Film Festival**, held in the Palazzo del Cinema and the Astra Cinema on the Lido every year in late August and September. As well as spotting the stars, you can sometimes get in to see films if you arrive at the cinemas really early—tickets are only sold on the same day as each showing.

traditional festivals

Venice's renowned **Carnival**, first held in the ten days preceding Lent in 1094, was revived in 1979 after several decades of dormancy. It attracts huge crowds, but faces an uphill battle against the inveterate Italian love of *bella figura*—getting dressed up in elaborate costumes, wandering down to San Marco and taking each other's picture is as much as most of the revellers get up to. Concerts and shows are put on all over Venice, with city and corporate sponsorship, but there's very little spontaneity or serious carousing, and certainly no trace of what Byron called the 'revel of the earth'.

Even so, a **Carnival mask** still makes a good souvenir, either in inexpensive papier mâché (*cartapesta*) or in leather. There are mask shops all over Venice, but for the real, traditionally crafted item, try **Giorgio Clanetti (Laboratorio Artigiano Maschere)**, Barbaria delle Tole 6657, Castello, near SS. Giovanni e Paolo.

In 1988 Venice revived another crowd pleaser, **La Sensa**, held on the first Sunday after Ascension Day, in which the doge married the sea (*see* p.84). Now the mayor plays the groom, in a replica of the state barge or *Bucintoro*. It's as corny and pretentious as it sounds, but on the same day you can watch the gondoliers race in the **Vogalonga**, or long row, from San Marco to Burano and back again.

Venice's most spectacular festival, **Il Redentore**, is held on the third Sunday of July, with its bridge of boats (*see* p.120). The greatest excitement happens the Saturday night before, when Venetians row out for an evening picnic on the water, manœuvring for the best view of the fabulous fireworks display over the Lagoon. For landlubbers (and there are thousands of them) the prime viewing and picnicking spots are towards the eastern ends of either the Giudecca or the Zattere.

More perspiration is expended in the **Regata Storica** (first Sunday in September), a splendid pageant of historic vessels and crews in Renaissance costumes and hotly contested races by gondoliers and a variety of other rowers down the Grand Canal. Another bridge of boats is built on 21 November, this time across the Grand Canal to the Salute, for the feast of **Santa Maria della Salute**, which also commemorates the ending of another plague, in 1631. This event provides the only opportunity to see Longhena's unique basilica as it would have been when it was built, with its doors thrown open on to the Grand Canal.

The Lagoon and its Islands

Pearly and melting into the bright sky, iridescent blue or murky green, a sheet of glass yellow and pink in the dawn, or leaden, opaque grey: Venice's Lagoon is one of its wonders, a desolate, often melancholy and strange, often beautiful and seductive 'landscape' with a hundred personalities. It is 56km long and averages 8km across; half of it, the Laguna Morta ('Dead Lagoon'), where the tides never reach, consists of mud flats except in the spring, while the shallows of the Laguna Viva are always submerged, and cleansed by tides twice a day. To navigate this treacherous sea, the Venetians have developed an intricate network of channels, marked by *bricole*—wooden posts topped by orange lamps—that keep their craft from running aground. When threatened, the Venetians only had to pull out the *bricole* to confound their enemies; and as such the Lagoon was always known as 'the sacred walls of the nation'. Keeping the Brenta and other rivers from silting it up kept engineers busy for centuries.

> *The city of the Venetians, by divine providence founded in the waters and protected by their environment, is defended by a wall of water. Therefore should anybody in any manner dare to infer damage to the public waters he shall be considered as an enemy of our country and shall be punished by no less pain that that committed to whomever violates the sacred border of the country. This act will be enforced forever.*
>
> 16th-century edict of the Maistrato alle Acque

The Venetian Lagoon

'Forever' unfortunately ended in the 20th century. New islands were made of landfill dredged up to deepen the shipping canals, upsetting the delicate balance of lagoon life; outboards and *vaporetti* churn up the gook from the Lagoon and canal beds, and send corroding waves against Venice's fragile buildings. These affect the tide, and increase both the numbers of *acque alte* and of unnaturally low tides that embarrassingly expose Venice's underthings—and let air in where it was never supposed to go, accelerating the rot and the subsidence of its wooden piles and substructures.

Then there are the ingredients in the water itself. The Lagoon is a messy stew of 60 years' worth of organic waste, phosphates, agricultural and industrial by-products and sediments—a lethal mixture that ecologists warn will take a century to purify, even if by some miracle pollution is stopped now. It's a sobering thought, especially when many Venetians in their 50s remember when even the Grand Canal was clean enough to swim in.

And in recent years, the Lagoon has been sprouting the kind of blooms that break a girl's heart—algae, 'green pastures' of it, stinking and choking its fish. No one is sure if the algae epidemic isn't just part of a natural cycle; after all, there's an old church on one Lagoon island called San Giorgio in Alga (St George in Algae). Crops of algae are on record in the 1700s and 1800s and at the beginning of this century, at times when water temperatures were abnormally high because of the weather. But other statistics are harder to reconcile with climatic cycles: since 1932, 78 species of algae have disappeared from the Lagoon, while 24 new ones have blossomed, these mostly microaglae thriving off the surplus of phosphates. These chemicals have now been banned in the Lagoon communities, leading to a noticeable fall in recent algae counts.

Once the largest of the 39 Lagoon islands were densely inhabited, each occupied by a town or at least a monastery. Now all but a few have been abandoned, many tiny ones with only a forlorn, vandalized shell of a building, overgrown with weeds. Occasionally one hears of plans to bring them back to life, only to wither on the vine of Italian bureaucracy. If you think you have a good idea, take it up with the Revenue Office (Intendenza di Finanza).

The Lido and South Lagoon

The Lido, one of the long spits of land that forms the protective outer edge of the Lagoon, is by far the most glamorous of the islands, one that has given its name to countless bathing establishments, bars, amusement arcades and cinemas all over the world. On its 12 kilometres of beach, poets, potentates and plutocrats at the turn of the century spent their holidays in palatial hotels and villas, making the Lido the pinnacle of *belle époque* fashion, so brilliantly evoked in Thomas Mann's *Death in Venice*, and Visconti's subsequent film. The story was set and filmed in the **Grand Hotel des Bains**, just north of the Mussolini-style **Municipal Casino** and **Palazzo del Cinema**, where Venice hosts its Film Festival.

The Lido is still the playground of the Venetians and their visitors, with its bathing concessions, riding clubs, tennis courts, golf courses and shooting ranges. The free beach, the **Spiaggia Comunale**, is on the north part of the island, a 15-minute walk from the *vaporetto* stop at San Nicolò (go down the Gran Viale, and turn left on the Lungomare d'Annunzio), where you can hire a changing hut and frolic in the sand and sea.

Further north, beyond the private airfield, the **Porto di Lido** is maritime Venice's front door, the most important of the three entrances into the Lagoon, where you can watch the ships of the world sail by. This is where the Doge would sail to toss his ring into the waves, in the annual ceremony of the 'Marriage of the Sea'. It is stoutly defended by the mighty **Forte di Sant'Andrea** on the island of Le Vignole, built in 1543 by Venice's genius of fortifications, Sanmicheli. In times of danger, a great chain was extended from the fort across the channel.

One of the smaller Lagoon islands just off the Lido, with its landmark onion-domed campanile, is **San Lazzaro degli Armeni** (*vaporetto no.20 from Riva degli Schiavoni, open to visitors daily 3–5pm*). This was Venice's leper colony in the Middle Ages, but in 1715 the then-deserted island was given to the Mechitarist Fathers of the Armenian Catholic Church after they were expelled from Greece by the Ottoman Turks. Today their monastery is still one of the world's major centres of Armenian culture and its monks, always noted as linguists, run a famous polyglot press able to print in 32 languages, one of the last survivors in a city once renowned for its publishing. Tours of San Lazzaro include a museum filled with relics of the ancient Christian history of Armenia, as well as memorabilia of Lord Byron, who spent a winter visiting the fathers and bruising his brain with Armenian. The fathers offer inexpensive prints of Venice for sale; or else they would appreciate a donation.

Sports and Activities

Despite dire reports about the state of the waters of the Adriatic, people still swim off the Lido without becoming mutants, but there is an alternative in the shape of the **swimming pool** on Sacca Fisola, at the west end of the Giudecca, © 041 528 5430. If you're interested in **sailing**, enquire at the sailing club, the **Compagnia della Vela**, near the Giardinetti in S. Marco, © 041 522 2593, for information on lessons and boat hire.

The Lido has the attractive 18-hole **Alberoni Golf Course**, Via del Forte Alberoni, © 041 731 015, and two tennis clubs, the **Tennis Club Venezia**, Lungomare Marconi 41/d, © 041 526 0335, and the **Campi Comunali di Tennis**, © 041 526 5689. You can also ride along the Lido, like Byron and Shelley, although it's no longer a romantic hooves-in-the-surf affair—enquire at **Circolo Ippico Veneziano**, Ca' Bianco, Lido, © 041 526 1820. If you prefer to **cycle** along the Lido, bikes can be hired at **Giorgio Barbieri**, Via Zara 5.

Where to Stay and Eating Out

luxury

★★★★★ **Excelsior Palace**, Lungomare Marconi 41, Lido di Venezia, © 041 526 0201, @ 041 526 7276. An immense confection, built in 1907 as the biggest and most luxurious resort hotel in the world and recently redesigned with as much flamboyance as ever. The outrageous exterior is part-Hollywood and part Moorish neo-Gothic. Private beach, swimming pool, tennis courts, golf, nightclub and private launch service to Venice are some of its amenities. Ogling the stars at the film festival is another. The restaurant, ✆ 041 526 0201 (*very expensive*), offers the classic turn-of-the-century Lido experience, with everything you could desire—including a traditional Venetian meal. *Closed mid-Nov–mid-Mar.*

very expensive

★★★★   **Des Bains**, Lungomare Marconi 17, Lido di Venezia, ✆ 041 526 5921, ✉ 041 526 0113. A grand old luxury hotel, now part of the Sheraton empire, that preserves much of its *belle époque* revelries in its magnificent Liberty-style salon, private *cabanas*, and large garden designed for dalliance. Thomas Mann stayed here on several occasions, and has Aschenbach sigh his life away on the private beach. There's also a salt-water swimming pool, tennis courts, perfect service, and a launch service into Venice. *Closed Dec–mid-Mar.*

★★★★   **Quattro Fontane**, Via delle Quattro Fontane 16, Lido di Venezia, ✆ 041 526 0227, ✉ 041 526 0726. The best of the smaller Lido hotels, it was formerly the seaside villa of a Venetian family. Its cool walled-in courtyard is inviting and tranquil, and the public and private rooms are furnished with antiques. Tennis court. Book well in advance. *Closed Nov–Mar.*

expensive

★★★   **Villa Parco**, Via Rodi 1, Lido di Venezia, ✆ 041 526 0015, ✉ 041 526 7620. A recently renovated villa a short way from the beach with a fine little garden for a bit of privacy. Children are welcome.

From the Lido to Chioggia

Tourist Information

Chioggia: Viale Po 16, Lido di Sottomarina, ✆ 041 554 0466, ✆ 041 554 0855.

Bus/ferries from the Lido or quicker buses from Piazzale Roma will take you to Chioggia at the southermost end of the Lagoon. The seldom used bus/ferry route (leaving roughly every hour) allows you to take in **Malamocco**, a tranquil fishing village named after the first capital of the Lagoon townships, a nearby islet that lost its status after Pepin and his Franks nabbed it in 810. The capital moved to the Rialto, leaving the original Malamocco to sink poetically into the sea during a tremendous storm in 1106.

Next to it, the small resort of **Alberoni** is home to the Lido Golf Course and the ferry to the next island reef, Pellestrina, which is even thinner. It has two sleepy villages, **San Pietro in Volta** and **Pellestrina**, where the *murazzi* or sea walls begin, the last great public works project of the Republic's Magistrato alle Acque. Built in response to to increased flooding in the 18th century, the 4km-long Murazzi are constructed of huge white Istrian blocks and built, as their plaque proudly states: *Ausu Romano—Aere Veneto* ('With Roman audacity and Venetian money'). From 1782 until 4 November 1966 they succeeded in holding back the flood.

Dusty **Chioggia** is one of the most important fishing ports on the Adriatic, a kind of populist version of Venice where the streets and canals are arrow-straight and full of working craft, many with brightly painted sails. The morning **fish market**, brimming with exotic denizens of the deep, is one of the wonders of Italy. On the map the town on its islands even resembles a fish, gutted and spread out flat, its straight narrow lanes lined up like bones.

The Venetians like to poke fun at Chioggia, which they consider a grumpy old place, and they like to wind up the inhabitants by calling the little Lion of St Mark on its column in Piazzettta Vigo (where the ferry deposits you) the 'Cat of St Mark'. Goldoni was amused enough by it all to make the town the setting of one of his comedies, *Le Baruffe Chiozzotte*. Almost nothing remains of medieval Chioggia thanks to the blockade and siege by the Genoese in the 1380 Battle of Chioggia. But if you take the first bridge left from the port and continue straight, you will eventually reach the church of **San Domenico**, containing Carpaccio's last painting, *St Paul*, signed and dated 1520, and a beautiful quattrocento crucifix on the altar.

Chioggia's other monuments are strung along the main **Corso del Popolo** (the fish spine). The fish market is just beyond a large 14th-century grain warehouse, the **Granaio**, with a relief of the Madonna on the façade by Sansovino. Further up the Corso, past a couple of low-key churches, is the **Duomo**, built by Baldassare Longhena after the 14th-century original, except for the campanile, burned in 1623. In the chapel to the left of the altar are some murky, unpleasant 18th-century paintings of martyrdoms, one of which is attributed to Tiepolo, although it's hard to swallow. However, the Gothic chapel of San Martino has a lovely polyptych (1349) that really might be by Paolo Veneziano.

And when you've had your fill of fish and the locals, you can stroll along the long bridge (or catch the bus at the Duomo) for a swim among the vivacious Italian families at Chioggia's lido, **Sottomarina**, which attracts mainly Italian families; from here it's a short drive down into the Po Delta, now a natural park.

Where to Stay and Eating Out

Chioggia ✉ 30015

All the hotels are at Sottomarina, where you'll find typical family-run seaside lodgings at the ★★★**Florida**, Viale Mediterraneo 9, ✆ 041 491 505, ✉ 041 496 6760 (*moderate; closed Nov–Jan*) or ★★★**Park**, Lungomare Adriatico, ✆ 041 496 5032, ✉ 041 490 111 (*moderate–inexpensive*).

Seafood lovers flock to the cat—**El Gato**, right behind the fish market in Campo S. Andrea 653, ✆ 041401806 (*expensive*), where the chef prepares the freshest of fish in the tastiest of Venetian styles. *Closed Mon and Tues lunch, Jan and mid-Feb*. At the old-fashioned **Trattoria Buon Pesce**, Stradale Ponte Caneva 625, ✆ 041 400 861 (*moderate*) start with *gnocchetti alla marinara* and follow it with oysters or crab. Prices are half what you'd pay in Venice.

Islands in the North Lagoon

San Michele

Most Venetian itineraries take in the islands of Murano, Burano and Torcello, all easily reached by inexpensive *vaporetti*. Lines 52 or 23 to Murano call at the cypress-studded cemetery island of **San Michele**, with its simple but elegant church of **San Michele in Isola** by Mauro Codussi (1469), his first-known work and Venice's first taste of the Florentine Renaissance, albeit with a Venetian twist in the tri-lobed front. It contains the tomb of Fra Paolo Sarpi, who led the ideological battle against the Pope when the republic was placed under the Great Interdict of 1607. Venice, considering St Mark the equal of St Peter, refused to be cowed and won the battle of wills after two years, thanks mainly to Sarpi, whose *Treatise on the Interdict* proved it was illegal. In return, he was jumped and knifed by an assassin: '*Agnosco stylum romanae curiae,*' he quipped ('I recognize the method [or the 'dagger'] of the Roman court'). His major work, the critical *History of the Council of Trent* (*see* p.70) didn't improve his standing in Rome, but made him a hero in Venice. Sarpi's main interest however, was science; he supported Copernicus and shared notes with Galileo, who was then lecturing at Padua, and also 'discovered' the contraction of the iris.

The **cemetery** itself is entered through the cloister next to the church (*open daily 8.30–4*). The Protestant and Orthodox sections contain the tombs of some of the many foreigners who preferred to face eternity from Venice, among them Ezra Pound, Sergei Diaghilev, Frederick Rolfe (Baron Corvo) and Igor Stravinsky. The gate-keeper provides a basic map.

Murano, the Island of Glass

The island of Murano (*vaporetti nos.52, 52 or 23 from S. Zaccaria or nos.12 or 13 from Fondamente Nuove*) is synonymous with glass, the most celebrated of Venice's industries. The Venetians were the first in the Middle Ages to rediscover the secret of making crystal glass, and especially mirrors, and it was a secret they kept a monopoly on for centuries by using the most drastic measures: if ever a glassmaker let himself be coaxed abroad, the Council of Ten sent their assassins after him in hot pursuit. However, those who remained in Venice were treated with kid gloves. Because of the danger of fire, all the forges in Venice were relocated to Murano in 1291, and the little island became a kind of republic within a republic—minting its own coins, policing itself, even developing its own list of NHs (*nobili homini*—noblemen) in its own *Golden Book*—aristocrats of glass, who built solid palaces along Murano's own Grand Canal.

But glass-making declined like everything else in Venice, and only towards the end of the 19th century were the forges once more stoked up on Murano. Can you visit them? You betcha! After watching the glass being made, there's the inevitable tour of the 'Museum Show Rooms' with their American funeral parlour atmosphere, all solicitude, carpets and hush-hush—not unfitting, as some of the blooming chandeliers, befruited mirrors and poison-coloured chalices begin to make Death look good. There is no admission charge, and there's not even too much pressure to buy. It wasn't always so kitschy. The **Museo**

Vetrario or Glass Museum (*open 10–5; closed Wed; adm*), in the 17th-century Palazzo Giustinian on Fondamenta Cavour, has some simple pieces from Roman times, and a choice collection of 15th-century Murano glass, especially the delightful 1480 *Barovier Nuptial Cup*; later glass tends to prove that Murano's glassblowers have long had a wayward streak.

Nearby stands the another good reason to visit this rather dowdy island, the Veneto-Byzantine **Santi Maria e Donato** (*open daily 8–12 and 4–7*), a contemporary of St Mark's basilica, with a beautiful arcaded apse. The floor is paved with a marvellous 12th-century mosaic, incorporating coloured pieces of ancient Murano glass, and on the wall there's a fine Byzantine mosaic of the Virgin. The relics of Bishop Donato of Euboea were nabbed by Venetian body-snatchers, but in this case they outdid themselves, bringing home not only San Donato's bones but those of the dragon the good bishop slew with a gob of spit; you can see them hanging behind the altar. Back on the Fondamenta dei Vetrai, the 15th-century **San Pietro Martire** has one of Giovanni Bellini's best altarpieces, *Pala Barbarigo* (1484), a monumental *Sacra conversazione* of the Madonna enthroned with SS. Mark and Augustine and Doge Barbarigo, that achieves a rare serenity that perfectly suits the subject.

Burano, the Island of Lace

Burano (*vaporetto no.12*) is the Legoland of the Lagoon, where everything is in brightly coloured miniature—the canals, the bridges, the leaning tower, and the houses, painted with a Fauvist sensibility in the deepest of colours. Traditionally on Burano the men fish and the women make Venetian point, 'the most Italian of all lace work', beautiful, intricate and murder on the eyesight. All over Burano you can find samples on sale (of which a great many are machine-made or imported), or you can watch it being made at the **Scuola dei Merletti** in Piazza Galuppi (*open Tues–Sat 10–4; adm*). 'Scuola' in this case is misleading; no young woman in Burano wants to learn such an excruciating art. The school itself was founded in 1872, when traditional lacemaking was already in decline. In the sacristy of the church of **San Martino** (with its tipsily leaning campanile) look for Giambattista Tiepolo's *Crucifixion*, which Mary McCarthy aptly described as 'a ghastly masquerade ball'.

From Burano you can hire a *sandola* (small gondola) to **San Francesco del Deserto**, some 20 minutes to the south. St Francis is said to have founded a chapel here in 1220, and the whole islet was subsequently given to his order for a **monastery** (*visitors welcome daily 9–11 and 3–5.30*). In true Franciscan fashion, it's not the buildings you'll remember (though there's a fine 14th-century cloister), but the love of nature evident in the beautiful gardens. Admission is free, but donations are appreciated.

Torcello, the Island of Ghosts

Though fewer than 100 people remain on Torcello (*vaporetto no.12; no.14 takes twice as long*), this small island was once a serious rival to Venice herself. According to legend, its history began when God ordered the bishop of Roman *Altinum*, north of Mestre, to take his flock away from the heretical Lombards into the Lagoon. From a tower the bishop saw a star rise over Torcello, and so led the people of Altinum to this lonely island to set up their new home. It grew quickly, and for the first few centuries it seems to have been the real metropolis of the Lagoon, with 20,000 inhabitants, palaces, a mercantile fleet and five townships; but malaria decimated the population, the *Sile* silted up Torcello's corner of the Lagoon, and the bigger rising star of Venice drew its citizens to the Rialto.

Torcello is now a ghost island overgrown with weeds, its palaces either sunk into the marsh or quarried for their stone; narrow paths are all that remain of once bustling thoroughfares. One of these follows a canal from the landing stage past the picturesque Ponte del Diavolo to the grass-grown piazza in front of the magnificent Veneto-Byzantine **Cathedral of Santa Maria Assunta** with its lofty campanile, founded in 639 and rebuilt in the same Ravenna basilica-style in 1008. The interior (*no longer a cathedral, although mass is celebrated every Sunday during the summer; open daily 10.30–6; adm*) has the finest mosaics in Venice, all done by 11th- and 12th-century Greek artists, from the wonderful floor to the spectacular *Last Judgement* on the west wall and the unsettling, heart-rending *Teotoco*, the stark, gold-ground mosaic of the thin, weeping Virgin portrayed as the 'bearer of God'.

Next to the cathedral is the restored 11th-century octagonal church of **Santa Fosca**, surrounded by an attractive portico, a beautiful and rare late Byzantine work. Near here stands an ancient stone throne called the **Chair of Attila**, though its connection with the Hunnish supremo is nebulous. Across the square, the two surviving secular buildings of Torcello, the Palazzo del Consiglio and Palazzo dell'Archivio, contain the small **Museo dell'Estuario** (*open daily 10–12.30 and 2–4; closed Mon and hols; adm*), with an interesting collection of archaeological finds and artefacts from Torcello's former churches.

Where to Stay and Eating Out

Murano ✉ 30121

Après all those empty glasses, take comfort over a chilled bottle of Soave and a plate of *spaghetti al vongole* at **Ai Frati**, Fondamenta Venier 4, ✆ 041 736 694 (*expensive*), a classic Venetian seafood restaurant. *Closed Thurs, Feb.*

Burano ✉ 30121

No frills **Raspo de Ua**, Via Galuppi 560, ✆ 041 730 095, ✆ 041 730 397 (*inexpensive*) offers six rooms above a restaurant and a chance to get to know Burano after the tourists have melted back into the Lagoon.

Torcello ✉ 30012

★★★**Locanda Cipriani**, Piazza S. Fosca 29, ✆ 041 730 150, ✆ 041 735 433 (*very expensive*). There are only six rooms in this recently renovated and infamous country house hotel, basking in the most rural and tranquil spot of the whole *comune* of Venice. Some have views over the hotel's blissful garden; you can sleep where Hemingway wrote his Venice novel, *Across the River and Into the Trees*— standing up because of haemorrhoids. All the rooms are spacious and fresh, and prices include half or full board. *Closed Jan.* The restaurant (*very expensive*) serves delicious seafood with all the Cipriani trimmings, and in summer you eat in the garden. *Closed Tues.*

Cavallino and Jesolo

One suspects these beach resorts closest to Venice owe part of their success to their total *lack* of any cultural 'obligations'. On the other hand, they have every facility for fun, Italian-style, from windsurfers and rollerblades to hire to water parks, horse-riding along the lagoon, bike trails and even covered *bocce* courts.

Tourist Information

Lido di Jesolo: Piazza Brescia 13, ✆ 042 137 0601, e-mail *apt@marconinet.it.*

There are two ports on the *litorale* linked to Venice: **Punta Sabbioni** (*vaporetto Line 14, from Riva degli Schiavoni and the Lido; car ferry Line 17, from Tronchetto*) and **Treporti** (*vaporetto Line 12*); frequent buses ply the strip between Jesolo with Punta Sabbioni. The **Litorale del Cavallino**, the 10km sliver of land that protects the northern part of the Lagoon, was long known as a semi-wild place of beach, dunes and pine forests. There's still some of that left, among its 28 camping grounds and umpteen hotels and restaurants. **Lido di Jesolo**, north from Punta Sabbioni, is a densely packed resort on a wide sandy beach, attracting some six million tourists a year.

Where to Stay and Eating Out

Because of the Adriatic's periodic pollution and algae problems, nearly all hoteliers have private pools as well as private beaches, including all those listed below.

Cavallino ✉ 30013

Quiet, out of the centre ★★★**Fenix**, Via F. Baracca 45, ✆ 041 968 040, ✆ 041 968 831 (*moderate*) is convenient for the pines, beach, or trips into Venice. *Open mid-May–Sept.* For lovely food, especially fresh, simply prepared seafood hot from the grill, book a table at the historic **Trattoria Laguna**, Via Pordelio 444, ✆ 041 968 058 (*expensive*), overlooking the lagoon. Make sure you save room for one of their famous desserts. *Closed Thurs out of season, and Jan–mid-Feb.*

Lido di Jesolo ✉ 30017

An elegant construction from the 1930s, ★★★★**Casa Bianca al Mare**, Piazzetta Casa Bianca 1, ✆ 042 137 0615, ✆ 042 137 1659 (*expensive*) is a lovely place to stay, set off by its own park. ★★★★**Grand Hotel Las Vegas**, Via Mascagni 2, ✆ 042 197 1515, ✆ 042 138 0581 (*moderate*) is attractive, modern, and right on the sea; all rooms have balconies, and the restaurant is one of Jesolo's best. *Open May–Sept.* ★★★**Christian**, Via Olanda 150, ✆/✆ 042 136 2264 (*moderate–inexpensive*) is similar, but simpler. *Closed Oct–Feb.*

Over the years, the river Brenta made itself universally detested by flooding the surrounding farmland and choking the Lagoon with silt, and in the 14th century the Venetians decided to control its antics once and for all. They raised its banks and dug a canal to divert its waters, and when all the hydraulic labours were completed in the 16th century they realized that the new canal was the ideal place for their summer *villeggiatura*; their gondoliers could conveniently row them straight to their doors, or, as Goethe and thousands of other visitors have done, they could travel there on the *Burchiello*, a water bus propelled by oars or horses. Over seventy villas and palaces sprouted up along this 'extension of the Grand Canal' and they were famous for their summer parties. Now, if only you could wave a magic wand and make the traffic disappear. The cars have replaced the fireflies that once made a summer's evening canal ride so magical, casting a glow bright enough to read by.

Getting Around

In *The Merchant of Venice* Portia, disguised as a young male lawyer, left her villa at Belmont on the Brenta Canal and proceeded down to Fusina to save Antonio's pound of flesh. For about the same price you can trace her route on the stately, villa-lined Brenta in a motorized version of the original public canalboat, the *Burchiello*, or on the simpler craft of *I Battelli del Brenta*; both lines make the day-long cruise from March to early November on Tuesday, Thursday and Saturday from Venice, and Wednesday, Friday and Sunday from Padua. The *Burchiello* motor-launch price includes admission into Villa Pisani, Barchessa Valmarana and La Malcontenta, guide, and coach back to the city of origin; book through Siamic Express, Via Trieste 42 (by Padua bus station), © 049 660 944, @ 049 662 830, *siamic@tin.it*; or through any travel agent or CIT office abroad. For the similar *I Battelli del Brenta*: Via Pellizzo 1, Padua, © 049 807 4340, @ 049 807 2830, *intercity.shiny.i/ battellidelbrenta*. Delta Tours, Via Toscana 2, © 049 870 0232, @ 049 976 0833, *deltatour@tin.it*, also run Brenta canal tours, stopping at Villa Pisana, Barchessa Valmarana and Villa Gradenigo in Oriago.

You can follow the Brenta on your own, less romantically and far less expensively, along the S11 road that follows the canal, by car or the half-hourly bus to Padua from Piazzale Roma. For La Malcontenta, however, you must take a different bus from Piazzale Roma which leaves only once an hour. Or hire a bike at Centre Bike, Via Mocenigo 3, Mira, © 041 420 110.

Villas along the Brenta

Sailing up from Venice and Fusina, the first grand sight is Palladio's temple-fronted Villa Foscari, better known as **La Malcontenta**, built in 1560 and as striking as it is simple (*open May–Oct, Tues and Sat 9–12 or by appointment, © 041 520 3966; adm exp; guided tours*). Viewed from the canal, it is a vision begging for a Scarlett O'Hara to sweep

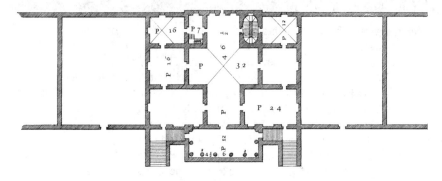

La Malcontenta, from Palladio's
Four Books of Architecture

down the steps—not surprising, as the villa was a favourite model for American plantation builders. Inside are some suitably delicate frescoes by Zelotti, Bernardino India and Battista Franco, one of which shows a sad woman—a possible source of the villa's name, although others say the unhappy one was the beautiful La Foscarina, who hated being cooped up here by her husband, far away from the fleshpots of Venice. Descendants of the original Foscari now own La Malcontenta, and have restored it beautifully.

Further up the canal, Oriago was the scene of early medieval battles between Venice and Padua. It still has the column that once marked their borders, as well as the late 16th-century Villa Gradenigo, with frescoes on the façade, which has recently been opened to canal-boating visitors. Mira Ponte, the next village, is the site of the 18th-century Villa Widmann-Foscari (*guided tours Tues–Sun, 9–6; adm exp*). If you only have time for one villa, don't make it this one—redone in French baroque after its construction, the villa contains some of its original furniture and gaudy murals by two of Tiepolo's pupils. The best parties, lasting up to eight days, were held nearby at Villa Corner, which had a facelift in the 1800s.

Mira's post office occupies the Palazzo Foscarini, Byron's address in 1817–19. While living here he composed the fourth Canto of *Childe Harolde* and cut off his last links with perfidious Albion, through his divorce and sale of the family home, consoling himself with a rag-tag collection of gondoliers, waiters, pets and black-eyed contessas who, Shelley sniffed, 'smelled so strongly of garlic that an ordinary Englishman cannot approach them'. You can visit the Barchessa Valmarana in Mira at Via Valmarana 11 (*open 9.30–12.30, 2.30–6, closed Mon*), the ornate wings of a demolished 18th-century villa belonging to one of Vicenza's most prominent families, decorated with baroque frescoes. In Dolo, on the other hand, 16th-century mills are a reminder that life wasn't all fun and games.

Byron Goes Swimming

Byron arrived in Venice in 1816, his heart full of romance as he rented a villa on the Brenta to compose the last canto of his *Childe Harolde's Pilgrimage*. The city's canals at least afforded him the personal advantage of being able to swim anywhere (his club foot made him shy of walking); on one occasion he swam a race from the Lido to the Rialto bridge and was the only man to finish.

It wasn't long before the emotional polish of *Childe Harolde* began to crack. To Byron's surprise, Venice didn't perfect his romantic temper, but cured him of it. He went to live in the Palazzo Mocenigo on the Grand Canal, in the company of 14 servants, a dog, a wolf, a fox, monkeys and a garlicky baker's wife, La Fornarina, who stabbed him in the hand with a fork—which so angered Byron that he ordered her out, whereupon she threw herself into the Grand Canal. Under such circumstances, all that had been breathless passion reeked of the ridiculous, as he himself admitted:

> *And the sad truth which hovers o'er my desk*
> *Turns what was once romantic to burlesque*

Venice, its women, its own ironic detachment and its love of liberty set Byron's mind free to write *Beppo: A Venetian Story*, spoofing Venice's *cavalieri serventi* (escort-lovers—even nuns had them) while celebrating the freedom of its people. He followed this with two bookish plays on Venetian themes, *Marino Faliero* and *The Two Foscari*, and most importantly began his satirical masterpiece, *Don Juan*.

Meanwhile debauchery was taking its toll: an English acquaintance wrote in 1818 that 'his face had become pale, bloated and sallow, and the knuckles on his hands were lost in fat'. Byron became infatuated with a young countess, Teresa Guiccioli, and left Venice to move in with her and her elderly husband in Ravenna. But, having tasted every freedom in Venice, Byron once more began to chafe; the Contessa was 'taming' him. He bundled up the manuscript of Don Juan and left, only to die of fever at the age of 36 in the Greek War of Independence.

'If you've got it, flaunt it,' was the rule in Venice, especially in the 1700s, when one of the grandest villas in all Italy went up at Stra: the Villa Nazionale (or Pisani), enlarged by Alvise Pisani, scion of the fabulously wealthy banking family, to celebrate his election as doge in 1735 (© 049 502 074, *hour-long guided tours June–Sept, Tues–Sun 9–6; until*

7.30pm many days in Aug; Oct–May, Tues–Sun 9–1.30; adm). The new doge had served as Venice's ambassador in Paris; he suggested that something in the Versailles mould might just do, complete with parterres and canals, and hired an architect with the delicious name of Frigimelica Preti to do the job. The villa was completed in 1760, but only after the original plans were scaled down (!). The Pisani sold their brick and mortar dream of grandeur to Napoleon, who gave it to his stepson and viceroy in Italy, Eugène Beauharnais. In June 1934 Mussolini chose it as the stage for his first meeting with Hitler, where he strutted about in full fig, offering the Führer tips on how to deal with Austria and those pesky socialists.

Although most of the villa has been stripped of its decoration, the ballroom makes up for the boredom with one of Tiepolo's most shimmering frescoes (the last he painted before leaving for Madrid), depicting, what else, the Apotheosis of the Pisani Family, who float about on clouds, hobnobbing with virtues and allegories of the continents. His son Giandomenico painted the chiaroscuro Roman scenes along the gallery. The vast park (the parterres were replaced in the 1800s with an English-style garden) contains the stables, a veritable equine Ritz, as well as innumerable pavilions and an expert-level box maze, planted before all the fuss, in 1721. Also on the canal in Strà, the 17th-century Villa Foscari-Negrelli-Rossi, Via Doge Pisani, is open for visits (*by appointment, ℂ 049 980 0335*); the architect is unknown and the frescoes attributed to Pietro Liberi and Domenico de Bruni.

South of Stra in Saonara, there's a treat for lovers of Romantic gardens: the Giardino Storico di Villa Valmarana (*ring ahead, ℂ 049 879 0879, ✉ 049 879 1380; adm exp*) laid out around a lake in 1816 by Padua's leading architect, Giuseppe Jappelli, with grottoes, waterfalls and statues. Noventa Padovana, between Stra and Padua and the *autostrada*, has another collection of villas, notably the Palladian-style Villa Giovanelli with its statues and temple portico inscribed 'Villaggio S. Antonio'.

A Patrician's Life

In the 1540s the great humanist Luigi (Alvise) Cornaro wrote a philosophical treatise 'On the Sober Life'. Cornaro was 83 at the time, and he was sick and tired of hearing people knock old age. While defending the glories of the golden years, he incidentally left behind one of the best accounts of how a nobleman in the Veneto might expect to spend his time:

Let them come and see, and wonder at my good health, how I mount on horseback without help, how I run upstairs and up hills, how cheerful, amusing, and contented I am, how free from care and disagreeable thoughts. Peace and joy never quit me... My friends are wise, learned, and distinguished people of good position, and when they are not with me I read and write, and try thereby as by all other means, to be useful to others. Each of these things I do at the proper time, and at my ease, in my dwelling, which is beautiful and lies in the best part of Padua, and is arranged both for summer and winter with all the resources of architecture, and provided with a garden by running water. In the spring and autumn, I go for a while to my hill in the most beautiful part of the Euganean mountains, where I have fountains and gardens, and a comfortable dwelling; and there I amuse myself with some easy and pleasant chase, which is suitable to my years. At other times I go to my villa on the plain. There all the paths lead to an open space, in the middle of which stands a pretty church; an arm of the Brenta flows through the plantations—fruitful, well-cultivated fields, now fully peopled, which the marshes and the foul air once made fitter for snakes than for men. It was I who drained the country; then the air became good, and people settled there and multiplied, and the land became cultivated as it now is, so that I can truly say: 'On this spot I gave to God an altar and a temple, and souls to worship Him.' This is my consolation and my happiness whenever I come here. In the spring and autumn, I also visit the neighbouring towns, to see and converse with my friends, through whom I make the acquaintance of other distinguished men, architects, painters, sculptors, musicians, and cultivators of the soil. I see what new things they have done, I look again at what I know already, and learn much that is of use to me. I see palaces, gardens, antiquities, public grounds, churches, and fortifications. But what most of all delights me when I travel, is the beauty of the country and the palaces, lying now on the plain, now on the slopes of the hills, or on the banks of rivers and streams, surrounded by gardens and villas...

Cornaro goes on to say that he has just written his first comedy, then gives some practical advice on draining marshlands and preserving lagoons, and writes of the joys of being a grandfather. When he turned 95, Cornaro added a postscript, saying that he owed part of his continued happiness to the fact that so many people had read his Treatise and were now enjoying their old age. He died, well over 100 years old, in 1565.

The Venetians were a notoriously long-lived race, and reading Cornaro one understands why: their lives were too delightful to give up easily. While other Italians mocked Venice for being a republic of old men, remember that they—the other Italians—were under the thumb of Spain, which wasn't half as much fun.

Where to Stay and Eating Out

Dolo ✉ 30031

Sleep in an antique bed under the frescoes at the ★★★**Villa Ducale**, Riviera Martiri della Libertà 75, ✆/✉ 041 420 094 (*expensive*); another plus is the garden setting with fountains.

Locanda alla Posta, Via Cà Tron 33, ✆ 041 410 740 (*expensive*) has been around a long time, and now has a wonderful new chef to wake it from its hibernation: great fish, delicately prepared, and other dishes too. *Closed Mon.*

Mira ✉ 30034

★★★★**Villa Margherita**, Via Nazionale 416, ✆ 041 426 5800, ✆ 041 426 5838 (*expensive*) offers another chance to live like a patrician; some of its charming rooms have terraces, and breakfast is served on the garden patio, just as it should be. The restaurant, **Margherita**, in a Liberty villa down the road, specializes in seafood and is also one of the best in the area. *Closed Tues eve, Wed, Jan.*

A less elaborate, 17th-century villa, ★★★**Riviera dei Dogi**, Via Don Minzoi 33, ✆ 041 424 466, ✆ 041 424 428 (*expensive–moderate*) has comfortable modernized rooms near the canal.

One of the traditional places to round off a Brenta Canal excursion is the lovely poplar-shaded veranda at **Nalin**, Via Nuovissimo 29, ✆ 041 420 083 (*expensive–moderate*). In business since 1914, the emphasis is on Venetian seafood, finely grilled, and there are good Veneto wines as well. *Closed Sun eve, Mon, Aug.*

History 150

The Cappella degli Scrovegni
  and the Museo Civico 152

Caffè Pedrocchi and the University 157

The Medieval Civic Centre 158

Padua

Where to Stay 163

Eating Out 164

Day Trips North of Padua 165

Day Trips South of Padua 171

Vicenza 175

Monte Bérico, Villa Valmarana
  and La Rotonda 184

Although only half an hour from Venice, Padua (Padova) refuses to be overshadowed by the old dowager by the sea, and can rightly claim its own place among Italy's most interesting and historic cities. Nicknamed *La Dotta*, 'The Learned', Padua is the brain of the Veneto, once home of the great Roman historian Livy and, since 1221, to one of Europe's most celebrated universities, which counts Petrarch, Dante and Galileo among its alumni.

Padua's churches, under the brushes of Giotto, Guariento, Altichiero, Giusto de' Menabuoi and Mantegna, were virtually laboratories in the evolution of fresco. But what Padua attracts most of all is pilgrims; it is the last resting place of St Anthony of Padua, and his exotic, seven-domed mosque of a basilica is the city's most striking landmark. If that's not enough, Padua is a delight to visit: it has more porticoed streets than any city in Italy except Bologna, some of which could easily serve as a setting for *The Taming of the Shrew*, which Shakespeare set in this lively, student-filled city.

History

According to Virgil, ancient Patavium was founded in 1185 BC by Antenor, a hero of the Trojan War, giving it a pedigree nearly as hallowed as Rome's. Unfortunately the archaeological record won't have it: Patavium was a simple Paleoveneto village on a branch of the Brenta river until the 4th century BC, when it became one of the Veneti's capitals. It sided with Rome against the Gauls in 45 BC, and grew into a prosperous Roman *municipium*. In 602 the Lombards burned it to the ground.

From the rubble Padua rose, a slow phoenix, to become an important *comune* by the 12th century. In the 13th century, it hosted one of the best characters of the day, St Anthony, and one of the worst, Ezzelino III da Romano, who robbed Padua of its independence while bleeding it white. In 1259 local *signori*, most importantly the Da Carrara, picked up where Ezzelino left off and fought over the pieces, then lost the city to the Scaligers of Verona in 1328. Doge Francesco Dandolo (after a deal reportedly made *under* his dining table) returned it to the Da Carrara in 1337, and as a bonus admitted them into Venice's Golden Book. For all the troubles, the 13th and 14th centuries were a golden age for Padua, in art, architecture and technology; it was the time of the famous Latin lecturer Vergerius, who made the university and Padua itself one of the earliest centres of Latin letters, and Giovanni Dondi (1320–89), who built Europe's first astronomical clocks (and whose descendants, after six centuries, still live just north of the cathedral, in Via Dondi dell'Orologio).

The Da Carrara, however, had ambitions beyond an entry in the *Libro d'Oro*. Francesco da Carrara allied himself with the King of Hungary and raised himself against Venice; in 1373 the Paduans proudly hung the banner of St Mark as a war trophy in the Basilica of Sant'Antonio. After three more decades of the usual betrayals, scheming and conspiring on both sides, Venice besieged Padua, then raging with plague, in 1405; the last of the Da

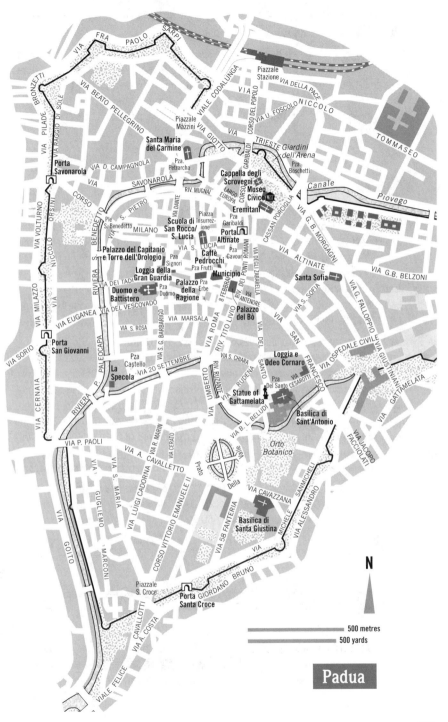

Padua

Carrara was heard shouting from the walls, inviting the devil 'to come and get him', as he was captured. He was later strangled in a Venetian prison.

Under the Venetians Padua continued to prosper, especially its university, which went on to become one of the chief medical schools in Europe. Many of Padua's students were involved in the Resistance in the Second World War, and the north part of the city was heavily bombed by the Americans (March 1944). But Padua is hardly one to forget its past—even long-gone buildings and streets are outlined on the pavement, giving the city a curious fourth dimension of time.

Getting There

Padua is easily reached by **train** from Venice (40min), Vicenza (45min) and other cities on the Milan–Venice line. Outside the train station, a booth dispenses tickets and directions for the city buses. The **bus station** is a 10-minute walk away in the Piazzale Boschetti, Via Trieste 40, ✆ 049 820 6844, and has buses every half-hour to Venice, and good connections to Vicenza, Este, Monsélice and other towns; **ACAP** city buses (✆ 049 824 1111) from the station serve Àbano Terme and Montegrotto Terme. **Landomas**, ✆ 049 860 1426, has direct connections to Marco Polo or Treviso airports from Padua and the Euganean hills—they'll pick you up at your door if you book a day in advance. **Radio taxi:** ✆ 049 651 333.

Besides **cruises** along the Brenta Canal (*see* p.143), **Delta Tours** also offers mini-cruises on *La Padovanella* around Padua itself on the river Piovego, recently made navigable again.

Car hire firms: Avis: Piazzale Stazione 1, ✆ 049 664 198. Europcar: Piazzale Stazione 6, ✆ 049 875 8590. Hertz: Piazzale Stazione 1/VI, ✆ 049 875 2202. Intercar: Via Fistomba 8, ✆ 049 807 3957. Maggiore: Piazzale Stazione 15, ✆ 049 875 2852. Padova Car e Eurodollar: Corso del Popolo 77, ✆ 049 875 8703.

Tourist Information

In the railway station, ✆ 049 875 2077 (*open Mon–Sat 9–7.30, Sun 8.30–12.30; Nov–Mar 9.20–5.45, Sun 9–12*); Riviera Mugnai 8, ✆ 049 875 0655, ✉ 049 650 794, e-mail *apt@padovanet.it*.

If you plan to visit most or all of the main attractions in Padua, a ***biglietto unico*** will save you money on admissions; you can buy it from any one of the participating sites.

The Cappella degli Scrovegni and the Museo Civico Eremitani

Open 9–6, until 7 in summer, closed Mon; same ticket for both; adm exp.

Padua deserves at least a whole day, but if you only have a couple of hours it's a short walk from the bus or railway station to its gem: Giotto's extraordinary, recently restored frescoes in the Cappella degli Scrovegni (or *Madonna dell'Arena*), a pearl sheltered by the crusty

Cappella degli Scrovegni

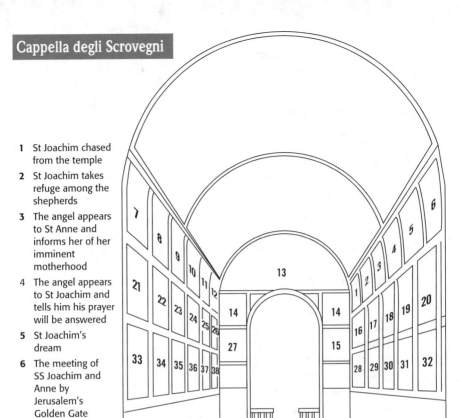

1 St Joachim chased from the temple

2 St Joachim takes refuge among the shepherds

3 The angel appears to St Anne and informs her of her imminent motherhood

4 The angel appears to St Joachim and tells him his prayer will be answered

5 St Joachim's dream

6 The meeting of SS Joachim and Anne by Jerusalem's Golden Gate

7 The birth of Mary

8 The Presentation of Mary at the Temple

9 Handing over the rod to St Simeon

10 The prayer for the blossoming of the rods

11 The wedding of Mary and Joseph

12 The Wedding Procession

13 God giving the Archangel Gabriel his orders

14 The Annunciation

15 The Visitation

16 The Nativity

17 The Adoration of the Magi

18 Presentation of Jesus at the Temple

19 The Flight into Egypt

20 The Massacre of the Innocents

21 Jesus among the Doctors of the Temple

22 The Baptism of Jesus

23 The Marriage at Cana

24 The Resurrection of Lazarus

25 The Entry of Jesus into Jerusalem

26 Chasing the Merchants from the Temple

27 Judas receiving the Thirty Pieces of Silver

28 The Last Supper

29 The Washing of the Feet

30 The Kiss of Judas

31 Jesus before Caiaphas

32 Jesus crowned with the Crown of Thorns

33 The Calvary

34 The Crucifixion

35 The Deposition

36 The Resurrection

37 The Ascension

38 Pentecost

shell of Padua's Roman amphitheatre. It is lucky to be there; bombs shattered the surrounding neighbourhood in the last war. In another close call, the Paduans, in a 19th-century fit of 'progress', knocked down the Palazzo Scrovegni and were about to demolish the chapel too, until an opportune campaign by *The Times* saved Giotto's masterpiece.

The Cappella degli Scrovegni

Giotto translated the art of painting from Greek to Latin.

Cennino Cennini, *Il Libro dell'Arte* (1400)

Nowadays he would not be allowed to paint a tennis court.

Charles (Président) de Brosses, *Lettres sur l'Italie* (1740)

We owe the Arena Chapel to Enrico Scrovegni, who built it in 1303 in expiation for the sins of his father, Reginaldo the usurer, who died shrieking for the keys to his safe to keep anyone from touching his money. Fortunately, he left enough of his filthy lucre behind for Enrico to build a chapel and commission Giotto, then at the height of his career, to fresco the interior with a New Testament cycle (1304–07), on the lives of the Virgin and her Son. In sheer power and inspiration these frescoes are the medieval equivalent of the Sistine Chapel, as revolutionary for the 14th century as Michelangelo's would be for the 16th. Giotto's fresh, natural narrative composition, solidly anchoring three-dimensional figures in their setting, derives its power not from divine trappings but sheer moral authority; his gift of portraying meaning and emotion in a glance or gesture conveys the story directly to the heart. Compare these frescoes to the Byzantine mosaics in San Marco, and you'll at once understand what Cennini was talking about.

Giotto's sons worked at his side and, like their father, were remarkably ugly. Their fellow Florentine Dante visited them while they worked, and couldn't help asking Giotto, 'How is it that you make painted figures so well, and real ones so badly?' Giotto returned at once, 'Because I make the former by day and the latter by night.' Dante laughed and, as a compliment to the artist, placed Reginaldo in the seventh ring of the *Inferno* (Canto XVII). Giotto, however, had no doubt where he was going; you'll find him fourth from the left in the front row of the elect in the powerful *Last Judgement* on the west wall. A delegation from heaven accepts Enrico's offering of the chapel, while on the far left a singularly harrowing pre-Dantesque Inferno is ruled by a big blue Satan munching and excreting sinners. Along the bottom of the frescoes note the monochrome *Vices and Virtues*, painted by Giotto in imitation of stone reliefs—history's first *grisailles*—while the frescoes in the apse, depicting the later career of the Virgin, are a slightly later work by Giotto's followers.

Museo Civico

The same ticket gets you into the Museo Civico, installed in the adjacent Augustine convent of the Eremitani, with its noteworthy **archaeological collection**: coins, vases and 14 funerary stelae from the 6th to 1st centuries BC, inscribed in bastard Etruscan. Padua is the only place in northern Italy where such stelae were discovered; apparently the local aristocracy wanted to put on airs by using the Greek alphabet. Other highlights are furnishings from the 8th-century BC tomb, and Roman busts of Augustus and a Silenus.

The **painting section** houses literally acres of art, not always in chronological order, but a gold mine for connoisseurs of lesser-known painters, mingled among the greats—including Giotto, whose *Crucifixion* was designed for the altar of the Cappella Scrovegni. In the next rooms are works by his follower Guariento, founder of the Paduan school, who painted the lovely but rather odd series of *Angels*, weighing souls and fighting the devil, each slightly different, as if they were frames from a film. The International Gothic style is represented by Lorenzo Veneziano, Jacopo Bellini (*Christ in Limbo*) and a charming but anonymous *millefleurs* Madonna (1408). The link in Padua from Giotto to the Renaissance was Francesco Squarcione, at least according to old art historians; a rather dry polyptych, one of only two documented works by his hand, is here.

This is followed by a charming *Expedition of the Argonauts* by Lorenzo Costa of Ferrara, and then a number of 16th-century Paduan paintings showing the influence of Andrea Mantegna (including Bartolomeo Veneto's all-dwarfing *Madonna* and Pietro Paolo Agabiti's *Madonna with SS. Peter and Sebastian*, with the face of a Hollywood starlet—Sebastian, that is). Lombard painters check in with Madonnas by Da Vinci's follower Bernardo Luino and Andrea Previtali. In Italy, a bride brought her trousseau in an ornate wedding chest or *cassione*; Titian as a youth decorated two with mythological scenes, and other works in the room show his later influence. Among the curiosities are three anonymous paintings of the *Influence by the Planets on the Activities of Man*.

In the next rooms you'll find Palma il Giovanni's rather bold *Santa Cristina*; portraits by Padua's leading female artist of the Renaissance, Chiara Varotari (1584–1663); a baroque *David and Goliath* by Pietro Muttoni della Vecchia (David, always so young and dashing in Renaissance paintings, has a grey beard here) and *Portraits of Philosophers* by the prolific Luca Giordano of Naples—his *Job* may be the best portrayal of a bad smell in Italian painting. In the 1600s, the nobility in the Veneto began to collect genre scenes and landscapes, bringing in artists from around Europe to cash in: especially represented here are Eismann and Philip Peter Roos, and the local painters they inspired, such as Antonio Marini of Venice, who specialized in battle scenes.

After these, the museum changes gear and returns to the 16th century with paintings by Domenico Campagnolo and Giampiero Silvio, both of whom worked in Padua; luminous Dutch paintings; and an enormous and fantastically detailed Brussels tapestry of *David Ordering Joab to Attack the Ammonites*. Il Romanino of Brescia weighs in with his masterpiece, a huge altarpiece of the *Virgin and Saints* (originally in Santa Giustina) as well as a *Last Supper*, with Judas clutching his money under the table. Other paintings to look for: Tintoretto's *Crucifixion* (with a battle in the background); *Dinner at the House of Simon*; the *Martyrdom of SS. Primo and Feliciano*, and a small *Crucifixion* against a black sky by Veronese; and works by 17th-century painter Il Padovinino (Alessandro Varotari) and his followers Pietro della Vecchia, Giulio Carpioni and Francesco Maffei. A portrait of Elena Lucrezia Cornaro Piscopia, painted in 1678 to honour her doctorate from Padua University, shares a room with what must be the campest portrait in all Italy: the 17th-century *Venetian Captain* by Sebastiano Mazzoni, matched only by its frame, carved with cupids, lions and a giant artichoke.

From the same century but from another world are the 'realist' works by Matteo di Pittocchi (Matteo of the Beggars); the paintings of tiny people being chased by snails and attacked by crabs by Faustino Bocchi (1659–1741); and the idyllic landscapes by Francesco Aviani (a Venetian proto-hippy, 1662–1715). There are striking 18th-century *trompe-l'œil* by a brother and sister team, Pietro and Caterina Leopoldo della Santa, and G.B. Tiepolo's *St Patrick Bishop of Ireland*, in a very non-Irish setting; also genre scenes by Pietro Longhi and Rosalba Carrara's *Portrait of a Young Priest*.

Some of the finest paintings are part of the **Quadraria Emo Capodilista**, a private collection donated to the museum in 1864 that includes Giorgione's *Leda and the Swan* and *Country Idyll*; Giovanni Bellini's *A Young Senator* and *Christ's Descent From the Cross*, the latter painted with his father Jacopo; and a *Mythological Scene* by Titian. Another donation, the **Museo Bottacin**, has more from the 18th century, and a fabulous coin collection. The *bronzetti* from the 14th–17th centuries that fill the halls were a speciality of Padua, especially those by Andrea Briosco, better known as Il Riccio ('Curly'). His famous *Drinking Satyr* is here, as well as works by Alessandro Vittoria, Niccolò Roccatagliata and a certain Il Moderno, whose name was probably invented by his agent.

The Eremitani, Santa Sofia and the Carmine

Next to the museum, the church of the **Eremitani** (1306; *open Mon–Sat 8.15–12.15, 4–6; Sun 9.30–12, 4–6*) lacked the luck of the Cappella Scrovegni and was shattered in an air raid in 1944. What could be salvaged of the frescoes has been painstakingly pieced together—frescoes by Giusto de'Menabuoi and Guariento (his *Story of SS. Augustine, Philip and James* in the second chapel to the right of the altar), and most importantly the magnificent **Ovetari chapel**, begun by Andrea Mantegna in 1454 at the age of 23. Mantegna was a precocious young man: the pupil and adopted son of Squarcione, he took his master/father to court at age 17 for exploiting him. He also found his unique style at an early age, with its remarkable clarity of line and colour and fascination with antiquity— Squarcione had an archaeological collection, but another influence on Mantegna was Padua itself, with its university and Latin letters. Painted 150 years after Giotto, *The Martyrdom of St Christopher and St James* still astonishes, thanks to Mantegna's wizardly use of scientific perspective to foreshorten the action from below and his use of Roman architecture to depict the power of the state—massive, hard, polished and pitiless, populated by remorseless, indifferent men.

Padua's oldest church, the 9th-century **Santa Sofia**, is to the east, at the corner of Via S. Sofia and Via Altinate; much rebuilt in the 11th century, it has a lovely Veneto-Byzantine apse and a precious polychrome *Pietà* (1430) by Egidio da Wienerneustadt. The quarter to the west of the Ermitani, Borgo Molino, was once an 'island' cut off by the Bacchiglione. Its centrepiece, the **Carmine** church, was rebuilt as the headquarters of a confraternity by Lorenzo da Bologna in 1494. Although it was heavily damaged in the air raids, the shells somehow missed the Sacristy and **Scuola del Carmine** (1377), with its interior covered by elegant *cinquecento* frescoes by Domenico Campagnola and Stefano dall'Arzere. Near here, just off Piazza Petrarca, the **Porta di Ponte Molino** and Torre di Ezzelino are leftovers from the 13th-century walls.

To Caffè Pedrocchi and the University

A short walk south from the Eremitani leads into Piazza Garibaldi, site of Padua's oldest surviving gate, **Porta Altinate**, 'captured from Ezzelino da Romano in 1256' as the plaque boasts. The streets all around, however, were torn up in 1926 to create big squares for big buildings flaunting the might of the Corporate State. A whole neighbourhood, Borgo Santa Lucia, was bulldozed to create **Piazza Insurrezione**, sparing the **Scuola di San Rocco** (1525; *open 9.30–12.30, 3.30–7.30, closed Mon; adm*) which, like the one in Venice, was built by a confraternity focused on plague prevention. Domenico Campagnola and Gualtiero Padovano frescoed it in 1537, although their work seems stale after Tintoretto's fireworks in Venice. Behind the Scuola, the church of **Santa Lucia** was also spared; founded in the 11th century, it has a fine painting of *San Luca* by G.B. Tiepolo on the left of the high altar. Via Santa Lucia still has a number of medieval houses; a remarkable one built over Via Marsilio da Padova is remembered as the **Casa di Ezzelino**.

South of Piazza Garibaldi and around the corner from another new square, **Piazza Cavour**, you'll find a stylish Egyptian-revival mausoleum with columned stone porches at either end. This is, in fact, the **Caffè Pedrocchi**, built in 1831 by Giuseppe Jappelli, and famous in its day for never closing (it couldn't—it had no doors) and for the intellectuals and students who came here to debate the revolutionary politics of Mazzini. When restorations are completed, you should be able to get a coffee again, as well as pay a visit the upper floor (*open Tues–Sun 9.30–12.30, 3.30–7, adm*). In Jappelli's adjacent neo-Gothic **Pedrocchino** (built to contain the overflow of clients) students turned words into deeds in 1848, clashing with the Austrian police. Look carefully and you can still see the bullet-scars.

At the far end of the complex, the 16th-century **Municipio** (the former Palazzo Comunale) hides behind an uncomfortable façade of 1904. Opposite is the seat of the **University of Padua**, Andrea Moroni's 16th-century **Palazzo del Bo'** ('of the ox', a nickname derived from the sign of a tavern that stood on this site in 1221) (*guided tours Mar–Sept, Tues, Thurs 9, 10, 11; Wed, Tues, Fri 3, 4, 5; adm*). The façade, attributed to Vincenzo Scamozzi, opens up to a handsome 16th-century courtyard. Galileo delivered his lectures on physics from an old wooden pulpit, which is still intact, and counted among his students Sweden's Gustavus Adolphus, who went on to mastermind the Protestant victories in the Thirty Years War. The golden Great Hall is covered with the armorial devices of its alumni; the steep claustrophobic **Anatomical Theatre** (1594) was the first permanent one anywhere. It was designed by Fabricius, tutor of William Harvey who went on to discover the circulation of blood—only one of scores of Renaissance Englishmen who earned degrees at Padua's School of Medicine. Other professors included Vesalius, author of the first original work on anatomy since Galen (1555), and Gabriello Fallopio, discoverer of the Fallopian tubes.

Before continuing to the Palazzo del Ragione, duck around the corner of the University to have a look at **Piazza Antenore**, with a pair of sarcophagi for a centrepiece. The one on columns supposedly contains what remains of Antenor, hero of the Trojan War and founder of ancient *Patavium*; the body was discovered in 1274, although modern scholars have had a peek and say Antenor was really a soldier from the 3rd century AD. The great Roman historian Livy was a son of the nearby Euganean hills, and the other sarcophagus commemorates his 2,000th birthday. Perhaps he'll get something nicer for his 3,000th.

The Medieval Civic Centre

Directly behind the Municipio (*see* above), the delightful medieval **Piazza delle Erbe** and **Piazza della Frutta** still host a bustling market every morning, divided by the massive, arcaded **Palazzo della Ragione** (*open 9–6, closed Mon; adm*). Constructed as Padua's law courts in 1218 and then rebuilt in 1306, its upper story or *Salone* is one of the largest medieval halls in existence, measuring 260 by 88ft, with an 85ft ceiling like a 'vaulting over a market square', as Goethe described it. Its great hull-shaped roof was rebuilt after a fire in 1756—an earlier blaze, in 1420, destroyed most of the frescoes by Giotto and his assistants, although some *Virtues* by de'Menabuoi survived. The rest were replaced with over 300 biblical and astrological scenes by Niccolò Miretto—one of the Renaissance's most important glorifications of astrology, which had had its own renaissance in the 13th century under Ezzelino's chief advisor and uncannily accurate astrologer, Guido Bonatto. Many of the later popes had astrologers; Petrarch roundly condemned them. Exhibitions are frequently staged under the eyes of Mars and Jupiter, but two exhibits never change: the *pietra del vituperio*, a cold stone block where the bankrupt had to sit bare-bottomed during three public meetings to absolve their debts, and a giant **wooden horse**, built for a joust in 1466, its fierce glance complemented by testicles the size of bowling balls.

Just to the west, the stately **Piazza dei Signori** saw many a joust in its day, and can boast Italy's oldest astronomical clock, built by Giovanni Dondi in 1344 and still ticking away, set in the tower of the **Palazzo del Capitaniato**. On the left is the fine Renaissance-style **Loggia della Gran Guardia** (or del Consiglio), completed by Giovanni Maria Falconetto in 1523; while behind Dondi's clock you'll find Padua University's Arts Faculty, the **Liviano**, built in 1939 by Gio Ponti. Ponti incorporated the upper floor of the old Da Carrara palace in the Liviano, with its remarkable **Sala dei Giganti** (*open Sept–June, Wed only, 9.30–12.30 and 3–6*), named after its huge 14th-century frescoes of ancient Romans and repainted by Domenico Campagnola in the 1530s; Altichiero added the more intimate 14th-century portrait of Petrarch sitting at his desk.

The Duomo and Baptistry

Around the corner from the square stands Padua's rather neglected **Duomo**, begun in the 12th century, but tampered with throughout the Renaissance—Michelangelo was only one of several cooks who spoiled the broth here before everyone lost interest and left the façade unfinished. The interior is neoclassical and serene, and the most memorable art is new, along the altar, where the smooth white figures of saints and trees melt into the stairs. In the 1370s Giusto de'Menabuoi frescoed the adjacent Romanesque **Baptistry** (*open 9.30–1 and 3–6; adm*), with over a hundred scenes; the dome, with its multitude of saints seated in the circles of paradise, is awesome but chilling.

The 15th-century bishop's palace to the left of the cathedral contains the **Pinacoteca dei Canonici** (entrance at Via Dietro Duomo 15) with portraits of the bishops by Bartolomeo

Mantagnana; a portrait of Petrarch, probably from life, was transferred here from the house he lived in while he served as a canon (*open only by appointment,* © *049 662 814*). Stroll down Via del Vescovado, one of Padua's most characteristic porticoed streets; among the palazzi, No.32, the **Casa degli Specchi** (1502), is especially handsome.

Saint Anthony: the Hammer of Heretics, and Much Much More

The sea obeys and fetters break
And lifeless limbs thou dost restore
While treasures lost are found again
When young or old thine aid implore.

13th-century Responsory of St Anthony

One of the busiest and most beloved of heavenly intercessors, Patron Saint of the Poor and a Doctor of the Church, Anthony of Padua was born in Portugal in 1195 (making him 13 years younger than St Francis). The son of a prominent family, he was baptised with the name Fernando Bulhom, and joined the Augustinians in Lisbon at the age of 15. Two years later he was sent to the monastery at Coimbra, where he studied theology for nine years.

In 1221 a band of Franciscan friars arrived in Portugal with the bodies of five of their comrades martyred in Morocco. This made a tremendous impression on the young monk; he at once went to the Franciscans and offered to join up if they would send him to Africa to evangelize and earn a martyr's crown. They accepted him, gave him the name Anthony and, as promised, took him back to Africa with them.

His dreams of martyrdom, however, were never to be. Anthony fell ill almost immediately and was sent home, although he never made it; his ship was blown wildly off course and wrecked on the coast of Sicily. He eventually found his way north to Padua, where he hoped to live a life of quiet contemplation. But his fate was in other hands, and took him to an ordination of Dominican and Franciscan priests in Forlì (although whether or not he himself was ordained as well is unclear). As the new priests dined together, it was suggested that someone give a sermon. Everyone turned shy and ducked, until Anthony, whom everyone presumed was uneducated, was coaxed into saying a few simple words. He began humbly enough, but as he spoke, his voice took on such tremendous power that the friars were convinced that the Holy Spirit had inspired his words.

Now revealed as a talented and well-educated preacher, Anthony was encouraged to abandon his hermit's existence. He became celebrated, not only for his words and conviction, but for practising what he preached. Not everyone was impressed; one day, when his listeners walked away bored, he preached to the fish in the river, who poked their heads out to hear his words. People, according to the chronicles, paid more attention after that.

Anthony travelled extensively to the towns of Northern Italy and France where the Albigensian heresy was the strongest; rather than condemning the heretics, he preached persuasively about Christian goodness, gentleness and justice. He was so successful in bringing the stray sheep back to the fold that he became known as 'the Hammer of Heretics', although 'Coaxer' might seem more apt. His miracles multiplied. To convince one doubter who challenged him, he had a mule kneel down before the Sacrament. He reattached a foot severed from a leg, and on a couple of occasions was even said to bring the dead back to life. Once when someone absconded with his favourite psalter, Anthony prayed that he would find the book again, and the thief at once brought it back. To this day he is famous for finding things; devotees who feel close to him often pray: 'Tony, Tony, turn around. Something's lost and must be found.'

Although at first cautious about his highly educated follower, fearing the pride of the sophisticated theologian, St Francis asked Anthony in 1224 to travel to his communities to instruct his friars in the gospel 'provided that in such studies they do not destroy the spirit of holy prayer and devotedness, as contained in the Rule'. He became the first Franciscan teacher, and chief superior of the order in Northern Italy. He met Pope Gregory IX in 1228 and preached, memorably; it was 'as if the miracle of the Pentecost was repeated.'

Back in Padua in 1230, the saint preached his last and most famous Lenten sermons. The crowds were so great—as many as 30,000 would show up to hear him—that Anthony would preach in the piazzas or the open fields, or even from the boughs of a walnut tree. A bodyguard was required to protect him from the people who wanted to snip or tear off a piece of his habit as a holy relic. He spent days fasting and hearing confessions, and died, exhausted, on June 13 1231. He was only 36.

Anthony was buried in a small Franciscan chapel, where his tomb at once became a centre of pilgrimages and miracles. The bishop of Padua petitioned the Holy See to canonize him, which it did on May 30 1232—an ecclesiastical speed record, which soon led to his nickname: in Padua Anthony isn't merely a saint, he is *The* Saint, Il Santo.

Basilica di Sant'Antonio

Open daily, 6.30am–7pm.

A suitably unique basilica to shelter his mortal remains was begun the year of his death, according to legend, by a friar who accompanied St Francis to Egypt. For pure fantasy it is comparable only to St Mark's: a cluster of seven domes around a lofty, conical cupola, two octagonal *campanili* and two smaller minarets—perhaps not what a monk vowed to poverty might have ordered, but certainly a sign of the esteem in which his devotees held and continue to hold him; even Francis, the patron saint of Italy, doesn't have anything approaching Il Santo's organization. Each year thousands of masses are celebrated in the Basilica, with many more expected for the Millennium; even the 50 father confessors on duty are often hard pressed to keep up with demand.

Inside pilgrims queue patiently in the **Cappella del Santo** to pray, press a palm against his tomb and study the votive testimonials and photos (happy babies, wrecked cars, including insurance-style charts of the collision), proof of The Saint's interventions. One of Anthony's many tasks is running Heaven's Lost Property Office, and he doesn't appreciate insincere petitions; in 1780 William Beckford wrote that he prayed Anthony to relieve him of a crush he had on a young son of the Cornaro family, but was disappointed, and left the basilica a 'frail, infatuated mortal'. With all of the activity surrounding the tomb, no one pays much attention to the 16th-century marble reliefs lining St Anthony's chapel, although they are exquisite works of the Venetian Renaissance: the fourth and fifth are by Sansovino, the sixth and seventh by Tullio Lombardo, and the last by Antonio Lombardo. Behind the saint's chapel the **Cappella di Conti** has richly coloured frescoes on the lives of SS. Philip and James by Florentine Giusto de'Menabuoi (1382).

The **high altar**, unfortunately dismantled and rearranged over the centuries, is mostly the work of Donatello (1443–50), crowned by his stone *Deposition*, over bronze statues of the Madonna and six patron saints of Padua and dramatic reliefs of the miracles of St Anthony below, each intricately crowded with figures in architectural perspectives that were to be a strong influence on Mantegna. The magnificent bronze **Paschal Candelabrum** (1519) is the masterpiece of Il Riccio, who spent nine years on the project. Although this work was designed for Easter, Christianity takes a back seat to the myriad satyrs, nymphs and other mythological creatures shown in relief, immersed in imaginative decorative motifs. Earlier in his career, Il Riccio helped his master Belluno (one of Donatello's assistants) cast the 12 bronze reliefs of Old Testament scenes on the choir walls. To the left of the altar, at the beginning of the ambulatory, note the **De Marchetti tomb** by Giovanni Comini (1690), an excellent example of the Hallowe'en-style tombs that were the rage in the baroque era—here a bust of dead man on a stack of books is topped by a skeleton blasting away on the trump of doom.

Behind the high altar, in the ambulatory, don't miss the **Treasury** where one of a hundred glittering gold reliquaries holds the tongue and larynx of Il Santo, found perfectly intact when his tomb was opened in 1981, the 750th anniversary of his death. In the right transept, the **Cappella di San Felice** contains

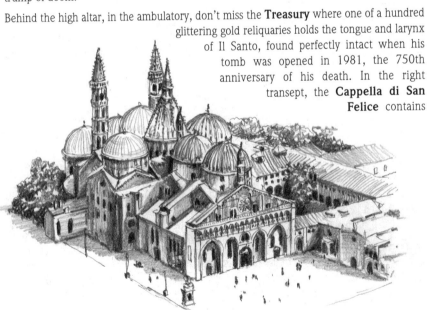

more beautiful frescoes and a remarkable *Crucifixion*, painted in the 1380s by Altichiero, the leading Giottoesque artist of the day. The basilica complex, big enough to require its own information office, includes several other exhibitions and museums in its cloisters. There's a free audio-visual (in Italian) on the saint's life, while the **Museo Antoniano** (*open 9–1 and 2–5, closed Mon; adm*) contains art made for the basilica over the centuries, including a lunette frescoed by Mantegna and a delightful 15th-century German reliquary in the shape of a ship.

Sharing the large piazza in front of the basilica, a bit lost among the pigeons and exuberant souvenir stands, is one of the key works of the Renaissance, Donatello's **Statue of Gattamelata** (1453), the first large equestrian bronze since antiquity and Padua's answer to Rome's Marcus Aurelius. The cool 'Honeyed Cat' was a *condottiere* who served Venice so well and honestly that the republic, in a rare moment of generosity, paid for this monument, which Donatello infused with a serene humanistic spirit, in marked contrast to Verrocchio's Colleoni statue in Venice. As a yardstick of taste, it is interesting to note that only 50 years after its completion the horse was being criticized for its realistic detail.

Flanking the piazza opposite Gattamelata, the **Oratorio di San Giorgio** (*closed for restoration*) was built in 1377, and beautifully frescoed by one of the leading heirs of Giotto, Altichiero of Verona, with help from Jacopo Avanzi. Until it reopens you can, however, visit the adjacent **Scuoletta del Santo**, an old confraternity with paintings on the *Life of St Anthony* by a variety of artists, some of which are winningly absurd; four, certainly not the best, are attributed to a teenage Titian (*open summer 9–1, 2.30–6.30, winter 10–1, 2–5, closed Mon; adm*).

Behind the basilica, on Via Cesarotti, the **Loggia and Odeo Cornaro** (1524 and 1530) are two Renaissance gems designed by Giovanni Maria Falconetto of Verona, whose refined use of ancient architectural orders exerted a major influence on Palladio. Built in the gardens of the humanist Alvise Cornaro (*see* pp.146–7), the Odeo was used for concerts and is decorated inside with exquisite stuccoes, while the Loggia saw performances of the plays of Ruzante (Angelo Beolco; *c.* 1496–1542), the Paduan dramatist who invented and played the role of Ruzante, 'the Joker', a satirically-minded peasant faced with one catastrophe after another; some of his works prefigure the *commedia dell'arte*.

Botanical Gardens, Europe's Biggest Square and La Specola

A few streets south of the Piazza del Santo, the **Orto Botanico** (*open April–Sept, Mon–Sat 9–1 and 3–6; Oct–Mar 9–1; adm*) is one of Europe's oldest botanical gardens, established in 1545; it retains the original layout, and even a few original specimens. At 'Goethe's palm', planted in 1585 and still flourishing, the great poet-scientist speculated on his Theory of the Ur-plant, that all plants evolved from one universal specimen.

Beyond, 'the largest piazza on the continent', **Prato della Valle**, was a swampy meadow converted into a square with a moat by the city's Venetian *procuratore* Andrea Memmo in 1775 to give Padua a new commercial centre. Today it does service as a municipal car park, flea market, amusement park and 'theatre of acting statues' for 79 illustrious men associated with Padua (and one woman, the Renaissance poet Gaspara Stampa, who gets a bust at the foot of Il Riccio). One statue, of Alberto Azzo II, was erected by an outsider—the brother of King George III, in honour of their illustrious ancestor from Este (*see* p.174); the tourist office publishes a booklet in English giving the biography of each worthy.

On one side stands the 393ft **Basilica of Santa Giustina**, the 11th-largest church in all Christendom (*open daily, 7.30–12, 3.30–7.30*), designed by Il Riccio with an exotic cluster of domes echoing St Antony's, but the façade is unfinished and the interior stillborn baroque: best bits are an altarpiece by Sebastiano Ricci in the second chapel on the left, the apse painting of the *Martyrdom of Santa Giustina* (1575) by Veronese and the 16th-century choir stalls. The left transept has a beautiful 14th-century tomb, the *Arca di S. Luca*, with alabaster reliefs made in Pisa. A door in the right transept leads to the original church, the 5th-century **Sacellum di San Prosdocimo**, burial place of Padua's first bishop, with a marble iconostasis; remains of the other previous churches lie beyond the monastery gate.

West of the basilicas, in Piazza Castello, Ezzelino da Romano rebuilt a castle in the medieval walls, now used as Padua's hoosegow. The tallest and oldest bit, the 144ft Torrelunga (1062), has had a rather more dignified career since 1767, when an astronomical observatory, **La Specola**, was added to the roof (*accessible round the back, off Riviera Tiso da Camposampiero; tickets for guided tours sold at Agenzia Next Tour, Via Bomporti 16, © 049 875 4949, on Tues, Wed, Fri 9pm–11pm*). Padua's massive and well-preserved Renaissance **walls**, considered impregnable in their day, were designed by Michele Sammicheli and finished in 1544. A few of the ornate gates, many in white Istrian stone, survive and are perhaps most easily seen from a bike saddle. The best are the **Porta Portello** (1519) to the northeast; the **Porta San Giovanni** and **Porta Savonarola** (1530, by Falconetto) to the west; and **Porta Santa Croce**, to the south.

Activities

Thanks to the students, there's always something happening. The tourist office's bi-monthly publication *Padova Today* lists events; every summer a series of concerts, exhibitions, open-air films and shows takes place around the city. The Prato della Valle sees a large general market every Saturday, and an antique market every third Sunday of the month.

Padua ✉ *35100*   ### Where to Stay

expensive

★★★★ **Donatello**, Via del Santo 102, © 049 875 0634, ✉ 049 8675 0829, by the basilica of Sant'Antonio: you can't miss it, as Donatello's Gattamelata points right to it. The rooms are air-conditioned and recently renovated.

★★★★ **Majestic Toscanelli**, Via dell'Arco 2, © 049 663 244, ✉ 049 876 0025, is also in the historic centre, but newer and more comfortable. It has every luxury, and a popular restaurant, specializing in Brazilian dishes.

★★★★ **Grande Italia**, Corso del Popolo 81, © 049 876 111, ✉ 049 875 0850, is in a beautiful Liberty building, conveniently opposite the railway station.

★★★ **Leon Bianco**, Piazzetta Pedrocchi 12, ✆ 049 875 0814, 🖷 049 875 6184, is small and cosy, right in the heart of Padua; from its roof terrace, where breakfast is served in summer, you can look down on the Caffè Pedrocchi.

★★★ **Al Cason**, Via Paolo Scarpi 40, ✆ 049 66236, 🖷 049 875 4217, friendly, cheaper and near the station, will make you feel at home, and fill you up with the classics in its restaurant.

★★ **Sant'Antonio**, Via S. Fermo 118, ✆ 049 875 1393, 🖷 049 875 2508, between the station and centre by the Porta Molino, has a friendly, family atmosphere.

★★ **Arcella**, Via J. D'Avanzo 7, ✆ 049 605 581, near the station but on the wrong side of the tracks, has friendly owners, limited parking and a/c.

★ **Pavia**, Via del Papafava 11, ✆ 049 661 558, is deservedly popular, clean, central and friendly.

★ **Junior**, Via L. Faggin 2, ✆ 049 811 756, is another ten-minute walk from the station, in the same area. It's homey and has no en suite baths, but easy parking.

The large, pleasant, city-run **Ostello Città di Padova** is at Via Aleardi 30, ✆ 049 875 2219, 🖷 049 654 210; IYHF cards required. To get there take bus 3, 8 or 11 from the station to the Prato della Valle. *Open all year.*

Eating Out

La cucina padovana features what the Italians call 'courtyard meats' (*carni di cortile*)—chicken, duck, turkey, pheasant, capons, goose and pigeon. Pork, rabbit and freshwater fish are other favourites. Try one of the various *risotti* for *primo*.

Antico Brolo, Corso Milano 22, ✆ 049 66455, not far from the historic centre, occupies an elegant 15th-century building, with a garden for outdoor dining on its Veneto and Emilian specialities; try the chateaubriand with balsamic vinegar; tourist menu L50,000. *Closed Mon and Sun lunch, some of Aug.* There's a good pizzeria down in the old wine cellar where you'll spend a lot less.

Dotto di Campagna, Via Randaccio, ✆ 049 625 469, in the suburb of Torre, 2km from the Padua-Est *autostrada* exit, offers elegant surroundings and inventive cookery based on the freshest of ingredients; for a first course try their famous *risotti* or *pasta fagioli*. Tourist menu L38,000. *Closed Sun eve, Mon, Aug.*

Da Giovanni, Via Maroncelli 22, ✆ 049 772 620 (bus 9 from the railway station): the crowds venture here, outside the city walls, for classic Paduan home cooking, featuring succulent boiled and roast meats. The home-made pasta is good, as are the locally raised capons. *Closed Sat lunch, Sun, Aug.*

Bertolini, Via Antichiero 162, ✆ 049 600 357, just north of the station, has been a favourite for 150 years; go for the hearty vegetarian and seasonal dishes and home-made desserts. *Closed Sat.*

Bastioni del Moro, Via Bronzetti 18, ✆ 049 871 006, just outside Padua's western walls (take Corso Milano from the centre) has had a recent facelift and serves up a delicious gnocchi with scallops and porcini mushrooms, indoors or in the summer garden; tourist menu L25,000, although prices soar if you order fish. *Closed Sun.*

Day Trips from Padua

Within an hour of Padua, you'll find medieval walled towns and castles built in the bad old days, along with the lush and lovely Euganean Hills with their spas, vines and villas. And last but hardly least, there's Vicenza in all its Palladian glory, just a hop to the west.

North of Padua

Some of the Veneto's best-known sites are north of Padua, in the charmed foothills of the Dolomites: there's Castelfranco Veneto, birthplace of Giorgione, and some outstanding villas, including Masèr, where Palladio and Veronese collaborated to create a unique work of art.

Getting Around

From **Padua** there are both buses and trains to Castelfranco, Fanzolo, Montebelluna and Cittadella. At **Castelfranco** change trains for Piombino Dese or take a bus for Riese Pio X. Frequent buses from **Montebelluna** serve Masèr (20km); or take a train from Padua for Cornuda railway station (3km from Masèr).

Tourist Information

Castelfranco Veneto: Via Francesco Maria Preti 39, ✆ 0423 495 000.

Piazzola sul Brenta and Piombino Dese: Palladian Villas

North from Padua, there's a choice of villas to see along the way. The SS47 follows the river Brenta to Cittadella, by way of **Piazzola sul Brenta** and the imposing **Villa Contarini** (*open 9–12 and 3–7, mid-Oct–Mar 9–12 and 2–5, closed Mon; adm*). Built in 1414, the villa was greatly enlarged in 1564 by Palladio for Marco Contarini, a Procurator of the Republic; later residents added the 17th-century *barchesse*, adorned with the full whack of Palladian statues and balustrades, on grounds that include an arcaded hemicycle, park and lake. The interior is more elaborate than the average villa as well, featuring special Music and Listening Rooms with excellent acoustics. Villa Contarini had an interesting career in the 19th century, when it was purchased by Silvestro Camerini, who made Piazzola into a model industrial/agricultural estate. One of its main products, jute, was still being processed in the 1960s.

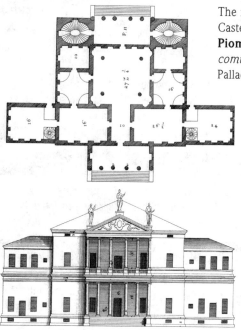

The more easterly SS307 from Padua to Castelfranco Veneto passes near **Piombino Dese**, a sprawling rural *comune*, but a must-see detour for Palladiophiles, for its **Villa Cornaro** of 1553 (*open by appointment only, ✆ 049 936 5017*), a block from the Piombino Dese train station. Built in 1553, this is among Palladio's most monumental and well-preserved villas, where he introduced one of his most original features—the two-storey projecting portico-loggia. It's also the only Palladian villa to preserve much of its original *intocato* cladding and tile floors; another unique feature is the grand Salon, where niches were designed to hold full-length statues of the Cornaro ancestors—a throw-

Villa Cornaro, from Palladio's Four Books of Architecture

back to the ancient Romans, who liked to keep wax models and masks of their forebears around the place. The harmonious interior was only frescoed in 1716 (after the Cornari relocated their famous art collection), when Procurator Andrea Cornaro commissioned 21-year-old Mattia Bortoloni to execute 104 fresco panels in stucco frames, using the newly fashionable 'light manner'. The subjects were carefully chosen by Cornaro, who eschewed the usual mythologies or allegories for scenes from the Old and New Testaments. Not what one expects in a country house, although the Bible may have been merely a vehicle to smuggle in a forbidden Masonic message: the frescos on the eastern wall of the main room especially abound with Masonic symbols.

Castelfranco Veneto and Around

Square, walled **Castelfranco Veneto** was built by Treviso in 1199 to counter the ambitions of Padua, and basks in the glory of having given the world the romantic, enigmatic genius Giorgione, or Zorzon as the locals called him, born here in 1478. Zorzon in gratitude (it seems like a pleasant enough place to have grown up in) left Castelfranco the masterpiece now hanging in the neoclassical **Duomo**: the *Castelfranco Madonna* (1504), a triangular composition of the Virgin, St Francis and the soldier-saint Liberalis, their remote figures inhabiting the same ineffable, dreamlike world as his paintings in the Accademia. The *Castelfranco Madonna* was subject to one of the more spectacular art heists in the 1970s; the thieves' demands for a ransom were repeatedly refused, and the painting was abandoned after a shoot-out with the *carabinieri*.

Next to the Duomo, the **Casa del Giorgione** (*open Tues–Sun, 9–12 and 3–6; adm*) is decorated with a fascinating *chiaroscuro* frieze of scientific instruments and symbols of the liberal and mechanical arts, attributed to Giorgione (who, according to one interpretation of the frieze's allegory, must have been Jewish); it also has photos of all his known works. During Zorzon's brief life Castelfranco built its most elaborate gate, the **Porta di Treviso**, with its clock and Venetian lion (1499). From here Borgo Treviso leads to the charming gardens of 19th-century **Villa Revedin Bolasco** (*open Tues and Thurs 2–5, Sun 10–12.30, 2–5.30*). Just west of Castelfranco, near Castello di Godego, a series of prehistoric earthen walls standing between 6 and 13ft high form a partially visible rhomboid known as the **Motte**; most have been found to have precise astronomical alignments.

After Treviso built Castelfranco, the Paduans founded the egg-shaped **Cittadella** 15km to the west. Its magnificent 13th-century **walls**, surrounded by a moat, are over a mile long and 40ft high; one of the 28 towers, the Torre di Malta, contained Ezzelino's infamous torture chamber ('...no man yet was ever sent to Malta/for treachery as foul as his shall be', *Paradiso* IX, 54). The Venetians added the fine lion with a kinky tail in the main square.

From Castelfranco you can also nip up to **Fanzolo**, 5km to the northeast, for another of Palladio's finest, **Villa Emo**, the only Palladian villa still owned by the family that commissioned it (*open April–Sept 3–7, Sun and hols 10–12.30 and 3–7; Oct–Mar, Sat and Sun only 2–6; adm exp*). Villa Emo has the typical Palladian five-part profile, with dovecotes surmounting the ends of the *barchesse* (now a hotel, *see* below); its temple front, with its tympanum stuccoed by Vittoria, was one of the first to have freestanding columns, not to mention a long ramp that enabled visitors to ride straight up to the door. Unlike many villas, this is still a working farm, and one with a famous pedigree—it was one of the first in Europe to grow maize (1536), used to fatten pigeons before it began to fatten the polenta-mad Venetians. The main rooms have brightly coloured mythologies by Giambattista Zelotti. Palladio also designed the long rows of brick farmworkers' cottages.

Close by, the little village of **Riese Pio X** is named for the Pontiff it produced, Pius X (Giuseppe Sarto, 1835–1914, canonized in 1951), whose home is now a museum. Although his policies were reactionary, he is remembered fondly in the Veneto. The story goes that his housekeeper took to wearing his old stockings, and found that they were not only holey but holy, and miraculously cured her bunions. When she told the pope, he laughed and said, 'They certainly don't do that for me!' Near Riese, **San Vito** has in its cemetery one of the most striking modern tombs in Italy, designed by Venetian architect Carlo Scarpa (1975) for himself and TV baron Giuseppe Brion. And although it's been abandoned since the 1700s, you can also have a look at what remains of the once-fabulous castle and gardens that Venice built in 1490 for Caterina Cornaro—the **Barco della Regina Cornaro**, in **Altìvole**.

Eating Out

Castelfranco Veneto ✉ 31033

Next to the walls, **Alle Mura**, Via Preti 69, ☏ 0423 498 098 (*expensive–moderate*) is an elegant place, with well prepared seafood dishes and a garden. *Closed Thurs.*

Just above Castelfranco, at Salvarosa, you can dine at little old **Ca' delle Rose**, on the Circonvallazione Est, in its famous restaurant, **Barbesin**, ✆ 0423 490 446 (*moderate*). The setting is as idyllic as the products of its kitchen, based entirely on fresh, seasonal ingredients; the veal with apples melts in your mouth. *Closed Wed eve and Thurs.*

In Galliera Vèneto, midway between Castelfrano and Cittadella, a former patrician hunting lodge serves as a setting for **Palazzino**, Via Roma 29, ✆ 0495 969 224 (*expensive–moderate*), a great place to try Renaissance dishes such as pheasant stuffed with truffles, accompanied by vegetables just plucked from the restaurant's garden. *Closed Tues eve, Wed, and Aug.*

Fanzolo ✉ 31050

There's fine dining in the restaurant in Palladio's ★★★**Villa Emo**, Via Stazione 5, ✆ 0423 476 414, 📠 0423 487 043, open to non-guests (*expensive; closed Mon, Tues lunch*).

Montebelluna and il Montello

The Roman *Mons Bellonae*, Montebelluno is proud to be the world capital of ski and hiking boots, celebrated in all their glory in the **Museo dello Scarpone**, located in the Villa Binetti-Zuccareda, one of a score of villas scattered about its hills above Piazza Garibaldi (Vicolo Zuccareda 1, *open 9–12 and 3–6*). Long before ski boots, however, what is now the centre of Montebelluno was an important medieval market; in Piazzetta di Mercato Vecchia, a column erected by the Venetians in 1593 honours the commercial concessions Montebelluno enjoyed from the 9th century until 1872. Another country house, the Villa Biagi, houses the **Museo Civico**, Via Piave 41, (*open Tues–Sun 9–12.30 and 2.30–5.30, summer 3.30–6.30; adm*) with remains of a Paleoveneti necropolis discovered just to the north of Montebelluna.

The **Montello**, the beautiful hilly district between Montebelluno and the Piave, was once the main source of oak timber for Venetian galleys, yet cut so carefully that 6,000 hectares of primordial forest remained intact until the 19th century; in this century about a third of that has been reforested. Because of its strategic location on the Piave, the Montello saw heavy action in the First World War, when Austro-Hungarian shells flattened **Nervesa della Battaglia** and turned its 12th-century **Abbazia di S. Eustachio** (where Giovanni della Casa compiled the first Index of Prohibited Books for the Church, in 1555) into the striking ruins that stand to this day. From Nervesa 'La Panoramica' skirts the top of the hills, farms and villas en route to **Crocetta del Montello**, near Masèr.

Villa Barbaro at Masèr

Open Mar–Oct, Tues, Sat, Sun, hols 3–6; Nov–Feb, Sat, Sun, 2.30–5; adm exp.

This unique synthesis of two great talents, Palladio and Veronese, was created in 1568 for two great patrons, the Barbaro brothers, Daniele (Patriarch of Aquileia and humanistic scholar) and Marcantonio (Venetian ambassador and amateur sculptor). Palladio used the Temple of Fortuna Virilis in Rome as his inspiration for the central residence, while the

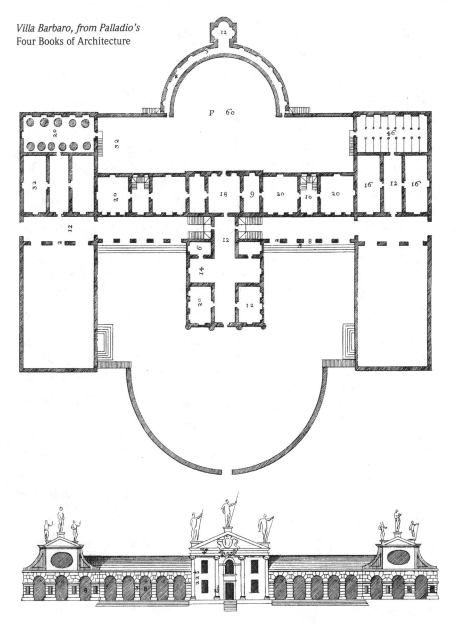

Villa Barbaro, from Palladio's Four Books of Architecture

barchesse are graceful wings with dovecotes rising at the ends, each with a sundial, forming the five-part profile that would inspire countless buildings (including the United States' Capitol). The horses frisking about the front lawn add to the patrician dignity, while the reliefs on the central pediment—the double-headed eagle of Byzantium (Aquileia, in this case) and two men astride dragons or sea monsters, each holding a woman in one arm and touching the horns of a central ox-head—add an air of mystery. Emblems like this were the rage in the Renaissance, full of puns and allegorical references for those in the know (which unfortunately doesn't include us).

Palladio taught Veronese about space and volume, and nowhere is this so evident as in these ravishing, architectonic *trompe-l'œil* frescoes, which repopulate the villa with the original owners and their pets, lingering as if the villa lay under the same spell as Sleeping Beauty's castle—an effect heightened by the slippers passed out to visitors at the door (to protect the original floors). Signora Barbaro and her sons gaze down from painted balconies; a little girl opens a door; a dog waits in a corner; painted windows offer views of imaginary landscapes; the huntsman in the far bedroom is Veronese, gazing across the row of rooms at his mistress. As delightful as these are, one tradition has it that Palladio was miffed that Veronese's *trompe-l'œil* detracted from the appreciation of the harmonic proportions of his rooms, and he punished the painter by completely snubbing him in the *Quattro Libri*. True or not, it's hard to disagree with Sir Henry Wotton, England's ambassador to Venice, who visited the Barbari and wrote admiringly that no house could be 'more artificial and delicious'. The back garden is taken up with a nymphaeum, guarded by giants sculpted by Marcantonio Barbaro. The striking, if crumbling, **Tempietto**, just across the road, is a miniature Barbaro pantheon designed by Palladio in 1580, inspired by his favourite Renaissance building, Bramante's Tempietto in Rome, and decorated with statues by Alessandro Vittoria and Orazio Marinali.

Other villas dot the road between Masèr and Àsolo, including the 17th-century **Villa Rinaldi**, a grand baroque stage set. Or there's a longer, enchanting route up through the **Forcella Mostaccin** (take the road into the mountains just south of Villa Barbaro). If you find yourself in these parts on 21 March, you can witness a curious old purification rite: the Trial of the Old Year ('*La Vecia*'), in which the past year is made to answer for all the ills that happened, in an Inquisition-style interrogation, and burned at the stake. **Masèr-Muliperte**, **Quinto di Treviso** and **Cavaso del Tomba** are the venues, and if their calendars seem out of whack, it's because the spring equinox was New Year's Day under the Serenissima.

Eating Out

Montebelluna ✉ 31044

Just south on the road to Barcon is the superb **Enoteca Marchi**, Via Castellana 177, ✆ 0423 303 530 (*expensive*), with an excellent wine list and great asparagus, duck and other Veneto favourites as well. *Closed Tues eve, Wed, and part of Aug.*

Masèr and Around ✉ 31010

Just up the road from Palladio's villa, dine in enchanting surroundings at **Da Bastian**, Via Cornuda, ✆ 0423 565 400 (*moderate*), where the pâté, risotto, Venetian-style snails and desserts are renowned. *Closed Wed eve and Thurs, some of Aug.*

Just north, in Cavaso del Tomba, you can also dine memorably at the romantic **Al Ringranziamento**, Via S. Pio X 107, ✆ 0423 543 271 (*expensive–moderate*) where the creative chef is a master at concocting delicious dishes: some you won't see anywhere else in the Veneto. *Closed Mon, Tues lunch, some of Aug.*

South of Padua

The landscape south of Padua is as flat as any of the pancake prairies of the Po, with the exception of the lush Euganean hills: a retreat of poets and the world-weary since Roman times, dotted with villas, spas, trails and country restaurants where Paduans head on Sundays. South of the hills you'll find a handsome trio of medieval towns, Monsélice, Este and Montagnana, all 'with pasts', as people used to say of women who dared to have fun.

Getting Around

The spas and towns in the **Euganean Hills** are easily reached from Padua by **bus**, or by **train** (to Terme Euganee). There are also regular **trains** from Padua to Monsélice (23km), Este (32km) and Montagnana (52km), which take about the same time as the buses, although you may have to change trains at Monsélice. Buses from Monsélice go to Arquà Petrarca (10km).

Tourist Information

Ábano Terme: Via Pietro d'Abano 18, ✆ 049 866 9055, ✆ 049 866 9053.
Montegrotto Terme: Viale della Stazione 60, ✆ 049 793 384, ✆ 049 795 276.
Monsélice: Piazza Mazzini, ✆ 042 972 380.
Este: Piazza Maggiore, ✆ 042 93635 (with bikes to hire).
Montagnana: Piazza V. Emanuele, ✆ 044 298 1320.

The Euganean Hills and Around

As soon as you leave Padua you'll spot them: the Euganean Hills or *Colli Euganei*, ancient volcanic islands, once surrounded by sea and now basking in the middle of the Veneto plain. Fertile, well watered by springs and defensible, they were settled early on in the Bronze Age by the Paleoveneti, who made Este their chief stronghold. Centuries later the Romans discovered the two key secrets of the Euganean Hills: wine (now *DOC Colli Euganei*) and hot mud. Livy, Suetonius and Martial all recommended the virtues of their hot mineral springs, which flow from the ground at 87°C, and they have been appreciated ever since: some 130 hotels built over thermal swimming pools provide health or beauty cures at **Ábano Terme** (from *Aponeus*, the Roman god of healing) and **Montegrotto Terme** (ancient *Mons Aegratorum*, 'mountain of the ill'), where the old Roman spa has been excavated. Children love Montegrotto's live butterfly zoo, the **Butterfly Arc**, with colourful species from around the world (*open April–Aug 9–12.30 and 2.30–5.30; adm*). In the same area, at Luvigliano near **Torréglia**, the vast **Villa dei Vescovi** (*open

Mar–Nov, Mon, Wed and Fri 10.30–12.30 and 2–6; adm), was designed by Giovanni Maria Falconetto (1579) for holidaying bishops: the interior has fine stuccoes, and the church houses a fine *Pala di San Martino* (1527) by Girolamo Santacroce of Bergamo.

From Torréglia, there's a road west to **Teolo**, Livy's birthplace. Here the **Museo di Arte Contemporanea** (*open daily exc Sat, 3–7*) in the Palazzetto dei Vicari was founded in honour of international art critic Dino Formaggio and houses works from many of Italy's finest living artists. Because of their unusual microclimate the Euganean hills are rich in flora, with over a thousand species, protected since 1989 under the auspices of a regional park. In Teolo you can join a 42km circular nature trail around the district or head north to visit the venerable Benedictine **Abbazia di Praglia** (*tours every half hour, 2.30–4.30 winter, 3.30–5.30 summer, closed Mon*), founded in 1117 but given the full Renaissance treatment, with a church by Tullio Lombardo and paintings by Bartolomeo Montagna, Giambattista Zelotti and others. The monks are famous for restoring old manuscripts and singing a mean Gregorian chant.

South of Torréglia, **Valsanzibio** was once the property of the Scrovegni money-bags and still maintains a quiet air of wealth, with an 18-hole golf course and the magnificent park and gardens at the **Villa Barbarigo** (*open 9–12, 2–7.30, until sunset in winter; adm exp*). Set in an enclosed valley, these are the grandest in the Veneto, laid out in the mid-1600s in the style of a Roman water garden (as at Tivoli) with fountains, waterfalls, nymphaea, pools, fishponds, and a domed rabbits' island; it also has one of Italy's finest garden mazes, as devilish to get through as the one at Stra.

Arquà Petrarca

Beyond Valsanzibio lies **Arquà Petrarca**, a jewel of hilltown in a lovely setting. In 1370, the world-weary Petrarch chose Arquà as his last home, accompanied by his daughter Francesca and her husband, and his stuffed cat, Laura II. His charming villa, the **Casa del Petrarca** (*open 9–12.30, 3–7; adm*), preserves much of its 14th-century structure and furnishings. Petrarch was *the* artsy trendsetter of the Middle Ages; his presence in Arquà attracted wealthy families from Padua and Venice, who built summer houses in the village—the first example of the lust for *villeggiatura* that would so transform the Veneto landscape over the next four centuries.

The house itself went through a number of owners, one of whom in the 16th century added delightful frescoes illustrating the sonnets (Petrarch chasing a goose, Petrarch being splashed...). With the exception of a radio mast, the view from the poet's study remains the same as it was over 600 years ago, and it isn't hard to imagine the plump old poet laureate sitting there, writing his *Letter to Posterity*, describing his life and career in some detail (he complains at having to wear spectacles after his 60th birthday). Famous signatures in the visitor's book are on display—Byron and his *contessa*, Teresa Guiccioli, came in 1818. Petrarch died here in 1374, while reading a book, and now occupies a huge Verona red marble sarcophagus in front of the church.

The fourth spa town in the Euganean Hills, **Battaglia Terme**, back on the SS16, is also a small industrial centre, with a severe villa-castle, **Il Catajo** (1570), the citadel of Venice's *condottiere* Pio Enea I degli Olbizzi. Sumptuous on the inside, with lively frescoes by

Giambattista Zelotti, it has an English garden with a charming elephant fountain; you can even hire it out for a party (© *049 526 541, otherwise open 15 Feb–Nov, Tues and Sun 2.30–6.30; adm*). East of Battaglia, two medieval Carrara properties merged to form a single *comune*, **Due Carrare**. The family citadel, **Castello di San Pelagio**, has a sumptuous interior and now a **Museo dell'Aria** (*open Tues–Sun 9–12.30, 2–6; summer 2.30–7; adm exp*) with exhibits dedicated to air travel, from mythology to space exploration. Carrara Santo Stefano is built around the Benedictine **Abbazia di Santo Stefano**, founded in 1027. Although the abbey was demolished in 1793 the church remains, with its beautiful 11th-century mosaic pavement and 14th-century marble tomb of Marsilio da Carrara (*open Sat 9–12, Sun 2–5, or by ringing ahead,* © *049 911 5027*).

Eating Out

Torréglia ✉ 35038

In nearby Torréglia, join the hungry Paduans at their favourite country restaurants: **Da Taparo**, Via Castelletto 42, © 049 521 1060 (*moderate*) with a beautiful terrace overlooking the hills to match its delicious Veneto cuisine (*closed Mon*); or **Antica Trattoria Ballotta**, Via Carromatto 2, © 049 521 2970, ✆ 049 521 1385 (*moderate*), in business since 1605 and one of the oldest in Venetia, with fine dining inside or in the garden; or the panoramic **Rifugio Monte Rua**, Via Mone Rua 29, © 049 521 1049 (*moderate*), where dishes change according to season. *Both closed Tues.*

Arquà Petrarca ✉ 35032

Near the centre of Arquà, at **La Montanella**, Via Costa 33, © 0429 718 200 (*expensive–moderate*), you can enjoy not only the garden and views, but exquisite *risotti* and duck with fruit; select your wine, olive oil and vinegar from special menus. *Closed Tues eve, Wed, 2 weeks each in Aug and Jan.*

Monsélice, Este and Montagnana

Spilling like an opera set down the southern slopes of the Euganean Hills, the natural citadel of **Monsélice** (*Mons silicis*) was first fortified by the Romans. In its heyday it bristled with five rings of walls and 30 towers, built in 1239 by Ezzelino da Romano to control the road between Padua and Este. Most of the walls fell victim to medieval Italy's biggest enemy—19th-century town planners. Nevertheless, the core of the citadel, Ezzelino's Ca' Marcello, was bought up in the early 1900s when it was on its last legs by industrialist and art patron Count Vittorio Cini, who beautifully restored it. Now part of the **Castello Cini** (*open April–11 Nov, guided tours at 9, 10, 11 and 2, 3, 4; summer 3, 4, 5; adm*), it houses the count's superb collection of medieval and Renaissance arms and antiques, and, they say, the ghost of Ezzelino's lover Avalda, who died here after a 17-year imprisonment.

The castle lies near the base of Vincenzo Scamozzi's striking **Via Sacra delle Sette Chiese** (1605), zigzagging up the hill passing the sumptuous **Villa Nani**, the Romanesque **Duomo** and seven **chapels** built by Scamozzi and frescoed by Palma Giovane (a miniature version of the Seven Churches of Rome, offering proportionately smaller indulgences). Near the top of the Via Sacra the elegant 16th-century **Villa Duodo and Esedra di San Francesco Saverio**, also by Scamozzi, is now a university centre of hydraulic studies. A path continues up to the **Rocca**, built by Frederick II, Ezzelino's boss, over a Lombard fort (*open Sat and Sun, book, © 042 972 931*). Just north of Monsélice in **Rivella**, the late *cinquecento* **Villa Selvatico-Capodilista** has an elegant, romantic garden designed by Jappelli in 1816. *Open April and October, Thurs–Sat 2–5, Sun 10–7.*

Monsélice's old rival, **Este** (ancient *Ateste*) is only 9km to the west. This was the capital of the Paleoveneti and, 2,000 years later, of the powerful 11th-century Lombard lord, Marquess Alberto Azzo II, whose son Guelfo IV became Duke of Bavaria, and whose later descendants included the Electors of Hanover and George I of England (Queen Victoria was proud to say her roots went back to Este); another branch of the family, famous as art patrons in the Renaissance, moved on to Ferrara. Like Monsélice, medieval Este was hotly contested real estate, and bristles with the towers of the **Castello dei Carraresi**, built by the lords of Padua in 1339 and now put out to pasture in a public garden.

Abutting the garden, the 16th-century Palazzo Mocenigo houses the excellent **Museo Nazionale Atestino** (*open 9–7, adm*), its frescoed ceilings gazing down at artefacts from the first Veneto civilization in the 10th century BC up to Roman times: don't miss the vigorous 9th-century BC rams' heads; the 7th-century BC *Situla Benvenuti*, a bronze vase decorated with warriors and fantastic animals; a superb collection of 6th–5th-century BC bronzes of warriors and horsemen; inscriptions in ancient Venetic, using the Etruscan alphabet; a rare gold medal issued by Augustus; and, a bit out of place, a luscious red-dressed *Madonna and Child* by Cima da Conegliano. Other highlights are the startlingly tilted 12th-century campanile of **San Martino**, the two grand clock towers in **Piazza Maggiore**, and Giambattista Tiepolo's altarpiece of *Santa Tecla vs. the Plague* in the **Duomo**. Behind the castle **Villa De Kunkler** was Byron's residence in 1817–18; here Shelley, his guest, wrote 'Lines Written among the Euganean Hills' after the death of his little daughter Clara:

> *Many a green isle needs must be*
> *In the deep wide sea of Misery,*
> *Or the mariner, worn and wan,*
> *Never thus could voyage on...*

Montagnana, 15km west, boasts some of the best-preserved medieval fortifications in Italy, the handiwork of Ezzelino da Romano and the Carrara family. The walls extend for two kilometres, defended by 24 intact towers—impressive but not effective; Venice lost and regained the town 13 times during the War of the Cambrai alone. Every September the walls form a picturesque backdrop to Montagnana's colourful Palio, inaugurated in 1259 to celebrate the liberation of the city from Ezzelino. Jutting out asymmetrically in the main piazza, the **Duomo** has a portal by Sansovino, a *Transfiguration* by Veronese, and a huge, anonymous painting of *The Battle of Lepanto*, to which the town contributed so generously with men and money that the Venetians paved the piazza in gratitude. The **Museo Civico A. Giacomelli** (*open Wed–Fri 10.30–12.30, Sat and Sun 10.30–1 and 3.30–6*), in the recently restored 12th-century **Castello di San Zeno**, has exhibits ranging from relics of prehistoric times to a whole room devoted to two native tenors, Giovanni Marinelli and Aureliano Pertile. Palladio mavens won't want to miss his **Palazzo Pisani**, by the Porto Padova.

Eating Out

Monsélice ✉ 35043

Modern **★★★Ceffri Villa Corner**, Via Orti 7, ✆ 0429 783 111, 📠 0429 783 100 (*moderate*) has a good restaurant featuring home-made pasta with a L30,000 tourist menu; fungi fiends head to elegant **La Torre**, Piazza Mazzini 14, ✆ 0429 73752 (*moderate, expensive* for truffles) for gratification. *Closed Sun eve, Mon, and part of July and Aug.*

Montagnana ✉ 35044

★★★Aldo Moro, Via G. Marconi 27, ✆ 0429 81351, 📠 0429 82842 (*moderate*) has fine rooms beside the Duomo, and a good restaurant serving the famous local *prosciutto dolce del montagnanese*, alone, with melon, or in a risotto. For lunch or dinner, find **Da Stona**, Via Carrarese 51, ✆ 0429 81532 (*inexpensive*), an excellent trattoria with tasty homecooking, *pasta e fagioli, prosciutto dolce*, and a good local wine list; tourist menu L19,000. *Closed Mon.*

Vicenza

'The city of Palladio', prettily situated below the Monti Bérici, is an architectural pilgrimage shrine and knows it. Where other Italians grouse about being a nation of museum curators, the Vicentini glory in it: Vicenza, after all, is the best example of what a gentry immersed in humanistic thought and classical philosophy could achieve in bricks and mortar. Their pride in their unique city was recently vindicated when UNESCO placed Vicenza on its list of World Heritage Sites.

History

A Paleoveneto centre, Vicenza was made a Roman *municipium* in the year 49 BC, and later suffered, like all the towns in the region, invasions by the Eruli, Ostrogoths, Visigoths and the Lombards, who made the town one of their 36 duchies. Later ruled by count-bishops, Vicenza became a free *comune* in 1164, although it wasn't strong enough to fight the neighbourhood bullies—the Da Carrara of Padua, the Scaligers of Verona and the Visconti of Milan. On 28 April 1404 the city offered herself on a platter to Venice, which wasn't one to look a gift horse in the mouth.

Under the Republic, the splendour of Vicenza's architecture earned it the nickname 'the Venice of the *Terra Firma*'. The works by Palladio and his followers drew an impressive list of visitors—among them Montaigne, Inigo Jones, Montesquieu and De Brosses; Goethe wrote that he could easily spend 'a month, following a course of lessons on architecture with old Scamozzi'. During the Second World War, air raids severely damaged the old town centre; restorers repaired all the major monuments and now, in a second wave, are

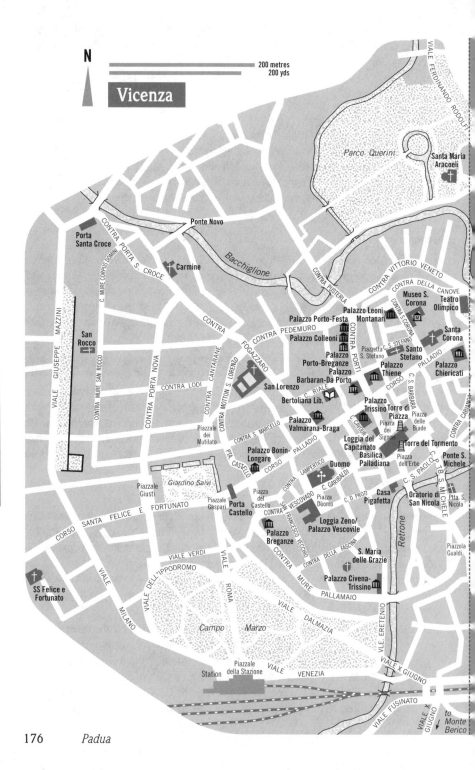

N

200 metres
200 yds

Vicenza

Santa Maria Aracoeli

Parco Querini

Ponte Novo

Porta Santa Croce

Bacchiglione

Carmine

San Rocco

Museo S. Corona
Teatro Olimpico

Palazzo Leoni-Montanari
Palazzo Porto-Festa
Palazzo Colleoni
Santa Corona
Palazzo Porto-Breganze
Palazzo Barbaran-Da Porto
Santo Stefano
Palazzo Thiene
Palazzo Chiericati
San Lorenzo
Bertoliana Lib.
Palazzo Trissino
Torre di Piazza
Piazza delle Biade
Palazzo Valmarana-Braga
Piazza dei Signori
Palazzo Bonin-Longare
Loggia del Capitanato
Torre del Tormento
Basilica Palladiana
Ponte S. Michele
Duomo
Piazza dell'Erbe
Piazzale dei Mutilato

Piazzale Giusti

Giardino Salvi

Casa Pigafetta
Oratorio di San Nicola

Piazzale Gaspari
Porta Castello
Piazza del Castello
Piazza Duomo

Loggia Zeno/ Palazzo Vescovile
Palazzo Breganze
S. Maria delle Grazie
Retrone
Piazzola Gualdi

SS Felice e Fortunato
Palazzo Civena-Trissino

Campo Marzo

Station
Piazzale della Stazione

to Monte Berico

aiming at 'minor' buildings, for these days the rouble rolls in Vicenza. The city (pop. 108,000) one of Italy's wealthiest, promotes itself as the *Città d'Oro*, thanks to its 800 gold-working firms (producing half of all Italy's goldwork); it was the birthplace of the inventor of the silicon chip, Federico Faggin, and produces machine tools, textiles, ceramics and shoes.

Getting There

Vicenza is on the main **rail** line between Verona (45mins) and Padua (35mins) and Venice (1hr). The station is on the south side of the town, at the end of Viale Roma. The FTV **bus station**, ✆ 0444 223 115, is alongside it: buses depart from here for Maròstica and other destinations in the region. You can rent a **bike** at the train station's *deposito bagagli*—part of the deal includes a free map with bike routes.

Leave your car in one of the two attended car parks, one at the west end of the town by the Mercato Ortofrutticolo and the other to the east by the stadium. Both are linked to the centre by special bus service every five minutes.

Tourist Information

Piazza Matteotti, 12; also Piazza Duomo 5, ✆ 0444 320 854, ✉ 0444 325 001.

Porta Castello to the Piazza dei Signori

The Viale Roma, the main road up from the station, enters the city proper through the **Porta Castello**, with its powerful 11th-century tower. It also has one of the most startling palaces in Vicenza: the **Palazzo Breganze**, designed by Palladio and partly built by his pupil Scamozzi before the monumentality of the design defeated him, leaving only two bays framed by three Corinthian columns the size of sequoias. Scamozzi also built the less exciting **Palazzo Bonin Longare** at No.13, in 1602, after his master's designs; the best part is the inner courtyard.

Map labels:

VIALE FERDINANDO RODOLFI
CONTRA PORTA S. LUCIA
VIA QUATTRO NOVEMBRE
VIA LEGIONE GALLIENO
Palazzo Angaran
Piazza XX Settembre
Palazzo Regaù
CONTRA S. DOMENICO
LEVA D'ANGELI
Ponte del Angeli
CONTRA XX SETTEMBRE
CONTRA PORTA PADOVA
Piazza Matteotti
CONTRA S. ANDREA
Corte di Roda
Piazza S. Pietro
San Pietro
VIA NAZARO SAURO
CONTRA SAN PIETRO
CONTRA DELLE BARCHE
VIALE GIURIOLO
Bacchiglione
CONTRA DELLA PIARDA
VIALE MARGHERITA
Retrone
Santa Chiara
Santa Caterina
CONTRA S. CATERINA
Piazzale T. Fraccon
VIA RISORGIMENTO NAZIONALE
BORGO BERGA
VIALE DANTE
to Villa Valmarana & La Rotonda

Contrà Vescovado begins by Palazzo Breganze and leads to the Gothic **Duomo**, its façade decorated with a diamond pattern that was carefully pieced together after the war. The side door on Contrà Lampertico is one of Palladio's few attempts at sacred architecture in Vicenza; he also designed the dome atop Lorenzo da Bologna's graceful tribune of 1482. Of the art, the most notable piece is in the fifth chapel on the right, a 1356 Lorenzo Veneziano polyptych. Excavations have revealed remains of the Duomo's 8th-century ancestor, a stretch of Roman road in the crypt and, out in the square, a **cryptoportico**, a U-shaped subterranean passage under what must have been a very large 1st-century AD house.

Opposite the Duomo, slip into the courtyard of the neoclassical Bishop's Palace to see the exquisite **Zeno Loggia** (1494) by Bernardino da Milano. Down Contrà Proti, turn at Via Pigafetta for the delightful Gothic **Casa Pigafetta** (1444), birthplace of Antonio Pigafetta, a local aristocrat who just happened to be in Spain in 1519 when Magellan was setting out on his world tour; Pigafetta went along and, unlike Magellan, survived; and wrote the definitive account of the voyage three years later. His motto '*Il n'est rose sans espine*' is inscribed on either side of the door. Beyond, to the left, lies the Piazza dei Signori.

Piazza dei Signori and Around

This kingly square is the heart and soul of Vicenza, its public forum from Roman times to this day. In the 1540s the Vicentines decided that the piazza's crumbling Gothic Palazzo della Ragione no longer matched their new Renaissance-humanist aspirations and decided to give it a facelift. Having rejected new designs proposed by such luminaries as Sansovino and Giulio Romano, they surprisingly hired the still relatively unknown Palladio to give it a new look in 1549. It was his first big break, and Vicenza would never be the same. The marble loggias he added to the building, ever after known as the **Basilica** ('hall of justice', as in Latin; *open Tues–Sat 9.30–12, 2.15–5; Sun 9–12.30; free if there's no exhibition*) were to be his only work in stone in the Veneto and would painstakingly remain a work in progress for decades, showcasing Palladio's talents in the heart of his adopted city throughout his life—it was only completed in 1619. The result perfectly fulfils its aims, with two tiers of rounded arches interspersed with Doric and Ionic columns that give an appearance of Roman regularity, although Palladio had to vary the size of the arches to compensate for the irregularities in the trapezoidal structure. The great copper keel of a roof (rebuilt after the war, when it caught fire and collapsed) is concealed behind a balustrade lined with the life-size classical statues that would become a hallmark of Palladio's work; stare at them long enough and the urge to shoot them off like ducks in a penny arcade becomes almost irresistible.

To see what Palladio was disguising, go behind the Basilica to **Piazza delle Erbe**, home to Vicenza's daily food and produce market, and its pleasant-sounding **Torre del Tormento**, the medieval prison. In the adjacent piazzetta stands a **statue of Palladio**, contemplating the Basilica with a finger on his chin, as if trying to figure out what he forgot. The truth is it was his favourite work, and he didn't mind saying so himself, writing that it ranked 'among the most noble and most beautiful fabrics that have been made since the ancient times.'

The Basilica shares Piazza dei Signori with two columns, as in Piazzetta San Marco in Venice, one topped with the Redeemer (1640) and the other with St Mark's lion (1473), and the needle-like **Torre di Piazza** (or Torre Bissara, after the barons who raised it in the 12th century); in the 14th century the civic authorities tamed it with a mechanical clock and in 1444 added its headdress. Opposite, the 16th-century **Monte di Pietà**, built in two sections, was frescoed in the 1900s with Liberty-style pin-up girls, some of whom still faintly survive moral outrage, war damage and Father Time. Next to this stands Palladio's **Loggia del Capitanato**, now the seat of the town council, which was built to celebrate the great victory at Lepanto on October 7 1571; the Contrà del Monte façade is decorated with reliefs of trophies and statues of War (symbolized by Venice) and Peace (Vicenza). If its grand brick columns and arches seem to be confined in too narrow a space, it's because the loggia was meant to extend over several more bays; the building boom that made Palladio's fortune ended in the late 1560s, leaving most of his designs incomplete. Inside, ask to see the Camera Bernarda, decorated with frescoes transferred from Villa Porto at Torri di Quartesolo.

South of the Retrone

From Piazza dei Signori, Via San Michele leads to the Retrone, one of Vicenza's two rivers, spanned here by the **Ponte San Michele** (1620). There are lovely views of the Retrone lapping the houses and, on the opposite bank, the **Oratorio di San Nicola**. This is remarkable for one of the creepiest altarpieces in Italy, *La Trinità* by the 17th-century Vicentine painter Francesco Maffei, whose feverish brush infected the Oratorio's walls as well with the assistance of Giulio Caprioni (*but unfortunately you have to find a guided tour to join to get in*).

Vicenza's Roman theatre, the 1st-century AD Teatro di Berga, was studied by Palladio but dismantled in the 1700s. Traces of it remain just south of S. Nicola, in and around picturesque **Piazzaola Gualdi**. Emperor Charles V stayed at the **Palazzo Gualdo** at No.10. Nearby, in Contrà Del Guanto, the octagonal **Oratorio di Santa Chiara e San Bernardino** (1451) is covered with a handsome wooden ceiling and has paintings by Giulio Carpioni. If it's closed, ring the bell at Via Burci 14.

Corso Palladio, Contrà Porti and Contrà Riale

Returning to the Piazza dei Signori, step behind the Loggia dei Capitanato to join **Corso Palladio**, the decumanus of ancient *Vicetia* and 'the most elegant street in Europe, not counting the Grand Canal in incomparable Venice'. This famous axis is lined with palaces, including, just to your right, Vincenzo Scamozzi's masterpiece, the **Palazzo Trissino**, with its Ionic portico and superb courtyard (begun in 1592, now the Municipio). A few doors down, the lovely late Gothic **Palazzo Da Schio** (1470s) is Vicenza's own 'Ca' d'Oro'.

Palladio himself is only dubiously linked to a couple of buildings on the street named after him; to find his work, turn up elegant **Contrà Porti**—the Roman *cardo*. One of his earlier works, **Palazzo Iseppo Da Porto** (1552) at No.21, is influenced by Raphael and contains frescoes by Giambattista Tiepolo. Next door, the sombre Gothic **Palazzo Porto-Colleoni** (No.19) hides an internal garden courtyard and an airy asymmetrical loggia; next to it, the late Gothic **Palazzo Porto-Breganze** (No.17), has a beautiful door added in 1481 and a precious mullioned window, the only one in Vicenza with Venetian reversed arches.

While building the Palazzo Porto-Festa, Palladio impressed the plutocrat Marc'Antonio Thiene, who had him redo his vast medieval **Palazzo Thiene** (now the Banca Popolare), a beauty treatment designed to create the most imposing residence in all Vicenza, although the project, like so many of Palladio's, was never completed. The Contrà Porti side of Palazzo Thiene is a fine work by Lorenzo da Bologna; around the corner is Palladio's part which, with its weighty sculpted windows, rustication and Mannerist classicizing, is his homage to Giulio Romano; Lord Burlington thought it was the most beautiful building in the world. Some of the interior retains its original and rather magnificent decoration; if the bank isn't too busy, ask to see the first floor's Rotonda with a domed vault and statues.

Opposite, on the corner of Contrà Riale, **Palazzo Barbaran-da Porto** was built from scratch by Palladio in 1570 and holds the **Museo Palladiano**, coinciding with a big exhibit in 1999 on Palladio's influences in Europe (*for more information, contact the Institute for Palladian Studies, © 0444 323 014*). Unlike the buildings he merely dressed in new clothes, the Palazzo Barbaran-da Porto is as symmetrical as pie, with two orders on the façade, Ionic on the ground level and Corinthian on the *piano nobile*; some of the frescoes inside are by Zelotti.

Continue down quiet Contrà Riale, where the convent of San Giacomo (1652) is now the **Bertoliana Civic Library**, repository of 400,000 volumes, 6,000 manuscripts and rare incunabula dating from the 13th to the 19th century, including Francesco Colonna's novel *Hypnerotaumachia Polifilo*, published in 1499 by the famous Venetian press of Aldus. Widely read in Renaissance Vicenza, the *Hypnerotaumachia* was the first antiquity-worshipping hodgepodge fantasy, full of nostalgia for ancient architecture, hieroglyphs and pagan sacrifices; a number of architects based designs on the imaginary buildings in its woodcuts. Have a look down Stradella San Giacomo, with its view of a graceful 18th-century loggetta set amid ivy and a magnolia. Contrà Riale gives on to lively Corso Forgazzero, where at No.16 Palladio's **Palazzo Valmarana-Braga** (begun in 1566) is distinguished by gigantic pilasters crowned by an attic, framed by two armoured *telamones* in high relief, symbolically 'imprisoned' and specially designed to be seen in perspective in the narrow street.

Santa Corona, Santo Stefano and Pietro Longhi

In lower Corso Palladio, a square opens by the early Gothic church of **Santa Corona** (*open 8.30–12, 2.30–6*), built by the Dominicans in the 1260s to entice the many locals who strayed into the Paterene heresy back to the Catholic fold. In later centuries it was adorned with beautiful art, especially Veronese's *Adoration of the Magi* (1573), the three kings dressed in gorgeous reds and yellows; and Giovanni Bellini's *Baptism of Christ* (1502), a lovely example of his late style set in a rugged, rather un-Venetian landscape. Note, too, the predella of Fogolino's *Madonna of the Stars*, featuring a rare portrayal of pre-Palladian Vicenza. The high altar (1670) is a massive bloom of inlaid marble and mother-of-pearl; the wooden choir stalls (1482–9) are lovely; and the altarpiece of the rococo Cappalla Thiene just to the right of the high altar has Giovanni Battista Pittoni's masterpiece, *SS. Peter and Paul and Pius V Adoring Mary*. Palladio designed the Valmarana Chapel; note how the plan and the front view refer to his Redentore in Venice.

Alongside the church, the **Museo Santa Corona** contains natural history exhibits on the region, as well as Lombard relics, fine Roman mosaics, and Vicenza's oldest goldwork—a lamina embossed with Paleoveneti warriors, *c.* 1500 BC (*open Tues–Sat 9–12.30 and 2.15–5; Sun 9–12.30; adm*). The nearby **Palazzo Leoni Montanari**, built 1676–94 (now the Banco Ambrosiano) is one of Vicenza's few baroque palaces and contains, in the recently restored Sala dell'Antica Roma, 14 paintings by Venetian genre master Pietro Longhi and his school (*open April–Oct, Sat only 10–12, 4–7*). From S. Corona, take Contrà S. Stefano to the baroque **Santo Stefano** to see one of Palma Vecchio's most beautiful paintings, *Madonna with SS. George and Lucy and Musical Angel.*

Palazzo Chiericati: The Pinacoteca

In Piazza Matteotti, at the north end of the Corso, Palladio designed his masterful **Palazzo Chiericati** (1550, finished only in 1670). For once not constricted by a narrow street, he created the lightest and airiest palace of the century, extending the double loggias of his villas into a double colonnade of two different orders, playing with voids and solids; the rooms may fulfil his rules on harmonic proportions, but are topsy-turvy compared to previous palaces, running parallel to the façade. Since 1855, when a new wing was added,

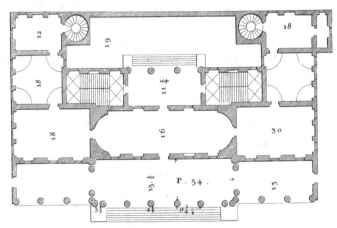

Villa Chiericati, from Palladio's
Four Books of Architecture

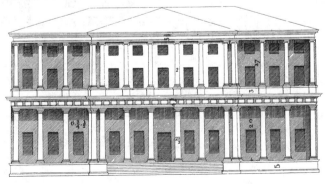

Palazzo Chiericati has been home to the *comune*'s **Pinacoteca** (*open Tues–Sat 9–12.30, 2.15–5; Sun and hols 9–12.30; adm*). The ground floor, containing a collection of contemporary Italian works (Carrà, De Pisis, Guidi, Lincini, Maccari, Oppi, Tancredi) retains its original stuccoes and frescoes, including a hilarious ceiling by Domenico Brusasorci, who took it upon himself to portray the sun god and his steeds in the position earthlings would see them at noon—all bums and bellies. The other paintings are in chronological order, with the oldest works in the 19th-century wing: there's a polyptych by Paolo Veneziano, a portrait of Pico della Mirandola by a follower of Bellini, a *Cavalry* by Hans Memling from a triptych, and works by the four top Vicentine painters of the *quattrocento*: Bartolomeo Montagna, Giovanni Buonconsiglio, Marcello Fogolino and Giovanni Speranza; Fogolino's *St Francis Receiving the Stigmata* incorporates another fine view of Vicenza.

The collection continues in the Palladian wing, with one of Bartolomeo Montagna's finest works, the *Madonna in Trono* with saints, and others by Cima da Conegliano and Veronese; an excellent *St Augustine and the Cripples* by Tintoretto; and works by Lorenzo Lotto, Giannantonio Fasolo, Zelotti, Jacopo Bassano and Sansovino (the terracotta *Madonna col Bambino*). The Flemish section includes Van Dyck's *Four Ages of Man* and Jan 'Velvet' Brueghel the Elder's *Madonna*. From the 17th century, there's the irrepressible Francesco Maffei (*Glorification of the Inquisitor Alvise Foscarini*) and Giulio Caprioni, along with Pietro and Marco Liberi and Francesco di Cairo; from the 18th century, Giambattista Piazzetta's *St Francis in Ecstasy*, landscapes by Marco Ricci, paintings by Francesco and Giambattista Pittoni, and two excellent Tiepolos (*Immacolata* and *Time Discovers Truth*) plus other paintings by his son Giandomenico.

Piazza Matteotti is the showcase for two more fine buildings: the **Palazzetto Giacomazzi-Trevisan**, the only rococo venture in this palazzo-ridden city, and **Palazzo Valmarano-Trento** (1718), a masterpiece by Francesco Muttoni, who kept up a regular correspondence with Lord Burlington to help him further Palladianism in England. Stretching along the north end of Piazza Matteotti, the **Palazzo del Territorio** began as a castle in the 13th century, and expanded to engulf the Teatro Olimpico.

Teatro Olimpico

Open 16 Mar–15 Oct, Mon–Sat, 9.30–12.20 and 3–5.30; Oct–Mar, Mon–Sat, 9.30–12.20, 2–4.30; Sun year round 9.30–12.20; adm.

This building was Palladio's swansong. As well as being one of the most original works of the Italian Renaissance, it is the oldest operational indoor theatre in the world (1580). Palladio was a member of the group of 25 literati, artists and dilettantes who founded the high-minded 'Olympic Academy' in 1555. The immediate inspiration for the Olimpico was a temporary wooden theatre that Palladio erected in the Basilica in 1561 for an opera, *L'Amor costante* by Alessandro Piccolomini, and a recital of his patron Giangiorgio Trissino's *Sofonisba*—monochrome frescoes in the Antiodeo show scenes from both works and document the ideas going through Palladio's mind. The architect's triumphant return to Vicenza from Venice in 1579 may have been the impetus to construct a permanent setting for the academy's plays and lectures, on the site of an old prison donated by the *comune*. For the seating and stage Palladio, as always, went back to his Vitruvius and the

Roman works he had seen during his sojourns: his cavea has 13 rows of seats arranged in a semi-ellipse, topped by a Corinthian colonnade and a balustrade decorated with statues of members of the Academy (note Giangiorgio Trissino in the centre) and reliefs of the Labours of Hercules.

Palladio died as the outer walls were going up, and the project was inherited by Vincenzo Scamozzi, who designed the rooms for academy use—the Odeo and Antiodeo—and, disregarding Palladio's plans for a stage screen with a triumphal arch and classical statues, built a stucco and wood stage set of a square and streets radiating out in flawless, fake perspective, representing Thebes, for the theatre's inaugural production in 1585, Sophocles' *Oedipus Rex*. But here Thebes has become a pure ideal, a Renaissance dream city, so perfect that no one ever thought to change the set, or bothered later, as the Council of Trent banned theatrical representations soon afterwards.

Visitors over the centuries have adored it. William Beckford leapt on stage in 1780 and recited Aeschylus, feeling that he had at last 'penetrated into a real and perfect monument of antiquity.' Another perfect and memorable moment occurred in 1987 during a visit by the Queen Mother, when her bodyguard fell off the stage and penetrated the orchestra pit. Since the 1930s the theatre has slowly been brought back to life and now, between April and October, you may be able to catch a play or ballet on its venerable boards.

Over the Bacchiglione

Behind the theatre, Ponte degli Angeli crosses over the Bacchiglione to Piazza XX Settembre, site of **Palazzo Angaran** (1480), Vicenza's finest pre-Palladian Renaissance palace; the beautiful ornate late Gothic **Palazzo Regaù** stands nearby, at the beginning of Contrà XX Settembre. This neighbourhood, an old craftsmen's district, is locally known as the 'Republic of San Zulian': on Contrà Sant' Andrea, the **Corte dei Roda** is a traditional complex of artisans' houses and courtyards. Just to the right of the Ponte degli Angeli, Contrà San Pietro leads to **San Pietro** (*open 8–12, closed Fri*), the church of a Benedictine monastery from the Carolingian era, rebuilt in the Renaissance. The interior is a colourful gallery of late 16th-century works by the Maganza family of Vicenza, and there's a beautifully decorated cloister of 1427. Ask the sacristan to unlock the handsome **Oratorio dei Boccalotti** (1414).

From Palazzo Angaran, take Contrà Santa Lucia to Porta Santa Lucia (1369) and turn left for the church of **Santa Maria Aracœli** (1680; *ring ahead © 0444 514 438*), built on a design by the great baroque genius Guarino Guarini of Turin. The façade's several levels are adorned with statues; within is a mighty drum topped by a well-lit dome. The hyper-ornate High Altar (1696) explodes around a painting on that favourite Renaissance subject linking Christianity to classical Rome, *The Triburtine Sibyl showing the Virgin and Child to Octavian*, attributed to Pietro Liberi. Just behind the church, Vicenza's prettiest public garden, the **Parco Querini**, is planted with pines and cedars of Lebanon; a statue-lined lane cuts through the lawns to a round island where the landscape designer Antonio Piovene built an elegant little Ionic temple (1820).

Outside the Historic Centre

North of the Duomo and Corso Palladio, **Corso Fogazzaro** is an ancient, atmospheric street where the porticoes have richly carved Gothic capitals and Vicenza holds a very popular antiques fair in spring and autumn. Here the Franciscan church of **San Lorenzo** (1280) has a grand façade and lovely marble portal, with a lunette of the *Madonna with Child and Saints* by Andriolo de Santi (1334). The interior is filled with sumptuous altars, frescoes and paintings dedicated by the noble families of Vicenza, notably the Pojana altar of 1474 in the right transept, and the chapel just left of the high altar, with a *Beheading of St Paul* by Bartolomeo Montagna. The 15th-century cloister is charming, and outside the apse you can see bits of Corso Fogazzaro's Roman predecessor. Further on, **Santa Maria del Carmine**, a Gothic church with a neo-Gothic façade, is decorated throughout with 15th-century bas-reliefs brought over from another church, and altars by Veronese and Jacopo Bassano.

Beyond the Carmine, Contrà di Porta Santa Croce continues towards the gate of the same name, built during the Scaliger tenure. Following along Contrà Mure Corpus Domini, you come to the area where Alberto della Scala commissioned 'architect Giovanni' to lay out the walled district of **Porta Nuova**, a grid that had broad green spaces inside the blocks, defended by a little fort or Rocchetta (1365). **San Rocco** (1530), on Contrà Mure Corpus Domini, was, like the Duomo, designed by Lorenzo da Bologna. The finely proportioned Renaissance interior is interrupted in the centre by the elegant cantoria, similar to Spanish churches. The walls and the altar are adorned with paintings by Giambattista Zelotti and Alessandro Maganza; don't miss the romantic cloister.

South, just outside Piazza Castello, the English-style **Giardino Salvi** contains a pair of loggias, one Palladian and one by Longhena (1649), reflected in the Seriola. Vicenza's oldest church, **SS. Felice e Fortunato** (*open Mon–Sat 9–12, 3.30–6.30*) is a ten-minute walk from here along Corso SS. Felice e Fortunato; built as a simple hall just after Constantine made Christianity the religion of the empire, it was remodelled in 398 with three naves and the Chapel of the Martyrium di Santa Maria Materdomini. Charlemagne visited the Benedictine monastery attached to the church; it was badly damaged by the Hungarians in 899 and rebuilt in the 1160s, with a battlemented bell tower and spire. In this century, the church has been un-restored as much as possible to its 4th-century appearance, revealing the original mosaics in the right aisle and the martyrium. The altarpiece, *St Valentine Healing the Sick* by Alessandro Maganza (1585), is the centre of the local celebrations on February 14.

Monte Bérico, Villa Valmarana and La Rotonda

Just to the south of the city rises Vicenza's holy hill, Monte Bérico. Buses make the ascent approximately every half-hour from the bus station, or you can walk up like a good pilgrim by way of Viale Eretenio, running parallel to the Retrone, stopping along the way to look at No.12, the elegant **Palazzo Civena-Trissino** (now the Eretenia Nursing Home), one of Palladio's earliest works (1540), showing the influence of Bramante and Raphael and an interest in their effects of *chiaroscuro* that would become a theme in his later work.

Nearby, in Via delle Grazie, the church of **Santa Maria delle Grazie** (1494, rebuilt 1595) has been restored (*open Tues, Wed, Fri and Sat 9–12, Thurs 3–6, Mon and Sun closed*) and contains paintings by Maganza, De Pieri, Marinali and Jacopo and Leandro da Bassano.

At the end of Via Eretenio, turn left in Viale X Giugno and head up through the half-mile-long covered walkway or **Portici**, built in the 18th century to shelter pilgrims, with superb views along the way over the city and the Villa Rotonda, down in the 'Little Valley of Silence.' The baroque **Basilica di Monte Bérico** (*open Mon–Sat 7–12 and 2.30–7; Sun 7–7*) that crowns the hill commemorates two apparitions of the Virgin in 1428, announcing the end of a plague that devastated Vicenza. It still does a brisk pilgrim trade, its polished, candle-flickering interior presided over by the painted marble statue of the Madonna of Monte Bérico, attributed to Antonino da Venezia; Vicenza's goldsmiths have crafted donations by the faithful into her fabulous necklace and a gold crown weighing eight pounds. The church possesses two first-class paintings: *La Pietà* by Bartolomeo Montagna, hanging near the altar, and the *Supper of St Gregory the Great* by Veronese, appropriately hung in the refectory (down the steps to the left), and carefully pieced together on Emperor Franz Joseph's orders after Austrian soldiers shredded it with their bayonets during the battle of Monte Bérico (10 June 1848), quashing Vicenza's popular revolt that had begun three months earlier.

Beyond the church, a pretty walk leads to Giovanni Antonio Selva's 18th-century **Villa Guiccioli**, the people's centre of resistance during the Battle of Monte Bérico. Now home to the **Museo del Risorgimento e della Resistanza** (*open Tues–Sat 9–12.30 and 2.15–5, Sun 9–12.30; April–Sept, Sun also 3.15–6; adm*) it houses documents on the city's history from the fall of Venice to 1945, including posters, paintings, weapons and so on; the large garden that surrounds it is now a romantic public park.

Walk back down the Portici as far as Via M. D'Azeglio (alternatively, from the centre of Vicenza take AIM bus 8 or 13); from here the narrow Stradella S. Bastian leads to the **Villa Valmarana**, nicknamed 'dei Nani' after the stone dwarfs on the wall, arty ancestors of the modern garden gnome (*open mornings May–Sept, Wed, Thurs, Sat and Sun 10–12; after-noons 15 Mar–April, 2.30–5.30; May–Sept, 3–6, Oct–15 Nov, 2–5; adm exp*). The villa's main attraction, however, is its sumptuous decoration by the Tiepoli, father and son, in frameworks painted by Mengozzi Colonna, master of illusionary architectural perspectives. Giambattista based his frescoes on the *Iliad*, *Orlando Furioso*, the *Aeneid* and Tasso's *Jerusalem Delivered*, concentrating on the scenes where the heroes face the hard choice between duty and love. Duty, of course, always wins out, but Tiepolo's heart is on the side of the nearly sacrificed Iphigenia and the forlorn Angelica, Dido and Armida. Son Giandomenico contributed the ceiling and a landscape in the main villa, and painted his masterpiece in the *Foresteria* (guest house): intimate, gently ironical scenes of rural life that seem to undermine his father's Grand Manner right under his nose. Two other rooms, the Gothic rooms and Carnival Room, are solo works by Mengozzi Colonna.

From there, a further five-minute walk along the Stradella Valmarana brings you to the celebrated Villa Almerico-Capra, better known as **La Rotonda** (*gardens open 15 Mar–early Nov, Tues–Sun 10–12 and 3–6; confirm for Fri, Sat, Sun, © 0444 321 793; adm. Interior open Wed only; adm exp*), designed by Palladio for a Monsignor Americo in

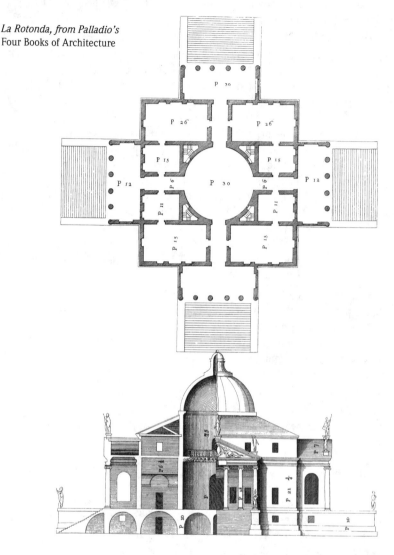

1567 and completed after his death by the faithful Scamozzi. Unlike Palladio's other villas which, under their classical skins, were functional farmhouses, the Villa Rotonda was built for sheer delight, for the Monsignor's garden parties and musical evenings, and, although no one knew it at the time, as the perfect setting for Joseph Losey's film *Don Giovanni*. One of the main interests of the Accademia Olimpica was mathematics, and La Rotonda is, if anything, an exercise in geometry—a circle in a cube, complemented by four symmet-rical porches: its location is so perfect that one critic wrote that Palladio planned the hill before the villa. The round central hall has stucco decorations and rather overblown

frescoes by Alessandro Maganza and Ludovico Dorigny; the four arms countain four iden-
tical suites of rooms. Alexander Pope, however, thought it ridiculous:

> *'tis very fine,*
> *But where d'ye sleep, or where d'ye dine?*
> *I find by all you have been telling*
> *That 'tis a house, but not a dwelling.*

There are two historic churches in the same area, southwest of Vicenza, on the route of
AIM bus 4 (although check at the tourist office for opening hours before setting out). The
first, simple single-naved Franciscan **San Giorgio in Gogna** (982) is immersed in the
greenery of Monte Bérico. It was far enough from the city to be the site of the *lazzaretto* or
fever hospital, and to be used for executions by the Austrians. It has only one painting, *The
Apparitions of the Virgin to Vincenza Pasini* (1620) by Alessandro Maganza, which has a
view of Vicenza at the time, as seen from the exact place where San Giorgio stands. The
same buses pass by the **Abbey of Sant'Agostino**, 5km southwest of Vicenza (near the
Vicenza West *autostrada* exit). Founded by the Lombards in the 7th century, rebuilt in
1357 and restored in 1942 by the parish priest, the church has a façade of tufa and bricks,
with an arched portal. The interior has 14th-century frescoes by the Veneto and Emilian
schools and a golden polyptych (1404) by Battista da Vicenza, commissioned by Ludovico
Chiericati to commemorate Vicenza's peaceful surrender to Venice. It was the parish
church of two holy men, St Lorenzo Giustiniani and Gabriele Condulmer, who became
Pope Eugene IV.

Vicenza ✉ *36100*   **Eating Out**

Whatever airs Vicenza puts on in the culture department become somewhat
draughty in the kitchen—this is polenta and *baccalà* (salt cod) country, whose
hearty and filling fare is not the most subtle on the stomach. But the locals
beg to differ: their *baccalà alla vicentina*, made of top-quality cod
endlessly pummelled with a wooden hammer, soaked for 36 hours,
sprinkled with cheese and browned in a mix of butter, oil,
anchovies and onions, then cooked over a slow flame, and seasoned with
parsley, pepper and milk, is 'a whole refined civilization…simmering in the pot'
according to writer Guido Piovene. A favourite way to eat polenta is sliced and
grilled, accompanied with *sopressa* sausage from Valli del Pasubio and Recoaro, or
pigeon roasted on embers.

Other specialities include potato gnocchi made with cinnamon and raisins, and
bigoli con l'arna, fat spaghetti with duck sauce, delicious accompanied by a glass of
red Tocai. Montecchio Maggiore is known for its *mostarda*, a spicy condiment of
fruit with mustard.

expensive

Nuovo Cinzia & Valerio, Piazzetta Porta Padova, ✆ 0444 505 213, for perfectly prepared
seafood: tagliatelle with salmon, cuttlefish risotto or grilled sole, followed by home-
made ice cream and crisp biscuits. *Closed Sun eve, Mon, Aug.*

Antica Trattoria Tre Visi, Corso Palladio 25, ✆ 0444 324 868. Luigi Da Porto, author of the original version of *Romeo and Juliet*, was born in a 15th-century palace that was converted into an inn some 200 years ago: it still serves food today and, with its fireplace and rustic fittings, is a charming place to enjoy good, basic Veneto cooking and homemade pasta dishes. *Closed Sun eve, Mon, July.*

Trattoria Framarin, Via Battista Framarin 48, ✆ 0444 570 407, a family-run place just west of the city walls, where you'll find delicious homemade pasta and a warm welcome. *Closed Sun, some of Aug.*

Vecchia Guardia, Contrà Pescherie Vecchie 11, ✆ 0444 321 231, near Piazza dell'Erbe, for pizza and straightforward meals (*closed Thurs*).

Antica Casa della Malvasia, Contrà delle Morette 5, near Piazza dei Signori, ✆ 0444 543 704, is basic, lively and very popular for real home cooking.

Righetti's bustling self-service canteen, a popular stop for a cheap lunch, has seats spilling on to Piazza Duomo. *Closed Sat, Sun.*

If you need something sweet and stylish, Vicenza has two historic *pasticcerias* near the Basilica—**Antica Offelleria della Meneghi**, Contrà Cavour 18, and **Sorarù**, Piazzetta Palladio 17.

The real gastronomic fireworks await just east of Montecchio Maggiore at Arzignano's **Principe**, Via S. Caboto 16, ✆ 0444 67131, ✆ 0444 675 921 (*expensive*), where one of Italy's top young chefs—trained in France—prepares superb, imaginative meals, accompanied by a selection of homemade breads, a chariot of French cheeses and delightful pastries. *Closed Sun some of Aug.* It's also a small hotel; *moderate*.

History	190
Getting Around	191
Tourist Information	191
Porta Nuova to the Arena	194
Around Piazza delle Erbe	194
North of the Adige: Veronetta	197
West of Piazza delle Erbe	198
East of Verona	201
Where to Stay	201
Eating Out	202
Day Trips North of Verona	205
Day Trips South of Verona	208

Verona

There is no world without Verona walls
But purgatory, torture, hell itself
Hence banished is banish'd from the world;
And world's exile is death.

Romeo and Juliet, Act III

Well, love does lead one to extremes, and although Verona isn't quite a world on its own, it is still fair to say that it's one of the choicest morsels on this planet. When Cupid's pilgrims alight here they sigh over 'Juliet's balcony' and other places concocted in response to a desperate need for shrines to the unlucky teenage couple. But the gorgeous rosy-pink city curling along the banks of the Adige has far more to offer than Romeo and Juliet and all the other star-crossed lovers singing their operatic hearts out in the Arena: evocative streets and romantic piazzas, sublime art, magnificent architecture, and all the gnocchi you can eat. According to Goethe, even the wind in Verona 'is charged with fragrance as if it had passed over a hill of roses'.

History

Blessed with a navigable river at the bottom of a busy Alpine pass, Verona was favoured by the Romans from the time of its colonization in 89 BC, and returned the favour by giving Rome the architect Vitruvius and the lyrical, lovesick poet Catullus. The city maintained its status as a regional capital under the Ostrogoths and Franks, and in 1107 became a free *comune* in league with Padua, Vicenza and Treviso. Freedom in the case of 12th-century Verona meant a free-for-all, as the city's nobility spiced up the national Guelph and Ghibelline rivalries with a sideshow of purely domestic feuds and vendettas that inspired the original *Romeo and Juliet* (by Luigi da Porto, 1529), and led to the *comune* actually inviting Ezzelino da Romano to take power as *podestà* in 1230. It was under his reign that Pope Gregory IX forced Verona to accept the Inquisition under Dominican Giovanni da Vincenza, who celebrated his arrival in 1233 by barbecuing 60 Cathars outside the Arena.

Ezzelino's successors, the della Scalas or Scaligeri, were a typical late medieval Italian family of exquisite gangsters, softening their lust for power with a refined taste for the arts. Bartolomeo della Scala was one of Dante's first and most generous patrons. His descendants' names were, however, uniquely canine, the better to terrify their opponents. 'Big Dog', Cangrande I (1311–29), was the greatest Ghibelline captain in Italy and gave such generous hospitality to Dante in exile that the poet dedicated his *Paradiso* to him (although one may well wonder if Dante's famous 'Letter to Cangrande' on how to read poetry ever arrived; most postmen who saw the name 'Big Dog of the Stair' written on the door would have walked straight past). Cangrande captured Vicenza, Padua and Treviso before dying suddenly aged 41; his heir Mastino II (the Mastiff) consolidated his gains while his own successor, the fratricidal Cansignorio (Lord Dog, 1359–75), presided over the construction of the family's last great monuments. In 1387 Verona was seized by the Milanese warlord Gian Galeazzo Visconti.

By the time Visconti died in 1402, Verona had had enough of *signori* and annexed itself to Venice. Yet relations with Venice had their ups and downs. In the Wars of the League of Cambrai, Verona opened its gates to the German army and didn't return to St Mark's fold until 1517. The Venetians, who had absolved them of their oath of allegiance under enemy attack, took them back, but made Verona foot the bill for a vast new system of fortifications. However (and notably unlike Venice) Verona had the spunk to resist Napoleon in 1797—only to be partly destroyed for its presumption. There then followed a long period of Austrian rule, until most of the city joined the new Kingdom of Italy with Lombardy in 1859, although the part of Verona on the north bank of the Adige (the border between Lombardy and Venetia) remained Austrian along with Venice until 1866. Bombed in the Second World War, Verona quickly rebuilt itself as suited its rank, not only as a *città d'arte*, but as one of the great post-war economic success stories of modern Italy.

Getting Around

Verona's **airport** Valerio Catullo, to the southwest at Villafranca, has daily flights to London on British Airways, and direct flights to Rome, Naples and Bari. For information © 045 809 5666. Every 20 minutes buses link the airport to Porta Nuova train station in Verona.

Verona is the junction of major **rail** lines from Venice (1hr 45min) and Milan (2hrs). The station, **Porta Nuova**, is a 15-minute walk south of Piazza Brà, along Corso Porta Nuova; alternatively, city buses nos.71 or 72 link the railway station with Piazza delle Erbe and Piazza Brà. A machine dispenses bus tickets opposite the station. The provincial APT **bus depot** is across the street from Porta Nuova railway station (© 045 800 4129) and has frequent departures to the mountains. The historic centre is closed to traffic from 7.30 to 10am and from 1.30 to 4.30pm with the exception of cars going directly to hotels. There are **car parks** near the train station, Arena and Corso Porta Nuova, the main entry point if you are coming from the A4. **Bicycles** can be hired on the southeast corner of Piazza Brà, © 045 504 901. **Taxis:** © 045 532 666

Verona urban (ATM, © 045 5887 1111) and APT buses offer an *Invito a Verona* pass (available at the bus depot, tourist office or museums) from mid-June–Oct, a daily or weekly scheme that includes unlimited travel and museum admissions.

Tourist Information

In the side of Palazzo Barbiera, Via Leoncino 61, © 045 806 8680 (next to the Arena), and Porta Nuova railway station, © 045 800 861 (*both open daily, closed Sun in winter*). For the **province:** Piazza delle Erbe 38, © 045 800 6997, @ 045 801 0682. **Internet:** *www.verona-apt.net*; e-mail: *veronapt@mbox.vol.it.* **Youth information:** Corso Porta Borsari 17, © 045 801 0795.

Note: on the first Sunday of every month admission is free to the Arena, the Museo Castelvecchio, the Teatro Romano, Juliet's tomb and the Museo Lapidaro Maffeiano.

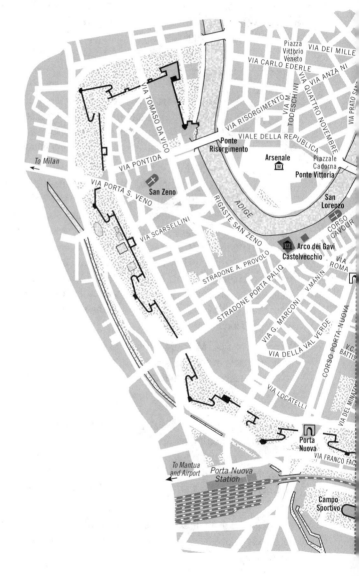

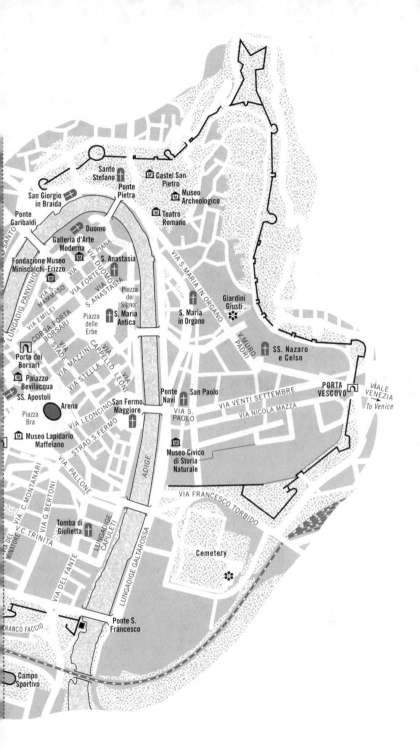

Santo
Stefano

Ponte
Pietra

Castel San
Pietro

Museo
Archeologico

San Giorgio
in Braida

Ponte
Garibaldi

Teatro
Romano

Duomo

Galleria d'Arte
Moderna

VIA PIANA

VIA DUOMO

S. Anastasia

VIA S. MARIA IN ORGANO

Fondazione Museo
Miniscalchi-Erizzo

VIA S.
MAMMASO

VIA FORTEMOSA

VIA
S.ANASTASIA

Piazza
dei
Signori

Giardini
Giusti

VIA EMILEI

Piazza
delle
Erbe

S. Maria
Antica

S. Maria
in Organo

LUNGADIG PANVINIO

CORSA PORTA
BORSARI

VIA
STADE

VIA MAZZINI

VIA CAPPELLO

VIA STELLA

V. MURO
PADRI

SS. Nazaro
e Celso

Porta dei
Borsari

VIA
LEONI

Palazzo
Bevilacqua

PORTA
VESCOVO

VIALE
VENEZIA

SS. Apostoli

Arena

San Fermo
Maggiore

Ponte
Navi

San Paolo

VIA VENTI SETTEMBRE

To Venice

Piazza
Bra

VIA LEONCINO

VIA S.
PAOLO

VIA NICOLA MAZZA

Museo Lapidario
Maffeiano

STRAD.S.FERMO

VIA. PALLONE

ADIGE

Museo Civico
di Storia
Naturale

VIA. C. MONTANARI

VIA. G.BERTONI

Tomba di
Giulietta

LUNGADIGE
CAPULETI

VIA FRANCESCO TORBIDO

V.C.TRINITA

A DEL
MINORE

LUNGADIGE GALTAROSSA

Cemetery

VIA DEL FANTE

RANCO FACCIO

Ponte S.
Francesco

Campo
Sportivo

193

Porta Nuova to the Arena

The first thing most people see of Verona, whether arriving by rail or road, is Sammicheli's Renaissance gate, the **Porta Nuova**, now stranded on a traffic island at the head of the Corso Porta Nuova. This avenue leads straight under another gate, Gian Galeazzo Visconti's **Portoni della Brà**, and into the heart of tourist Verona: the large, irregular **Piazza Brà**, the favourite promenade of the Veronese and tourists, milling about a broad swathe of café-filled pavements (the Liston) curving around the **Arena** (*open 9–7, closed Mon; during opera season 8.15–3.30; adm; for opera information* see *p.204*). Built in the 1st century AD and, after the Colosseum, the best-preserved amphitheatre in Italy, the elliptical Arena measures 456 by 364ft and seats 25,000—the only substantial change was wrought by earthquakes, which shattered the outer arcade with the exception of the four arches of the wing, or *ala*. Dressed in pink and white marble, the Arena is lovely enough to make one almost forget the brutal sports it was built to host. During the Middle Ages, Verona kept up Roman traditions by using it for public executions; in the Renaissance it hosted knightly tournaments, and in the baroque era it was used for bull-baiting. Since 1913, the death and mayhem has been purely operatic, with sets in Karnak proportions.

Opposite the Arena in Piazza Brà rises the 17th-century **Palazzo della Gran Guardia**, with a Visconti tower peeking over its shoulder; on the corner of Via Roma, at No.28, the **Museo Lapidario Maffeiano** (*open 9–3, Tues–Sun; adm*), established in 1714, was one of the first museums in the world dedicated to ancient inscriptions.

Around Piazza delle Erbe

> *This is the vegetable market, and that day it was alive with delightful figures of women and girls, with faces from which gazed great languid eyes, with soft appetising bodies, marvellously golden and unashamedly dirty, made for the night far more than the day.*

> Heinrich Heine

From Piazza Brà, **Via Mazzini** (the first street in Italy to ban cars) is the most direct route to the core of medieval and Roman Verona, the **Piazza delle Erbe**. The market square that so entranced Heine occupies the old forum and still fulfils its original purpose, selling fast food, souvenirs and overpriced vegetables, although you'd be hard pressed these days to find an unashamedly dirty tomato of any kind. Four monuments on the piazza's spine poke their heads above the rainbow lake of parasols—a Lion of St Mark; a 1368 fountain built by Cansignorio topped by a Roman statue known as the 'Madonna Verona'; a 16th-century loggia called the 'Berlina' where malefactors were tied and pelted with rotten produce; and an elegant Gothic stone lantern.

A colourful panoply of buildings encases the square, including the charming **Casa Mazzanti**, formerly part of a Scaliger palace and brightened with 16th-century frescoes, and the 12th-century **Torre de Lamberti**, 275ft high, reached by a lift from the courtyard of the Palazzo della Ragione (*see below, open Tues–Sun 9–7; adm*). The shorter **Torre del Gardell** at the other end of the piazza was another work of Cansignorio. Six ancient gods blithely pose atop the adjacent yellow sandstone **Palazzo Maffei** (1668), while a battlemented red-brick palace, built in 1301 for a merchants' association, still does duty as Verona's Chamber of Commerce after 700 years.

From Piazza delle Erbe, the **Arco della Costa** ('of the rib'—named after a whalebone hung in the arch) leads into stately **Piazza dei Signori**, the civic centre of Verona, presided over by a grouchy statue of Dante (1865). The striped **Palazzo della Ragione** has a lovely Romanesque-Gothic courtyard, the Cortile del Mercato Vecchio, which forms a pretty setting for a series of free summer classical/jazz/blues concerts. Behind Dante, the **Loggia del Consiglio** (1493) is the city's finest Renaissance building, decorated with yellow and red frescoes and statues of five ancient celebrities of Verona (one of whom, Pliny the Elder, was pinched from Como). The adjacent crenellated **Tribunale** (law courts), formerly a Scaliger palace, has a portal by Sammicheli; in the courtyard, and in adjacent Via Dante, you can peer down through glass into Verona's Roman streets, revealed in the 1980s **Scaliger excavations**. The underground corridors are used for photo exhibitions (*open 10–7, closed Mon*).

The arch adjoining the Tribunale leads to the grand Gothic pantheon of the della Scala, the **Scaliger Tombs** or *Arche Scaligere*, which Ruskin considered the crowning achievement of Veronese Gothic. The three major tombs portray their occupants in warlike, equestrian poses on top, and reposing in death below, although a copy replaces the best one, the horseman atop the Tomb of Cangrande (d. 1329), built into the wall of the 12th-century **Santa Maria Antica**. Don't miss the crowned dogs next to Cangrande's effigy, standing like firemen holding up ladders, the della Scala emblem. More ladders adorn the fantastical pinnacles of the tomb of 'Lord Dog' Cansignorio (d. 1375), the more sedate one of Mastino II (d. 1351), and the web of their wrought-iron enclosure. The rather plain 14th-century house in the same Via delle Arche Scaliger belonged to the Montecchi family (Shakespeare's Montagues), and has been known ever since as the **Casa di Romeo**.

The tour groups, however, are all over the **Casa di Giulietta**, near the Piazza delle Erbe at Via Cappello 23 (*open 9–7, closed Mon; adm*). Although the association is slim (the 13th-century house was once an inn called 'Il Cappello', reminiscent of the dal Cappello family, the original of the Capulets), it was restored on the outside in 1935 to fit the Shakespearian bill, with lovely windows and *de rigueur* balcony; inside you can peruse lovelorn graffiti of modern youth, ripe postcards, and photos of Italian girlhood's new Romeo, Leonardo di Caprio. The well fondled bronze statue of Juliet in the courtyard is a bit busty for a 13-year-old, but girls grew up faster back then.

Sant'Anastasia, Modern Art and the Duomo

North of the Scaliger Tombs, it's hard to miss Gothic **Sant'Anastasia**, Verona's largest church, begun in 1290 but never completed; in its woebegone façade only the fine portal, with frescoes and reliefs of St Peter Martyr, hints of its builders' good intentions. The interior, however, is beautiful but, just coming in from the bright sun, many people start at what appears to be two men loitering under the holy water stoops; these are the *Gobbi*, or hunchbacks. The three naves are supported by massive marble columns and decorated by an all-star line-up of artists: there's the beautiful Fregoso altar by Sammicheli (the first on the right), and excellent frescoes from 1390 by Verona native Altichiero, in the Cavalli Chapel in the right apse (note how the horse-head helmets that the worshippers wear on their backs resemble the dragon head on Cangrande's statue). The next chapel has 24 terracottas by Michele da Firenze on the *Life of Jesus*; paintings by the school of Mantegna fill the Pellegrini chapel, and, to the left of the high altar opposite a large 15th-century *Last Judgement*, the tomb of Cortesia Serego (1429) has an equestrian statue by Tuscan Nanni di Bartolo and frescoes by Michele Giambono. Best of all, in the sacristy, there's a fairytale fresco of *St George at Trebizond* (1438) by Pisanello, one of his finest works, although his watchful, calculating princess seems more formidable than any dragon.

Nearby, in Via Piana, the medieval Palazzo Forti which once lodged Napoleon now houses the **Galleria d'Arte Moderna** (*open 9–7, closed Mon*) where frequent exhibitions share the walls with Italian masters (Hayez, Fattori, De Pisis, Boccioni, Vedova, Manzù) of the 19th and 20th centuries.

A few streets down Via Duomo, almost at the tip of the river's meander, stands Verona's **Duomo**, consecrated in 1187, Romanesque at the roots and Renaissance in its windows and octagonal crown. The portal, supported on the backs of griffons, was carved by the great 12th-century Master Nicolò of San Zeno (*see* below). Look for the chivalric figures of Roland and Oliver guarding the west door and, on the south porch, a relief of Jonah being swallowed by the whale, and another of a dog biting a lion's buttocks; lastly, be sure to walk around to see the apse, made of volcanic tufa and one of the finest Romanesque works in the Veneto.

Inside, there's the beautifully carved Tomb of St Agatha (1353) in the Cappella Mazzanti, and an *Assumption* by Titian in the first chapel on the left. Painted in 1540, it shows us a very different Virgin from Titian's famous goddess whirlwinding to heaven in Venice's Frari—this one is looking down sympathetically at her friends on earth. In the second chapel on the right, Liberale da Verona contributed a delightful *Adoration of the Magi*, its foreground dominated by frolicking children, rabbits and dogs. A pope is buried in the choir—Lucius III, who preferred Verona to Rome, and made the city the papal seat from 1181 to 1185.

The pretty cloister has a few remains of the Duomo's pre-Romanesque predecessor (victim of an earthquake), and in its ancient baptistry, **San Giovanni in Fonte**, there's an eight-sided font big enough to swim in, carved in 1200 from a single piece of marble and decorated with beautiful reliefs. The chapter library, the **Biblioteca Capitolare**, at Piazza del Duomo 10 (*open 9.30–12.30; also Tues, Fri 4–6; closed Thurs, Sun and July*) was founded in the 5th century as a *Scriptorium* and justifiably claims to be the oldest library still operating in Europe; it contains a magnificent collection of medieval manuscripts.

Head away from the cathedral, down Stradone Arcidiacono Pacifico/Via Sole to Via S. Mamaso 2A, for the **Fondazione Museo Miniscalchi-Erizzo**, a private, ecletic collection of furniture, paintings, weapons and more stored in a frescoed 15th-century palace (*open Tues–Sat 4–7, Sun 10.30–12.30 and 4–7; adm exp*).

The north bank of the Adige, locally known as 'Veronetta', was that part of the city that remained in Austrian hands until 1866. It's due a whole morning unto itself: if you cross over the Ponte Garibaldi, just down from the Duomo, the first landmark is the large dome of **San Giorgio in Braida** (1477) to your right, worth a closer look inside to see Paolo Veronese's *Martyrdom of St George*. Follow the Adige down to **Santo Stefano**, an important palaeochristian church, pieced together in the 12th century from 5th–10th-century columns and capitals, and brightened with 14th-century frescoes, some by Altichiero. The bridge here, **Ponte Pietra**, was built by the Romans and blown up in the Second World War along with Verona's other bridges. The Veronese dredged up as much of its original stone as they could when they rebuilt it.

In ancient times, the citizens of Verona would trot over the Ponte Pietra to attend the latest plays at the picturesque **Teatro Romano** (*open 8–1.30 Tues–Sun; adm*). Actually, they still do: the cavea and arches, carved out of the cypress-clad hill of San Pietro in the time of Augustus, are in good enough nick to host a summer theatre season. A lift goes up to the **Archaeology Museum** (*same hours and ticket*), occupying a convent built on top of the theatre and containing a collection of small bronzes, portrait busts and a few mosaics. Further up still, the **Castel San Pietro** was built by the Austrians over Roman and Visconti-era fortifications, and has famous views over Verona at sunset.

South, on the Interato dell'Acqua Morta, **Santa Maria in Organo** has a façade (1533) by Fra Giovanni da Verona; the talented friar also made the extraordinary *intarsia* choir stalls, lectern and cupboards (in the sacristy) depicting scenes of old Verona, *trompe-l'œil* birds, animals, musical instruments and flowers. Across the street that runs behind the church are the cool **Giardini Giusti** (*open 9am–dusk; adm*) described by Thomas Coryate, the court jester of King James I's son Prince Henry, as 'a second paradise, and a passing delectable place of solace'. That was in 1611, the date of the enormous cypresses, formal box hedge parterres, fountains and grotto topped with a leering mask. The hillside was re-landscaped in the 19th century in the more romantic English style, making it a favourite setting for newlywed photos.

Continuing south, **Santi Nazaro e Celso** (1484) on Via Muro Padri contains 16th-century frescoes and a painting of the eponymous saints by Montagna, while **San Paolo** (rebuilt 1763), on Via San Paolo, boasts Veronese's beautiful *Madonna and Saints*, painted before he had to move to Venice, supposedly on the run after committing murder. On the river bank, at Lungadige Porta Vittoria 9, there's the elegant Palazzo Pompei, built in 1530 by Sammicheli and now housing the **Museo Civico di Storia Naturale** (*open 8–7, Sun 1.30–7; closed Fri; adm*), with an excellent fossil collection.

San Fermo Maggiore and Juliet's Tomb

From Piazza delle Erbe, Via Cappello/Leoni leads past the picturesque ruins of the 1st-century BC **Porta dei Leoni** (incorporated into a building), marking the beginning of the Roman *cardo maximus*. This leads to the splendid vertical apse of **San Fermo Maggiore**, an architectural club sandwich: it consists of two churches, one built on top of the other.

The Romanesque bottom was begun in 1065 by the Benedictines, while the upper Gothic church, with its attractive red and white patterns, was added by the Franciscans in 1320, along with the façade. Walk around to see the apse, a harmonious *mélange* of both styles.

The upper church is covered with a lovely wooden ceiling of 1314 and fine 14th-century frescoes—the *Crucifixion* in the lunette over the door is by Turone. The first chapel on the right has a charming if mutilated fresco of scroll-bearing angels, by Stefano da Verona; in the right transept the Renaissance Cappella Alighieri has a pair of tombs by Sammicheli; and the left transept has good frescoes on the *Life of St Francis* by Liberale da Verona. The **Cappella delle Donne** contains one of Caroto's best altarpieces (*Madonna and Saints*, 1528) and a beautiful tomb, the *Monumento Brenzoni* (1439) by Florentine Nanni di Bartolo, with statues and a graceful fresco of the *Annunciation* and *Archangels* by Pisanello (1462). The lower church has more frescoes and columns and capitals inspired by classical models.

The so-called **Tomba di Giulietta** (*open 8.15–7; closed Mon; adm*) is back near the river on Via del Pontiere, not far from the Piazza Brà. Even the Veronese admit no connection with any tradition here, except that the Romanesque cloister and the 14th-century red marble sarcophagus would make a jolly good stage set for Shakespeare's last scene. A small **museum of frescoes** is an added attraction, including lovely 16th-century allegorical and mythological scenes by Paolo Farinati.

West of Piazza delle Erbe

From Piazza delle Erbe, Corso Porta Bórsari leads to an impressive Roman customs house, the twin-arched **Porta dei Bórsari** ('Gate of the Duty-collectors') built in the 1st century AD on the Via Postumia. A small temple to Jupiter stood nearby on Via Diaz, its foundation now traced in porphyry (the temple itself was relocated to Verona's Cimiterio Monumentale); bits of the Roman walls are just to the right. Back then, once you passed out of the Porta dei Bórsari, you'd find the Via Postumia chock-a-block with tombs, but now this is **Corso Cavour**, one of Verona's most elegant thoroughfares, embellished with palaces from various epochs. The best is Sammicheli's refined if unfinished **Palazzo Bevilacqua** (1588, No.19), with its ornate, rhythmic alteration of large and small windows, columns and pediments; at No.44 his **Palazzo Canossa** is from the same period, but was finished only in 1675.

Opposite Palazzo Bevilacqua, the lovely Romanesque church of **San Lorenzo** (1117) preserves its upper, women's gallery (*matroneum*) reached by way of two cylindrical towers. To the left and a bit back from the Palazzo, another venerable church, **SS. Apostoli**, was founded in the 5th century and rebuilt several times since (especially after the Second World War); the oldest surviving bit is a votive chapel dedicated in the 6th century to Saints Teuteria and Tosca, modelled after the Mausoleum of Galla Placidia in Ravenna. Further down, Corso Cavour opens up into a small square with yet another Roman arch: the simple but elegant **Arco dei Gavi**, designed by Vitruvius in honour of a local family. The French demolished it in 1805, but in 1932 the local *fascisti* put it back together again.

Castelvecchio and its Museum of Art

Next to the arch, Cangrande II's fortress of **Castelvecchio** (1355) has weathered centuries of use by other top dogs, from the Venetians to Napoleon and the Nazis, to become Verona's excellent civic **museum of art** (*open Tues–Sun 9–7; adm*). Exhibits are arranged chronologically: among the oldest treasures in the first five rooms you'll find goldwork from the 4th–7th centuries, a sarcophagus (1179) carved with vivid reliefs of SS. Sergius and Bacchus, the *Archivolto di Peregrinus* (1120), and expressive 14th-century Veronese sculpture, especially a stark, painful *Crucifixion* by the Maestro di S. Anastasia. Two other statues are attributed to his circle, *St Catherine* and *St Cecilia*, patroness of music, holding her invention—a portable organ—under her arm.

Beyond the collection of old town bells and detached frescoes wait excellent 14th-century paintings: *SS. James and Anthony* by Tommaso da Modena, a polyptych by Altichiero, and another by Turone, one of Verona's first documented painters. The museum is especially rich in lovely Madonnas, beginning with two straight out of fairytales, the *Madonna of the Quail* by Pisanello and the *Madonna of the Rose-garden* by Stefano da Verona; others are by Jacopo Bellini and Michele Giambono. A *Pietà* by Tuscan Filippo Lippi and early Flemish works offer a change of pace, before Room 15 returns to Venetian art with the *Madonna della Passione* by Carlo Crivelli and Andrea Mantegna's *Holy Family*. Local Renaissance painters Liberale da Verona, Francesco Morone and Francesco Bonsignori fill the next rooms, followed by another beautiful *Madonna* by Giovanni Bellini and Carpaccio's *SS. Caterina and Veneranda*.

Next comes Verona's mascot, the striking 14th-century equestrian **statue of Cangrande I** from the Arche Scaligere, displayed outside the first-floor window of the Napoleonic wing. The pyjama-clad steed, complete with an equine hood ornament and deathly eyes, and the moronically grinning 'Big Dog' himself, with his ghastly dragon-helmet slung over his back, make an unforgettable pair, straight out of a malevolent pantomime. But this was the great Ghibelline captain to whom Dante dedicated his *Paradiso*; and, as with the Veneto's other great equestrian statues, of Gattamelata and Colleoni, a physical resemblance to the hero was irrelevant. Beyond Cangrande are paintings by Veronese (who left little in his native town), Tintoretto,

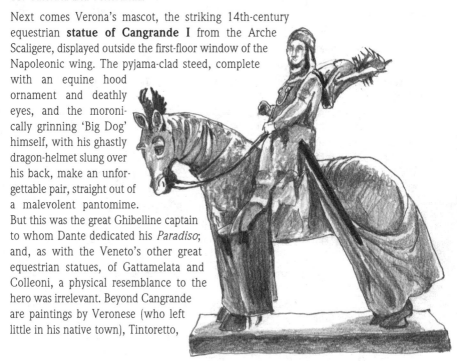

Giovan Francesco Caroto (including his well-known *Child with Sketch*, a happy insight into Renaissance childhood), both Tiepolos, Guardi and Longhi. Among the minor works, look for the strange, haunting *Orfeo* by 17th-century artist Roelandt Savery. A room in the keep displays the garments and trappings found in Cangrande's tomb in the 1920s.

Behind the castle, Cangrande II's **Ponte Scaligero** spanning the Adige repeats the attractive 'swallowtail' battlements of the Castelvecchio; like the Ponte Pietra it was blown up in the war and meticulously reconstructed in the 1950s, in the indomitable Italian spirit of *dov'è era, come era* ('where it was, as it was'), using the original stone.

Basilica of San Zeno Maggiore

A 15-minute walk west from the Castelvecchio, mostly along the riverbank, or bus 32 or 33 from Corso Porta Borsari, will take you to the superb **Basilica of San Zeno** (*open 7–12.30, 3.30–6.30*), one of the finest Romanesque buildings anywhere. First built in the 4th century next to a Benedictine monastery (of which only the massive brick tower on the left survives), the basilica took its present form between 1120 and 1398. Its magnificence demanded a legend: beneath its lofty campanile (finished in 1149) lies the tomb of a personage no less than Venice's old nemesis—Pepin the Short, king of the Franks.

For centuries San Zeno was the symbol of Veronese liberty, the custodian of its *carroccio* or war wagon. All medieval Italian cities had them to take into battle, drawn by oxen and equipped with altars and priests to pray for their enemy's discomfort, and drums and trumpets to rally their own troops. Capturing another *comune*'s *carroccio* was the most devastating blow an army could inflict. Florence, for instance, got Fiesole's, and the mortified city never recovered.

The rich façade of San Zeno has a perfect centrepiece: a 12th-century rose window of the *Wheel of Fortune* by Maestro Brioloto. Below, the beautifully carved porch (1138) by Masters Nicolò and Guglielmo shows scenes from the months, the miracles of San Zeno, the *Hunt of Theodoric* (driving a stag straight to Hell) and other allegories. The **bronze doors** with their 48 panels are a 'poor man's Bible' and one of the wonders of 11th-century Italy. Even after a millennium, they have an unmatched freshness and vitality: in the Annunciation scene Mary covers her face in fear and anguish while the angel Gabriel does his best to comfort her; in the Descent into Hell Christ and a large, leering Satan fight a tug-of-war for souls. Other scenes seem strange to us, especially the one of two nursing mothers on the lower left-hand door, one suckling twin children, the other, what look to be twin crocodiles. In the 18th and 19th centuries, Grand Tourists found the doors appalling: 'To this low level did art fall during the Carlovingian decadence and the Hungarian invasions,' sniffed Hippolyte Taine; but Ruskin thought they beat any Renaissance work in Venice hands down.

The vast interior, divided into three naves by Roman columns and capitals, has a beautiful Gothic ceiling, 13th- and 14th-century frescoes and, on the altar, the magnificent triptych of the *Madonna, Angels and Saints* (1459) by Andrea Mantegna, a work that brilliantly combines the master's love of classical architecture and luminous colouring. Although the French returned the painting after Napoleon carted it off, they kept the predella, and the panels displayed here are copies of the originals in the Louvre and Tours. In the crypt below, the body of St Zeno glows in the dark. Also spare a glance for the handsome cloister, completed in 1313.

Just East of Verona: the Madonna di Campagna

Of the many surviving gates in Verona's walls, the furthest from the centre is the easterly 16th-century **Porta Vescovo** on the far side of monumental cemetery. Viale Venezia out from here leads to the suburb of **San Michele Extra**, built around a long-gone 8th-century Benedictine monastery. In the 1500s a fresco of the Madonna on a wall performed so many miracles that the bishop commissioned Michele Sammicheli to design a church to house it: this was the round and rather startling **Sanctuario della Madonna di Campagna** (1562), one of Longhena's inspirations for La Salute. It became the aim of a very popular all-night pilgrimage on the first Sunday of each May, until the authorities noticed that the pilgrims were having far too much May Day-style fun along the road, and abolished it all in 1804.

Verona ✉ *37100*   ***Where to Stay***

There are plenty of soulless chain hotels on the fringes of the city, but not really enough nice places in the centre, especially during opera season in July or August, so do book. Rooms are also tight in March, when Verona hosts an agricultural fair.

very expensive

★★★★ **Due Torri Baglioni**, Piazza Sant'Anastasia 4, ✆ 045 595 044, ✉ 045 800 4130. Goethe and Mozart slept here, and would feel just at home today, at least in the rooms appointed with 18th-century antiques. The public rooms are equally resplendent, the ceilings adorned with 17th-century frescoes, the banquet rooms with circus scenes.

★★★★ **Colomba d'Oro**, Via C. Cattaneo 10, ✆ 045 595 300, ✉ 045 594 974, in a quiet, traffic-free street near the Arena, offers very comfortable air-conditioned rooms behind its old stone façade, and secure parking, but no restaurant.

★★★★ **Accademia**, Via Scala 12, ✆/✉ 045 596 222. A restored 16th-century palace houses this excellent, atmospheric choice smack in the centre.

expensive

★★★ **Giulietta e Romeo**, Vicolo Tre Marchetti 3, ✆ 045 800 3554, ✉ 045 801 0862, centrally located on a quiet street near the Arena, has recently been renovated and offers fine rooms (and parking facilities), but no restaurant.

★★★ **De' Capuleti**, Via del Pontiere, ✆ 045 800 0154, another good choice in the historic centre, has air-conditioning and satellite TV for news junkies.

★★★ **Novo Hotel Rossi**, Via delle Coste 2, ✆ 045 569 022, ✉ 045 578 297, is very convenient and simpatico if you're arriving by train; some rooms fall within the *moderate* category.

★★★   **Italia**, Via Mameli 58, ✆ 045 918 088, 🖷 045 834 8028, can offer tranquil rooms on the other side of the Adige, near the Roman Theatre; rooms are modern and comfortable and priced right.

moderate

★★   **Sammicheli**, Via Valverde 2, ✆ 045 800 3749, 🖷 045 800 4508, is convenient for opera-goers (about 150 yards from the Arena), with easy parking, and colour TVs in each room.

★★   **Torcolo**, Vicolo Listone 3, ✆ 045 800 7512, 🖷 045 800 4058, in the same area, is welcoming, convenient and not too noisy, on its quiet little square.

★★   **Scalzi**, Via Scalzi 5, ✆ 045 590 422, 🖷 045 590 069, a family-run place, has similar amenities in a fairly quiet spot just south of the Castelvecchio.

inexpensive

★   **Catullo**, Via Valerio Catullo 1, ✆ 045 800 2786, for cheaper rooms with or without bath in the centre; some even have balconies.

If you have an IYHF card, however, you can't beat the **Ostello Verona**, a 16th-century villa with frescoes in Via Fontana del Ferro 15, ✆ 045 590 360, just beyond the Castel di San Pietro (take bus no.72 to the first stop across the river). Beds are up in the newer wing. The reception stays open year-round, 24 hours a day, but you won't be allowed in until 5pm; get there early in summer.

Verona ✉ *37100*   *Eating Out*

The Veronese have long gastro-memories. They've been fond of potato gnocchi (served with melted butter and sage) since the late 16th century, when the ingredients were distributed after a great famine, and, like the Parisians, attribute their weakness for horsemeat to a siege when horses were all there was left to eat; it's served in stew called *pastissada de caval*. In summer look for Italy's finest peaches.

very expensive

Il Desco, Via dietro San Sebastiano 7, ✆ 045 595 358, is the king of the Veronese restaurant scene, in a 15th-century palace, not far from the Ponte Nuovo. Expect exquisite dishes based on seasonal ingredients: gnocchi with ewe's milk cheese, red mullet with black olives and rosemary, goose liver in a sauce of sweet wine and grapes. *Closed Sun, hols, part of Jan and June.*

Arche, Via delle Arche Scaligere 6, ✆ 045 800 7415, located near the Scaliger tombs, has been run by the same family for over a hundred years, and has long been the classic place to go for a special meal in an aristocratic setting. The freshest of fish is brought in daily from Chioggia and imaginatively prepared by the maestro in the kitchen. Excellent wine list. *Closed Sun, Mon lunch.*

expensive

I Dodici Apostoli, Corticella San Marco 3, ✆ 045 596 999, is an even older favourite, located a couple of streets from Piazza delle Erbe, offering a traditional Renaissance setting—complete with frescoes of Romeo and Juliet. The name is derived from 12 18th-century 'apostles' of the kitchen who gathered here to dine. Some of the delicacies served today are adapted from Roman or Renaissance recipes; the *salmone in crosta* (marinated salmon in pastry) is famous. *Closed Sun eve, Mon, two weeks June and July.*

Nuovo Marconi, Via Fogge 4, ✆ 045 591 910. For a glamorous gourmet experience, sit outside in Piazza dei Signori and have your every culinary care tended to by the elegant waiters. The food is as rooted in tradition as the surroundings: tagliolini with crab, gnocchi with pumpkin, and fine scampi and duck. *Closed Sun, part of June and July.*

Bottega del Vino, Via Scudo di Francia 3 (off Via Mazzini), ✆ 045 800 4535, a century-old place, prepares traditional recipes using organically grown ingredients, with pasta made on the premises, customized to accompany a huge list of wine from around the world. *Closed Tues, except during opera season.*

Maffei, Piazza delle Erbe 38, ✆ 045 801 0015, is another beauty, both ancient and elegant and serving a melt-in-the-mouth cheese flan and risotto with pumpkin and *amarone*. *Closed Sun, Mon in July and Aug.*

moderate

Greppia, Vicolo Samaritana 3, ✆ 045 800 4577, near Juliet's house, serves up traditional and Veronese favourites in a quiet little square. *Closed Mon, June.*

Alla Strueta, Via Redentore 4 (near the Roman Theatre), ✆ 045 803 2462, was an old workers' *osteria* now featuring delights on the order of smoked goose breast, gnocchi and, yes (or rather, neigh!), *pastissada de caval.* Prices are lower over the Adige in Veronetta. *Closed Mon and Tues lunch, Aug.*

Alla Pergola, Piazzetta Santa Maria in Solaro 10, ✆ 045 800 4744, a traditional and reliable old favourite, housed in a deconsecrated medieval church off Via Garibaldi. *Closed Wed, Aug.*

inexpensive

Giardino, Via G. Giardino 2, ✆ 044 834 330. You'll find a number of places around the Liston offering cheap, run-of-the-mill tourist menus, but for something special head north into the Borgo Trento quarter for this exceptionally friendly trattoria serving delicious homemade *tortelli di formaggio*, grilled cutlets and Italian cheesecake (*tortine di ricotta*); tables are few, so book.

Osteria Morandin, in Via XX Septembre 144 (in Veronetta just off Interrato dell'Acqua Morta) is another old standby, with a good choice of wines and a few dishes to go along. *Closed Sun.*

Stop for a coffee at the historic **Antico Cafè Dante**, Via Fogge 1; for traditional Veronese pastries, **Cordioli**, Via Cappello 39, takes some beating. *Closed Wed.*

Verona bills itself as the 'city for all seasons' and offers a wide-ranging cultural programme throughout the year. Big events take place in the Arena, especially the Stagione Lirica, the **opera and ballet** festival founded in 1913, with performances almost daily in July and August. If you're travelling on a tight schedule, it's best to reserve your seat before coming to Italy: **Liaisons Abroad** in London, ✆ 0171 384 1122, can arrange tickets before you go. Alternatively, for programme details and reservations, contact the **Ente Lirico Arena di Verona**, Piazza Brà 28, ✆ 045 8051811, *www.arena.it*; tickets sales are next to the Arena at Via Dietro Anfiteatro 6/b, ✆ 045 800 5151, ✉ 045 801 3287. If you get an unnumbered seat, plan on arriving an hour earlier to get yourself situated. And bring a cushion. At the same time Verona also hosts a **Shakespeare festival** (in Italian) in the Roman Theatre: same address as above for information and tickets.

From December to April there is **drama** in the Teatro Nuovo, and also more **opera and concerts** in the Teatro Filarmonico, sponsored by the Ente Lirico. From mid-December to mid-January Verona uses the arcades of the Arena for a massive show of Christmas cribs (*presepi*) from around the world. In the spring the city hosts one of Italy's oldest **carnivals**, first recorded in 1530; the last Friday of carnival is known as the 'Bacchanal of Gnocchi', presided over by the Papà dello Gnoco, who walks about with a giant potato dumpling on a fork. All listings are in the tourist office's free *Passport Verona*. For discos, films and more casual artistic events, *Siri-Sera* is a broadsheet fly-posted weekly in cafés and around town.

There are a number of **art galleries** around the Piazza delle Erbe, while the area between the Via Ponte Pietra, Via Duomo, Sottoriva, and Corso S. Anastasia is called the 'little city of antiques'. But buyer beware: the region is Italy's largest producer of reproductions.

Unlike the Venetians, the Veronese like to be out and about in the evening and have their own expression for pub-crawling, '*andar per goti*' (going Goth-ing), after a memorable binge by Theodoric's bunch back in the 5th century. The bars in Piazza Brà and Piazza delle Erbe are the busiest. Old-fashioned **Al Carro Armato**, Via San Pietro Martire 2a, ✆ 045 803 0175, near the Piazza de' Signori, is one of the most atmospheric; **Le Vecete,** near Piazza delle Erbe at Via Pellicciai 32, ✆ 045 594 681, is a favourite wine bar (*closed Sun*).

Day Trips from Verona

Getting Around

Verona has an excellent **bus** network (*see* p.191), with APT services to Bosco Chiesanuova, Negràr, Fumane, Volargne and destinations towards Lake Garda; and to Villafranca di Verona and Valéggio sur Mincio. There are **trains** to Isola della Scala and Legnano.

Tourist Information

Bosco Chiesanuova : Piazza Chiesa, 34, ℂ/⌕ 045 705 0088.

For guided tours of **Lessinia Natural Park**: Via Ca' di Cozzi 41 (Verona) ℂ 045 915 155 ⌕ 045 915 970.

Lessinia Natural Park

North of Verona, the soft foothills of the Dolomites make up the Lessinia, now a Regional Natural Park, and one famous for rocks, in formations, fossils and flintstones. In the 13th century Lessinia was settled by Bavarians, whose descendants still speak a kind of medieval German, or Cimbra. Although traditionally a poor area, the inhabitants enjoyed a golden age in the 1600s, manufacturing flintlocks. You can learn more about them, their folklore, costumes, and the huge *tromboni* (a kind of arquebus) that they blast on holidays, at the small ethnographic museum (ℂ 045 784 7026) in Giazza, one of Lessinia's prettiest villages with its medieval German houses. **Bolca**, southeast of Giazza, caused a sensation in the Renaissance when the discovery of a rich bed of fossilized fish was cited as proof of Noah's Flood. They are also extremely beautiful and delicate, and in the local fossil museum (ℂ 045 656 5111).

A winding road loops east to the next valley and **Bosco Chiesanuova**, Lessinia's modest winter sports centre. From here, follow the road to **Velo Veronese**, the starting point for a visit to **Camposilvano**, its fossil museum, and the **Valley of the Sphinxes** (*Valle delle Sfingi*), named for its striking chasms and landforms, made of layer upon layer of red ammonite. In recent years a beautiful stalactite cave was discovered in adjacent Roverè: **Grotta di Roverè 1000**, open for visits (ℂ 045 783 5777).

Another pretty place to aim for is west, at **Molina**, where the Parco delle Cascate has paths along the waterfalls. North, beyond **Fosse**, the slopes of Corno d'Aquilio are pierced by the **Spluga della Preta**, one of the world's deepest chasms, its floor halfway to hell—2,906ft down. Lessinia's wealth of flint first attracted people in the Lower Palaeolithic age (500,000 BC). Shelters and flint workshops have been discovered on the ridges and in the caves; some can be seen in the prehistory museum at **Sant'Anna d'Alfaedo**, along with a 20ft-long fossilized shark. South of Sant'Anna, not far off the road to Fane, don't miss the **Ponte di Veja**, a spectacular natural 170ft arch, the inspiration for the Malebolge bridge in Dante's *Inferno*.

Valpolicella

The cherry-scented prince of Veronese wines, Valpolicella was the *vino retico* quaffed by all the emperors from Augustus to Theodoric, and hails from 19 *comuni* west of Verona and south of Lessinia. The Molinara, Rondinella and Corvina grapes that grow so well here are vinified in different ways—the familiar stuff sold in your supermarket

at home (*Superiore*), and three others, made from well-ripened grapes left to dry for several months: *Recioto della Valpolicella*, a fine dessert wine with a bittersweet aftertaste, not unlike port; DOCG *Amarone*, left longer in the vat to become a dry, powerful (16°) wine of great character that can be aged up to 20 years, one of the best and most distinctive wines in Italy; and *Ripasso*, wine fermented on the lees of the *Recioto* to take on some of nuances of *Amarone*.

The region of Valpolicella is sliced by torrents and dotted with Romanesque churches and villas. **Negràr**, one of the main centres, has a handsome 12th-century campanile and park at Villa Rizzardi. Just west in **Pedemonte**, Palladio's **Villa Serego poi Boccoli** was built in 1565–9, its two prominent wings bearing a continuous double portico of Ionic columns. West, in a hamlet of the same name, the 12th-century church of **San Floriano** is one of the prettiest in the area, with a frieze and an arcade on its tufa façade. **Fumane**, another important wine village to the north, has a number of stately homes and a landmark, the 16th-century **Villa della Torre** (on the road to Càvolo). The name of the architect has been forgotten, although the originality of the design suggests Giulio Romano; based on the concept of an ancient Roman villa, the rooms are off a peristyle court with a fountain. Other features include pools resembling Roman *piscinae*, a little octagonal temple, and towering dovecotes.

Further west, **Sant'Ambrogio** produces Verona's famous red marble in addition to red wine; nearby, in the lovely old hilltop hamlet of **San Giorgio**, the parish church was founded in the 7th century and expanded in the 1100s. The ciborium over the altar also dates from the 600s, and among the frescoes there's a fascinating 11th-century *Last Judgement*. The cloister has Byzantine-Romanesque capitals, and leads to the 14th-century frescoed Sala della Collegiata. In such ancient surroundings, perhaps it's not surprising that the parish maintains a custom long forgotten elsewhere in Italy: the distribution of fava beans after a funeral, symbolic of the afterlife. North of Sant'Ambrogio on the Adige, **Volargne** merits a detour for its riverside **Villa del Bene**, built in the 1400s and enlarged by Sammicheli in the next century. He enclosed the courtyard at the entrance, and added the portico and loggia to the façade, a second courtyard, and dovecotes; the interior has fine frescoes by Caroto and Domenico Brusasorci, including—rather bizarrely for a villa— scenes of the Apocalypse.

Up the Rear Slopes of Monte Baldo

Just west of Sant'Ambrogio (*see* above) is one of your last chances for a long time to cross the Adige and the A22 into the eastern valleys of Lake Garda's **Monte Baldo** (*see* below). Once over the Adige, turn north at **Affi**, a village made of rounded stones from the Adige, for **Rivoli Veronese**, a small village set in a morainic amphitheatre. This is the origin of the famous Rue de Rivoli in Paris, laid out by Napoleon to celebrate his great victory over the Austrians here on 14 January 1797. The village's privately run **Museo Napoleonico** (*open daily 9–12 and 2.30–6; adm*) has a relief model of the battle, weapons, documents, and a copy of the Treaty of Campoformio signed that same year, giving the Republic of Venice to Austria in exchange for Belgium.

Carry on north for **Caprino Veronese**, a medieval new town and later a favourite area for *villeggiatura*. One summer house, the 17th-century **Villa Carlotti**, now serves as the town hall and **Museo Civico** (*Tues, Wed, Fri, Sat 10–12*), where you can visit the 'Room of Dreams' with its caryatids and frescoes, and another chamber containing a magnificent 14th-century statue group called *Il Compianto* ('The Lamented One'), where life-size figures of Joseph of Arimathea, St John, Nicodemus and the holy women mourn a strikingly dead cadaverous Christ.

From Caprino you can turn up the sometimes vertiginous road west for **San Zeno di Montagna**, with views over Lake Garda, or meander west towards **Platano**, where an enormous ancient plane tree predates even the 15th-century Palazzo Nichesola, with its high chimneys. The main road continues north by way of the striking **Santuario della Madonna della Corona**, set up on a nearly inaccessible rocky spur under a cliff, where a statue of Our Lady of Sorrows appeared in a blaze of light just as the Turks captured Rhodes from the Knights of St John in 1522, having apparently flown there to escape the infidels. The shrine was built in 1540 and 556 steps were dug out of the side of the mountain for pilgrims; thousands still come to pay their respects on 19 September, although most now drive up the paved road.

Further north, **Ferrara di Monte Baldo** was an iron-mining centre and is now an excursion centre, with skiing and a botanical garden sheltering some of the many rare species that thrive in Monte Baldo's unique micro-climate. You won't, however, see the species the Italians like best—black truffles, which thrive under the big mountain's oaks.

Eating Out

Bolca/Altissimo ✉ 36070

Just east of Bolca in Altissimo, dine superbly at **Casin del Gamba**, an old hunting lodge 2km from the centre at Via Pizzati 1, Roccolo, ✆ 0444 687 709 (*expensive*), where the chef prepares dishes entirely based on the season, accompanied by a great wine list and masterful desserts. *Closed Sun eve and Mon, part of Jan and Aug.*

Pedemonte ✉ 37020

Not far from Palladio's villa in Valpolicella, the lovely Relais & Château ★★★★**Villa del Quar**, Via Quar 12, ✆ 0456 800 681, ✆ 0456 800 604 (*very expensive*) has been beautifully restored; its restaurant, **Arquade**, occupies in part the villa's chapel and emphasizes the best of the region's cuisine, with the occasional French touch. *Closed Mon out of season, and Jan 6–mid-Mar.*

Sant'Ambrogio di Valpolicella ✉ 37010

Once you've looked at the vines, stop at **Groto de Corgnan**, Via Corgnano 41, ✆ 045 773 1372 (*expensive–moderate*) to sit around the fire and sip them with dishes specially concocted to bring out their best—the wine list includes the finest Amarones. *Closed Sun and Mon lunch.*

Day Trips South of Verona: La Pianura Veronese

Six hundred years ago, Verona's well-watered breadbasket (in this case, rice basket) was crossed by one of the wonders of Europe: the *Serraglio*, a mini-Great Wall of China, built in the mid-14th century by the Scaligers to defend Verona from Mantua and other bullies coming from the south. Stretching 16km, fortified with 200 towers, these thick walls, complete with moats and towers, were the most advanced fortifications of the day. But by the time the Venetians inherited the *Serraglio* in the 15th century they were not terribly impressed with its ability to stand up to the artillery of the day, and concentrated their defences at Legnano and Peschiera del Garda; now only traces of the great walls remain.

The *Serraglio*'s eastern hub was **Villafranca di Verona**, a town founded by Verona along the road to Mantua in 1185 as an agricultural colony and fortified camp. Laid out in an elongated grid, with an elevated **castle** on one end, its plan is reminiscent of the *bastides* or *villefranches* ('free towns' with tax exemptions to attract settlers) founded by England and France during the Hundred Years War. There were a number of these in the Veneto, but this is the only one to keep its walls intact.

Just as impressive, in its way, is the massive **Villa Canossa** at **Grezzano**, 4km southeast, a neo-Palladian ranch built in 1776, in the centre of an enormous rice plantation. One of Verona's four DOC wines, *Bianco di Custoza*, is grown to the west of Villafranca at **Custoza**, a peaceful town of cypress-fringed roads and vineyards, but a jinx for Italy: the two war cemeteries recall major defeats by the Piedmontese (1848) and the Italians (1866) at the hands of the Austrians.

The source of all the moisture in these parts is the Adige and Lake Garda's main drain into the Po, the river Mincio. On its banks, **Valéggio sul Mincio** started out as another Veronese colony and was given a 14th-century castle and a bridge by the Visconti during their brazen attempt to seize all of Italy. Most of all they were interested in the possibilities of diverting the Mincio: they intended either to drain the lakes of Mantua downstream to make it easy to conquer, or to flood the plain inside the *Serraglio* in case Mantua attacked. In 1393 they invested an enormous sum in the project at **Borghetto** (a *frazione* of Valéggio), building at the end of the Scaliger's *Serraglio* the 1,980ft-long **Ponte Rotta**, a cross between a fortified bridge and a dyke, with a system of portcullises that could be used to shut off the river's flow. It's still there, a bit overgrown but one of the surviving engineering marvels of the Middle Ages. Nearly six centuries later another Visconti, Luchino, found Borghetto's romantic, 19th-century atmosphere the perfect setting for his film *Senso*.

In fact, everything here is on a big scale. There's the **Cavour Parco Acquatico** south of town, a water fun park in a tropical garden with palms and sandy beaches, set in an enormous botanical park with lakes and beautiful old trees (*② 045 795 0904, open May–Sept, 9.30am–7pm; adm L18,000 adults, L13,000 children*). In Valéggio itself, the old grounds of the Villa Maffe became in the early 19th century the **Sigurtà Gardens** (*open Mar–Nov daily 9–6; adm L30,000 per car*). This was the 40-year project of Dr Count Carlo Sigurtà, 'Italy's Capability Brown', who, granted water rights from the Mincio, used them to transform a barren waste into 123 acres of Anglo-Italian gardens along a 7km lane; parking areas along the route allow you to get out and walk along the waterlily ponds, topiary gardens and valleys of roses.

One of the strangest encounters of any kind in Italian history occurred just north of Valéggio, in **Salionze**. Word had reached Pope Leo the Great that Attila the Hun had laid waste to the Veneto and was on his way to do the same to Rome. Leo rode forth to prevent Attila from coming any closer and met up with the Hunnish warlord in Salionze. Their meeting is faithfully recorded on Leo's tombstone in St Peter's: the Pope told Attila that he would get a fatal nosebleed if he came any closer. But there's a snag—Attila doesn't understand Latin. Fortunately SS Peter and Paul come down from the clouds to translate, and the Hun, suitably impressed, turns on his heel and retreats—it's as good an explanation as any for why Attila suddenly turned back from his stated goal. These days Salionze sees few Huns or popes, but probably the occasional nosebleed from kids zooming down the vertiginous waterslides at **Acquapark Altomincio** (*open mid-May to late Sept, 10–7; adm L16,000, children L13,000*).

The Eastern Plain: Legnano and Cologna Veneta

Halfway between Verona and Rovigo, **Legnano** is the biggest town and industrial centre of the Pianura. Two mighty floods of the Adige and Second World War bombardments have obliterated everything but a 16th-century tower, a last reminder that for a thousand years Legnano was a key in the Veneto's defences and a corner of the Austrian 'Quadrilateral'. It was also the birthplace of Antonio Salieri (1750–1825), the composer and director of the Viennese Opera, who did *not* poison Mozart, at least according to the locals (and most historians); Legnano's theatre is named in his honour.

Cologna Veneta, east of the Adige, was another agricultural colony, founded by the Romans this time, back in 170 BC; originally the main crop was hemp, although now the town specializes in *mandorlato* (nougat; try it at Rocco Garzotto & Figlio, Via Quari Destra 57). The historic centre is well preserved, around a picturesque 19th-century cathedral with an altarpiece of the *Nativity* by Bartolomeo Montagna. The neighbouring **Civico Museo Archaeologico** (*open Mon–Fri 9–12, exc Tues; Sat 4–6, Sun 9–12, 4–6*) has a good assortment of finds, not only from Roman times but also from the Paleoveneti and the Bronze Age (8th century BC). In nearby Pressana, **Villa Querini Stampalia** is an example of a villa that expanded over the years into a handsome mix of late Gothic and Renaissance elements.

Eating Out

This is prime grazing land, for people, that is: Valéggio, famous for its homemade tortellini, has over 40 restaurants, and the Pianura has two gourmet shrines.

Valéggio sul Mincio ✉ 37067

A charming 17th-century inn, the **Antica Locanda Minicio**, Via Michelangelo 12, Borghetto, ✆ 045 795 0059 (*expensive*) adds culinary expertise to a delightful setting—depending on the season you can dine by the fireplace or out on the banks of the Mincio. The dishes have a touch of Mantua in them, which isn't a bad thing. *Closed Wed eve, Thurs, some of Feb and Nov.*

But many give the Tortellini de Valéggio crown to **Borsa**, Via Goito 2, ℂ 045 795 0093 (*moderate*) where the river and lake fish make a good *secondo*. *Closed Tues eve, Wed.*

Isola della Scala ✉ 37063

The 'Gilded Cage' or **Gabbia d'Oro**, 6km from Isola at Gabbia south of Verona, ℂ 045 733 0020 (*very expensive–expensive*), occupies an old inn, elegantly restored if not always easy to find on these arrow-straight country roads. The reward: Veronese regional cuisine at its finest, prepared with the best and freshest ingredients, although you may want to avoid some of the fussier dishes on the menu. *Closed Tues and Wed, Jan and Aug.*

Isola Rizza ✉ 37050

Lost in the middle of an ugly industrial area north of Legnano, next to a *panettoni* bakery, **Perbellini**, Via Muelle 10, ℂ 045 713 5352 (*very expensive–expensive*) is an island of classic refinement and masterful cuisine, every dish from *antipasti* to dessert a pure delight, with service to match. *Closed Sun eve and Mon, part of Jan, July and Aug.*

atrium: entrance court of a Roman house or early church.

badia: *abbazia*, an abbey or abbey church.

baldacchino: baldachin, a columned stone canopy above the altar of a church.

barchesse: wings of a Veneto villa, originally used as farm buildings for storing grain or other supplies

basilica: a rectangular building, usually divided into three aisles by rows of columns. In Rome this was the common form for law courts and other public buildings, and Roman Christians adapted it for their early churches.

campanile: a bell tower.

cardo: transverse street of a Roman castrum-shaped city.

cartoon: the preliminary sketch for a fresco or tapestry.

caryatid: supporting pillar or column carved into a standing female form; male versions are called **telamons**.

castrum: a Roman military camp, always nearly rectangular, with straight streets and gates at the cardinal points. Later the Romans founded or refounded cities in the form, hundreds of which survive today (Verona and Padua are clear examples).

cavea: the semicircle of seats in a classical theatre.

cenacolo: fresco of the Last Supper, often on the wall of a monastery refectory.

centro storico: historic centre.

ciborium: a tabernacle; the word is often used for large, free-standing tabernacles, or in the sense of a baldacchino.

chiaroscuro: the arrangement or treatment of light and dark in a painting.

comune: commune, or commonwealth, referring to the governments of the free cities of the Middle Ages. Today it denotes any local government, from the *Comune di Roma* down to the smallest village.

condottiere: the leader of a band of mercenaries in late medieval and Renaissance times.

confraternity: a religious lay brotherhood, often serving as a neighbourhood mutual aid and burial society, or following some specific charitable work.

cupola: a dome.

Artistic, Architectural & Historic Terms

decumanus: street of a Roman castrum-shaped city parallel to the longer axis, the central, main avenue called the Decumanus Major.

duomo: cathedral.

forum: the central square of a Roman town, with its most important temples and public buildings. The word means 'outside', as the original Roman Forum was outside the first city walls.

fresco: wall painting, the most important Italian medium of art since Etruscan times. It isn't easy: first the artist draws the sinopia (q.v.) on the wall. This is covered with plaster, but only a little at a time, as the paint must be on the plaster before it dries. Leonardo da Vinci's endless attempts to find clever shortcuts ensured that little of his work would survive.

Ghibellines: one of the great medieval parties, supporters of the Holy Roman Emperors.

gonfalon: the banner of a medieval free city; the *gonfaloniere*, or flag bearer, was often the most important public official.

Guelphs (*see* Ghibellines): a great medieval political faction, supporters of the Pope.

intarsia: work in inlaid wood or marble.

intonaco: the stucco-like material covering the brick substructure of Palladio's villas.

narthex: the enclosed porch of a church.

palazzo: not just a palace, but any large, important building.

palio: a banner, and the horse race in which city neighbourhoods contend for it.

Pantocrator: Christ 'ruler of all', a common subject for apse paintings and mosaics in areas influenced by Byzantine art.

piano: upper floor or story in a building; *piano nobile*, the first floor.

pieve: a parish church, especially in the north.

podestà: a mayor or governor from outside a *comune*, usually chosen by the emperor or overlord, like Venice; although sometimes a factionalized city would itself invite a *podestà* in for a period to sort it out.

polyptych: an altarpiece composed of more than three panels.

predella: smaller paintings on panels below the main subject of a painted altarpiece.

presepio: a Christmas crib.

quadriga: chariot pulled by four horses.

quattrocento: the 1400s—the Italian way of referring to centuries (duecento, trecento, quattrocento, cinquecento, etc.).

rocca: a citadel.

Sacra Conversazione: Madonna enthroned with saints.

scuola: the headquarters of a confraternity or guild, usually adjacent to a church.

sinopia: the layout of a fresco (q.v.), etched by the artist on the wall before the plaster is applied. Often these are works of art in their own right.

terra firma: Venice's mainland possessions.

thermae: Roman baths.

tondo: round relief, painting or terracotta.

transenna: marble screen separating the altar area from the rest of an early Christian church.

triptych: a painting, especially an altarpiece, in three sections.

trompe-l'œil: art that uses perspective effects to deceive the eye—for example, to create the illusion of depth on a flat surface, or to make columns and arches painted on a wall see real.

tympanum: the semicircular space, often bearing a painting or relief, above a portal.

The fathers of modern Italian were Dante, Manzoni and television. Each had a part in creating a national language from an infinity of regional and local dialects; the Florentine Dante, the first to write in the vernacular, did much to put the Tuscan dialect in the foreground of Italian literature. Manzoni's revolutionary novel, *I Promessi Sposi*, heightened national consciousness by using an everyday language all could understand in the 19th century. Television in the last few decades is performing an even more spectacular linguistic unification; although the majority of Italians still speak a dialect at home, school and work, their TV idols insist on proper Italian.

Perhaps because they are so busy learning their own beautiful but grammatically complex language, Italians are not especially apt at learning others. English lessons, however, have been the rage for years, and at most hotels and restaurants there will be someone who speaks some English. In small towns and out-of-the-way places, finding an Anglophone may prove more difficult. The words and phrases below should help you out in most situations, but the ideal way to come to Italy is with some Italian under your belt; your visit will be richer, and you're much more likely to make some Italian friends.

Italian words are pronounced phonetically. Every vowel and consonant is sounded. Consonants are the same as in English, except the 'c' which, when followed by an 'e' or 'i', is pronounced like the English 'ch' (*cinque* thus becomes cheenquay). Italian 'g' is also soft before 'i' or 'e' as in *gira*, or jee-ra. 'H' is never sounded; 'z' is pronounced like 'ts'. The consonants 'sc' before the vowels 'i' or 'e' becomes like the English 'sh' as in 'sci', pronounced shee; 'ch' is pronounced like a 'k' as in Chianti, kee-an-tee; 'gn' as 'ny' in English (*bagno*, pronounced ban-yo); while 'gli' is pronounced like the middle of the word million (Castiglione, pronounced Ca-stee-lyon-ay).

Vowel pronunciation is: 'a' as in English father; 'e' when unstressed is pronounced like 'a' in fate (as in *mele*), when stressed can be the same or like the 'e' in pet (*bello*); 'i' is like the 'i'

Language

in machine; 'o', like 'e', has two sounds, 'o' as in hope when unstressed (*tacchino*), and usually 'o' as in rock when stressed (*morte*); 'u' is pronounced like the 'u' in June.

The accent usually (but not always!) falls on the penultimate syllable. Also note that in the big northern cities, the informal way of addressing someone as you, *tu*, is widely used; the more formal *lei* or *voi* is commonly used in provincial districts.

Useful Words and Phrases

yes/no/maybe	*si/no/forse*	Good night	*Buona notte*
I don't know	*Non lo so*	Goodbye	*Arrivederla* (formal),
I don't understand (Italian)	*Non capisco (italiano)*		*arrivederci, ciao* (informal)
Does someone here speak English?	*C'è qualcuno qui che parla inglese?*	What?/Who?/Where?	*Che?/Chi?/Dove?*
Speak slowly	*Parla lentamente*	When?/Why?	*Quando?/Perché?*
Could you assist me?	*Potrebbe aiutarmi?*	How?	*Come?*
Help!	*Aiuto!*	How much?	*Quanto?*
Please	*Per favore*	I am lost	*Mi sono smarrito*
Thank you (very much)	*(Molte) grazie*	I am hungry	*Ho fame*
You're welcome	*Prego*	I am thirsty	*Ho sete*
What do you call this in Italian?	*Come si chiama questo in italiano?*	I am sleepy	*Ho sonno*
		I am sorry	*Mi dispiace*
It doesn't matter	*Non importa*	I am tired	*Sono stanco*
All right	*Va bene*	I am ill	*Mi sento male*
Excuse me	*Mi scusi*	Leave me alone	*Lasciami in pace*
Be careful!	*Attenzione!*	good	*buono/bravo*
Nothing	*Niente*	bad	*male/cattivo*
It is urgent!	*È urgente!*	It's all the same	*Fa lo stesso*
How are you?	*Come sta?*	fast	*rapido*
Well, and you?	*Bene, e lei?*	slow	*lento*
What is your name?	*Come si chiama?*	big	*grande*
Hello	*Salve* or *ciao* (both informal)	small	*piccolo*
		hot	*caldo*
Good morning	*Buongiorno* (formal hello)	cold	*freddo*
		up	*su*
Good afternoon, evening	*Buonasera* (also formal hello)	down	*giù*
		here	*qui*
		there	*lì*

Shopping, Service, Sightseeing

I would like...	*Vorrei...*	money	*soldi*
Where is/are...	*Dov'è/Dove sono...*	newspaper (foreign)	*giornale (straniero)*
How much is it?	*Quanto viene questo?*	pharmacy	*farmacia*
open	*aperto*	policeman	*poliziotto*
closed	*chiuso*	police station	*commissariato*
cheap/expensive	*a buon prezzo/caro*	post office	*ufficio postale*
bank	*banca*	sea	*mare*
beach	*spiaggia*	shop	*negozio*
bed	*letto*	room	*camera*
church	*chiesa*	tobacco shop	*tabaccaio*
entrance	*entrata*	WC	*toilette/bagno*
exit	*uscita*	men	*Signori/Uomini*
hospital	*ospedale*	women	*Signore/Donne*

Time

What time is it?	*Che ore sono?*	today	*oggi*
month	*mese*	yesterday	*ieri*
week	*settimana*	tomorrow	*domani*
day	*giorno*	soon	*fra poco*
morning	*mattina*	later	*dopo/più tardi*
afternoon	*pomeriggio*	It is too early	*È troppo presto*
evening	*sera*	It is too late	*È troppo tardi*

Days

Monday	*lunedì*	Friday	*venerdì*
Tuesday	*martedì*	Saturday	*sabato*
Wednesday	*mercoledì*	Sunday	*domenica*
Thursday	*giovedì*		

Numbers

one	*uno/una*	twenty	*venti*
two	*due*	twenty-one	*ventuno*
three	*tre*	twenty-two	*ventidue*
four	*quattro*	thirty	*trenta*
five	*cinque*	thirty-one	*trentuno*
six	*sei*	forty	*quaranta*
seven	*sette*	fifty	*cinquanta*
eight	*otto*	sixty	*sessanta*
nine	*nove*	seventy	*settanta*
ten	*dieci*	eighty	*ottanta*
eleven	*undici*	ninety	*novanta*
twelve	*dodici*	hundred	*cento*
thirteen	*tredici*	one hundred & one	*centouno*
fourteen	*quattordici*	two hundred	*duecento*
fifteen	*quindici*	one thousand	*mille*
sixteen	*sedici*	two thousand	*duemila*
seventeen	*diciassette*	million	*milione*
eighteen	*diciotto*	a thousand million	*miliardo*
nineteen	*diciannove*		

Transport

airport	*aeroporto*	port station	*stazione marittima*
automobile	*macchina*	railway station	*stazione ferroviaria*
bus/coach	*autobus/pullman*	seat (reserved)	*posto (prenotato)*
bus stop	*fermata*	ship	*nave*
customs	*dogana*	taxi	*tassì*
platform	*binario*	ticket	*biglietto*
port	*porto*	train	*treno*

Travel Directions

I want to go to...	*Desidero andare a...*	Have a good trip	*Buon viaggio!*
How can I get to...?	*Come posso andare a...?*	near	*vicino*
		far	*lontano*
Do you stop at...?	*Ferma a...?*	left	*sinistra*
Where is...?	*Dov'è...?*	right	*destra*
How far is it to...?	*Quanto siamo lontani da...?*	straight ahead	*sempre diritto*
When does the ... leave?	*A che ora parte ... ?*	forward	*avanti*
What is the name of this station?	*Come si chiama questa stazione?*	backwards	*indietro*
		north	*nord*
When does the next ... leave?	*Quando parte il prossimo...?*	south	*sud*
		east	*est/oriente*
From where does it leave?	*Da dove parte?*	west	*ovest/occidente*
		round the corner	*dietro l'angolo*
How long does the trip take?	*Quanto tempo dura il viaggio?*	crossroads	*bivio*
		street/road	*strada*
How much is the fare?	*Quant'è il biglietto?*	square	*piazza*

Driving

bicycle	*bicicletta*	motorbike/scooter	*motocicletta/Vespa*
breakdown	*guasto* or *panne*	narrow	*stretto*
bridge	*ponte*	no parking	*sosta vietata*
car hire	*noleggio macchina*	parking	*parcheggio*
danger	*pericolo*	petrol/diesel	*benzina/gasolio*
driver	*guidatore*	slow down	*rallentare*
driving licence	*patente di guida*	speed	*velocità*
garage	*garage*	This doesn't work	*Questo non funziona*
map/town plan	*carta/pianta*	toll	*pedaggio*
mechanic	*meccanico*	Where is the road to...?	*Dov'è la strada per...?*

Italian Menu Vocabulary

Antipasti

These before-meal treats can include almost anything; among the most common are:

antipasto misto	mixed *antipasto*
bruschetta	garlic toast (sometimes with tomatoes)
carciofi (sott'olio)	artichokes (in oil)
crostini	liver pâté on toast
frutti di mare	seafood
funghi (trifolati)	mushrooms (with anchovies, garlic, and lemon)
gamberi ai fagioli	prawns (shrimps) with white beans
mozzarella (in carrozza)	cow or buffalo cheese (fried with bread in batter)
olive	olives
prosciutto (con melone)	raw ham (with melon)
salami	cured pork
salsicce	sausages

Minestre (Soups) and Pasta

These dishes are the principal typical first courses (*primi*) served throughout Italy.

agnolotti	ravioli with meat
cacciucco	spiced fish soup
cannelloni	meat and cheese rolled in pasta tubes
cappelletti	small ravioli, often in broth
crespelle	crêpes
fettuccine	long strips of pasta
frittata	omelette
gnocchi	potato dumplings
lasagne	sheets of pasta baked with meat and cheese sauce
minestra di verdura	thick vegetable soup
minestrone	soup with meat, vegetables, and pasta
orecchiette	ear-shaped pasta, often served with turnip greens
panzerotti	ravioli filled with mozzarella, anchovies and egg
pappardelle alla lepre	pasta with hare sauce
pasta e fagioli	soup with beans, bacon and tomatoes
pastina in brodo	tiny pasta in broth
penne all'arrabbiata	quill-shaped pasta with tomatoes and hot peppers
polenta	cake or pudding of corn semolina
risotto (alla milanese)	Italian rice (with stock, saffron and wine)
spaghetti all'amatriciana	with spicy sauce of salt pork, tomatoes, onions and chilli
spaghetti alla bolognese	with ground meat, ham, mushrooms, etc.
spaghetti alla carbonara	with bacon, eggs and black pepper
spaghetti al pomodoro	with tomato sauce
spaghetti al sugo/ragù	with meat sauce
spaghetti alle vongole	with clam sauce
stracciatella	broth with eggs and cheese
sagliatelle	flat egg noodles
tortellini al pomodoro/panna/in brodo	pasta caps filled with meat and cheese, with tomato sauce/with cream/in broth
vermicelli	very thin spaghetti

Carne (Meat)

abbacchio	milk-fed lamb
agnello	lamb
anatra	duck
animelle	sweetbreads
arista	pork loin
arrosto misto	mixed roast meats
bistecca alla fiorentina	Florentine beef steak
bocconcini	veal mixed with ham and cheese and fried
bollito misto	stew of boiled meats
braciola	chop
brasato di manzo	braised beef with vegetables
bresaola	dried raw meat similar to ham
capretto	kid
capriolo	roebuck
carne di castrato/suino	mutton/pork

carpaccio	thin slices of raw beef served with a piquant sauce
cassoeula	winter stew with pork and cabbage
cervello (al burro nero)	brains (in black butter sauce)
cervo	venison
cinghiale	boar
coniglio	rabbit
cotoletta (alla milanese/alla bolognese)	veal cutlet (fried in breadcrumbs/with ham and cheese)
fagiano	pheasant
faraona (alla creta)	guinea fowl (in earthenware pot)
fegato alla veneziana	liver (usually of veal) with filling
lepre (in salmi)	hare (marinated in wine)
lombo di maiale	pork loin
lumache	snails
maiale (al latte)	pork (cooked in milk)
manzo	beef
ossobuco	braised veal knuckle with herbs
pancetta	rolled pork
pernice	partridge
petto di pollo	boned chicken breast
(alla fiorentina/bolognese/	(fried in butter/with ham and cheese/
sorpresa)	stuffed and deep fried)
piccione	pigeon
pizzaiola	beef steak with tomato and oregano sauce
pollo	chicken
(alla cacciatora/alla diavola/	(with tomatoes and mushrooms cooked in wine/grilled/
alla Marengo)	fried with tomatoes, garlic and wine)
polpette	meatballs
quaglie	quails
rane	frogs
rognoni	kidneys
saltimbocca	veal scallop with prosciutto and sage, cooked in wine and butter
scaloppine	thin slices of veal sautéed in butter
spezzatino	pieces of beef or veal, usually stewed
spiedino	meat on a skewer or stick
stufato	beef braised in white wine with vegetables
tacchino	turkey
trippa	tripe
uccelletti	small birds on a skewer
vitello	veal

Pesce (Fish)

acciughe or alici	anchovies
anguilla	eel
aragosta	lobster
aringa	herring
baccalà	dried salt cod
bonito	small tuna
branzino	sea bass
calamari	squid

cappe sante	scallops
cefalo	grey mullet
coda di rospo	angler fish
cozze	mussels
datteri di mare	razor (or date) mussels
dentice	dentex (perch-like fish)
dorato	gilt head
fritto misto	mixed fried delicacies, usually fish
gamberetto	shrimp
gamberi (di fiume)	prawns (crayfish)
granchio	crab
insalata di mare	seafood salad
lampreda	lamprey
merluzzo	cod
nasello	hake
orata	bream
ostriche	oysters
pescespada	swordfish
polipi/ polpi	octopus
pesce azzurro	various types of small fish
pesce di San Pietro	John Dory
rombo	turbot
sarde	sardines
seppie	cuttlefish
sgombro	mackerel
sogliola	sole
squadro	monkfish
tonno	tuna
triglia	red mullet (rouget)
trota	trout
trota salmonata	salmon trout
vongole	small clams
zuppa di pesce	mixed fish in sauce or stew

Contorni (Side Dishes, Vegetables)

asparagi (alla fiorentina)	asparagus (with fried eggs)
broccoli (calabrese, romana)	broccoli (green, spiral)
carciofi (alla giudia)	artichokes (deep fried)
cardi	cardoons, thistles
carote	carrots
cavolfiore	cauliflower
cavolo	cabbage
ceci	chick peas
cetriolo	cucumber
cipolla	onion
fagioli	white beans
fagiolini	French (green) beans
fave	broad beans
finocchio	fennel
funghi (porcini)	mushrooms (boletus)

insalata (mista, verde)	salad (mixed, green)
lattuga	lettuce
lenticchie	lentils
melanzane (al forno)	aubergine/eggplant (filled and baked)
patate (fritte)	potatoes (fried)
peperoni	sweet peppers
peperonata	stewed peppers, onions, etc., similar to ratatouille
piselli (al prosciutto)	peas (with ham)
pomodoro (i)	tomato(es)
porri	leeks
radicchio	red chicory
radice	radish
rapa	turnip
sedano	celery
spinaci	spinach
verdure	greens
zucca	pumpkin
zucchini	courgettes

Formaggio (Cheese)

bel paese	a soft white cow's cheese
cacio/caciocavallo	pale yellow, often sharp cheese
fontina	rich cow's milk cheese
groviera	mild cheese (gruyère)
gorgonzola	soft blue cheese
parmigiano	Parmesan cheese
pecorino	sharp sheep's cheese
provolone	sharp, tangy cheese; dolce is less strong
stracchino	soft white cheese

Frutta (Fruit, Nuts)

albicocche	apricots
ananas	pineapple
arance	oranges
banane	bananas
cachi	persimmon
ciliege	cherries
cocomero	watermelon
composta di frutta	stewed fruit
datteri	dates
fichi	figs
fragole (con panna)	strawberries (with cream)
frutta di stagione	fruit in season
lamponi	raspberries
macedonia di frutta	fruit salad
mandarino	tangerine
mandorle	almonds
melagrana	pomegranate
mele	apples

melone	melon
mirtilli	bilberries
more	blackberries
nespola	medlar fruit
nocciole	hazelnuts
noci	walnuts
pera	pear
pesca	peach
pesca noce	nectarine
pinoli	pine nuts
pompelmo	grapefruit
prugna/susina	prune/plum
uva	grapes

Dolci (Desserts)

amaretti	macaroons
cannoli	crisp pastry tubes filled with ricotta, cream, chocolate or fruit
coppa gelato	assorted ice cream
crema caramella	caramel-topped custard
crostata	fruit flan
gelato (produzione propria)	ice-cream (homemade)
granita	flavoured ice, usually lemon or coffee
Monte Bianco	chestnut pudding with whipped cream
panettone	sponge cake with candied fruit and raisins
panforte	dense cake of chocolate, almonds and preserved fruit
Saint-Honoré	meringue cake
semifreddo	refrigerated cake
sorbetto	sorbet/sherbet
spumone	a soft ice cream
tiramisù	sponge fingers, mascarpone, coffee and chocolate
torrone	nougat
torta	cake, tart
torta millefoglie	layered pastry with custard cream
zabaglione	whipped eggs, sugar and Marsala wine, served hot
zuppa inglese	trifle

Bevande (Beverages)

acqua minerale con/senza gas	mineral water with/without fizz
aranciata	orange soda
birra (alla spina)	beer (draught)
caffè (freddo)	coffee (iced)
cioccolata (con panna)	chocolate (with cream)
gassosa	lemon-flavoured soda
latte	milk
limonata	lemon soda
succo di frutta	fruit juice
tè	tea
vino (rosso, bianco, rosato)	wine (red, white, rosé)

Cooking Terms, Miscellaneous

aceto (balsamico)	vinegar (balsamic)
affumicato	smoked
aglio	garlic
alla brace	on embers
bicchiere	glass
burro	butter
cacciagione	game
conto	bill
costoletta/cotoletta	chop
coltello	knife
cucchiaio	spoon
filetto	fillet
forchetta	fork
forno	oven
fritto	fried
ghiaccio	ice
griglia	grill
in bianco	without tomato
limone	lemon
magro	lean meat or pasta without meat
marmellata	jam
menta	mint
miele	honey
mostarda	candied mustard sauce, eaten with boiled meats
olio	oil
pane (tostato)	bread (toasted)
panini	sandwiches
panna	cream
pepe	pepper
peperoncini	hot chilli peppers
piatto	plate
prezzemolo	parsley
ripieno	stuffed
rosmarino	rosemary
sale	salt
salmi	wine marinade
salsa	sauce
salvia	sage
senape	mustard
sartufi	truffles
tazza	cup
tavola	table
tovagliolo	napkin
tramezzini	finger sandwiches
umido	cooked in sauce
uovo	egg
zucchero	sugar

General and Travel

Barzini, Luigi, *The Italians* (Hamish Hamilton, 1964). A perhaps too clever account of the Italians by an Italian journalist living in London, but one of the classics.

Goethe, J.W., *Italian Journey* (Penguin Classics, 1982). An excellent example of a genius turned to mush by Italy; brilliant insights and big, big mistakes.

Haycraft, John, *Italian Labyrinth* (Penguin, 1987). An attempt to unravel the Italian mess.

Hutton, Edward, *Venice and Venetia* (Hollis & Carter).

McCarthy, Mary, *Venice Observed* (Penguin, 1986). Brilliant evocations of Italy's great art city, with an understanding that makes many other works on the subject seem sluggish and pedantic; don't visit without it.

Morris, Jan, *Venice* (*The World of Venice* in the USA, Harcourt Brace, 1995). A beautifully written classic on the World's Most Beautiful City.

Nichols, Peter, *Italia, Italia* (Macmillan, 1973). Account of modern Italy by an old hand.

History

Burckhardt, Jacob, *The Civilization of the Renaissance in Italy* (Harper & Row, 1975). The classic on the subject (first published 1860), the mark against which scholars still level their poison arrows of revisionism.

Ginsborg, Paul, A *History of Contemporary Italy: Society and Politics 1943–1988* (Penguin, 1990). A good modern account of events up to the fall of Rome.

Hale, J.R. (ed.), *A Concise Encyclopaedia of the Italian Renaissance* (Thames and Hudson, 1981). An excellent reference guide, with many concise, well-written essays.

Hibbert, Christopher, *Benito Mussolini* (Penguin, 1965).

Morris, Jan, *The Venetian Empire* (Faber & Faber, 1980). A fascinating account of the Serenissima's glory days.

Norwich, John Julius, *A History of Venice* (Penguin, 1983). A classic, wittily written account of the Serenissima.

Procacci, Giuliano, *History of the Italian People* (Penguin, 1973). An in-depth view from the year 1000 to the present—also an introduction to the wit and subtlety of the best Italian scholarship.

Rand, Edward Kennard, *Founders of the Middle Ages* (Dover reprint, New York). A little-known but incandescently brilliant work that can explain Jerome, Augustine, Boethius and other intellectual currents of the decaying classical world.

Further Reading

Zorzi, Alvise, *Venice: City—Republic—Empire* (Sedgwick & Jackson, 1980). Beautifully illustrated, with a large section on Venice's dealings in the Veneto and eastern Mediterranean.

Art and Literature

Boccaccio, Giovanni, *The Decameron* (Penguin, 1972). The ever-young classic by one of the fathers of Italian literature. Its irreverent worldliness still provides a salutary antidote to whatever dubious ideas persist in your mental baggage.

Calvino, Italo, *Invisible Cities, If Upon a Winter's Night a Traveller* (Picador). Provocative fantasies that could only have been written by an Italian. Something even better is his compilation of *Italian Folktales*, a little bit Brothers Grimm and a little bit Fellini.

Cellini, *Autobiography of Benvenuto Cellini* (Penguin, trans. George Bull). Fun reading by a swashbuckling braggart and world-class liar.

Clark, Kenneth, *Leonardo da Vinci* (Penguin).

Dante Alighieri, *The Divine Comedy* (plenty of good translations). Few poems have ever had such a mythical significance for a nation. Anyone serious about understanding Italy and the Italian world-view will need more than a passing acquaintance with Dante.

Gadda, Carlo Emilio, *That Awful Mess on Via Merulana* (Quartet Books, 1980). Italy during the Fascist era.

Gilbert/Linscott (ed.), *Complete Poems and Selected Letters of Michelangelo* (Princeton Press, 1984).

Lauritzen, Peter and Wolf, Reinhart, *Villas of the Veneto* (Pavilion, 1988). Lush pictures and light descriptions.

Levi, Carlo, *Christ Stopped at Eboli* (Penguin, 1982). Disturbing post-War realism.

Levy, Michael, *Early Renaissance* and *High Renaissance* (both Penguin, 1975). Old-fashioned accounts of the period, with a breathless reverence for the 1500s—but still full of intriguing interpretations.

Littlewood, Ian, *A Literary Companion to Venice* (St Martin's Press, 1995). Concentrated dose of Venetian inspiration.

Murray, Linda, *The High Renaissance* and *The Late Renaissance and Mannerism* (Thames and Hudson, both 1977). Excellent introduction to the period; also Peter and Linda Murray, *The Art of the Renaissance* (Thames and Hudson, 1963).

Petrarch, Francesco, *Canzoniere and Other Works* (Oxford, 1985). The most famous poems by the 'First Modern Man'.

Steer, John, *A Concise History of Venetian Painting* (Thames and Hudson, 1984). A well-illustrated introduction.

Vasari, Giorgio, *Lives of the Artists* (Penguin, 1985). Readable, anecdotal accounts of the Renaissance greats by the father of art history, also the first professional philistine.

Wittkower, Rudolf, *Art and Architecture in Italy 1600–1750* (Pelican, 1986). The bible on baroque; erudite and full of wit.

Main page references are in **bold**; page references to maps are in *italic*.

Ábano Terme 171
abbeys
  di Praglia 172
  di S. Eustachio 168
  di Sant'Agostino 187
  di Santo Stefano 173
Accademia (Venice) 109–11
accommodation 33–6
  see also under individual
  places (where to stay)
Acquapark Altomincio 209
activities and sports 30–1, 136,
  163
Affi 206
air travel
  domestic 10–11
  international 2–4
Aistulf, King 42
Alberoni 137
Alberto Azzo II 174
  statue 163
d'Alema, Massimo 52
Alemanni 40
Alexander III, Pope 44
Alexander IV, Pope 67
Alticheiro 59
Altissimo 207
Altìvole 167
Amarone 206
d'Annunzio, Gabriele 49, 50
Antenor 38, 157–8
Anthony of Padua 159–60
antiques 30, 121
Antonello de Messina 59
Arquà Petrarca **172**, 173
art and architecture **54–64**
  baroque 57–8
  Dark Ages 54–5
  directory of artists 59–64
  Gothic 55–6
  Mannerism 57
  Middle Ages 54–5

Paleoveneti 54
Palladian 71–5
  Renaissance 56–7
  rococo 57–8
  Roman 54
  Romanesque 55
  Romanticism 58
  Veneto-Byzantine 55
  villas 72–3
Ateste 39
Attila the Hun 40, 209
Austrian wars 48–9
bank opening hours 28
Barbarigo Villa 172
Barbaro brothers 168
Barbaro Villa 168–70, *169*
Barco della Regina Cornaro 167
baroque age 47, 57–8
Basaiti, Marco 59
Bassano, Jacopo 59
Bastiani, Lazzaro 59
Battaglia Terme 172–3
beaches 31
Belisarius, General 41
Bella, Gabriel 59
Bellini, Gentile 59
Bellini, Giovanni 56, 59, **68–9**
Bellini, Jacopo 59
Bene, Villa del 206
Berlusconi, Silvio 51–2
Bianco di Custoza 208
bicycles 15–16
Black Death 45
Bolca **205**, 207
Bon, Bartolomeo 59
Bonifazio Veronese 59
Bonino 59
book shops 121
Bordone, Paris 59
Borghetto 208
Bosco Chiesanuova 205
Bossi, Umberto 52

breakfast 22
Brustalon, Andrea 59
Burano **140**, 141
Burlington, Lord 74–5
buses and coaches 6, 13
Byron, Lord 145
Cambrai, League of 46
Campagnola, Domenico 60
camping 36, 126–7
Camposilvano 205
Canaletto, Antonio 58, 60
Cangrande I (Big Dog) 190
  statue 199
  tomb 195
canoeing 31
Canossa Villa 208
Canova, Antonio 60
Cansignorio (Lord Dog) 190
  tomb 195
Caorle 21
Caprino Veronese 207
car hire 14–15, 94
car travel 6–7, 13–15
Carlo Alberto, King 48
Carlotti Villa 207
Caroto, Giovanni 60
Carpaccio, Vittore 60
Carriera, Rosalba 60
Castagno, Andrea del 60
Castelfranco Veneto 165,
  166–8
Castello di San Pelagio 173
Catena, Vincenzo 60
Cavallino 142
Cavaso del Tomba 170
Cavour Parco Acquatico 208
Charlemagne, Emperor 42
Charles of Anjou 44
Charles V, Emperor 46, 69
Charles VIII of France 46
charter flights 2–3, 4
Chioggia 137, **138**

Index

Neoclassicism 58

Bragadin, Marcantonio 117

Chioggia, War of 45, 76

de Chirico, Giorgio 60
Christian Democrats 51
Cima da Conegliano, Giovanni
   Battista 60
Cisalpine Gaul 39
Cisalpine Republic 47
classical music 130
Clement V, Pope 45
Clement VII, Pope 69
climate 18
coaches and buses 6, 13
Codussi, Mauro 60
Colleoni, Bartolomeo 117
   statue 117
Cologna Veneta 209
communism 51
comuni 43
Congress of Vienna 48
Constantine, Emperor 40
consulates 19–20
Contarini, Marco 165
Contarini Villa 165
Cornaro family 166
   Luigi 146–7
Cornaro Villa 166
Council of Ten 85
Council of Trent 46, **69–71**
Counter-Reformation 46
crime 18–19
Crivelli, Carlo 60
Crocetta del Montello 168
Crusades 43, 44
currency *see* money
customs formalities 7–8
Custoza 208
cycling 15–16
Da Carrara family 150
Dark Ages 41–2, 54–5
De Kunkler Villa 174
De Pisis, Filippo 60
Diocletian, Emperor 40
disabled travellers 19
discount flights 4
Doge of Venice 107
Doges' Palace 105–8
Dolo 145, 147
Donatello 60
driving in Italy 6–7, 13–15
Due Carrare 173
Duodo Villa 174

E111 forms 26
economy 51–2
embassies 19–20
emergencies 26, 95
Emo Villa 167
Este 171, **174**
Euganean Hills 171
Eurostar 5
evening meals 23
Ezzelino III da Romano 44,
   66–7
Falconetto, Giovanni Maria 60
Fanzolo **167**, 168
Fascism 49–51
fashion shops 121–2
Ferrara di Monte Baldo 207
festivals **20–2**, 132–3
Fini, Alberto 52
First Crusade 43
First World War 49–50
Fogolino, Marcello 61
food 22–5
   shopping 122
   see also under individual
      places (eating out)
football 30
Forcella Mostaccin 170
Forte di Sant'Andrea 136
Foscari Villa 143–4
Fosse 205
Fourth Crusade 44
Franks 40
Frederick I Barbarossa 43–4
Frederick II, Emperor 44, 66, 67
Fumane 206
Galzignano Terme 21
Gambellara 21
Garibaldi, Giuseppe 48, 49
Gattamelata, statue 162
Gauls 39
Genoa 85
Gentile da Fabriano 68
Ghibellines 43–4
Giambellini *see* Bellini, Giovanni
Giambono, Michele 61
Giardino Storico di Villa
   Valmarana 146
Giorgione 57, **61**
Giotto di Bondone 61, 154
Giovanni da Verona 61

glass-making 139
Golden Book 85
Goldoni, statue 109
gondolas 91
Gothic art and architecture 55–6
Gradenigo Villa 144
Gramsci, Antonio 51
Great Interdict 47
Gregory IX, Pope 66
Gregory VII, Pope 43
Grezzano 208
Grotta di Roverè 1000 205
Guardi, Francesco 58, **61**
Guariento 61
Guelphs 43–4
Guggenheim, Peggy 111
Guiccioli Villa 185
Habsburgs 45
Henry IV, Emperor 43
history **38–52**
   baroque age 47
   comuni 43
   Dark Ages 41–2
   Fascism 49–51
   Guelphs and Ghibellines 43–4
   Napoleon Bonaparte **47–8**,
      86
   Padua 150, 152
   post-war Italy 51–2
   prehistory 38–9
   Renaissance 45
   Risorgimento 48–9
   Romans 39–40
   Venice 83–7
   Verona 190–1
   Vicenza 175, 177
   World Wars 49–51
hitchhiking 15
Honorius, Emperor 40
hostels **35**, 126–7
Ice Man 38
Il Catajo 172–3
Il Riccio 63
insurance
   motor 6, 14
   travel 26
international driving licence 6–7
irredenta 49
Isola Rizza 210
Isola della Scala 210

Jacobello del Fiore 61
Jappelli, Giuseppe 61
jazz clubs 131–2
Jesolo 142
Jesuits 77
Jews 119
Jones, Inigo 74
Juliet's tomb 198
Julius II, Pope 76
Justinian, Emperor 41
Kingdom of Illyria 47
lace 140
League of Cambrai 46
Lega Lombarda 52
Legnano 209
Leo the Great, Pope 209
Lepanto, Battle of 47
Lessinia Natural Park 205
Liberale da Verona 61
Lido 135–7
Lido di Jesolo 142
Lombard League 44
Lombardo, Pietro 61
Lombardo, Tullio 61
Lombards 42
Longhena, Baldassare 61
Longhi, Pietro 58, 61
Lonigo 20
Lorenzo Veneziano 61
Lotto, Lorenzo 61–2
Luvigliano 171–2
Maffei, Francesco 62
Maggior Consiglio 85
Malamocco 137
Manin, Daniele 48
Mannerism 57
Mansueti, Giovanni 62
Mantegna, Andrea 62, 68, 156
Maróstica 21
Masegne, Jacobello dalle 62
Masegne, Pier Paolo dalle 62
Masèr **168–70**, 170–1
Masèr-Muliperte 170
Massari, Giorgio 62
Mastino II 190
  tomb 195
Mazzoni, Sebastiano 62
Menabuoi, Giusto de' 62
Messina, Antonello da 68
Middle Ages 54–5

Mira Ponte 21, **144–5**, 148
Molina 205
money 8, 27
Monsélice 171, **173–4**, 175
Montagna, Bartolomeo 62
Montagnana 171, **174–5**
Monte Baldo 206, 207
Monte Bérico 184
Montebelluna 165, **168**, 170
Montegrotto Terme 171
Montello 168
Monteverdi, tomb 112
motorcycles 15–16
motoring in Italy 6–7, 13–15
motoscafi 90–1
Murano **139–40**, 141
murazzi 137
museums
  Accademia (Venice)
  Antoniano (Padua) 162
  Archaeology (Venice) 105
  Archaeology (Verona) 197
  Art (Verona) 199–200
  di Arte Contemporanea
    (Teolo) 172
  Bottacin (Padua) 156
  Byzantine Religious Painting
    (Venice) 115
  Civico (Montebelluna) 168
  Civico (Padua) 154–6
  Civico di Storia Naturale
    (Verona) 197
  Comunità Israelitica (Venice)
    119
  Correr (Venice) 104
  Diocesano (Venice) 116
  dell'Estuario (Torcello) 141
  of frescoes (Verona) 198
  Galleria d'Arte Moderna
    (Venice) 114
  Galleria d'Arte Moderna
    (Verona) 196
  Galleria Franchetti (Venice)
    118
  Lapidario Maffeiano (Verona)
    194
  Marciano (Venice) 103
  Miniscalchi-Erizzo (Verona)
    196
  Natural History (Venice) 114
  Nazionale Atestino (Este) 174

opening hours 28
Oriental Art (Venice) 114
Palladiano (Vicenza) 180
del Risorgimento e della
  Resistanza (Vicenza) 185
Santa Corona (Vicenza) 181
dello Scarpone
  (Montebelluna) 168
del Settecento Veneziano
  (Venice) 112
Storico Navale (Venice) 116
Vetrario (Murano) 139–40
Mussolini, Benito 50–1
Muttoni, Francesco 62
Nani Villa 173
Napoleon Bonaparte **47–8**, 86
national holidays 27
Nazionale (Pisani) Villa 145–6
Negràr 206
Neoclassicism 58
Nervesa della Battaglia 168
Norico 40
Odoacer 40
opening hours 28
opera 130
Oriago 144
Orient Express 5
Orseolo, Doge Pietro 84
Otto the Great 42
Padua 150–88, *151*
  activities 163
  Anatomical Theatre 157
  Baptistry 158
  Basilica di Sant'Antonio
    160–2
  Basilica of Santa Giustina 163
  Caffè Pedrocchi 157
  Cappella degli Scrovegni
    152–4, *153*
  Carmine church 156
  Casa degli Specchi 159
  Casa di Ezzelino 157
  day trips (north) 165–71
  day trips (south) 171–5
    see also Vicenza
  Duomo 158
  eating out 164–5
  Eremitani 156
  festivals 20, 21
  getting there 152
  history 150, 152

Padua (*cont'd*)
La Specola 163
Liviano 158
Loggia della Gran Guardia 158
Loggia and Odeo Cornaro 162
Municipio 157
Museo Antoniano 162
Museo Bottacin 156
Museo Civico 154–6
Oratorio di San Giorgio 162
Orto Botanico 162
Ovetari chapel 156
Palazzo del Bo' 157
Palazzo del Capitaniato 158
Palazzo della Ragione 158
Pedrocchino 157
Piazza Antenore 157–8
Piazza Cavour 157
Piazza delle Erbe 158
Piazza della Frutta 158
Piazza Insurrezione 157
Piazza dei Signori 158
Pinacoteca dei Canonici 158–9
Porta Altinate 157
Porta di Ponte Molino 156
Prato della Valle 162–3
Quadraria Emo Capodilista 156
Santa Lucia 157
Santa Sofia 156
Scuola del Carmine 156
Scuola di San Rocco 157
Scuoletta del Santo 162
statue of Alberto Azzo II 163
statue of Gattamelata 162
tourist information 152
University of Padua 157
where to stay 163–4
Paleoveneti 38, 54
Palladio (Andrea di Pietro della Gondola) 57, 62, **71–5**, 143–4, 183
La Rotonda 185–6
Palazzo Chiericati 181
statue 178
Villa Barbaro 168–70
Villa Cornaro 166
Palma Giovane 62

Palma Vecchio 62
Paolo Veneziano 62
Patriarchate of Aquileia 43
Paul III, Pope 70
Pedemonte **206**, 207
Pellestrina 137
Pepin, King of the Franks 42
petrol 14
photography 29
Piazzetta, Giambattista 62
Piazzola sul Brenta 165
Pigafetta, Antonio 178
Piombino Dese 166
Pisanello, Antonio 62
Pisani, Alvise 145–6
Pisani (Nazionale) Villa 145–6
Pittoni, Giovanni Battista 62
Pius X, Pope 167
Platano 207
political terrorism 19
politics 51–2
Ponte Rotta 208
Pordenone 62
post offices 29–30
post-war Italy 51–2
Praglia Abbey 172
prehistory 38–9
Prodi, Romano 52
Prussia 49
Querini Stampalia Villa 209
Quinto di Treviso 170
Raetia 40
rail travel 5–6, 11–13
rainfall 18
Raphael 68
Recioto 206
Renaissance 45, 56–7
restaurants 23–4
     see also under individual
     places (eating out)
Ricci, Sebastiano 63
Riese Pio X 167
Rinaldi Villa 170
Risorgimento 48–9
Rivella 174
Rivoli Veronese 206
Rizzo, Antonio 63
rococo 57–8
Romanesque art and architecture 55

Romans 39–40, 54
Romanticism 58
rowing/canoeing 31
S. Eustachio 168
Sack of Rome 46
St Mark's Basilica *100*, 100–3
Salieri, Antonio 209
Salionze 209
Saló 51
Salzano 21
Sammicheli, Michele 63
San Floriano 206
San Francesco del Deserto 140
San Giorgio 206
San Lazzaro degli Armeni 136
San Michele 139
San Pietro in Volta 137
San Vito 167
San Zeno di Montagna 207
Sansovino, Jacopo 57, 63
Sant'Agostino 187
Sant'Ambrogio di Valpolicella **206**, 207
Sant'Anna d'Alfaedo 205
Santo Stefano 173
Santuario della Madonna della Corona 207
Saonara 146
Sarpi, Fra Paolo 70–1
     tomb 139
Scala (Scaligeri) family 190
Scamozzi, Vincenzo 57, 63
Scrovegni, Enrico 154
scuola 78
Sebastiano del Piombo 63
Second World War 51
Selvatico-Capodilista Villa 174
Serego poi Boccoli Villa 206
Serenissima 75–8
Serraglio 208
Serrata 85
shopping 30, 120–3
     opening hours 28
Sicilian Vespers 44
Sigurtà Gardens 208–9
Spiaggia Comunale 135
Spluga della Preta 205
sports and activities 30–1, 136, 163
Squarcione, Francesco 63

Stefano da Verona 63
Stra 145–6
student travel 3, 4
telephones 31
tennis 31
Teolo 20, 21, **172**
terrorism 19
theatre 130
Theodoric of the Ostrogoths 41
Tiepolo Conspiracy 85, **108**
Tiepolo, Giambattista 63
Tiepolo, Giandomenico 63
Tintoretto 57, **63**, 114
Titian 57, **64**
  tomb 112
Tommaso da Modena 64
Torcello 55, **140–1**, 141–2
Torre, Villa della 206
Torréglia **171**, 173
tour operators 8–10
tourist offices 32–3
trains 5–6, 11–13
Trent, Council of 46, **69–71**
Trieste 51
Trissino, Giangiorgio 71
Tron, Doge Nicolò 112
Tura, Cosmè 64
Turone 64
United Italy 48–9
Urban IV, Pope 44
vaccinations 26
Valéggio sul Mincio **208**, 209–10
Valley of the Sphinxes 205
Valmarana Villa 185
Valpolicella 205–6
Valsanzibio 172
vaporetti 90–1
Velo Veronese 205
Venet/Venetic 38–9, 88
Venetian Lagoon 133–42, *134*
  Alberoni 137
  Burano **140**, 141
  Cavallino 142
  Chioggia 137, **138**
  eating out 136–7, 138, 141–2
  Forte di Sant'Andrea 136
  Jesolo 142
  Lido 135–7
  Lido di Jesolo 142

Malamocco 137
Murano **139–40**, 141
murazzi 137
Pellestrina 137
pollution 135
San Francesco del Deserto 140
San Lazzaro degli Armeni 136
San Michele 139
San Pietro in Volta 137
Spiaggia Comunale 135
sports and activities 136
Torcello **140–1**, 141–2
where to stay 136–7, 138, 141–2
Veneto-Byzantine art 55
Venice 75–8, *80–1*, **82–148**, *92–3*, *96–7*
  Accademia 109–11
  addresses 88
  Arsenale 115
  Brenta Canal 143–8
  Bridge of Sighs 107
  buses 94
  Ca' Foscari 98
  Ca' d'Oro 95, 118
  Ca' Pésaro 114
  Ca' Rezzonico 98, 112
  Caffè Quadri 98
  Campanile 104, 120
  Campo dei Mori 119
  Campo San Bartolomeo 109
  Campo Santa Margherita 112
  Campo Santo Stefano 109
  Cannaregio 118–20
  car hire 94
  Carmini 112
  Casino 130
  Corte Prima del Milion 117
  Corte Seconda del Milion 117–18
  Dogana di Mare 98, 111
  Doges' Palace 105–8
  Dorsoduro 111–12
  eating out 24, 127–30
  emergencies 95
  entertainment 130–3
  festivals 20, 21, 22
  Florian's 98
  Fóndaco dei Tedeschi 98

Fóndaco dei Turchi 95, 114
Fondamenta delle Zattere 111
Fondazione Querini-Stampalia 116
Frari 112
Galleria d'Arte Moderna 114
Galleria Franchetti 118
Gesuati 111
Gesuiti 118
getting around 90–4, *92–3*
getting there 88–9
Ghetto 119
Gobbo di Rialto 109
gondolas 91
Grand Canal 95–8, *96–7*
Great Gateway 115
Guggenheim Collection 111
hiring boats 91
history 83–7
Hotel Danieli 114
Il Redentore 120
La Fenice 109
La Giudecca 120
La Pietà 115
Lagoon *see* Venetian Lagoon
Libreria 105
Lista di Spagna 120
Madonna dell'Orto 118–19
Memorial to Vittorio Emanuele II 114
Mercerie 108
motoscafi 90–1
museums
  Archaeology 105
  Byzantine Religious Painting 115
  Comunità Israelitica 119
  Correr 104
  Diocesano 116
  Galleria d'Arte Moderna 114
  Galleria Franchetti 118
  Marciano 103
  Natural History 114
  Oriental Art 114
  del Settecento Veneziano 112
  Storico Navale 116
music 130–2

Venice (cont'd)
palazzo
Corner 98
Corner-Spinelli 98
Grassi 98
Grimani 98
Labia 119–20
Mastelli 119
Mocenigo 98
Pésaro 95
delle Prigioni 107
Vendramin-Calergi 95
Paolin 109
Parco delle Rimembranze 116
Peggy Guggenheim Collection 111
Piazzetta Giovanni XXIII 104
Piazzetta San Marco 104–5
Piazza San Marco 98–108, *99*
Ponte dell'Accademia 98
Ponte dell Guglie 119
Ponte di Rialto 95, 109
Porta della Carta 105
post office 95
Procurate Nuove 98
Procurate Vecchie 98
Public Gardens 116
public transport 90–4, *92–3*
Rialto 108–9
Rialto Markets 98
Riva degli Schiavoni 114
St Mark's Basilica *100*, 100–3
San Giacomo di Rialto 109
San Giorgio dei Greci 115
San Giorgio Maggiore 120
San Giovanni in Brágora 115
San Giovanni Crisostomo 118
San Moisè 109
San Pietro di Castello 116
San Polo 112
San Rocco *113*, 113–14
San Salvatore 108
San Sebastiano 111
San Zaccaria 114–15
San Zanipolo 117
San Zulian 108
Santa Maria Formosa 116
Santa Maria dei Miracoli 117
Santa Maria della Salute 98, 111

Santa Maria Zobenigo 109
Sant'Alvise 119
Santi Giovanni e Paolo 117
Santo Stefano 109
Scuola Grande dei Carmini 112
Scuola Grande di San Giovanni Evangelista 114
Scuola Grande di San Marco 117
Scuola Grande Tedesca 119
Scuola Levantina 119
Scuola di San Giorgio degli Schiavoni 115
Scuola di San Rocco *113*, 113–14
Scuola Spagnola 119
shopping 120–3
statue of Bartolomeo Colleoni 117
statue of Goldoni 109
Tomb of Doge Nicolò Tron 112
Torre dell'Orologio 104
tourist information 94
transport system 90–4, *92–3*
vaporetti 90–1
water-taxis 91
when to go 82–3
where to stay 123–7
Zecca 105
Verona 190–210, *192–3*
Arco della Costa 195
Arco dei Gavi 198
Arena 194
Basilica of San Zeno 200–1
Casa di Giulietta 195
Casa Mazzanti 194
Casa di Romeo 195
Castel San Pietro 197
Castelvecchio 199
Corso Cavour 198
day trips (north) 205–7
day trips (south) 208–10
Duomo 196
eating out 202–3
entertainment and nightlife 204
festivals 20, 21, 22
Fondazione Museo Miniscalchi-Erizzo 196

Galleria d'Arte Moderna 196
getting around 191
Giardini Giusti 197
history 190–1
Loggia del Consiglio 195
museums
Archaeology Museum 197
Art Museum 199–200
Civico di Storia Naturale 197
of frescoes 198
Galleria d'Arte Moderna 196
Lapidario Maffeiano 194
Miniscalchi-Erizzo 196
Palazzo Bevilacqua 198
Palazzo Canossa 198
Palazzo della Gran Guardia 194
Palazzo Maffei 195
Palazzo della Ragione 195
Piazza Brà 194
Piazza delle Erbe 194
Piazza dei Signori 195
Ponte Pietra 197
Ponte Scaligero 200
Porta dei Bórsari 198
Porta dei Leoni 197
Porta Nuova 194
Porta Vescovo 201
Portoni della Brà 194
San Fermo Maggiore 197–8
San Giorgio in Braida 197
San Lorenzo 198
San Michele Extra 201
San Paolo 197
Santa Maria Antica 195
Santa Maria in Organo 197
Sant'Anastasia 195–6
Santi Nazaro e Celso 197
Santo Stefano 197
Santuario della Madonna di Campagna 201
Scaliger excavations 195
SS. Apostoli 198
Teatro Romano 197
Tomba di Giulietta 198
Torre del Gardell 194
Torre de Lamberti 194
tourist information 191

Verona (*cont'd*)
   Tribunale 195
   Veronetta 197
   Via Mazzini 194
   where to stay 201–2
Veronese (Paulo Caliari) **64**, 111
Verrocchio, Andrea del 64
Vescovi, Villa dei 171–2
Vespers 44
Vicenza 175–88, *176*
   Abbey of Sant'Agostino 187
   Basilica 178
   Basilica di Monte Bérico 185
   Bertoliana Civic Library 180
   Casa Pigafetta 178
   Contrà Porti 179
   Corso Fogazzaro 184
   Corso Palladio 179
   Corte dei Roda 183
   cryptoportico 178
   Duomo 178
   eating out 187–8
   festivals 20, 21, 22
   getting there 177
   Giardino Salvi 184
   history 175, 177
   La Rotonda 185–7, *186*
   Loggia del Capitanato 179
   Monte Bérico 184
   Monte di Pietà 179
   museums
      Palladiano 180
      del Risorgimento e della
      Resistanza 185
      Santa Corona 181
   Oratorio dei Boccalotti 183
   Oratorio di San Nicola 179
   Oratorio di Santa Chiara e San
      Bernardino 179
   Palazzetto Giacomazzi-
      Trevisan 182
   palazzo
      Angaran 183
      Barbaran-da Porto 180
      Bonin Longare 177
      Breganze 177
      Chiericati *181*, 181–2

Civena-Trissino 184
Da Schio 179
Gualdo 179
Leoni Montanari 181
Porto-Breganze 179
Porto-Colleoni 179
Regaù 183
del Territorio 182
Thiene 180
Trissino 179
Valmarana-Braga 180
Valmarano-Trento 182
Parco Querini 183
Piazza delle Erbe 178
Piazza dei Signori 178–9
Piazzaola Gualdi 179
Pinacoteca 182
Ponte San Michele 179
Porta Castello 177
Porta Nuova 184
Portici 185
San Giorgio in Gogna 187
San Lorenzo 184
San Pietro 183
San Rocco 184
Santa Corona 180
Santa Maria Aracoeli 183
Santa Maria del Carmine 184
Santa Maria delle Grazie 185
Santo Stefano 181
SS. Felice e Fortunato 184
Teatro Olimpico 182–3
Torre di Piazza 179
Torre del Tormento 178
tourist information 177
Villa Guiccioli 185
Villa Valmarana 185
Zeno Loggia 178
Vienna, Congress of 48
Villa Guiccioli 185
Villa Valmarana 185
Villafranca di Verona 208
villas
   architecture 72–3
   Barbarigo 172
   Barbaro 168–70, *169*
   del Bene 206

Canossa 208
Carlotti 207
Contarini 165
Cornaro 166
De Kunkler 174
Duodo 174
Emo 167
Foscari 143–4
Gradenigo 144
Nani 173
Nazionale (Pisani) 145–6
Querini Stampalia 209
Rinaldi 170
Selvatico-Capodilista 174
Serego poi Boccoli 206
   della Torre 206
   dei Vescovi 171–2
   Widmann-Foscari 144
visas 7
Visconti, Gian Galeazzo 190–1
Vittoria, Alessandro 64
Vittorio Emanuele II 49
   memorial 114
Vittorio Emanuele III 50
Vittorio Veneto 50
Vivaldi 115
Vivarini 64
Vò 21
Volargne 206
War of Chioggia 45, 76
watersports 31
when to go 18, 82–3
where to stay 33–6
   Padua 163–4
   Venetian Lagoon 136–7, 138,
      141–2
   Venice 123–7
   Verona 201–2
Widmann-Foscari Villa 144
wines 25–6
   Bianco di Custoza 208
   Valpolicella 205–6
World Wars 49–51
youth travel 3, 4
Zelotti, Giambattista 64
Zorzon 166

Also Available from Cadogan Guides...

Country Guides

Antarctica
Belize
Central Asia
China: The Silk Routes
Egypt
France: Southwest France;
    Dordogne, Lot & Bordeaux
France: Southwest France;
    Gascony & the Pyrenees
France: Brittany
France: The Loire
France: The South of France
France: Provence
France: The Côte d'Azur
Germany: Bavaria
India
India: South India
India: Goa
Ireland
Ireland: Southwest Ireland
Ireland: Northern Ireland
Italy
Italy: The Bay of Naples and Southern Italy
Italy: Italian Riviera
Italy: Lombardy, Milan and the Italian Lakes
Italy: Rome and the Heart of Italy
Italy: Tuscany and Umbria
Italy: Venetia and the Dolomites
Japan
Morocco
Portugal
Portugal: The Algarve
Scotland
Scotland's Highlands and Islands
South Africa, Swaziland and Lesotho
Spain
Spain: Southern Spain
Spain: Northern Spain
Syria & Lebanon
Tunisia
Turkey
Western Turkey
Yucatán and Southern Mexico
Zimbabwe, Botswana and Namibia

City Guides

Amsterdam
Brussels, Bruges, Ghent & Antwerp
Bruges
Edinburgh
Florence, Siena, Pisa & Lucca
Italy: Three Cities—Rome, Assisi, Padua
Italy: Three Cities—Rome, Florence, Venice
Italy: Three Cities—Rome, Naples, Sorrento
Japan: Three Cities—Tokyo, Kyoto, Ancient
    Nara
London
London–Brussels
London–Paris
Madrid
Manhattan
Paris
Prague
Rome
Spain: Three Cities—Granada, Seville,
    Cordoba
St Petersburg
Venice

Island Guides

Caribbean and Bahamas
NE Caribbean; The Leeward Is.
SE Caribbean; The Windward Is.
Jamaica & the Caymans

Greek Islands
Crete
Mykonos, Santorini & the Cyclades
Rhodes & the Dodecanese
Corfu & the Ionian Islands

Madeira & Porto Santo
Malta, Gozo and Comino
Sicily

Plus...

Take the Kids Travelling
Take the Kids London
Take the Kids Paris and Disneyland
Bugs, Bites & Bowels
London Markets

Available from good bookshops or via, in the UK, **Grantham Book Services**, Isaac Newton Way, Alma Park Industrial Estate, Grantham NG31 9SD, ℡ (01476) 541 080, @ (01476) 541 061; and in North America from **The Globe Pequot Press**, 246 Goose Lane, PO Box 480, Guilford, Connecticut 06437–0480, ℡ (800) 243 0495, @ (800) 820 2329.